CW00822514

Sky Over Scapa

1939-1945

Sky Over Scapa

1939-1945

Gregor Lamb

First edition:published by Byrgisey

This edition published by
Bellavista Publications,
3 Sabiston Crescent, Kirkwall,
Orkney, KW15 1YT

Printed and Bound by Cromwell Press Ltd., Aintree Avenue,
White Horse Business Park, Trowbridge, Wiltshire, BA14 0XB

© Gregor Lamb, 1991 & 2007

ISBN 0 9550586 3 5

Frontispiece:

771 Squadron Pilots Johnny Treloar and Charlie Buxton in the snow at Twatt, January 1945

Dedicated to all those who sojourned among us

Contents

Chapter 1	Early Aviators	17
Chapter 2	The Military Airfields of Orkney	29
Chapter 3	In the Front Line	47
Chapter 4	The Resident Squadrons	59
Chapter 5	The Carrier Men	105
Chapter 6	A Posting to Orkney	139
Chapter 7	Epilogue: the Return	181
Appendix I	Aircraft Crash Records	187
Appendix II	Aviation War Diary	197
	List of Abbreviations	276
	References	277
	Index	279

Acknowledgements

I am not sure that I should thank Orkney farmer Sandy Scarth for his initiative in suggesting that the Control Tower of Twatt airfield should be preserved. He made a lot of work for me! Had I put the same effort for four years into breeding beef cattle I would have a fine herd by this time and might have made a lot of money but then a piece of Orkney history would have vanished. Orcadians owe him a sincere debt of gratitude.

My first duty is to acknowledge the help of Ronald Gilbert, Chief Executive of Orkney Islands Council who, though on holiday, made special arrangements to prevent the demolition of the Control Tower of Twatt airfield in Orkney and unwittingly set in motion a wide ranging research project which has culminated in this book. Tom Eggeling, Director of Planning to Orkney Islands Council must also be congratulated for his foresight in seeing in the wartime eyesores which scattered throughout the Orkney landscape some things worthy of preservation to commemorate the huge impact which war had on these islands.

I would especially like to thank Captain 'Hank' and wife Deborah Rotherham of Canada who, on hearing of a plan to preserve something of the Royal Naval Air Station at Twatt, flew to Orkney to give the project their blessing. Without their initial input of enthusiasm, the book would have remained a dream. Hank has an outstanding memory and carefully typed out for me detailed notes of his experiences in Orkney to supplement the material in his own book, *"It's Really Quite Safe"*. Many initial contacts were made through Hank, especially a close friend of his, Duncan Hamilton of Marston Magna in Somerset who, by showing me his wonderful collection of photographs of war-time Hatston, gave me the idea of building up a Photographic Archive. Duncan was most generous in his support and a most convivial host who spared much of his time to help. He loved Orkney and devoted a long, very amusing chapter in his autobiography *Touch Wood* to his time at Hatston.

Nicholas Horne was a photographer at Skeabrae and, after the war, continued in his profession. On his retirement he cleared out a lot of chaff and was uncertain what to do with a useless album of photographs he had taken on the station. By good fortune he happened to mention this to a close friend, Ralph Faulkner, an ex-Fleet Air Arm man who had come to retire in Orkney. In this way, unique photographs of Skeabrae were saved. There is a great shortage of wartime RAF photographs throughout Britain; some squadrons disappeared without leaving any photographic record so we are particularly fortunate in this regard. Sadly there are no squadron photographs in the collection but nevertheless we do have a record of life on this famous wartime station and I should like to thank sincerely Ralph and Nicholas for presenting the album to Orkney Archives.

A rich collection of photographs was also loaned by Patrick Hill, son of Lt.Cdr. Peter Hill, head of photography at Twatt. The collection included rare colour ciné film shot in Orkney during the war and therefore valuable archival material. Also from the same Photograph Section at Twatt, Wren Photographer Celia Green loaned an album in which the Wrens were well represented. The Royal Navy was very proud of the high standard of photography in this department and judging by the evidence, this is very true.

Mrs. Anne Bell and David Richards, librarians at the Fleet Air Arm Museum at Yeovilton in Somerset provided every facility at their disposal, (including coffee!), to assist with the tracking down of Scapa related photographs in their very fine library. Dr. Graham Mottram of the Museum there has also shown keen interest in the project and was intimately connected with the identification of war-time aircraft on the seabed off Orkney. By way of gratitude to these members of the Museum it gives me much pleasure to be able to donate copies of the whole collection of Fleet Air Arm photographs to the Museum. Scapa Flow is now well represented there!

Among the other large private photograph collections which have been loaned I must acknowledge the help of Keith Remmington and Muriel Wears of Gosport who were both stationed at Twatt. They met there and married and in common with all those couples who spent their war time years in Orkney, they have vivid memories of life in the islands and were able to provide a tape for Orkney Sound Archive. Chief Petty Officer Pilot Eric Haslam and Wren Peggy Harrison of Oxford also met at Twatt and provided many unusual photographs and very helpful notes on the station. New Zealander, Cyril Burke, latterly CO of 771 Squadron at Twatt and now resident in Australia sent his whole album at enormous expense to Orkney to be copied. Cyril also very kindly donated, unsolicited I might add, £25 to the project. This was handed over to Tom Eggeling, Director of Planning, as unofficial trustee of project funds. From Canada unique photographs were sent by Jean-Paul Fournier. French-Canadian, Jean-Paul, was the Royal Navy's first helicopter pilot. It does not appear to be recorded in Naval history that the Royal Navy's first operational helicopter was assembled and flown in Orkney at Twatt airfield, consequently such photographs are most valuable. I was particularly pleased to be contacted by John Molyneux, son of Commander H. Molyneux, CO of 771 Squadron at Twatt. John very kindly loaned for copying the family album which contained many rare and fine photographs.

Sergeant Pilot Jackie Brown (alias 'Cyclops') was a pilot at Skeabrae and made a return visit to the islands in 1988. He had lost an eye in a dog fight but managed to get permission to continue flying and eventually rose to the rank of Air Commodore! He called on me and expressly asked for the RAF to be represented in any museum or interpretation centre likely to be established. He gave me a copy of his 'vignette' of life in Orkney as seen through the eyes of a young Hurricane pilot. It is beautifully written and I hope that one day it will be published in its own right. I have used several extracts from 'Cyclops' paper in this book, quite moving descriptions of Orkney which help us see a fighter pilot in a different light. 'Cyclops' was so interested in the Orkney project that he undertook to write up a history of Skeabrae based on the Station Diary in the Public Record Office at Kew. This was of inestimable help to me in the early stages of the research and I am most appreciative of the contribution made by 'Cyclops' to this study.

Bill Reid, a pilot with 771 Squadron at Twatt from 1942 until 1943 wrote for me a brief reminiscence. 'My memories of Twatt after so long are largely of wind, red hot cast iron stoves, more wind, the Balfour and Beatty men, still more wind—and Highland Park Whisky.' So many references were made to Balfour Beatty, the firm of constructional engineers who did so much to mould war-time Orkney that I contacted them to let them know they had not been forgotten. I was delighted to receive a letter from Mr. A. J. Wivell, Director and General Manager who replied to say that two of his office colleagues began their Civil Engineering careers in Orkney and that his father also worked there. He sent good wishes for the success of the project and an 'interim' goodwill contribution of £150! I should like to thank Mr. Wivell for this generous contribution and acknowledge the enormous war-time effort of Balfour Beatty who, among other projects, undertook the building of the Churchill Barriers to block off the eastern approaches to Scapa Flow. Balfour Beatty, a name familiar to many in Britain today for its association with major roadworks is still a household name in Orkney today but for another reason.

Many others have written reminiscences for me and have loaned photographs and personal mementoes all of which have helped to build up a picture of life in Orkney for the serviceman and woman during the war. I have kept detailed notes of all other service contributors but if I have omitted any, may I please be forgiven. These include Con Ardern (née Watson), Bournemouth, Wren, (Twatt); W. Atkins, Gwynnedd, 825 Squadron, (Hatston); Margaret Boden (née Baikie), Cornwall, Wren, (Hatston); Sqdn.Ldr. Ian Blair, Essex, 602 Squadron Pilot, RAF, (Skeabrae); Margaret Bramwell (née Bennett), Salisbury, Wren, (Twatt); Lt. Alan Bristow, Surrey, 771 Squadron Helicopter Pilot, (Twatt); Capt. Eric Brown, Sussex, 802 Squadron Pilot, (Twatt); Norman Brown, Orkney, Observer, 700 Squadron, (Twatt); Lt.Cdr. Cyril Burke, Australia, CO 771 Squadron, (Twatt); Doug Cole, Norfolk, TAG, 771 Squadron, (Twatt); D. Coll, Herts, Met. Officer, (Twatt); Pat Condor, Wren, (Hatston); Lt.Cdr. John Cooper, Surrey, Pilot, 809 Squadron (Twatt), later CO, 882 Squadron, (Hatston); J. Crooks, Hull, (Twatt); Cdr. Michael Crosley, Isle of Wight, Pilot, 800 Squadron, (Hatston), 804 Squadron, (Hatston), (Twatt), CO 880 Squadron, (Skeabrae), (Grimsetter); E. Trevor Dole, Signals, (Twatt); Leading A/M G. F. Edwards,

Southampton, (Twatt); E. M. Evans (née Dunnett), Bolton, WAAF, (Skeabrae); Capt. H. St. J. Fancourt, Hampshire, CO (Hatston); PO Ralph Faulkner, Orkney, 856 Squadron, (Hatston); R. G. Fletcher, Suffolk, 845 Squadron, (Hatston); Lt. Jean-Paul Fournier, Canada, Pilot, 771 Squadron, (Twatt); Barbara Fry (née Murray), Dorset, Wren, (Twatt); E. J. Gilberd, New Zealand, Pilot, 771 Squadron, (Twatt); P. Godley, Devon, 771 Squadron, (Twatt); T. Halhead, Lancashire, TAG 771 Squadron, (Hatston); Douglas Haskey, Pilot/Observer, Orkney, 821 Squadron, (Hatston); Bernard Hazelton, Essex, TAG, (Twatt); Ruby Heyman-Nicoll, Netherlands, Wren, (Twatt); Leading Stoker Jack Holden, Orkney, (Twatt); Sub.Lt. Ian Houghton, Ross-shire, Pilot, 771 Squadron, (Twatt); PO Ron Howarth, TAG, Swordfish Squadron, (Hatston); Arthur Howes, Sutton Coldfield, TAG, 846 Squadron, (Hatston); Lt. C. G. Hyde, Dorset, Pilot, 771 Squadron, (Twatt); Air Mechanic Leslie Jessett, Norfolk, 771 Squadron, (Twatt); R. I. Kennedy, Bristol, 771 Squadron, (Twatt); Ken Knowles, Leicester, TAG, (Twatt); Eric Lambeth, Norwich, 771 Squadron TAG, (Twatt); W. C. Larkins, Canada, 771 Squadron, (Twatt); Mick Lawrence, Secretary, Fleet Air Arm Officers' Association, London; Petty Officer Barbara Ledger-Lomas (née Hayward), Liverpool, Wren, (Twatt); Catherine Mair, Cheltenham, NAAFI, (Twatt); Norman Mills, Gwynnedd, 823 Squadron, (Hatston); Pat Molony, Herts, 771 Squadron TAG, (Twatt); Lt. Leonard Page, Canada, 771 Squadron Helicopter Pilot, (Twatt); Iris Page (née Turner), Canada, Wren, (Twatt); Celia Pemberton (née Green), London, Wren Photographer, (Twatt); William Pitman, Wiltshire, Air Mechanic, 809 Squadron, (Twatt); Lt. Bill Reid, Surrey, Pilot, 771 Squadron, (Twatt); Eleanor Robertson (née Irvine), Shetland, WAAF, (Skeabrae), (Grimsetter); Sam Sephton, Hull, (Twatt); Arthur (Tiny) Small, Suffolk, Radio Operator, (Twatt); Dick Stark, Nottingham, 771 Squadron TAG, (Twatt); Harry Stephens, Surrey, Radio Mechanic, 700 Squadron, (Twatt); Roy Stevens, Hampshire, 800 Squadron, (Hatston); Gretta Taylor, Sutherlandshire, WAAF, (Skeabrae); John Thompson, Nottingham, Chief Air Radio Officer, (Hatston); Allan H. Thomson, Aberfeldy, 830 Squadron TAG,, (Hatston); Sonia Thorpe (née Morrison), Nottingham, Leading Wren Air Mechanic, (Twatt); Mary Treby, Essex, Wren, (Twatt); Fl/Lt. Mike Walker, Herts, Signals Officer, (Skeabrae); Commander D. C. B. White, former Director, Fleet Air Arm Museum, Yeovilton; G. R. S. Williams, South Glamorgan, Radar Mechanic, (Twatt); Trevor Wiren, brother of Lonsdale Wiren, New Zealand, 878 Squadron, (Hatston); Frank Wyles, Leading Air Fitter, (Hatston).

I should like to single out for special mention three people not directly concerned with Orkney but who have been very helpful. Ray Sturtivant's *The Squadrons of the Fleet Air Arm* is an outstanding reference book and has been of great value to me in piecing together the history of the Fleet Air Arm in Orkney. I sincerely acknowledge the assistance I have received from this book and from Ray Sturtivant personally. Ron Pankhurst of Exeter is an authority on Fleet Air Arm casualties and very generously supplied me with all the data relating to Orkney during World War II. Keith Bryers of Ross-shire shares an interest in aircraft accidents and he too provided me with all his relevant research.

Two Orcadians deserve special mention. Alec Strutt of Kirkwall is an experienced diver and came by chance upon a Grumman Avenger aircraft on the seabed off Hatston. A Royal Naval expedition confirmed this and photographed the find which, by the way, still remains a mystery*. So far no reference has been found of this aircraft ditching off Hatston. This discovery sparked off in Alec a great interest in war-time military aircraft. I thank Alec for his interest in the project. It is recorded that five aircraft were raised from the seabed in Scapa Flow during the war but I can assure Alec that there are many more lying out there and waiting to be discovered. Lastly I would like to thank Orcadian farmer Tom Johnston of Bryameadow Farm, Twatt. Tom has lived all his life alongside the 'drome' as it is known locally and is a great authority on the history of the station. He has woven a spider's web round the airfield and succeeds in catching any unsuspecting serviceman or woman who tries to creep back unobtrusively. Through Tom I have made many valuable contacts. Without him, this book would have been the poorer.

Gregor Lamb
South Waird
Marwick
Birsay
Orkney

8th November 1990

*later information suggests that the wreckage may be of Grumman Avenger IC TBF FN899 of 832 Sqdn. Hatston which ditched near the Station on 16th November 1943.

Acknowledgements, 2007 Edition

Many readers have contributed to the revision of this text but I should particularly like to thank R. C. B. Ashworth of Padstow, Cornwall and J. Meaden of Cheltenham, Gloucester, both experts in the field of military aviation who made a rigorous study of the first edition of this book and who pointed out many errors. I am most grateful to them for their help. I should also like to take the opportunity to apologise to H. E. (Red) Duthie, formerly of 801 Sqdn. Skeabrae who wrote, quoting Mark Twain, to say 'the report of my death was an exaggeration.' New Zealanders are tough guys and he in fact survived the serious accident at Skeabrae on 05/12/41. One can only reply facetiously to a 'dead' man and so it seemed appropriate to quote Mark Twain once again when I answered Red's letter expressing the hope that readers would say of me, 'There was things which he stretched, but mainly he told the truth.' 'Red' magnanimously wrote some superb recollections of his time there, many of which are incorporated in this revised edition. Perhaps the reader should be reminded that practically all the details of such accidents have been built up, not through official records, but through personal and often sad recollections of squadron comrades. In the likelihood that I have written off other aircraft and crew with a flourish of my pen, I further apologise.

Many servicemen and women who read the first edition and noticed minor errors or omissions or felt that they had a story to tell about their time in Orkney wrote to the author, sometimes at great length. Their contributions have greatly enriched the text. The principal correspondents include John Sheppard, R.N., Hesta Geo; Sqdn.Leader Derek Yapp, No. 253 Sqdn. Skeabrae; First Officer Mary Barton (formerly Foster-Barham) WRENS, Twatt; Inga Deacon (née Marchant), WAAF; John Laing, RN Hatston; Ken Knowles, R.N. Hatston; 'Crusty' Pye, 880 Sqdn. Grimsetter; Lt. Observer Frank Walker, 771 Sqdn. Twatt; Jean Williams, WAAF Fighter Direction Station, Kirkwall; David Corkhill 700 and later 819 Sqdn. Hatston and Twatt; Michael Harvey 881 Sqdn. Hatston; Anthony Liskutin, DFC, AFC and John Sigmund, 313 Sqdn. (Czech.), Skeabrae. I should like to express my sincere appreciation to all of them for their help. The reader will find references to their contributions scattered throughout the book.

It was perhaps through the Czechs that an early copy of *Sky Over Scapa* found its way to the newly liberated Czechoslovakia (as it was then) and I was surprised to get a letter from a young Czech asking me if the British authorities knew of the remains of a British bomber which crashed in the mountains near to where he lived. I was able to pass the information on to Duxford but this was not followed up by me. Jack Campbell was Customs and Excise Officer in Kirkwall during the war and wrote a most interesting account of his time there. He was intimately connected with Kirkwall Arts Club through which he made many naval friends and it was through them that I was introduced to him. It can be imagined that the job of a Customs and Excise Officer in Orkney in the early stages of the war was not an enviable appointment, at a time when ships of all nations were seized on the high seas and shepherded into Kirkwall Bay by the Royal Navy to check for trade with Germany.

Lastly, a special thanks to Jeremy Lewis, biographer of Allen Lane, founder of Penguin Press, It was he who helped to clear up for me the intriguing association between Hesta Geo Radar Station in Birsay and the Lane family by which the call sign of that station became 'Penguin'. Allen's Brother, Richard, was the first occupant of the station and it was he who chose the call sign. Allen himself was well known to Orcadian writer Eric Linklater whose novel *Poet's Pub* was one of the first ten novels chosen to launch Penguin Press in 1935.

The opportunity has been taken in this edition to upgrade and correct details of Crash Records in or near Orkney in World War II and to add the little that is known about earlier accidents. Also included as an Appendix is the author's *Aviation Diary, Orkney, 1939 - 1945* which was originally produced to help in the writing of *Sky over Scapa*. Several military enthusiasts expressed an interest in the diary itself and a small number of copies were privately printed. Its inclusion in this book now makes the information more widely available.

Through research into the flying services in Orkney during World War II the author has made many lasting friends who have welcomed our family into their homes, with whom we have stayed and who have stayed with us. The original publication of this book was timely since a great number of them and some of my most important contributors have passed away but it is comforting to think that in remembering their years spent in the sky over Scapa, in the servicing echelons or the executive branches, that they themselves will not be forgotten.

Gregor Lamb, 23rd January 2007

Introduction

In October 1986, at a meeting of the Community Council of the parish of Birsay in Orkney, Councillor and farmer Sandy Scarth drew the attention of the members to the fact that, next day, the Control Tower of Twatt Aerodrome was to be blown up. He was of the opinion that since this was one of the last vestiges of World War II still extant, it was of historical interest and should be preserved. The Council concurred and it was agreed that steps should be taken immediately to prevent its demolition. It fell to the writer, also a member of the Council, to act on behalf of the Community Council and appeal to Orkney Islands Council to preserve the Control Tower of the Royal Naval Air Station at Twatt as testimony to the enormous contribution made to the war effort by the Fleet Air Arm in Orkney. Ronald Gilbert, Chief Executive of Orkney Islands Council, was sympathetic to the Council's request and instructions were given to the army demolition team to preserve the Control Tower. The arrival of the messenger was timely for holes had already been drilled into the tower and the charges implanted.

The Community Council was now left to decide what to do with the building. Civil Engineer, Mike Austin, established that it was structurally sound but even simple refurbishment was far beyond the budget of the Community Council. Little was known of the history of the Tower or indeed of the Airfield and, again, on behalf of the Council, the writer offered to undertake some simple research. An approach was made to the Director of the Fleet Air Arm Museum at Yeovilton in Somerset with a hint that the Orkney site might make a small museum or interpretation centre. From here a message was passed on to Captain 'Hank' Rotherham a retired naval officer living in Quebec, Canada. Hank Rotherham was the first permanent Station Commander at Twatt and he had just recently written a book about his naval experiences, devoting a considerable amount of space to his time spent in Orkney. Hank was very excited about the project and made arrangements to fly to Orkney with his wife.

Thus the Orkney Fleet Air Arm Museum became airborne. A brief news item in the *Daily Telegraph* brought in some letters of encouragement and several photographs. Word got round through service magazines and at service reunions and a file of correspondence built up including letters from Australia, New Zealand and Canada. By coincidence a local diver, Alec Strutt, found an intact Grumman Avenger at the bottom of Kirkwall Bay and the prospect of this aircraft being the centrepiece of a display gave new life to the project.

In the summer of 1988 the writer had a visit from Air Commodore 'Cyclops' Brown, a former Skeabrae pilot. 'Cyclops' had heard of the project and made the not unreasonable suggestion that, since RAF Skeabrae was very close to Twatt and there had been a high degree of cooperation between these two stations during the war, the project might perhaps be extended to include reference to the Royal Air Force as well. From this point onwards the net was spread wider and contact was made with RAF personnel. By doing so interest was increased twofold and the writer was particularly pleased to make contact with members of the Norwegian Hurricane Squadron which had been based in Orkney during the war. The project now took a new turn—to accumulate as much material as possible relating to the flying services in Orkney during World War II.

Meanwhile the photographic collection built up. At the beginning of the project there was only one photograph in Orkney Archives relating to the flying services in World War II and arrangements were made for Archives to copy any which were loaned to the writer. In this way a superb collection of over 800 photographs has been made, mostly copied from private collections but 70 were very generously donated by the Fleet Air Arm Museum at Yeovilton. Others were purchased from the Public Records Office at Kew and from the Imperial War Museum.

Orkney Islands Council meanwhile had begun to establish an Interpretation Site at Lyness, the administrative headquarters of Scapa Flow during World War II and accordingly Birsay Community Council approached Orkney Islands Council to enquire whether the Islands Council had had a change of heart over the future of certain war-time buildings. The Council replied positively indicating that they saw the project envisaged at Twatt as being complementary to their own scheme at Lyness. The Lyness Interpretation Centre would focus on warships, the Twatt Centre on military aircraft. This was followed immediately by a proposal to buy not only the Control Tower but also nine acres of the surrounding land, the aim being to recreate, piecemeal, certain features of the old station.

Cooperation from all parties had been so great that the writer decided to bring together many wartime reminiscences and photographs and weave them into a history of the *Sky Over Scapa, 1939-1945*. It was in this way that the book had its beginnings. The book is intended to complement that excellent reference book *This Great Harbour, Scapa Flow*, by William Hewison. Unlike William Hewison the writer has no particular qualifications to write a book of this nature. He was only two years old when war broke out. As a student he did help to dismantle the giant Torpedo Building at the Royal Naval Base at Lyness and translated correspondence between the contractors, Tait of Dounby and a German firm in Lübeck to where, ironically, the building was to be transported. The only other qualification of marginal relevance possessed by the writer is a certificate to say that he had failed the officer training course at the Britannia Royal Naval College, Dartmouth!

A chronological approach has been adopted within each chapter with the exception of the chapter entitled *A Posting to Orkney* where chronology is less significant. It is important for the reader to realise that this book does not vaunt war. Set in a European perspective, it merely tells the story of airmen and islanders in six tragic years of history. Without Scapa Flow, its deep-water anchorage, the war would have passed Orkney by. Instead it became, at one point, the focus of interest in Europe and, as the war progressed, well over a hundred thousand men and women from all three services must have passed through the islands, playing a part in their defence or taking temporary advantage of the enormous support structure which had been established there. If the reader can visualise from the pages of this book, something of the bustle and excitement of war and its effect on a small island community but at the same time give thought to the private, sometimes agonised lives of those who came to Scapa, then the writer will have succeeded in his aim.

*　　*　　*　　*

After the enormous interest shown in the preservation of Twatt Control Tower in the 1990s when unsolicited donations were made by interested parties in the hope that the plan would become a reality, it is regrettable that Orkney Islands Council purchased only the Control Tower and land but did nothing to preserve what remained. As this 2007 edition goes to press, it is learned that Birsay Heritage Trust has assumed this responsibility and it is hoped that, with the tower being made safe and maintained and the site becoming more accessible, it will, in the years to come, be a permanent reminder of the role played by aviation in the islands in World War II. Meanwhile it is hoped that the donations which, for eighteen years, have been languishing in the safe keeping of Orkney Islands Council, will now be directed to a fund for which they were intended.

Time is like a river made up of the events which happen, and its current is strong; no sooner does anything appear than it is swept away, and another comes in its place, and will be swept away too.

MARCUS AURELIUS, MEDITATIONS, IV. 43

Chapter One

Early Aviators

It is not generally known that, in World War II conflict began not in the south of England as one might expect but in the island group to the north of Scotland known as Orkney. In his introduction to *Action Stations (No. 7)*, David Smith writes, 'The Battle of Orkney was fought and won long before the Battle of Britain began'. In the war, this small group of islands played a part out of all proportion to its size. Why was this so?

In the 14th century, Orkney and parts of Northern Germany whence the threat now came, had been part of the same kingdom and their peoples, loyal subjects of the King of Denmark. Now fate had ranged them on opposing sides. Orkney had been given in bond to the Scottish Crown and with the Union of the Crowns and Parliaments had become part of Great Britain. Schleswig-Holstein and Lower Saxony had become *länder* of the German State and later of the German Reich. On 3rd September 1939 Britain declared war on the Reich and already the small island community of Orkney had begun a series of preparations which were to leave no part of the islands undefended and would eventually swell its population to a remarkable 60,000. Within a year the islands had been turned into an impenetrable fortress; no other part of Britain of similar size was protected with such rigour.

To understand the frenetic activity in the air over Scapa Flow in World War II we have to look briefly at the history of Orkney. In the 1930s Orkney had a population of 22,000. It was a farming community with an economy based on beef cattle and it was known nationally for its egg production. It had no manufacturing industry, no minerals, no part of its land surface was of any strategic value and, as part of Britain, it was about as far away from Germany as it was possible to get. At first sight it would appear to be of little value to Germany or indeed to any enemy. Despite these negative attributes, the islands had played a significant part in European history and indeed pre-history. There had been dense settlement here in Neolithic, Bronze Age and Iron Age times and even today the landscape is studded with monumental remains of highly organised societies who vied for territorial control of these low,

windswept islands. Harassed Norsemen settled here and established an Earldom which at its height controlled most of the north of Scotland and western Britain. What brought these people here? For all those who have left their mark in the history of Orkney, the principal attraction must have been, not the land, good as it is, but the water. The islands offered rich fishing grounds and in an otherwise hostile coastline, shelter.

Although the first record of warships in Orkney dates from the 12th century, Orkney must have been associated with navies from the earliest times. The historian Adam Bede speaks of the subjugation of Orkney by the Romans and, if true, this could have been achieved only through an impressive display of naval power for it is known that the Picts themselves had a considerable fleet of warships. For these fleets, the place of assembly must have been Scapa Flow, the vast natural anchorage in the south of Orkney encircled by The Mainland of Orkney to the north and a profusion of islands to the south, east and west. 'Scapa' takes its name from the narrow neck of land to the north-east of this stretch of water and 'Flow' is the Old Norse word *flói* which we find used for bays in Iceland. The first written record of warships in Scapa Flow dates from the year 1154 when Earl Rognvald and Earl Harald brought a fleet of fourteen into the north-east corner of the anchorage. Meanwhile, to the south-east, another smaller fleet of seven warships commanded by Sweyn Asleifsson slipped in and prepared to do battle. More than a hundred years pass before we find our next record, a fleet of 120 Norse vessels anchored in Scapa Flow. In the flagship *Kristsuðin* was King Håkon Håkonsson of Norway hosted by the Earl of Orkney, taking stock of men and materials, recruiting volunteers and hiring ships in preparation for the showdown with King Alexander of Scotland over the disputed territories in the west of Scotland.

After a period of 500 years, Scapa Flow came to the fore again. During the Napoleonic Wars a marine surveyor's report looked seriously at Scapa Flow as a fine roadstead where battleships could rendezvous but there is no evidence that his proposals received consideration. However extensive use was made of

Scapa Flow by merchant shipping. The reason for this was plain. Britain had two enemies; to the west the rebel colonists of North America and, to the east, France. Unarmed British merchant shipping vessels hugged the coast as far as possible to avoid the attentions of American and French privateers but for deep water journeys, they wisely waited for naval escorts. The Compulsory Convoys Act of 1803 was introduced to protect merchant shipping and for voyages in northern Europe where timber and forest products made up much of the trade, merchantmen gathered in Longhope, a long arm of Scapa Flow, where they cast anchor. To guard the vessels in the bay, two defensive points which took the form of Martello Towers were built and a battery of guns erected. When the man-of-war appeared, the vessels would slip their moorings and the journey eastwards in convoy began.

By the beginning of last century, there was intense rivalry between the navies of Britain and the rising German nation. The report of the 18th century marine surveyor which recommended Scapa Flow as a Fleet Anchorage was brought down and dusted. Gradually there were occasional visits of naval vessels to Scapa Flow but not until April 1909 could it be truly said that 'The Fleet's in'. Under the command of Admiral Sir William May, the battleship HMS *Dreadnought* led into Scapa Flow a fleet of 82 ships, not insignificant vessels by any means, for more than half of them were destroyers. Here they remained for a month. At a stroke the population of the islands was increased by almost 70%. The following year the Fleet returned, this time with 90 warships. Wherever possible, victualling was done from the islands themselves and for the first time

Orkney merchants were to experience the boom in trade brought by war. As a small instance of this, all baker's yeast for the Fleet requirements was sourced from Jolly, a small bakery in the parish of Harray. The provenance of such yeast in interesting. It was known as 'Parisian barm' and was brought home to Orkney by a soldier who had served in the Napoleonic War!

The arrival of this enormous British Fleet in Scapa Flow coincided with two remarkable feats of aviation both of which, in the long term, were to bring great changes to the islands. One occurred in Germany and ended by default in Orkney. On 3rd December 1910, a 1,500 cubic metre balloon belonging to the German Touring Club of Munich and named appropriately *Touring Club*, took off from a field near the village of Gersthofen, now the site of Augsburg airport. In the basket were three men, Herr Distler, the pilot and Touring Club manager, Captain Wilhelm Jördens, a retired army officer and Captain Ernst Metzger, all from Munich. There was nothing remarkable about this flight; ballooning had been a sport for more than 120 years and some seven years earlier the Wright Brothers in America had already pioneered flight with a heavier than air machine. The simple aim of the balloonists was to stay aloft for twenty four hours. Everything went well for the lift-off and there were high hopes that their mission would be accomplished but sadly, what the balloonists did not know was that they had launched themselves into the eye of a vicious depression.

When they were at altitude they soon became enveloped in cloud, the wind began to change in direction and to blow more and more strongly. Darkness fell suddenly and the balloonists were

The first to arrive in Orkney by air; Left, Distler; Centre, Jördens. ORKNEY ARCHIVES.

conscious that they were being blown at high speed across country but whither, they had no idea. They spent a frightening night cowering in the basket with the wind screaming in the ice-covered ropes above them and after 15 hours aloft, when dawn slowly began to appear, they thought they could hear the sound of the sea. At 8 o'clock on Sunday morning the storm finally forced the balloon down and they began furiously to throw away bags of sandbag ballast but it was too late. A towering wave struck the basket, washing Captain Metzger overboard. It was ironical that the loss of this one crew member saved the lives of the others for with Metzger gone the balloon rose into the air again The gale continued to blow relentlessly and for them there was no let up. At last they saw a flashing lighthouse beacon and knew that they were nearing land again. When more lights appeared they decided that it had to be land underneath them and that it was safe to open the valve and make a descent. Quickly they pulled the ripping cord to deflate the balloon and this time by good luck that same wind which had blown them across Europe pulled the deflating balloon and its trailing basket shorewards but the furious gale continued to keep the deflated casing airborne and since the grappling hook had been jettisoned earlier to give them additional lift, the helpless crew was dragged overland at high speed. The basket careered along through fences and stone walls for almost a mile until it struck a wall and was held fast, coming to rest upside down at the edge of a quarry.

Gradually the English speaking visitors established that they had made landfall in Orkney, just to the east of Kirkwall. They quickly recovered from their ordeal and two days later they set sail on the steamer on the first leg of their journey back to Germany. They had made the longest flight ever over an ocean, a distance of more than 500 miles and they had moreover set a record which no one else can beat—they were the first of many foreigners to arrive in Orkney by air. It is a remarkable coincidence that they took off from an area which is now Augsburg Airport and, had they landed two minutes earlier, they would perhaps have touched down on the site of the present day Kirkwall Airport at Grimsetter!

The other related aerial feat occurred 3,000 miles away in Chesapeake Bay, USA where American aviator, Eugene Ely, made the first successful flight from a ship at sea. A year later he landed on a specially adapted cruiser and in this way opened up new possibilities for naval warfare. But the landing on was still technically a very risky operation and, meanwhile it was the development of the so-called hydroaeroplane which was favoured by the American and British governments. In 1912 Lt. C. R. Samson RN in a Short S.27 floatplane took off from a specially extended platform over the foredeck of the battleship HMS *Africa* in Sheerness Harbour, and made a successful landing at Eastchurch. Later the aircraft landed in the sea beside the parent vessel, was winched back on board and prepared for another flight. This was the modest beginning of what later became the Catapult Flights of 700 Squadron of the Royal Navy which reached their peak in the middle years of World War II.

Left: the author's uncle, Theodore Lamb, Flight/Lt. Pilot in the Royal Flying Corps, 1916; he had 500 hours solo flying experience, none of which was in Orkney.

The year 1911 brought Winston Churchill to the office of First Lord of the Admiralty. The success of Samson's flight led him to believe there was a considerable future for naval aviation but Churchill considered the first obstacle in the way of its development was the name 'hydroaeroplane' or, sometimes, 'hydroplane'. Churchill suggested the name 'seaplane' and the name stuck.

The Royal Flying Corps was formed in 1912, consisting of a Military Wing, a Naval Wing and a Central Flying School and in the same year the old light cruiser HMS *Hermes* was converted as a parent ship for seaplanes with platforms fore and aft for launching and stowing. In August 1913 HMS *Hermes* was in Scapa Flow with two aircraft embarked, one of British manufacture, the other French and Orcadians watched with great interest the comings and goings of the heavier than air machines, the first of many hundreds to fly over Scapa Flow. Winston Churchill, in his capacity as First Lord of

the Admiralty, was in Scapa Flow at the time and was privileged to view the anchorage from above when he had a flight round Scapa Flow in one of *Hermes'* seaplanes. Churchill was a keen aviator himself and already an experienced flier; indeed his family was seriously worried that his passion for flying might end in disaster. There is little doubt that Churchill was involved in, if not responsible for, the Admiralty declaring in June 1914 that it was to break away from the Royal Flying Corps and form its own independent Royal Naval Air Service. It was from this small beginning that, what later came to be called the Fleet Air Arm, developed.

On 1st August 1914, with war now inevitable, the Fleet, consisting this time of 96 warships, took refuge in Scapa Flow and was later joined by a flotilla of 18. At this time Scapa Flow was anything but a safe haven and the Fleet remained extremely jittery until all the anti-submarine booms and blockships had been put in place. Joining the 'Grand Fleet' as it came to be known on the outbreak of war, five aircraft arrived, three seaplanes and two aeroplanes. They were aircraft of the newly formed Royal Naval Air Service. A Fleet Aircraft Repair Base was set up near the farm of Nether Scapa in the north-east corner of the anchorage but in the most exposed place possible, wide open to gales from the south-west. Within three months one such gale struck the islands doing extensive damage not only to the temporary buildings but also to the aircraft. A more sheltered repair facility was sought and this led to the construction of a base at Houton in the north of Scapa Flow although it did not become operational until 1917.

Another development in aerial reconnaissance made its mark in Orkney. This was the so-called kite balloon. It was merely an extension of the long established observation post on the crow's nest. A balloon, beneath which hung a basket with an observer, was secured to a ship with a long hawser. At Caldale to the west of Kirkwall, huge hangars, originally intended to house and maintain airships were adapted to service and inflate these balloons. Balloons of a type used to protect warships from aerial attack were also serviced here towards the end of the war; this establishment had a staff of almost 200. The remains of this large station is still in evidence. Yet another kite balloon station was built at Houton in Orphir. Apparently an attractive proposition from the observer's point of view, kite observation balloons were not a success. They could scarcely ever be flown in windy Orkney and moreover could be lethal when an electrical storm threatened since the storm tended to discharge through the balloon which of course was hydrogen filled. Several were ignited by lightning in Scapa Flow, though the observers, remarkably, survived. One observer was less fortunate the hawser

Royal Naval Air Station, Houton, Orkney, 1918. PRO.

Airship sheds from SE; Caldale Air Station, Orkney, WW1. Kent.

Observers in a basket suspended below a Kite Balloon; the observer on the right is using a telephone, WWI.
Copyright Unknown.

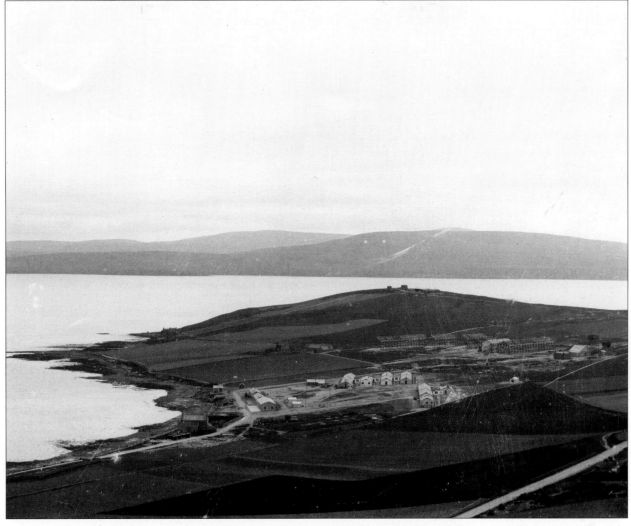

Houton Kite Balloon Station, Orkney, 1918, WW1. KENT.

supporting the kite sheared in the strong wind and balloon, basket and observer disappeared into the northern mists. Although a parachute was a standard piece of equipment in such balloons in case it was brought down by gunfire, the heavy clothing worn by the observer to protect him against atmospheric cold would have made survival in the cold North Sea impossible.

Meanwhile seaplane development continued apace with the commissioning of HMS *Campania* as an aircraft carrier in 1915. At first capable of carrying six seaplanes she was later modified to carry twelve and her inclined deck extended to 200 feet. Much of the early experimental work with this carrier was carried out in Scapa Flow. Seaplanes were clumsy, slow and unmanoeuvrable compared with aeroplanes and it was an experiment by Royal Naval pilots in Scapa Flow itself which was, much later, to spike the development of the seaplane as a ship-borne aircraft. In Scapa Flow in 1917, one of the most significant advances in naval aviation was made. HMS *Furious* had been launched in 1916 as a light battle cruiser and during later construction, was modified as an aircraft carrier though initially

the facilities she offered aviators were extremely primitive, being equipped only with a flying-off deck forward. When *Furious* arrived in Scapa, pilots in their Sopwith Pups could now get plenty of practice flying off but there was one great handicap. There was no airstrip anywhere in Orkney where naval aeroplanes (as distinct from seaplanes) could land. The only choice for the Sopwith pilot was to ditch or to find a reasonably flat piece of land where he could park his aeroplane until it was retrieved. The ditching of aircraft, though profligate, had to be seen in perspective for these early bi-planes cost little more than a battleship shell!

To facilitate more flexible use of aeroplanes, the urgent need for a land base became apparent and a small naval airfield was established at Smoogro on the north coast of Scapa Flow.

Pilots were able to get much needed flying practice from this airfield for the Fleet was in Scapa Flow for long periods of time. Aircraft were towed back to the ship on crude rafts towed by a picket boat and were hoisted on board again by crane. Now *Furious* was a fast warship, capable of a top speed of

Fellow pilots holding back the aircraft as Squadron Commander Dunning in a Sopwith Pup lands safely on HMS Furious in Scapa Flow in 1917. This was the first ever landing on a vessel underway. COPYRIGHT UNKNOWN.

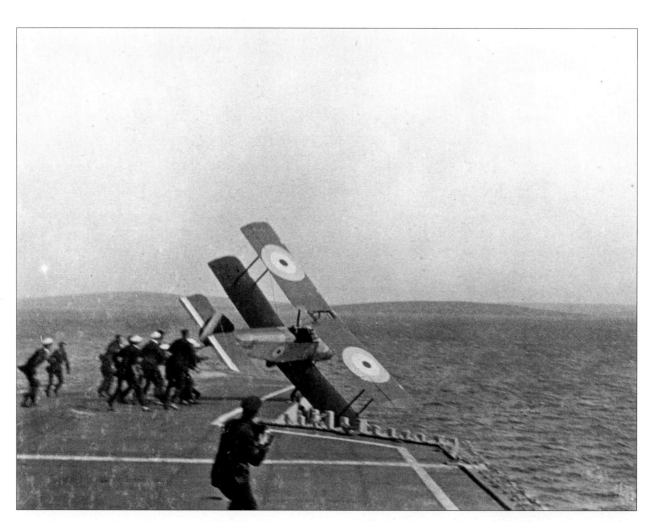

Despite desperate attempts by fellow officers, Squadron Commander Dunning goes over the side and is drowned while attempting a second landing on HMS Furious in Scapa Flow. COPYRIGHT UNKNOWN.

31 knots in the open sea and it occurred to the Smoogro pilots that, if the carrier sailed into a reasonably strong natural wind of around 25 knots, it might be possible to land on the flying-off deck. It was decided to attempt something which had never been done anywhere in the world before—a landing on the deck of a moving carrier. *Furious* was not the ideal vessel to land on for the deck was after all a flying-off deck and was of course placed immediately in front of the funnels. The aviator would not only have to negotiate the funnels but also to pilot his frail craft through the extreme turbulence around that part of the vessel. Neither was Scapa Flow the ideal place for such an experiment. The maximum stretch of water was a little over ten miles and it would have taken some time for the carrier to get up speed and some time for it to slow down; moreover the anchorage was crowded with warships. At least wave height in the anchorage was normally fairly low and there would have been little heave on *Furious'* landing platform. Ideally the experiment should have been conducted in the open sea but this would have run the risk of a U-boat attack.

On 5th August 1917 aircraftmen prepared Squadron Commander Edwin Dunning's Sopwith Pup for the epic flight. Many admirals and indeed generals were on board that day awaiting the outcome, such was the significance of this new development. Carrier arrester wires were still unheard of so grappling ropes were fixed to the wing struts to enable the deckhands to restrain the aircraft if it touched down. Conditions were not ideal when he took off from Smoogro; the natural wind speed was only 21 knots and to make his task more difficult, *Furious'* maximum attainable speed was only 26 knots. He did however land on successfully with the help of the grappling party and history was made.

Five days later, it was decided that further trial landings should take place involving several naval pilots. Again Dunning was the first to take off and landed successfully but the wind blew his aircraft back and the elevator was damaged by the coamings of a lift hatch. He was not happy about this performance and ordered Flight Commander Geoffrey Moore (who was just about to take off) out of his aircraft, jumped in and took off again. As he came in to land, the eight appointed officers ran to grab the toggles but Dunning was clearly not confident of his success, waved them off and opened up his engine to go round once more. Unfortunately the engine choked, the aircraft stalled and dropped on deck where the wind caught it. By this time he had travelled beyond the grappling party who rushed

Houton Seaplane Station, WW1. Kent.

Royal Naval Air Station, Stenness, Orkney, 1918. PRO.

after him but, despite heroic efforts, only the tail toggles could be held. The aircraft slewed to starboard and went over the side. Dunning's aircraft was kept afloat by an airbag in the tail but he was trapped in the cockpit. Remarkably there were no rescue craft positioned for this experiment and the carrier had to steam past the wreckage at 26 knots. It took 20 minutes for the 20,000 ton ship to heave to by which time Dunning had drowned. Deck-landing trials were immediately discontinued while their Lordships considered the next move. Dunning's experiment had not been in vain however. A Committee of Enquiry into Naval Aviation meeting in 1917 recommended that the minimum length of a landing deck should be 300 feet (91.4m) and no less than the full width of the vessel. Thus was born the first flush-deck carrier, HMS *Argus*, and the way was open for development of Royal Naval aeroplanes which were faster, lighter, more manoeuvrable and with longer endurance.

The Royal Navy still considered that the seaplane had a vital role to play as a land-based aircraft and consequently two seaplane bases were built in Orkney, one in Stenness, the other in Orphir. The Stenness base was established on the southern shore of the Stenness Loch beside the farm of Netherbigging. Flights 309, 310 and 311, consisting of 18 Felixstowe F3 seaplanes operated from here and the staff of 200 were billeted partly in the Standing Stones Hotel and partly in a hutted camp. The hotel became the Headquarters of the Royal Naval Air Service serving Scapa Flow. However the Stenness Loch proved too shallow* and too exposed for a seaplane base and eventually the more sheltered base at Houton in Orphir on the edge of Scapa Flow was favoured. Originally intended only as a repair and maintenance base, Houton, when fully developed had slipways, hangars, concrete aprons, repair shops, its own generating plant and accommodation for a staff of 600. Apart from a good number of Short seaplanes, 36 'Large America' type Curtiss flying boats were planned for this station; at one point 25 flying boats could certainly be mustered though they were not by any means always serviceable.

The presence of so many of these massive machines with wing-spans of almost 100 feet (30m.) must have been an impressive sight at Scapa in these early days of aviation. After the seaplane base was moved to Houton, the Standing Stones Hotel in Stenness, though now inconveniently placed, was retained as the Headquarters of the Naval Air Service.

The purpose of the seaplane base was to provide anti-submarine patrols in the waters to the north of

Orkney, between North Ronaldsay and Fair Isle. To counter the menace of German U-boats, an anti-submarine boom had been placed across the English Channel and now to gain access to the Atlantic, U-boats took the northern route through the Fair Isle Channel. Usually in the faint light of dusk or dawn, they would break water and check their compasses by Fair Isle since their compasses were still not gyroscopic. To monitor the reported positions of U-boats, in the Operations Room at the Headquarters in Stenness, a large map of the North Atlantic covered the wall and on it were plotted the positions of British and enemy submarines. The Headquarters was commanded by Captain Oliver Swan, (later Air Vice-Marshal), a pioneer of seaplane development. The Short seaplanes and Curtiss and Felixstowe flying boats were used on patrols, some of which lasted more than five hours. Few could have envied the lot of the pilots of these frail aircraft in open cockpits, usually in inclement weather, their only lifeline initially being the two obligatory pigeons which they carried with them in a basket and which, in an emergency, flew back to the pigeon loft at Houton. Flight/Lt. T. Crouther Gordon records a not untypical entry in his diary:

12th September (1918) The Admiral at Longhope called for patrols and two flying boats were despatched but it was a dreadful day for flying. The sea was rough, the wind was high and the air was very bumpy. In addition there was no U-boat to be seen. Four hundred gallons of petrol and nothing to show for it! The language of the pilots was not suitable to be recorded in my diary.

The stormy weather wreaked havoc on land too; despite the relatively sheltered position of Houton, a storm on 6th October 1918, lifted a brand new flying boat worth £14,000 (an enormous amount of money at that time) off its cradle and completely destroyed it. The planes seemed to have had little success in finding their quarry despite numerous reports of enemy submarine presence in the Fair Isle Channel. Moreover, since naval aviation was in its infancy, the appropriate infrastructure to maintain an operational fleet of seaplanes had yet to be established. On one occasion there was only one flying boat available for anti-submarine patrol and an old Short seaplane had to be brought into use as well.

It is well known that, apart from its engagement with the German Navy at Jutland in 1916, the Grand Fleet rarely left the anchorage in Scapa Flow, nevertheless development of the Royal Naval Air Service in the islands went ahead. Towards the end of the war, a new airfield at Swanbister in Orphir on the northern edge of Scapa Flow was begun and, even after the Armistice, work was still progressing there. Considerable progress was made in Naval Aviation

Seaplanes continued to appear in Scapa in the inter-war years; here a Supermarine Southampton III, S1058 lies on the beach near the old Royal Naval Air Station at Nether Scapa. KENT.

during the war and there is no doubt that Scapa Flow played a large part not only in developing roles for aircraft but also in developing new roles for warships with the advent of aerial warfare. There was still some prejudice in the Senior Service against aviators; indeed there was still evidence of this in World War II but, despite this, aircraft clearly had operational value at sea and were here to stay. The Royal Navy had 2,900 aircraft in 1918, the same year in which the world's first purpose-built aircraft carrier HMS *Hermes* was laid down and, ironically, the same year in which the Royal Naval Air Service merged with the Royal Flying Corps to form the Royal Air Force.

By 1918 elements of the Grand Fleet had moved south to Rosyth though Scapa Flow continued to be maintained fully as a naval base. However, by November in that same year many of the warships were back again, on this occasion shepherding upwards of 70 warships of the German Hochseeflotte which, under the terms of the Armistice were to be interned in an Allied port. It was a remarkable assemblage of warships. Overhead flew an escort of Royal Naval planes from the Air Station at Houton. As the world was soon to learn, the German warships were, before long, to disappear beneath the surface of Scapa Flow. There was no further need for a Grand Fleet presence in the anchorage and gradually it moved south once more to Rosyth with its accompanying aircraft. At times, 100,000 Royal Naval personnel had been based in Scapa Flow and Orcadian farmers and merchants had fed them. The prosperity brought by war had now gone. Between 1922 and 1923 what had been the old Royal Naval Air Service Stations were sold off and a blighted landscape of concrete and iron remained. No one could have predicted that, within 15 years, the whole cycle would begin again with even greater intensity.

The superstructure of SMS Hindenburg remains above water after the scuttling of the German Fleet in Scapa Flow in 1919. KENT.

The Military Airfields of Orkney

Four hundred and forty four military airfields were built in Britain during World War II. Four of these airfields were established in Orkney and five 'dummy dromes', altogether quite a number for such a small area. The Orkney airfields were extremely busy and, at their height, could launch 15 squadrons of aircraft. In this chapter we trace the convoluted evolution of these stations and their post-war history.

Early in 1938, the Directorate of the Naval Air Division suggested that a survey of sites suitable for the location of a military airfield should be undertaken in Orkney in view of the fact that Scapa Flow was intended to be used as a base for the Home Fleet in the event of possible hostilities with Germany. By August 1938, twenty-nine sites had been examined in Orkney by the Air Ministry and, of these, it was considered that Skeabrae was possibly the only suitable location. Between 15th and 21st September 1938, the Admiralty visited Orkney and considered four sites. These were Skeabrae, Hatston, Wideford near Kirkwall and Quoyburray in Tankerness. Wideford, at that time used by Scottish Airways, was considered incapable of expansion. Quoyburray was low lying, wet, and had little to recommend it. Hatston had the advantage that it could be developed in the dual role of aerodrome and seaplane base. Skeabrae might also be developed in this way, the seaplane base being established in the north end of the Harray Loch. The decision was taken to establish the first purpose built military airfield at Skeabrae and, accordingly, Mr. James Wood the proprietor of the farm of Garson in Sandwick, and Mr. John Kirkness of the farm of Hammerclait, were given verbal notice by military surveyors that their lands were to be immediately requisitioned. They were visited again in mid September by the Admiralty for an on-site assessment of the alternatives. There was no further immediate action and we find both these farmers writing to the Air Ministry in October 1938 anxious about their future. Mr. Wood was unsure whether to buy sheep to make up his breeding stock; he had no desire to buy in sheep and have to resell them immediately at a loss. Mr. Kirkness wanted an

assurance that his property would no longer be required 'now that peace seems assured'. The proprietors were not to know that, as a result of the September visit, doubts were cast in the minds of the Admiralty experts about the suitability of Skeabrae. Its remoteness from Kirkwall and the difficulties in establishing a seaplane base at the north end of the Harray Loch counted against it. Moreover Kirkwall clearly needed a proper civil airport, the Wideford site often being fogbound and incapable of extension. The intention of Scottish Airways to develop Hatston as an alternative civil airport seemed to weigh heavily in favour of this site. In December 1938, plans to develop Skeabrae were abandoned and Hatston was chosen as the first purpose-built Royal Naval Air Station in Great Britain. The Sandwick farmers could not have been very happy about the two months' delay in the reply to their letter only to be told then that their lands were no longer wanted.

The lands of Hatston extending to 320 acres were purchased by the Admiralty for £25,000 and in February 1939, work was begun on the construction of the airfield. Unlike Skeabrae, it had the added advantage that seaplanes, at that time very important in naval aviation, could land alongside. What appeared at first sight to be a difficulty—the main Kirkwall to Stromness road passed through the middle of the site—was to be used to advantage as one of four runways to be constructed. Because of the climate and the nature of the underlying soil, all runways were to have tarmacadam surfaces and, in what was surely to be a unique arrangement, the local council was contracted to construct them. For the first pilots who landed at Hatston, hard runways came as a great surprise to them for the norm at that time was the grass landing strip. Hatston was one of the first aerodromes in Britain to have a tarmacadam surface but not the first as quoted in David Smith's *Action Stations*. Gosport and Odiham in England already had bitumen surfaces in 1938. The main road was to be diverted, at the Admiralty's expense, to the south of the station. Four Bellman hangars were planned along with workshops, storage space, compass swinging bases, a magazine and tanks for

Jock Douglas from Harray was the last person to use the Hatston section of the main Kirkwall to Stromness road before it was closed off to make a runway; in the background lie foreign vessels impounded by the Royal Navy to check for contraband goods bound for Germany.

50,000 gallons of aviation fuel. To man this station the requirements were 70 officers, 38 Chief Petty Officers, 36 Petty Officers and 290 other ratings, a complement of 434, for all of whom hutted accommodation had to be provided. All in all it was a major project since Hatston had to be started from scratch.

On 25th August 1939, Hatston runways were considered operational and Fleet Requirement Unit, 771 Squadron moved in to begin its long association with Orkney. The first aircraft to land was Swordfish R5A from Evanton piloted by Lt.Cdr. Mortimer and with TAG Harry Davison. The very next day 800 Squadron Skuas disembarked from HMS *Ark Royal*, the first of seventy two Royal Naval squadrons to do so in the following six years. On 2nd October, the

Royal Naval Air Station, Hatston. FAA.

Aerial photograph of Hatston under snow; shows clearly the main Kirkwall/Stromness road which served initially as the main runway. FAA.

station was commissioned as HMS *Sparrowhawk*. At the commencement of hostilities, the Royal Navy, in terms of aviation, was reasonably prepared. Churchill was not happy that there was no RAF presence to protect the Fleet in its Home Base but seemed satisfied that the Navy itself would provide two squadrons of fighter aircraft when the Fleet was in Scapa and a visit to the anchorage on 14th September 1939 confirmed his impression that this was adequate. The dramatic turn of events in October which resulted in the penetration of the Scapa defences by a U-boat and the later bombing of the Fleet caused an immediate reassessment of the position. As Churchill says in his *The Gathering Storm*,

These events showed how necessary it was to perfect the defences of Scapa against all forms of attack before allowing it to be used. . . . On October 31st, accompanied by the First Sea Lord, I went to Scapa* to hold a second conference on these matters in Admiral Forbes' flagship. The scale of defence for Scapa upon which we now agreed included . . . substantial fighter protection . . . organised both in the Orkneys and at Wick on the mainland.
*it was in fact the Clyde [G.L.]

Control Tower, Hatston with Avenger in foreground; notice the plan of the runways is marked on the tower! The last three windows on the left of the long building are the Signals Distribution Office; this building also housed the WT Office; Teleprinter Room, Cypher Office, Met. Office to the right as well as offices for the Air Signals Officer, Commander Flying, Staff Officer (Air) and the old Ops. Room. PRO.

The immediate outcome of this was the proposal to build in Orkney a second airfield for the Royal Navy and two landing strip aerodromes for the RAF. In November 1939, the Admiralty immediately took up its option on Skeabrae and so, almost a year after they had been told their land was not wanted, the farmers of Garson, Hammerclait and Grind in Sandwick were given very short notice to leave their properties. On 8th December, the bulldozers moved in, in some cases before the farms were properly vacated. The former occupiers looked on in disbelief as battering rams knocked out the windows battens of wood were carried into their houses and secured to chains which passed through the window holes. These in turn were fixed to bulldozers which quickly pulled the walls out and the whole building collapsed. As in the case of Hatston a main road also had to be diverted. Plans for the new Skeabrae station were modest—the construction of a one squadron (12 aircraft) site. As for the RAF, the Air Ministry (Aerodrome Branch) considered sites at Grimsetter, Twatt and Birsay. Birsay was eliminated as being too exposed, Twatt was considered too near the Royal Naval Air station being developed at Skeabrae. The decision was taken to construct a station at Grimsetter in Tankerness on the East Mainland. In the interim, RAF Coastal Command at Wick took over operational control of the northern Royal Naval squadrons, 803 Skuas and Rocs at Wick and 804 Gladiators at Hatston.

With the return of the Fleet to Scapa in March 1940, the German bombers returned too, this time in force. On 16th March, the whole of 804 Squadron from Hatston got airborne in the gathering darkness to intercept a bombing raid on Scapa Flow and, indeed, on their own station. They failed to make contact with any enemy aircraft and had great difficulty in returning to base. On Monday 8th April upwards of two dozen German bombers attacked the Flow and this time RAF Hurricanes of No. 605 Squadron from Wick came to the aid of the defences. On Wednesday 11th April, the day after the German invasion of Norway, 60 enemy bombers made a determined raid on Scapa and again the Wick Hurricanes went into action. In this great air battle over Orkney, seven enemy bombers were brought down.

Despite the threat of more and bigger attacks on Scapa, perhaps even an invasion, there was still no RAF presence in Orkney and no immediate prospect either, pending the completion of Grimsetter scheduled for the Autumn. There was a desperate need for the faster RAF fighters to be stationed locally and immediately. A solution was found by transferring the new Royal Naval Air Station at Skeabrae to the Royal Air Force. On 2nd May 1940 it was handed over, in an incomplete state, to the RAF. Despite the transfer, the RAF was still dithering about the development of Skeabrae for we

Hatston was situated right at the edge of the sea and the rescue launch was frequently required! Air Mechanics on board the launch in Kirkwall Bay. HAMILTON.

find that, on 14th May, a directive was sent to the Admiralty to the effect that Skeabrae was no longer needed since Castletown in Caithness was now operational. The outcome of that message is not recorded. Castletown did receive its first squadron, 504 Hurricanes on 21st June but development of Skeabrae went ahead nevertheless, plans being modified to make it into a station capable of handling two Fighter Squadrons. Runways of Royal Naval air stations were a mere 30 yards wide and this meant extending them in width to the standard 50 yards required by the RAF.

These modified plans, coupled with acute labour shortages in the islands meant that it was 15th September before the first aircraft landed at what was still a very incomplete station. By this time the Battle of Britain was at its height and so, though the RAF station was at last operational, no RAF squadrons could be spared! 804 Squadron of the Royal Navy with Grumman Martlets was called upon to fill the gap and took over the defending role. They had to wait until 7th January 1941 before they were at last relieved of their duties by No. 3 Squadron of the Royal Air Force.

The Royal Navy, now one airfield short was, in turn, hard pressed to carry out its duties. Between 23rd and 24th May 1940, Admiralty surveyors were already in the islands looking at the alternative sites available and, the following month, it was decided to construct a new station at Twatt in the parish of Birsay with plans to accommodate one reinforcing fighter squadron but this was very soon changed to accommodate one and a half squadrons. The landowners concerned got even less warning than their Sandwick counterparts. The farm of Hyval was to be immediately demolished followed by Festigarth, Skogar, Newhall and North Newhall.

The RAF was not happy about the Royal Navy choosing a site in such close proximity to Skeabrae, the airfields being barely two miles distant. It was considered that, without some measure of Flying Control, it was inevitable that with the wind blowing from a north-westerly or south-easterly direction, aircraft landing at one station would collide with aircraft taking off at the other. The RAF proposed that it be responsible for Flying Control in the immediate area of both stations. The Royal Navy objected most strongly to this and thus began between these two services, a series of sharp exchanges. The Royal Navy could not, understandably, tolerate a situation in which a junior officer in Flying Control at Skeabrae might countermand the order of a carrier Admiral to embark his squadrons immediately. The RAF felt so strongly about the issue that they suggested the Royal Navy move to their station at Grimsetter! The argument was never resolved. Both services controlled their aircraft independently and, as a

Walrus taxying up slipway, Hatston, 1941; in background can be seen neutral shipping brought into Kirkwall Harbour from the North Atlantic by the Royal Navy to check on contraband materials bound for Germany. FANCOURT.

King George VI at Hatston, 1941; note Maryland aircraft in background. FANCOURT.

matter of fact, the only collision which occurred over Skeabrae during the war involved RAF aircraft and the only incident at Twatt was a mid-air collision between two Royal Navy planes. Twatt was commissioned on 1st April 1941 as HMS *Tern*, a satellite of Hatston and the first aircraft, a detachment of four Sea Hurricanes of 880 Squadron landed on. At first it acted as an overflow for frontline squadrons disembarked at Hatston but, with the arrival of USS *Wasp* in Scapa Flow in April 1942 and the disembarkation of three of her squadrons for an extended period while she ferried Spitfires to beleaguered Malta, Twatt assumed a new role. Fleet Requirements Unit 771 was transferred to Twatt and was subsequently joined two months later by 700 Squadron. Previously, on 31st March, Twatt had been elevated to an independent command. Meanwhile in the East Mainland, RAF Grimsetter became operational on 17th October 1940 as a satellite of Skeabrae. In the early 1940s it was clear that the busy Orkney skies needed a proper control centre and accordingly all Fighter Operations shed their Coastal Command control and were transferred from Wick to Kirkwall where a Fighter Direction Station was established.

At the age of 21 Jean Williams a WAAF from Nottingham was posted here as a Fighter Plotter She describes the experience:

We were the first airwomen at the camp which was situated on both sides of the Holm Road. The domestic site was on one side of the road and on the other were the Admin. Offices, the Officers' Mess and the Operation block. The WAAF site was alongside the RAF quarters but divided by a swamp and masses of barbed wire! It was a brand new site of Nissen and wooden huts, completely self contained, comprising sleeping and recreation quarters, guard room, NAAFI, sick quarters, hairdressers, etc. and far superior to that which many of us had experienced; here the ablution huts were attached to the sleeping huts and that was five star living!

The Ops Room was typical of the early period. The Ops table was in the centre with the plotters around it. On a raised dais facing the centre sat the Controller and his assistants and on the opposite wall was a large board giving all the information of the readiness of the RAF squadrons in that area. On each side were the desks of the Navy and Ack-Ack Officers and at a smaller table sat the D/F plotters. The whole appearance was of DIY but very efficient nevertheless.

In January 1944 we moved to the purpose built bunker off the Deerness Road where everything was far more technical and far more spacious but no more efficient. The controller and other officers were now behind glass, high above the Ops room and there were offices for the Navy, Army, signals, etc.

The Ops Room plotted all aircraft, day and night, but only controlled RAF squadrons. I vaguely remember a German aircraft being shot down over Scapa Flow but I do remember talking down a lost aircraft and being unable to help another lost pilot. Night flying from Hatston was always a busy time for the plotters and I seem to remember a couple of aircraft ditching in Kirkwall Bay. Our tour of duty was for nine months but I don't know of any WAAF in Ops who did not volunteer for a second tour, despite the fact that about 95% of the Ops WAAF came from the south of England! I was very upset when I left Orkney in February 1945 but was determined to return. I eventually did so in 1983 and since then I have been back twice. Of course it is no longer a fortified island but it really hasn't changed; the magic is still there.

Grimsetter was used regularly by squadrons based at Skeabrae but it was not until 11th June 1942 that the first squadron, No. 132 moved in.

Five decoy airfields were also constructed in Orkney during the war. On The Mainland, two were established in the parish of Birsay at Deasbreck and at the Burn of Grid. The other 'dummy dromes' were built on the island of Sanday on the Plain of Fidge, at Sacquoy Head in Rousay and at Cot-on-Hill in the south-east of Shapinsay. All these dummy airfields relied on flare paths as means of deceit and individual generating stations had to be provided. Even the large RNAS Station at Twatt did not have its own flare path until the end of the war! Some decoy stations also had 'dummy fires' which could be lit to deceive the enemy into believing that important targets had been hit. The enemy showed no interest in these decoy airfields although an enormous amount of effort had gone into their planning and we find that by September 1942 the Sanday and Rousay sites had already been abandoned. In December 1942, in Army manoeuvres, the Deasbreck facilities were actually, by accident, shelled and destroyed! Not only did the enemy show no interest in the decoys, they showed surprisingly little interest at all in Orkney airfields. Only Hatston saw a little enemy action—and that was in the early stages of the war. Grimsetter was bombed once; Skeabrae and Twatt were left untouched.

As the war shifted its focus in Europe the functions of the stations changed. There was no likelihood of further aerial bombardment and even less of airborne invasion. The RAF, having wanted only one station in Orkney in the first place found itself with two, one of which, Grimsetter, was, by 1943, considered surplus to their requirements. The Royal Navy on the other hand found itself from time to time hard pressed for squadron accommodation. Hatston regularly had to accommodate five squadrons of disembarked aircraft and the runways were considered inadequate for the new 845 and 846 Avenger Squadrons which were about to arrive. Twatt, with 700 Squadron and 771 Squadron both of which had the largest number of aircraft of any of the Royal Naval squadrons was crowded with aircraft

The purpose built Fighter Direction Station in Kirkwall, locally known as the 'Black Building', as it is today; its future remains in doubt.

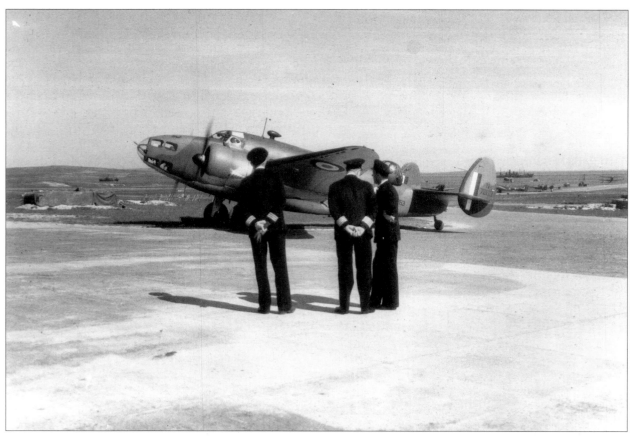

Duke of Kent visiting Hatston, 16.05.41; being met by Capt. Fancourt and Commander Rotherham; the aircraft, a Lockheed Hudson I, N7263, normally a Coastal Command patrol bomber, is seen here as an aircraft of the 'King's Flight' with special passenger seats, an extra hand-operated gun in the nose, a D/F (Direction Finder) in a streamlined cover on the roof and a special blister on the pilot's left side window to improve downward and rearward view. FANCOURT.

and could rarely accept front line disembarkations. Consequently, on 6th July 1943, Grimsetter was transferred to the Royal Navy, initially as a satellite of Hatston but on 15th August became an independent command when it was commissioned as HMS *Robin* and a major rebuilding programme begun which would equip the Station to cope with three disembarked squadrons. The first opportunity to use the station came in September when Hatston was again swamped by aircraft, this time from the American carrier USS *Ranger* which joined the British Fleet at Scapa. 846 Squadron with its twelve Avengers were displaced from Hatston and took up residence at Grimsetter. By October the Royal Navy had upgraded the station with the addition of new officers' quarters, recreational block and galleys.

The inadequacy of Hatston as an airfield became increasingly apparent as the war went on and with the Royal Navy now operating from three stations there was a real need to rationalise. On 30th March 1944 the proposal was made to develop Twatt as the only suitable airfield in Orkney where disembarked squadrons of Home Fleet aircraft could train together. After the arrival of 771 Squadron, Twatt had already been expanded from a one and a half to a three squadron station. New proposals included demolition of the Control Tower and the construction

of a superior Fearn type tower, more squadron hangars, workshops, offices and upgrading of the accommodation to accept 1,872 personnel including 438 Wrens. A large frontline training unit accommodating three squadrons of Fighters, each with fourteen aircraft and two squadrons of Torpedo Bombers with twelve aircraft each was envisaged. To make this possible, the whole of the Fleet Requirements Unit, 771 Squadron, the largest squadron in the Royal Navy and now combined with 700 Squadron, was to move to a new station. In July, the former Coastal Command station, Dounreay in Caithness was acquired for this purpose and established as a satellite of Twatt as HMS *Tern II* but as the war progressed attention shifted to the Far East and, as a consequence, the huge expansion plans for Twatt were barely implemented. On 5th December 1944 the plans were abandoned and it was decided merely to make some minor cosmetic changes to the station.

With the cessation of hostilities in Europe on 8th May 1945, the writing was already on the wall for Orkney's military airfields. In their quick demise there were echoes of their tortuous beginnings. No squadrons were based at Grimsetter after April 1945 and, at the end of July, the Royal Navy was happy to transfer it back to the Royal Air Force to become a satellite of Skeabrae. 846 Squadron Avengers, the last operational squadron to be based at Hatston left on 19th July for Crail and two weeks later Hatston became a satellite of Twatt as HMS *Tern II*. With the departure of No. 603 Squadron from Skeabrae in July, Skeabrae itself came under the wing of Twatt and, for a short time the commander of Twatt was responsible for the control of four stations— Grimsetter, Skeabrae and Dounreay, in addition to his own! Hatston was soon however to become Kirkwall's first civilian airport, a position it held until 1948 when, with the arrival of Dakotas, it became necessary to transfer the airport to Grimsetter which eventually came to be known as Kirkwall Airport. Hatston airfield was taken over by Kirkwall Town Council and the Officers' and Ratings' accommodation was used to solve the town's immediate post-war housing problem. Some of the hangars were converted to civilian use and the idea gradually developed of Hatston as Orkney's first Industrial Estate. Twatt became a reserve station under Lossiemouth until 1949 when both it and its satellite Skeabrae were placed on a Care and Maintenance basis but an end was in sight. With the announcement in June 1956 of the closure of Scapa Flow Royal Naval Base, there was clearly no future

Skeabrae; aerial photograph from 5,000 feet; 29.04.43 at that time No. 66 Spitfire Squadron, No. 234 Spitfire Squadron and 1476 Anson Advanced Ship Recognition Flight were based there. HORNE.

RAF Skeabrae showing, encircled, defended positions.
HORNE

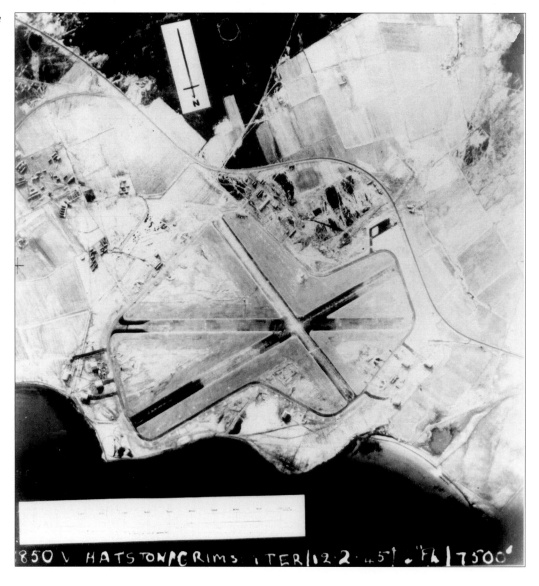

Aerial photograph of Grimsetter. 12.02.45. FAA.

for the Royal Naval Air Stations. Both Skeabrae and Twatt were sold off in 1957. All timber and Nissen buildings were removed and the land reverted to what could only be described as limited agricultural use because of the vast amount of concrete, pipework and brickwork left on and in the airfields.

But Skeabrae and Twatt were not dead by any means—only apparently unconscious since in the 1970s military surveyors again appeared warning the new proprietors and indeed the contiguous proprietors that their lands were to be requisitioned for a new airfield which this time would combine both the old RAF and Fleet Air Arm Stations. At that time relations between Britain and Iceland were strained over fishing rights, the so-called 'Cod War' and it was feared that NATO was to be asked to pull out of its base at Keflavik. The new NATO base was to be in Orkney. The fishing dispute was finally solved and the plan to redevelop Skeabrae and Twatt abandoned. Shortly afterwards with the advent of North Sea oil both airfields came to the fore again when it was planned to construct a huge airfield there to handle trans-Atlantic oil-related freight. Like the many schemes which mushroomed at this time, the trans-Atlantic air freight port came to nothing. In the mid 1980s when oil prices were high and the development of the Atlantic fields became a real possibility, the British Helicopter Advisory Board recommended that Twatt be considered as a

helicopter base. Unfortunately the price of oil dropped steeply curtailing further offshore exploration and so Twatt airfield, the first British proving ground of helicopters, was denied a new lease of life. Now that the Atlantic fields are in production it is ironic that long-range helicopters from Aberdeen often fly directly over the Twatt and Skeabrae airfields on their way north-west!

Meanwhile memories of Skeabrae airfield were kept alive by those dissatisfied with the present civil airport at Grimsetter. As a site for a civil airport, Grimsetter was a bad choice, its only advantage being proximity to Kirkwall. A serious disadvantage is experienced in April and May when the warmer waters of the Atlantic meet the cold North Sea and a dense bank of fog creeps in over the eastern part of the archipelago and closes Kirkwall Airport. Meanwhile Skeabrae and, indeed Twatt to the west of the long chain of hills which act as a barrier to the fog, bask in sunshine! In 2005 science came to the rescue of Grimsetter where a new Instrument Landing System was installed, sealing the fate of Twatt and Skeabrae.

In 1986 Government monies could be directed to the removal of wartime relics and consequently, with the permission of the new landowners, the final demolition process was begun. Ironically what had been an eyesore for forty years was, by this time, being seen by some people in a completely new light.

RNAS Grimsetter. FAA.

A.	Aircraft standings	E.	Control building	I.	Ground signals	M.	Sick Bay
B.	Armoury	F.	E.R.S. hangar	J.	Hangars	N.	Test butt
C.	A.R.S. hangar	G.	Equip. & Erect: hangar	K.	Pens	O.	Workshop
D.	Compass base	H.	Explosives area	L.	Radar test base	P.	Apron

Aerial photograph of Twatt Airfield. FAA.

RNAS Twatt. FAA.

A. Aircraft standings
B. Armoury
C. A.R.S. hangar
D. Compass base
E. Control building
F. E.R.S. hangar
G. Equip: & Erect: hangar
H. Explosives area
I. Ground signals
J. Hangars
K. Pens
L. Radar test base
M. Sick Bay
N. Test butt
O. Workshop
P. Apron

So, when the parish of Birsay, a community which had been totally involved in the war objected to the demolition of Twatt airfield, the Orkney Islands Council was taken aback. An appeal was made for the retention of the Control Tower at least to form the basis of a small museum. A sympathetic Council agreed and, at the eleventh hour, when the demolition charges were already implanted, a stay of execution was granted. This triumph was followed by an immediate reversal of Council policy. The Control Tower was to be preserved as an Interpretation Centre to commemorate the work of both the Royal Navy and the RAF in Orkney and, on the surrounding nine acres of land, parts of the station were to be reconstructed, piecemeal. This generous gesture by the Islands' Council meant that few tears were shed when, half a century after its stormy birth, the Control Tower of nearby Skeabrae, the last remaining structure on that airfield, was razed to the ground.

Plan of Control Tower (Protected Control Building or 'PCB'), Twatt, 1940. PRO.

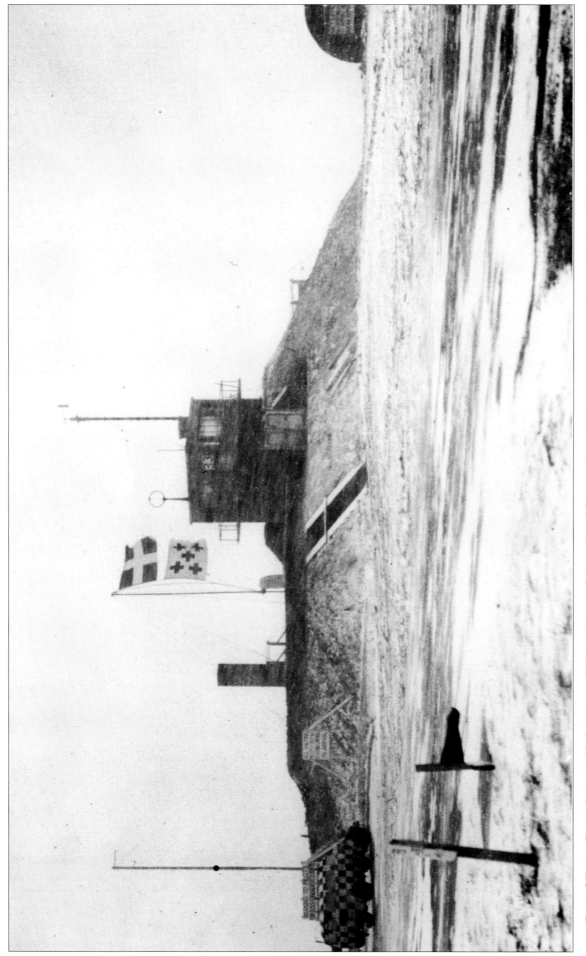

Control Tower, Twatt, January 1945; it was a PCB or Protected Control Building; underneath lay a mass concrete Communications Block; the two flags flying are the Affirmative Flying flag and the Negative Flying flag; when flown together as in this photograph it was interpreted by pilots and TAGs as "You can fly if you don't want to"! The chequered vehicle is a crash tender. PEMBERTON.

Twatt Airfield 1945, looking south-west; the Control Tower is on the extreme right; there are four Boston bombers on the tarmac. HILL.

Wrens inside the Control Tower, Twatt, 10.06.45; standing, with the field glasses is Watchkeeper L/Wren Radio Mechanic Iris Page (née Turner) who married Len Page, 771 Sqdn. helicopter pilot; foreground, June Millard, Fighter Direction. PAGE.

Result of a mid-air collision between Roc piloted by Lt. Tony Thackara and Henley piloted by Sub.Lt. Ted Gilberd what appears to be a wing of the Roc is in fact the tail plane of the Henley; 12.03.43. BURKE.

Flying Control Officer Sub.Lt. Paul Congdon in Control Tower, March 1944. PEMBERTON.

In the Control Tower, Twatt, 10.06.45 Left to Right, Rosemary Gornall, SDO Watchkeeper; Wren Teleprinter operators Hilda Smith and unknown Wren. HILL.

Four Blackstone Diesel engines in the Power Station at Linklater in Sandwick; this station served both Skeabrae and Twatt. HILL.

Armourers at Twatt, 10.06.45; Dorothy Resker and Ruby Heymans; the caption reads 'Shooting a Line' because this was not a duty of the Wren! PEMBERTON.

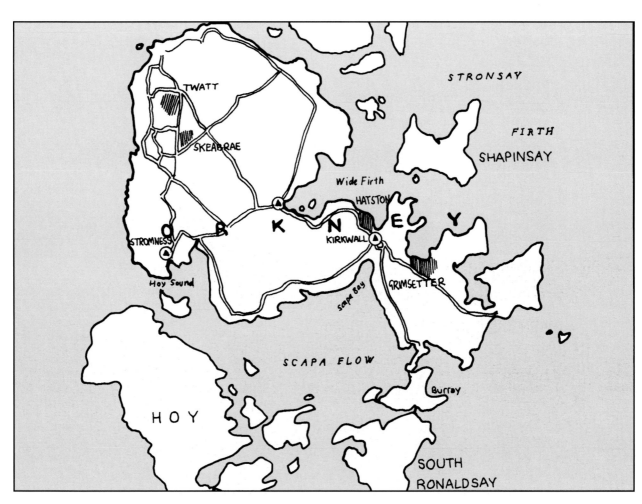

Military Airfields of Orkney. FAA.

In the Front Line

The harbingers of war knocked early on Orkney doors. In 1936 surveyors on the island of Hoy explored the possibilities of siting fuel tanks there and a year later surface tanks with 100,000 gallon capacity were constructed near Lyness. In June 1938, the first submarine booms were placed in position in Scapa Flow and in September the Commander-in-Chief of the Home Fleet, Admiral Forbes, hitherto in a position to choose between Rosyth and Scapa Flow as the base of the Home Fleet, cast the die in favour of Scapa Flow. Farmers in the parish of Sandwick were told that their lands were to be immediately requisitioned for an airfield.

To Orcadians it was clear that Britain was on a war footing but, despite the obvious preparations, life went on in its usual unhurried style, after all wasn't Orkney just about as far away from German soil as it was possible to get? So, in their customary leisurely way, Orkney County Council started to convert a main road into the Royal Navy's first purpose-built runway and Orcadians went about their age old crafts of raising cattle, cutting peat, mowing meadow hay, buying and selling. In the endless summer days of 1939, little did they know that the Air Staff now predicted that the Luftwaffe were capable of dropping over 400 tons of bombs in Orkney in one day and, before long, Orcadians would be in the front line.

800 Squadron Skua, L2933 taking off from Ark Royal, 1939. Stevens.

By 25th August 1939, Hatston airfield was considered operational. 771 Squadron Fleet Requirements Unit moved in and, the next day, Skuas of 800 Squadron disembarked from HMS *Ark Royal*. By 31st August there were 44 warships in Scapa Flow and, with the invasion of Poland on 1st September, most of them put to sea including the *Ark Royal* with its Skua squadron; the pawns in the war game were taking up position. On Sunday 3rd September, war was declared. There was little stir among Orcadians; the story is told that when a venerable Stromnessian learned of the outbreak of war, he remarked, 'My, thir gotten a graand day fur hid'. By contrast there was a flurry of activity around the great battleship HMS *Nelson* which had been left to guard the Flow. A crated consignment was lowered into an awaiting drifter which ploughed through a choppy Scapa Flow to Scrabster. A heavily guarded truck drew up and sped the case to Thurso where the vaults of the National Bank were already open and waiting. The doors were firmly shut—at least the uniform of Admiral Nelson was safe!

At 10 pm on 5th September, Churchill held a conference on Scapa Flow. In his book *The Gathering Storm* he says:

> There were now in 1939 two dangers to be considered; the first, the old one of submarine incursion; the second, the new one of the air. I was surprised to learn at my conference that more precautions had not been taken in both cases to prepare the defences against modern forms of attack. . . . The new danger from the air had been almost entirely ignored. Except for two batteries of anti-aircraft to defend the naval oil tanks at Hoy and the destroyer anchorage, there were no air defences at Scapa. One airfield near Kirkwall was available for the use of naval aircraft when the Fleet was present, but no provision had been made for immediate RAF participation in the defence and the shore radar station, although operative, was not wholly effective. Plans for basing two RAF fighter squadrons at Wick had been approved but this measure could not become effective before 1940. I called for an immediate plan of action. Our air defence was so strained, our resources so limited, and our vulnerable points—including all vast London—so numerous, that it was no use asking for much. On the other hand protection from air attack was now needed only for five or six great ships, each carrying a powerful anti-aircraft armament of its own. To keep things going, the Admiralty undertook to provide two squadrons of naval fighter aircraft whilst the Fleet was in Scapa. . . . I felt it my duty to visit Scapa at the earliest moment. . . .

and so he did on 15th and 16th September. His heart must have sunk when he arrived back in London to be told that the aircraft carrier HMS *Courageous* had been torpedoed in the Bristol Channel with the loss of 500 lives. Worse was to come.

Two weeks later, on 1st October 803 Squadron equipped with Skua fighter dive-bombers flew off *Ark Royal* and took up station at Hatston to protect Scapa Flow against aerial attack. On 6th October they were inspected by King George VI who, earlier in the day, had sped into the safety of Scapa Flow in the cruiser HMS *Aurora* with a large destroyer escort. But was Scapa really safe? Between 9th and 12th October vapour trails criss-crossing the sky high above Scapa signalled the arrival of German reconnaissance aircraft in the form of stripped down Luftwaffe Ju-88 bombers travelling at an altitude of 30,000 feet or more. Dönitz had requested intelligence on the number of warships in the base and the aerial photographs showed an aircraft carrier, five heavy ships and ten cruisers. On October 14th tragedy struck and Orcadians heard the resounding booms of German munitions only half a mile from their shores. U-47 under the command of Lt.Cdr. Günther Prien, had slipped into the anchorage through a partially blocked channel and one hour later the battle cruiser HMS *Royal Oak* went to the bottom of Scapa Flow with the loss of over 800 men. Most of the Home Fleet with the exception of HMS *Iron Duke*, the flagship of the Admiral commanding Orkney and Shetland, quickly put to sea and dispersed, seeking shelter in a variety of Scottish sea lochs and estuaries. Despite all the lessons learned in World War I, Scapa Flow defences could be breached from the sea. Was it safe from air attack?

On 17th October the Luftwaffe struck. It was no Air Show by any means. Only four Ju-88 bombers of this massive army of the air made the 900 mile journey from Sylt. Diving in from 11,000 feet they bombed and sank HMS *Iron Duke* but not without loss. The first enemy aircraft of the war to fall to anti-aircraft fire was shot down by Orkney gunners over Hoy and the only surviving member of the crew taken prisoner. Three hours later a more threatening formation of 15 high level bombers arrived and released their bombs over Scapa Flow, narrowly missing the 12,000 ton accommodation liner *Voltaire*. At this stage in the war only military targets were attacked but one bomb fell, by mistake, on the island of Hoy, the first part of the British Isles to be hit by a German bomb in World War II. From this small beginning, it was difficult to believe that, in under a year, with the Battle of Britain at its height, 372 bombers escorted by 642 fighters would attack London. . . . Mercifully Orkney was far beyond fighter support range. But what of the Royal Navy's own fighters in the Scapa engagement? The slow Skuas of 803 Squadron at Hatston made no contact with the enemy.

On 31st October Churchill held a conference with Admiral Forbes at his temporary Headquarters in the Clyde. Both were resolved to retain Scapa as the base of the Home Fleet; new defence measures included, among other things, 'substantial fighter protection . . . organised both in the Orkneys and at Wick on the mainland'. As a matter of fact Churchill was not making any new request. He had previously asked for two fighter squadrons to defend Scapa and so far only one, which had proved to be completely inadequate, had been provided. Another month was to pass before the second squadron, 804 with Gladiators, was formed at Hatston. Meanwhile, in a juggling operation, 803 Squadron was moved alternately between the Royal Naval Air Station at Hatston and the RAF Station at Wick on the other side of the Pentland Firth until finally they both came together at Hatston in early February 1940.

Reinforcement of Scapa Flow defences went on apace. November gales were the first enemy to test the structures. Radar and wireless masts were blown down. Referring to this gale Captain Loriston-Clarke R.N. in his short history of Hatston commissioned by the Flag Officer, Orkney, at the end of the war wrote wryly:

> It was a matter of departmental pride that the Meteorological Hydrogen Balloon Filling Tent was the last to become airborne.

As for the squadrons, they were persistently airborne maintaining regular patrols in case, in the absence of warships, the defences themselves, especially the submarine boom nets and Hatston airfield came under attack. Squadron readiness still left something to be desired. The pilots of 804 Squadron lived in the luxury of the Royal Hotel in a narrow street a mile from the station and had to cycle to the airfield, an altogether hopeless arrangement. Some luxury was sacrificed when the whole squadron moved on to the airfield but it was then possible to have a flight of three at immediate readiness, one at readiness, one at stand-by and the fourth off duty. Sightings of German aircraft were few but on 22nd November 1939 a reconnaissance aircraft passed low over Hatston station! In December 1939 Wick became a Sector Station with headquarters in a primary school classroom. It controlled all fighter operations over Scapa Flow including initially the Royal Navy squadrons at Hatston.

Within weeks of the outbreak of war the first accidents involving British aircraft occurred in Scapa Flow when four Walrus aircraft catapulted off HMS *Southampton*, HMS *Newcastle*, HMS *Glasgow* and HMS *Sheffield* and flying in formation were struck by a 50 mph squall. Three were badly damaged as they tried to land in Stromness harbour. On 28th December two Sea Gladiators of 804 Squadron collided and Pilot Lt.Cdr. J. C. Cockburn, had to bale out when his aircraft became uncontrollable. The

first fatal accident occurred two weeks later when a Skua of 803 Squadron spun in off a turn near Stronsay killing the midshipman pilot and his air gunner. These were the first of 187 accidents, many of them fatal, in the busy airspace of Orkney during World War II.

In January, anticipating a return of the Fleet, German reconnaissance was stepped up and when weather conditions were right, almost daily flights appeared. These consisted of modified Ju-88s coming over high and fast to see what was sitting in Scapa—and to sample the weather. Unfortunately because of their height and speed, they were far beyond the interception capabilities of 803 and 804 Squadrons who had to be content to watch the vapour trails in the sky! On the ground, British squadron strength was increasing with the arrival of 800 Squadron disembarked from HMS *Ark Royal* in mid February and the positioning of two squadrons of RAF aircraft, Nos. 43 and 605 at Wick. To guard against dive-bombers, 950 Barrage Balloon Squadron of the RAF moved to Scapa; initially capable of flying over fifty balloons, this squadron grew to become the largest in Britain with a capability of flying over 80 balloons most of which were based on land but others were on trawlers which were anchored at strategic points in Scapa Flow. Anti-submarine patrols were also stepped up in early 1940 when a number of merchant ships were torpedoed in Orkney waters. Off Copinsay the U-57 sank the 5,000 ton steamer *Loch Maddy* bound from Vancouver to Leith with a cargo of wheat. Later the same submarine in the same location torpedoed the *Daghestan*, a merchant vessel of 5,000 tons. The U-23 torpedoed the 10,000 ton Danish tanker *Danmark* as she lay at anchor in Inganess Bay. Despite frequent patrols there were no successful spottings of submarines by the Skua and Sea Gladiator squadrons based at Hatston.

By early March, every defensive precaution considered necessary had been taken. On 6th March HMS *Hood* arrived at Scapa from Rosyth and, the next day, Churchill embarked on the flagship HMS *Rodney* in the Clyde for the voyage back to the base of the Home Fleet. It must have been an impressive sight as five capital ships, a cruiser squadron and twenty destroyers sailed north through the Minches. But any doubts Churchill might have had about the reduced capabilities of the Luftwaffe in the highly defended Scapa area were immediately dispelled when German aircraft dropped mines in the approaches to the base and brought the Fleet to a standstill off Orkney for twenty four hours. Churchill had to transfer to a destroyer for a speedy passage to Scapa and in the middle of this operation an air raid warning went and the warships swung into action stations. Churchill was impressed:

the whole ship flashed into activity as all the ack-ack batteries were manned and other measures were taken.

In the event, the aircraft did not appear but the Premier must have been left in no doubt that he was in the front line.

Churchill was impressed by the security at Scapa too. Orkney had been turned into a so-called *Protected Area* and it was impossible for any civilian to enter or leave the islands without a special pass. In addition to the barrage balloons, the five squadrons of fighter aircraft at the ready and the Fleet's own guns, two new airfields were under construction, 52 Heavy Anti-Aircraft guns and 20 Light Anti-Aircraft guns were in position and manned by almost 10,000 troops. In his *The Gathering Storm* Churchill wrote:

> more than six months of constant exertion and the highest priorities had repaired the peace-time neglect.

It took German intelligence one week to assess the new military situation and adopt counter measures. The Allies had no knowledge at the time of Germany's intention to invade Norway and the absolute necessity for the enemy to destroy not only the Home Fleet but the base itself which, with the occupation of Norway, would lie a mere three hundred miles from German territory.

Meanwhile in Orkney, the week ending Saturday 16th March had been windy and practically all the barrage balloons had been grounded. This was unfortunate because in the gathering darkness Shetland radar picked up what was clearly a formation of enemy aircraft approaching Orkney from the east. Ten minutes later they flew in low over Scapa Flow and Hatston Royal Naval Air Station. Estimates put the number of aircraft as high as 35, mostly Heinkel 111s, but because of the twilight conditions, it was difficult to be precise. A hundred high explosive and incendiary bombs fell on land, half of them in error in the parish of Stenness where James Isbister, the first of many British civilians to die in the war, was killed.

Most of the other bombs fell near Hatston blasting eight foot wide craters and miraculously just missing the bomb dump. The only casualty was one of the ground crew of 800 Squadron at Hatston who was out walking a mile from base and who was hit in the head by shrapnel. Many of the Hatston servicemen were in the audience at a performance of Kirkwall Amateur Dramatic Society's 'Tilly of Bloomsbury' which had the distinction of being the first show to go on under an air-raid! It hit the national dailies with 'The show went on . . .'. In fact the cast had no idea that there was an air-raid. The stage manager was furious about the noise which he thought came from the off-stage cast in the club below and the cause of the row was explained only when the show was interrupted by naval Lt. Davis who came in and announced that an air-raid had been going on for some time and that certain servicemen should return to base immediately!

The attack on Scapa Flow was more successful. The cruiser HMS *Norfolk* was hit and holed, three of her officers were killed and six ratings injured. Three days later Whitleys and Hampdens of Bomber Command launched a retaliatory attack on a German land target striking at the minelaying seaplane base at Hörnum on the island of Sylt. These were the opening shots in bombing campaigns which would soon engulf most of Europe.

The attack on the Scapa area lasted three quarters of an hour. Despite extensive anti-aircraft fire from the Fleet and the shore batteries supported by searchlights, no enemy aircraft were shot down. As for the fighter defences, their performance was very poor. The RAF squadrons from Wick made no contact at all. The Gladiators and Skuas from Hatston were scrambled with the same lack of success. In his book *Operation Skua*, Major R. T. Partridge wrote:

> The whole squadron (804) got airborne but, in the gathering darkness, no contacts were made and we all had a hell of a job landing back at the airfield as there were no flares or runway lighting.

Both the Royal Navy and RAF blamed inadequate cover from Netherbutton Radar Station which was not surprising because in his November conference with Admiral Forbes the C-in-C of the Home Fleet, Churchill had attached the lowest priority to radar. The defences had been tested and had been found to be inadequate; clearly the capabilities of the Luftwaffe had been underestimated. On 19th and 20th March, Admiral Forbes received instructions to put to sea with the whole of the Home Fleet because of the danger of a night attack when the moon was full. A solution to aerial bombardment, now apparently the most serious threat, was immediately sought. Until shore based radar could be improved, a warship linked to the shore batteries and Fighter Control and with up-to-date radar was to be positioned in Scapa Flow. The guns of the Fleet and shore stations, instead of aiming at individual targets were now to fire a three minute barrage, virtually a continuous wall of shellfire on the approach of enemy aircraft. Thus was born the famous *Scapa Barrage,* probably the loudest sustained noise that has ever been heard in Britain!

Meanwhile German aircraft kept their distance

HAVOC OF ENEMY AIR ATTACK ON STENNESS HOMES

Picture on left shows Mr. James W. Isbister of Bridge of Waithe, Stenness, who was killed in the March 16 air raid. Above is an interior view of the havoc created by the bombs in the home of Miss Isabella McLeod. Miss McLeod was wounded, but extricated herself from the wreckage. Below is seen the rear of the property occupied by Mr. Alfred G. Linklater, who was wounded, and whose wife and infant son escaped injury.

[Scenes by William S. Thomson, Photographer, Kirkwall: Portrait, by courtesy of Mrs. Isbister, from a Jerome (Glasgow) re-printed picture, originally taken two years ago by Mr. James W. Sinclair, Photographer, Kirkwall. All blocks by courtesy of the *Daily Record and Mail*, Glasgow]

Reproduced from The Orcadian of March 28, 1940, by kind permission of James Miller.
The original caption reads: Picture on left shows Mr. James W. Isbister of Bridge of Waithe, Stenness, who was killed in the March 16 air raid. Above is an interior view of the havoc created by the bombs in the home of Miss Isabella McLeod. Miss McLeod was wounded, but extricated herself from the wreckage. Below is seen the rear of the property occupied by Mr. Alfred G. Linklater, who was wounded, and whose wife and infant son escaped injury.
[Scenes by William S. Thomson, Photographer, Kirkwall: Portrait by courtesy of Mrs. Isbister, from a Jerome (Glasgow) re-printed picture, originally taken two years ago by Mr. James W. Sinclair, Photographer, Kirkwall. All blocks by courtesy of the *Daily Record and Mail,* Glasgow.]

but the staff of Hatston Royal Naval Air Station feared the worst when a series of horrendous explosions rocked their establishment and the nearby town of Kirkwall. Believing it to be another German attack the whole airfield was in confusion as riggers scrambled to get their aircraft ready. But the unseen enemy on this occasion was the Orkney wind. Two Air Fitters had been returning bombs to the bomb dump; apparently the wind had turned the vanes of one to make it live and the whole dump with nineteen 100lb. bombs and one 500 lb. bomb had gone up. Air Mechanic Black was killed instantly and the other had a miraculous escape.

Scapa Barrage was tested on 2nd April when 12 Heinkel bombers approached Scapa Flow again at dusk. The formation immediately broke up on meeting the wall of fire. The attack lasted a mere ten minutes and no damage was done. Six days later on 8th April yet another twilight attack was made, on this occasion with 24 bombers flying between 12,000 and 20,000 feet to avoid the barrage. By this time the new radar was in place and the aircraft were picked up 80 miles out to sea. They were intercepted first by No. 43 Squadron Hurricanes from Wick and in the ensuing dog-fights three Heinkels were shot down. The remainder succeeded in reaching Scapa where they attempted to bomb Lyness and the boom defences but intense gunfire brought down another four, one of the Heinkels limping to Wick airfield where it force-landed with two dead crewmen.

This raid was a prelude to the invasion of Norway though no one knew it at the time. The position of Orkney and Scapa Flow now assumed critical importance. The front was moving nearer.

On 10th April, the boot was on the other foot. An attack on the German Fleet in Norway was planned, not on this occasion at the highest level in the Admiralty but in the Operations Room at Hatston Royal Naval Air Station by Lt. William Lucy, Officer Commanding 803 Squadron at Hatston. A fearless officer, he was clearly sick of the endless routine of convoy patrols and of chasing enemy aircraft which he had no hope of catching. He had read intelligence reports of a German cruiser in Bergen harbour and succeeded in persuading Major R. T. Partridge, who was by this time Officer Commanding 800 Squadron to take part in a dive bombing raid on Bergen. The Commanding Officer of the station gave his approval and at 5 am on the morning of 10th, sixteen heavily armed Skuas took off from Hatston on an extremely risky mission. Meeting only light anti-aircraft fire the 16 aircraft made a simultaneous attack on what turned out to be the cruiser *Königsberg* in Bergen harbour. Fortunately the attack was completely successful. The raid made history for the *Königsberg* was the first major warship ever to be sunk by aircraft. The mission was not without loss. Roy

Stevens, an armourer attached to 800 Squadron writes:

It was a long time before we were warned to stand by to receive our aircraft back at Hatston. They arrived in formation, circled and took up approach positions, touching down in turn and taxying up to the hangar. Two Skuas were missing. One which returned had had a large chunk of its starboard tail-plane shot away—by its own gunner! In another, the observer had just stood up over the target area to mark the bomb's effect when a bullet came up through the seat and made its exit through the roof. He was a lucky chap. One of the missing Skuas had not been seen since the attack went in; the other had disappeared from the formation in cloud during the return journey so both were presumed lost. We did our rearming jobs and hung round just in case one or both turned up. Time went by and eventually the fitters said that the Skua's endurance limit had gone so we might as well pack up and leave. Then we heard it—a Skua's engine—and there was a Skua coming towards Hatston. Straight in it came on to the grass and before it could taxi to the hangar, the engine stopped for lack of petrol. This was the aircraft which got lost over Bergen. The other was never seen again. This raid, the first of many, cost us one aircraft and its gallant crew.

Although the operation was successful, the timing was unfortunate because the Germans had

Type 277S Radar, South Ronaldsay. PRO.

819 Sqdn. Swordfish at Hatston, 11 March 1942 being loaded with dummy torpedoes prior to a dummy attack on HMS Atmah, a target vessel; the aircraft in the foreground appears to be V4356. FANCOURT.

plans of their own for 10th April. Several German reconnaissance aircraft arrived in the late afternoon flying quite low. Both 800 and 803 Squadrons were resting after their mission and it fell to 804 Squadron Gladiators from Hatston and No. 605 Squadron Hurricanes from Wick to intercept. 804 Squadron diary for 10th April reads:

> A tremendous day for HMS *Sparrowhawk*, the first and we hope by no means the last. 804 Squadron began their fun at 16.05 hours when Yellow Section flew off to Copinsay. There were a great many plots on the board, the weather fine with layers of cloud varying in density up to about 10,000 feet. About 16.40 hours, P/O Sabey saw a Do-17 and the section gave chase. Sub.Lt. Fell got in a burst at about 500 yds. as the Do-17 disappeared into the cloud but followed him in. P/O Peacock went in above the cloud and as he came out so did the Do-17, 400 yds. away. Peacock got in a burst before the enemy aircraft dived away back into the clouds. We were later informed that Do-17 was crying SOS with a leaking petrol tank and did not reach his base. At 16.45 hours Red Section was sent to patrol between Copinsay and Burray. As soon as it got there, Carver saw a Heinkel 111K* about ten miles east going north-east. Hot pursuit was begun and as the Section followed, Hurricanes could be seen on

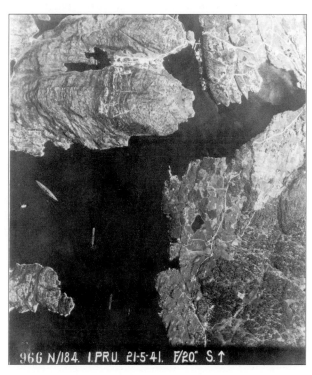

RAF reconnaissance photograph of Bismarck at Bergen 21.05.41; this famous early reconnaissance photograph was taken by Pilot Officer Michael Suckling, flying from Wick and refuelling at Sumburgh. FANCOURT.

the cloud dodging Heinkel's tail. After a few minutes the enemy aircraft began climbing, twisting and diving. By the time Red Section arrived and got within range, No. 43 Squadron had done their job. The enemy aircraft's motors were idling and he dived down to 20 feet over the sea. For two or three miles, he held at 20 feet with a dark oil streak trailing behind him on the sea and finally flopped, port wing first. Six Hurricanes and Red Section flew around the wreck as three of the crew swam for it.

* these bombers were wrongly named at the beginning of the war; should read He111P.

At dusk the radar picked up formations of 60 German bombers coming in from the east. They turned out to be Heinkel 111s and Ju-88s. Again 800 and 803 Squadrons were out of commission and 804 Squadron Gladiators went out to meet the attackers. The Squadron diary records the contribution of the Fleet Air Arm in this, the greatest of the air battles over Orkney:

At 20.45 hours, the evening blitzkrieg began. Red were scrambled to Copinsay where 15 to 20 enemy aircraft were reported approaching from the east at 18,000 feet between Copinsay and Burray. By 21.00 hours all Sections were in the sky and the party had started, the guns putting up an ugly barrage. Yellow had the first chase after an enemy aircraft which was in a long dive towards Kirkwall and which peppered Kirkwall and Hatston with front guns. Yellow Section could not, unfortunately, keep pace though P/O Sabey optimistically gave the enemy aircraft a burst at very long range in order to ease his repressed fighting spirit.

At 21.00 hours Red Section dived down to 11,000 feet about four miles east of Burray. Unfortunately Red 2 was left behind in the dive. As soon as they flattened out, a bomber crossed 200 yds. ahead from port to starboard. Carver and Ogilvy turned, pursued and loosed off nearly all ammunition, gradually closing in from 300 to 200 yards. The enemy fired back narrowly and finally turned and dived away to the south-east, with smoke coming from his starboard motor.

During this party, Blue Section were lurking further west and came galloping up on seeing the shooting. Plenty of enemy aircraft were coming in so Smee chose a back one and stuffed himself under its tail. He and his Section rattled away with such good effect that the enemy aircraft was last seen in a flat right hand spiral going down towards South Ronaldsay. Unfortunately no wreckage was found and so the very probable result could not be

Maryland AR 717 at Hatston: with Noel Goddard as Pilot and Hank Rotherham as Observer; a similar aircraft flew from Hatston to Bergen and confirmed that the Bismarck had sailed into the Atlantic; in peacetime Noel Goddard was Chairman of the Cotswold Aero Club, one of the oldest aero clubs in the U.K.; foreground left Lt. Martin standing highest on the wing, Lt. Duncan Hamilton, Senior Air Engineer, Hatston. HAMILTON.

confirmed. By 21.50 hours the party was over and 11 Gladiators returned. The twelfth was one of Blue Section who, shortly afterwards, could be heard calling, "Where am I?" Nifty* told him and led him back to Wick where he spent the night.

 * Fighter Control, Wick

No. 605 Squadron from Wick were quickly on the scene again. In the interception they shot down two and probably damaged another four. The enemy formations were broken up yet, despite this, 20 aircraft ran the gauntlet of the Scapa Barrage where another three were shot down. Those that did get through dropped 500lb. and 1,000 lb. bombs aimed mainly at the boom nets. The cruiser HMS *Suffolk* was hit and several of the crew killed but the vessel itself sustained only minimal damage. The whole engagement lasted about an hour. For the very first time all the defensive measures had worked well. Had the two Skua squadrons been in action there is no doubt that the enemy casualties would have been much heavier. The Skuas had been immediately rearmed after the Bergen sortie but, fortunately for the Germans, the aircraft remained on the ground, their crews exhausted from the early morning mission. No damage was done to the boom nets and Scapa remained a safe haven. The enemy had failed again in its attempt to smash the Home Fleet and its base and both remained a piercing thorn in the German side throughout the war. It was the last mass bombing raid to take place over Scapa. The Battle of Orkney had been won.

Offensive missions continued to be conducted by both sides, the Royal Navy continuing to use Hatston for this purpose. Single Skuas of 800 Squadron were despatched with the simple brief 'hit anything of military value'. There were a number of such missions in April supported by Blenheims of No. 254 Squadron of the Royal Air Force which was based temporarily at Hatston. All these raids proved to be quite ineffectual and jeopardised the lives of highly skilled pilots who were badly needed elsewhere and the missions were therefore discontinued. Only two further offensive operations were conducted from Hatston. In May 1940 Skuas of 806 Squadron took part in a bombing operation on Bergen, the targets being oil tanks and coastal shipping and in the same month, Swordfish of 821 and 823 Squadron took off from Hatston for a revenge attack on the German battleship *Scharnhorst* steaming south at high speed off the Norwegian coast. The *Scharnhorst* and *Gneisenau* had earlier sunk the aircraft carrier HMS *Glorious* on passage from Norway to Scapa and among the considerable losses was half of 823 Squadron which had been aboard at the time. Unfortunately the torpedo attack was unsuccessful, the *Scharnhorst* accounting for yet another

Ju-88 shot down by 804 Sqdn. Skeabrae in Sandwick, 25 December 1940. Fancourt.

Swordfish. The last Skua raid against Bergen from Hatston was around October 1940. All subsequent operations against the enemy in Norway were carrier based with the exception of a brilliant piece of reconnaissance work in May 1941 which was again conceived at Hatston.

On 21st May 1941, Pilot Officer Michael Suckling flying from Wick in a long-range reconnaissance Spitfire located in a fjord just south of Bergen the *Bismarck*, the most powerful battleship in the world. There was fear among the Allies that she would strike out into the Atlantic where she could do untold damage. For two months Captain H. St. J. Fancourt, Commanding Officer of Hatston had been training 828 Squadron Albacores for this great moment. He asked the RAF for another reconnaissance to confirm that the *Bismarck* was still in the fjord but, because of poor weather, they were unable to comply. Not to be outdone, he asked for volunteers from the Station's own 771 Fleet Requirements Unit to attempt such a reconnaissance. It was not all part of 771 Squadron's duties to conduct reconnaissance and certainly not at such a distance but the Commanding Officer of 771 Squadron, Noel Goddard, a most experienced pilot, volunteered along with his TAG, J. W. Armstrong and Air Gunner Milne. There was no experienced Observer available and to fill the breach Commander Hank Rotherham, the Station Executive Officer and trained Observer, stepped in. Their charge was a Maryland bomber, one of two attached to 771 Squadron at Hatston. 828 Squadron Albacores meanwhile moved to Sumburgh in Shetland ready for the torpedo strike.

The reconnaissance was a complete success. The Maryland came through almost unscathed to transmit the urgent message *Battleship and cruiser have left*. The Fleet slipped its moorings in Scapa and headed for the Atlantic. Station Commander Fancourt was not disappointed that his Albacore Squadron was untested. He writes:

> When they had established that the *Bismarck* had sailed, there was nothing more I could do from Hatston. I am glad to say that I did not send in the Torpedo Bomber Squadron. It would have been a very difficult operation in the circumstances.

The importance of this daring mission was recognised by the Admiralty who awarded Rotherham as Captain of the aircraft an immediate DSO, Goddard an immediate DSC and Armstrong a DSM. Rotherham gives an excellent account of this reconnaissance in his book, *"It's Really Quite Safe"*.

After the air battle of 10th April 1940, German initiatives in the Scapa area were sporadic and half-hearted. Radar installations in Sanday and Deerness were bombed and minelaying operations around the coast continued. RAF Wick, outside the area of the Scapa Barrage was less fortunate. It was bombed several times. Aircraft and hangars were destroyed and there were several casualties including 11 civilians in Wick itself. Reconnaissance patrols in and around the islands continued, the lone aircraft sometimes appearing completely by surprise. On 25th December 1940 a Ju-88 suddenly appeared over the West Mainland of Orkney. 804 Squadron equipped with their new Grumman Martlets were by this time stationed at Skeabrae and took off in pursuit of the intruder. The Station Diary has this entry:

> 25th December first blood was drawn, an enemy aircraft, a Junkers 88 was sighted two miles west of base by Lt.Cdr. Carver in an 804 Squadron patrol just after the men had finished their Christmas Dinner. After an interesting and exciting chase, Sub.Lt. Parke put a burst from the stern in the starboard engine and white and black smoke was seen to come from it. After the fourth pass, the enemy aircraft was seen to be flying on only one engine and Carver noticed it losing height after each burst. After the last burst, the aircraft landed with the undercarriage retracted. The crew of four, one of whom was injured, was taken to Kirkwall for interrogation; all the guns of the enemy machine showed stoppages. The Ju-88 was brought down in a field near Flotterston in Sandwick, the first enemy aircraft of the war to be shot down by a British pilot flying an American aircraft. The aircraft suffered only minimal damage and was stored in a hangar at Skeabrae for some time before being transferred south.

Norman Goodfellow, pilot in 804 Sqdn., has vivid memories of that rousing day. He himself had only come off readiness 10 minutes earlier and he remembers the scene as crowds of cheering people, some brandishing turkey drumsticks and beer mugs, streamed across the countryside to see this wonderful Christmas present. No wonder it was known as the 'Great turkey shoot!'

Although the threat of aerial bombardment declined, there was no let up in security. After the invasion of Norway, airborne invasion was considered imminent. To add to the inconvenience already experienced by Orcadians with the introduction of the special pass required for travel to or from Orkney, a 11pm. to 5pm. curfew was introduced in July 1940 when fear of airborne invasion was at its height. Large troop concentrations in Norway betokened the worst. The main Kirkwall to Stromness Road at Binscarth was reduced in width by the placing of huge concrete blocks on either side and a man-hole in the space was prepared for a heavy explosive charge in the event of an invasion when the main island artery in this narrow col between the hills would be severed. The writer can well remember the family treating a severely injured motor cyclist who with the much reduced headlights permitted during the war, had crashed into one of these concrete blocks. Despite the turmoil and concern around them, Orcadians could scarcely believe that their island was likely to be invaded, one veteran declaring that the invasion of Orkney would be impossible because there were far too many barbed-wire fences!

Considerable relief was felt when the enemy in Norway turned eastwards into the Soviet Union. At last the pressure was off. There is little doubt that the war in the north prepared the services well for the terrible events of the Autumn of 1940 in England. Many lessons must have been learned and copious amendments made to service manuals. Vigilance still needed to be maintained in the north nevertheless for the nature of the conflict was constantly changing. After the successful paratroop and glider invasion of Crete in 1941 preparations were made in Orkney for a similar eventuality. In an Army Co-operative Exercise Hotspur gliders towed by Hawker Harts were used at Skeabrae to demonstrate the implications of this new type of warfare.

So far civilian targets in Britain had been immune. A report on air attacks involving the civilian population of Orkney up to 1944 said:

In all, 228 bombs and two parachute mines have fallen on land in the county in 16 attacks. Hoy has suffered the largest number of attacks, having been bombed five times but other islands in and around Scapa Flow have also suffered. South Ronaldsay has been bombed three times, Flotta twice and Burray once. The North Isles have not escaped; Sanday has been bombed twice and Shapinsay once. At Auskerry the lighthouse came under attack and, to the west of Orkney, Sule Skerry light was also bombed. Casualties have been remarkably light—altogether three people in Orkney have been killed, 11 seriously injured and five slightly injured.

Civilians in the northern front line had come out well. When the Luftwaffe turned its attention to the south of England and the destruction of non-military targets was considered legitimate, the outcome was rather different.

At the age of 85, Capt. Hank Rotherham performs an official duty in Quebec; it was he who volunteered to act as navigator on the risky flight from Hatston to Bergen to determine whether the Bismarck had sailed: he was later the first CO of RNAS Twatt.

Blockships proved inadequate to protect the Home Fleet in Scapa Flow after the sinking of the Royal Oak; the eastern approaches to Scapa Flow were sealed off by a causeway which came to be known as the Churchill Barriers.
BALFOUR BEATTY.

Chapter Four

The Resident Squadrons

Eight days before war broke out, the arrival of 'X' Flight of 771 Squadron at Hatston heralded the first of 89 squadrons of aircraft to use the military airfields of Orkney between 1939 and 1945. Almost all these squadrons were based in Orkney; only a few were in transit or diverted through bad weather. Though based in Orkney, these squadrons were not necessarily resident. A resident squadron was a squadron posted to Orkney to perform particular duties, be it for example, target towing, interception, air-sea rescue, convoy protection or communications. All 19 RAF squadrons were resident. Of the 70 Royal Naval Squadrons, it would be generally true to say that all aircraft disembarked from carriers were not resident but this is only a rule of thumb. Some squadrons such as 801, 828 and 1770 flew to Orkney and trained for long periods before embarking on a carrier in the early years of the war; others such as 800 and 801 disembarked from carriers to play a role for many months in the defence of Orkney when RAF fighters were fully committed to the South of England. These were, properly, front-line squadrons and are considered under disembarked aircraft. Of Royal Naval squadrons, there were, in reality, only three squadrons resident in Orkney. As might be expected, these were squadrons in the 700 non-combative series, 771 Squadron, Fleet Requirements Unit which spent the whole of the war in Orkney, 700 Squadron, the Headquarters of all Catapult Flights, which spent most of the war years there and 712 Squadron, a Communications Squadron formed at Hatston in 1944 to replace the reduced communications facility available when 700 Squadron merged with 771 Squadron in March 1944. 712 Squadron was a small squadron flying Expeditor, Dominie, Sea Otter and Traveller aircraft, formed at Hatston in August 1944 and whose principal role was to ferry high ranking officers and, sometimes, urgent supplies from Orkney to the Scottish Mainland and will not be discussed here.

If there is any squadron which can lay claim to a long association with the Orkney Islands, it must surely be 771 Squadron of the Royal Navy. The complete Squadron was in residence at Hatston by 28th September 1939 flying in from Portland and Lee-on-Solent, in the case of the latter station, a timely move for, within a year, Lee-on-Solent was to be devastated by Stuka dive-bombers. When Hatston was chosen as the Royal Navy's first purpose built airfield, it could scarcely be envisaged that five squadrons of aircraft would frequently be disembarked there in addition to the busy 700 Squadron and 771 Fleet Requirements Unit Squadron. The disembarkation of front-line Fighter and Torpedo Bomber Squadrons received the highest priority and this meant that the resources of Hatston were usually stretched to the limit. A real crisis occurred in April 1942 when the carrier USS *Wasp* was loaned to Britain to ferry Spitfire aircraft to Malta. Three of *Wasp's* four squadrons of aircraft had

Lt.Cdr. Michael Le Fanu, Fleet Gunnery Officer; Scapa Twatt photographers have decorated him suitably; how were they to know that he was to rise to the rank of Admiral of the Fleet! MOLYNEUX.

Ratings ashore from ships in Scapa man the guns at Yesnaby, the so called 'Northern Range'. HILL.

Modified Roc towing a drogue over Hatston. HAMILTON.

to be disembarked somewhere in Britain for five weeks and the aircrew's rigorous training programmes had to be continued in that time. The only station capable of maintaining the crews at the highest standard of war-readiness was Hatston. Consequently, to make room for the Americans, it was decided that 771 Squadron should move to the new Royal Naval Air Station at Twatt which had been coping with the overspill of fighters from Hatston for almost a year. Here the Squadron remained until 24th July 1945 when it once again made the long journey south, on this occasion to Zeals in Wiltshire.

771 Squadron was an FRU or Fleet Requirements Unit sometimes jokingly referred to as 'Scapa Services'. Its duties were multifarious but its primary role was in training, especially in providing gunnery practice for the Fleet in Scapa Flow or for the Naval A.A. Range, the so-called Northern Range, at Yesnaby to the north of Stromness. Drogues and, later, winged targets, were towed behind a variety of aircraft, not always successfully. The winged target when out of control could prove a dangerous hazard. TAG Eric Lascelles says that he was in a Martinet which took off with a winged target; the cable broke and the target dived straight into a henhouse producing what he described as 'a snowstorm of white hens'. The falling canvas drogue on the other hand was welcomed by Orcadians since whoever salvaged it and returned it to a Naval Air Station was given a £3 reward, the equivalent of a week's wages in those days!

Initially Swordfish, Skuas and Rocs were used for target towing purposes but later Chesapeake, Defiant and Martinet were introduced. 771 Squadron pilots logged up long hours of flying for there were few days in busy Scapa Flow when some ship or other did not require practice. Chief P/O Pilot Haslams's log records the names of 83 ships with which he exercised in the last 18 months of the war, many of them allied. These exercises were not without risk. Many pilots refer to the experience of training the gunners on the Soviet battleship *Arkhangelsk*. This battleship had originally been the British HMS *Royal Sovereign* but was transferred to the Soviets in July 1944. Admiral Levchenko and some of the new crew arrived at Scapa from the Soviet Union in early May aboard the carrier HMS *Fencer* as part of Convoy RA59. The Soviets arrived armed with many crates of vodka and with such a cargo they received a rapturous welcome. Attitudes changed however after the first sea to air gunnery practice when the Twatt pilots saw the shells bursting in front of their aircraft instead of around the drogue which was streaming 6,000 feet behind them! Nevertheless the training given the Soviet crew by the Twatt pilots proved very useful since, shortly after the battleship arrived in the Soviet Union, a direct hit was scored in its first encounter with an aircraft. Unfortunately the aircraft was American! By this time the *Arkhangelsk* was lying in Vaenga Bay a few miles below Murmansk. The American pilot had been on a special mission to Norway from Scotland and, damaged by enemy fire, had sought what he thought was the friendly airfield at Graznaya! The Soviets, seeing the aircraft fly from the direction of

Miles Martinet target towing aircraft over Orkney. REMMINGTON.

16 foot winged target towed by a Martinet in flight over Orkney. HASLAM.

32 foot winged target at Twatt. HASLAM.

occupied Norway naturally assumed it was an enemy aircraft.

A similar function of 771 Squadron was to provide air to air firing practice for both embarked and disembarked squadrons. Again drogues were used and streamed to a length of 1,000 feet, such exercises being carried out at sea outside shipping lanes. There were also 'throw-off shoots' when the big guns of the naval ships were offset 20° and practice shells fired at aircraft making simulated attacks. Ciné photography was used to evaluate such exercises and 771 Squadron at Twatt established one of the finest photographic departments in the Royal Navy. Colour ciné of World War II activities in Orkney originated here at Twatt and are now valuable archival material.

There were similar Army Co-operative Exercises. Huge Army Artillery garrisons were stationed in Orkney throughout the war and since it was their principal duty to ensure that no enemy aircraft reached Scapa Flow, they needed constant practice. Approximately one third of all sorties made by 771 Squadron were for the benefit of the Army. Once a month there was an exercise code-named *Chutney* when as many aircraft as serviceable got airborne together and attacked the Home Fleet at anchor in Scapa Flow. The exercises consisted of dummy high-level bombing, dive-bombing, strafing and torpedo attacks. Accidents were not uncommon. In one such exercise on 14th August 1944 a pilot pulled up too late from a dive and his aircraft, a Miles Martinet, hit the superstructure of one of the capital ships and crashed into the sea. Both he and his TAG were killed. Perhaps one of the strangest incidents of the war occurred on the island of South Ronaldsay on 22nd October 1943 when the crew of a Blackburn Roc of 771 Squadron at Twatt were rescued by the enemy! The Roc was on a dive-bombing and fighter direction exercise with HMS *Royalist* when the engine failed. Having a young midshipman on board, the pilot decided to crash land his aircraft rather than bale out. TAG Doug Cole relates what happened:

> We braced ourselves for what we knew was going to be a pretty heavy landing. The next I can recall is seeing very swarthy looking men with axes hacking round my head. They were dressed in strange clothing with huge red discs on their backs and they were jabbering away in a foreign language. In my stupor I thought this couldn't be any place on earth. Next I remember lying on the grass and a lady appearing from nowhere and offering me a cigarette. I asked her who these people were who got me out and she replied that they were Italian prisoners of war!

These Italian prisoners of war were employed in

"The CO's compliments, and—er—he says please can we have our winged target back?" HOLDEN.

building what came to be known as the Churchill Barriers, the causeway which was built to link all the islands to the east of Scapa Flow to prevent the intrusion of enemy submarines.

Frank Walker was an Observer with 771 Squadron at Twatt in the summer of 1943 and he tells an amusing story:

The pilot of a Chesapeake or Roc flying over Scapa Flow experienced engine trouble and told the TAG to put on his parachute. In the confusion of the moment, the TAG accidentally and unknowingly pulled out his intercom plug and pulled the rip cord of his parachute but gathered the parachute in his arms. He called up his pilot to tell him what had happened but getting no reply (since he had pulled out his intercom plug!) he supposed the pilot had already baled out so he jumped. He fell some way, alarmed at the fact that his parachute hadn't opened then realised he was still clutching it to his bosom! He let go and, lucky fellow, drifted down gently into Scapa Flow. Kicking off his heavy boots, he released the parachute harness and swam clear. A passing launch was well placed to pick up not only the TAG, but also his parachute and even one of his boots. Meanwhile the aircraft engine picked up again and the pilot returned to base where he was astonished to find that his TAG was no longer with him but he could offer no explanation for his disappearance! I

The cruiser HMS Newfoundland, steaming at 18 knots off Orkney photographed by Twatt aircraft. HILL.

*Sea Gladiator,
771 Sqdn. Twatt,
1943.* MOLYNEUX.

Early morning 'Met' flights were a feature of every station; TAG Richard (Dick) Stark ready for the flight with a rather bulky barometer! STARK.

A 771 Sqdn. pilot looks down on the cruiser HMS Ceylon off Orkney. HASLAM.

was ordered to carry out an enquiry and report which I did. I have no recollection of the names.

In the twelve months leading up to D day, the official history of Royal Naval Air Station, Twatt, written up at the end of the war by a Wren officer records that 771 Squadron carried out over 4,000 exercises and flew almost 11,000 hours so it does not surprise us to learn that, in their time in Orkney, this squadron had more than 50 recorded accidents and probably many more unrecorded. Altogether 18 aircrew lost their lives in Squadron operations in Orkney.

Few Royal Naval pilots had the opportunity to fly multi-engined aircraft during the war, but for 771 Squadron pilots this was commonplace. As early as October 1940, two Martin Maryland bombers, originally intended for the French Air Force, were attached to 771 Squadron at Hatston. By early 1945 the Squadron at Twatt could boast six bombers. One important use of these aircraft was in the checking of Radar Calibration, the size of the bombers giving a very good radar response. Cruisers and battleships were fitted with Air Warning Radars which gave range, bearing and height and it was the function of 771 Squadron bombers to make passes at nine levels between 200 and 40,000 feet to check the accuracy

of the radars. In unheated bombers at this latter altitude for long periods of time, even with the regulation clothing, could sometimes be difficult for the crews. Frank Walker recalls some of these flights at Twatt with 771 Squadron:

Above 10,000 feet it was usually below freezing point even in summer and sometimes well below— indeed it was then I learned that -40F = -40C or near enough. We had no artificial heating and relied upon inner and outer Sidcot suit, flying boots and gloves for warmth. For an hour or two this was comfortable enough. Now the pencil I used for navigation had a metal gadget on the end which was used to set the wind on the Course and Speed Calculator and once after descending below 10,000 feet, I took off the oxygen mask and absent-mindedly put the pencil in my mouth. The metal tip was probably -20C and took the skin off my tongue, palate and cheek! The ground crew would never believe how cold it was but apart from this illustration I really impressed them one day. We had flown through very heavy rain after take off and since there were gaps in the perspex of the nose, water drove in and gathered in the rectangular depressions in the trap door where my feet rested. On landing, the rigger came out with the ladder and opened the trap door to let me out. Each of my feet was encased in a neat brick of ice about 16" x 8" x 8" and I told him to stand clear while I banged them off. He was most impressed! I suppose my feet had been in those blocks for 1½ hours but I had not felt any discomfort.

Calibration was a particularly valuable service not only for HM ships but also for the Station itself which, in keeping with its training role, established its own Fighter Direction Centre at Hesta Geo on the north coast of Birsay on 10th May 1943. Its Radio Call sign was 'Penguin' since its original operator was Dick Lane, RNVR officer and brother of Allen Lane who founded Penguin Books in 1935! Allen Lane himself was in Orkney early in the war to take part in a Brain's Trust. The publication of his books was considered a reserved occupation and Allen did not enlist. However the other brother, John, also joined the RNVR, served on the aircraft carrier *Avenger* and spent much of September and October in Scapa Flow and at Hatston when preparations were being made for the North African landings. Unfortunately he was one of many lost when the *Avenger* was torpedoed off North Africa on 15th November 1942.

One week after the establishment of the Fighter Direction Centre in Birsay, a Fighter Direction School with associated Link Trainer and Fisher Gun Trainer facilities were opened at Twatt. The purpose of the School was to exercise fighter aircraft and also ship's fighter director teams. In this it was highly successful for more than 1,000 officers and 3,000 ratings passed through this School in its two years' existence.

With such heavy commitments, it isn't surprising to learn that 771 Squadron was the largest in the Royal Navy. In July 1942 it already had 19 aircraft; by May 1945 increasing workload had raised the total to 51 which included 23 Martinet target towing aircraft, 16 Corsair single seater fighters, 6 Boston bombers, 3 Blenheim bombers and three helicopters. After November 1942 Twatt was considered too crowded to accept disembarked front-line fighters and from then on most of the overspill went to RAF Grimsetter or RAF Skeabrae. Eventually the problem was solved in July 1943 by transferring Grimsetter to the Royal Navy.

Pilots had to be very adept at handling a great variety of types of aircraft. Between January 1943 and August 1945, Cyril Burke RNZNVR, CO of the squadron, logged up 537 flying hours in 14 different types of aircraft 30% of those being multi-engined experience. There was little time to study the niceties of each machine. Chief P/O Pilot Eric Haslam writes that, with single seater aircraft, he was given pilot's notes to read about an hour before the first flight. On his third Hurricane flight, exercising with HMS *Nelson* and HMS *Argonaut*, he crashed on landing due to a ground loop but was excused from blame due to 'inexperience on type'. In accident enquiries

this judgement was common. There was even little time for accident enquiries and there was probably more than a grain of truth in the notice displayed in a Commander (Flying)'s Office.

> *I sometimes feel that, if I could stop the paperwork caused by accidents, I could then stop the accidents which caused this paperwork which now prevents me stopping accidents.*

In addition to its many fixed-wing aircraft, it is a little known fact that 771 Squadron was the first squadron in the Royal Navy to experiment with helicopters, indeed the Royal Navy's first operational helicopters were assembled and flown at Twatt. On 8th May 1944, three R-4 Sikorsky helicopters had arrived in Britain for evaluation by the Royal Navy at MAP (Ministry of Aircraft Production). One of these crashed due to mechanical failure but trials continued with the other two. The trials showed that the helicopter was of some value to the Royal Navy and the first operational machines were attached to 771 Squadron at Twatt. Lt. Jean-Paul Fournier RCN qualified as a fixed wing pilot in the Fleet Air Arm and after serving in TBR squadrons ashore and on the carrier HMS *Indomitable* was posted to the US Coastguard Station at Floyd Bennett, New York, for a course on helicopters. There he became the first Canadian to solo on helicopters. On the completion of his course he returned to the UK and, in January 1945, was posted to Twatt where he found five or six crated R-4 Sikorsky helicopters and a maintenance crew of six or seven already there. The helicopters were assembled and test flown there but this development was so innovative that he had no terms of reference and initially was at a loss to know what to do. The machines were looked on as toys with little practical use.

In this honeymoon period there were pleasure trips in which the pilot landed on the gun-turret of the battleship HMS *Duke of York* and flew Admiral Tovey C-in-C of the Home Fleet to a local stream to do some fishing. That was a success. When the Captain of the battleship HMS *King George V* went for a joy ride in Scapa Flow, things did not go so well. The helicopter with floats was unserviceable so, at the last minute, the wheeled version was substituted. The helicopter landed on the front gun turret of the battleship and took its captain aboard for a short local flight. Unfortunately, on the return flight, the engine cut out but the pilot was able in time to declutch the blades and change their pitch. In this way they continued to turn and the helicopter landed gently on the water close to the battleship. Without floats it began to submerge slowly. The pilot and the Captain released themselves, came to the

As part of an Army Co-operative Exercise, Lt.Cdr. Molyneux plans a flight with Norwegian Army Officers in Blenheim, Twatt, July 1943. MOLYNEUX.

In No. 5 Mess Twatt occupied by TAGs and Naval Photographers, 16.03.45. The Scots Guards gave a concert in The Orcadia, the Station recreation building, and two of the band members visited the Mess; RN photographer. Walter 'Bing' Crosby is attempting to play the pipes; the tall rating in the background is Fred Fenson. HILL.

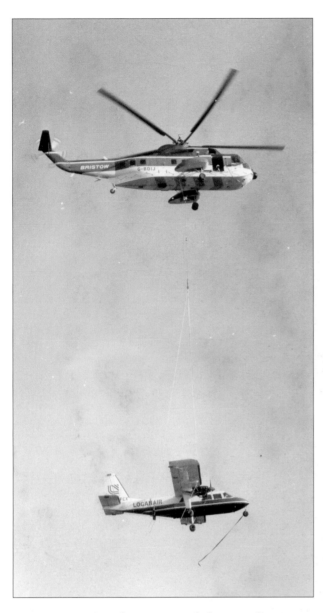

Eric Bristow's early training on helicopters began at RNAS Twatt; little did he know that, forty years later, a helicopter bearing his name would salvage a stricken Loganair aircraft from Rousay! ORKNEY ARCHIVES

surface, and were picked up by the ship's boat. The Captain was subsequently piped aboard, soaked to the skin, in front of all his crew! A signal to Twatt confirmed that he wasn't very pleased. The Station itself found a valuable use for the helicopter when the CO gave permission for the pilot to go round the farms collecting eggs!

After a month, Jean-Paul Fournier was joined by a second helicopter pilot who had the great misfortune during a demonstration flight to collide with a parked Blenheim. The machine was a write-off but it was ingeniously set up by the workshops as a demonstration unit with cut-out opened sections of gear box and engine for the benefit of mechanics and pilots. With the arrival of the replacement helicopter pilot, Alan Bristow, later to become an international figure in the helicopter world, Fournier set about a

proper evaluation of the helicopter in the Royal Navy. Soon it was found that the helicopter, though not giving such good radar response, was invaluable for Ship Radar and Fire Control Calibration because of its high degree of manoeuvrability. It also began to show its value in direct ship to shore communications, a capability which battleships and cruisers lost after the demise of the Catapult Squadrons of 700 Squadron. Its Air-Sea Rescue potential was yet to be discovered but by landing an engineer on isolated Stroma in the Pentland Firth to attend to a faulty radar responder it showed its value in reaching isolated areas speedily and efficiently. The photographic possibilities of the helicopter were seen quickly by the excellent Photographic Section who, among other things, produced a magnificent diorama of RNAS Twatt, from a hovering helicopter, surely a unique visual record of a war-time RNAS station.

To maintain such a big and complex squadron of aircraft required workshop facilities of a very high standard. An engine repair shop, aircraft repair shop and general engineering shop, all capable of work up to major inspections of engines and major repairs to aircraft were established at Twatt. Truly of 771 Squadron could be said 'You bend it, we mend it.' In March 1945 Twatt could boast having 20,000 items recorded in its Stores Ledgers. These items included 745 different types of bolt, 389 of them British, 356 American, and six miles of cable! In the last year of the war, 70 aircraft were repaired in the Twatt workshops but even from the very beginning when the squadron was based at Hatston the workshops there were kept extremely busy. Aside from the job of repairing aircraft, it was also the job of 771 Squadron to salvage and transport crashed aircraft. 56 Royal Naval crashes are recorded on land in Orkney during the war years though doubtless there were many more; as many off-shore ditchings occurred. 771 Squadron were also required to repair aircraft damaged in deck-landing crashes at sea. For this the RNAS stations in Orkney were served by a very poor infrastructure, the damaged aircraft being landed at Scapa Pier, hoisted by a hand-worked crane and then transported over narrow twisting roads to the workshops.

One of the last tasks of 771 Squadron was to escort, triumphantly, the surrendering German U-boats which made their way to Scapa or Loch Eriboll in Sutherland. On the cessation of hostilities in Europe the Fleet moved east to the Pacific theatre. There was no further need for aircraft whose main duty was to support the Fleet and so on 24th July 1945 this massive squadron became airborne and headed off in stages to the south of England.

700 Squadron of the Royal Navy formed at Hatston on 21st January 1940, and was one of a number of Royal Naval squadrons which formed

Formation of 18 Corsairs of 771 Squadron, Twatt, lining up for an 'attack' on the Home Fleet. HILL.

there during the hostilities. 700 Squadron was not, however, a completely new Squadron but a bringing together, under one command, of the widely scattered 700 Series of Flights which had been formed in mid July 1936. In early September, just before the outbreak of war, some of these 700 Flights made a spectacular entry into the Orkney skies—but all did not go well. In his book *The Supermarine Walrus*, G. W. R. Nicholl writes:

As tension built up towards the Munich crisis in September, ships of all naval commands were alerted to stand by to take up their allotted war stations. The 2nd Cruiser Squadron of the Home Fleet—HMS *Southampton*, HMS *Newcastle*, HMS *Sheffield*, HMS *Glasgow* and HMS *Cornwall*—moved to Scapa Flow and all the Walruses were bombed up in readiness with 100lb. anti-submarine bombs. One afternoon, the Squadron Commander Lt.Cdr. Shattock led four of these aircraft in a formation flight over the Flow in what was known as a 'balbo', a flying display named after the Italian Air Marshal who had led a spectacular flight of flying-boats across the South Atlantic a few years earlier. (The Squadron Commander was clearly not familiar with weather conditions in Orkney where, in a space of fifteen minutes, the wind speed can rise from calm to 50 mph. G.L.) All the aircraft were caught in such a squall; three landed in Stromness harbour, all being severely damaged. An exception was Sub.Lt. J. W. R. Groves who landed HMS *Sheffield's* Walrus L2269 in the Flow. The sea was too rough for the ship to recover him; the best that could be done was to stream astern a line to which the aircraft was made fast; thereafter she had to ride out the storm from that afternoon until 09.00 the next day!

Two 771 Sqdn. Corsairs on dispersal at Twatt, 1944. HASLAM.

Bristol Blenheim IV R2782 flying over Sma Geo, Marwick, Birsay, 31.03.45; it can be seen that this aircraft is being used for training in the absence of undernose gun blister and gun in upper turret. REMMINGTON.

Boston III in flight over Orkney, 31.03.45; Boston T8B appears to be W8392. Before transfer from the RAF to the FAA, one Boston had been experimentally fitted with a searchlight known as a Turbinlite which accounts for the flat nose. This aircraft (T8E) is likely to be W8317. The flat nose gave less drag than expected, the projecting Townend Ring causing the airflow to cling to the surface instead of becoming turbulent. REMMINGTON.

Hesta Geo, Birsay Fighter Direction Centre, transmitting and receiving station; its Radio Call sign was 'Penguin', its original occupant being Richard Lane, brother of Allen Lane, founder of Penguin Books! PRO.

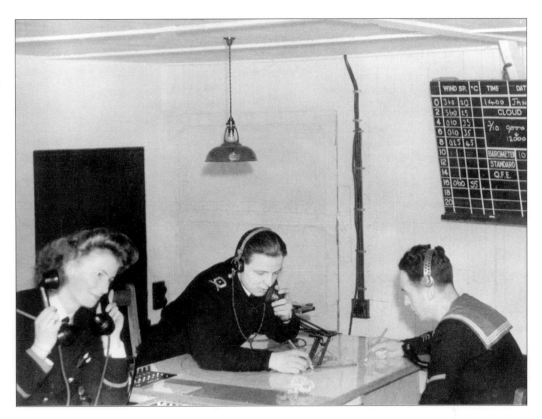

In the Fighter Direction School, Twatt, January 1945; 3rd. Officer Sheila Tucker and Johnny Treloar plotting. PEMBERTON.

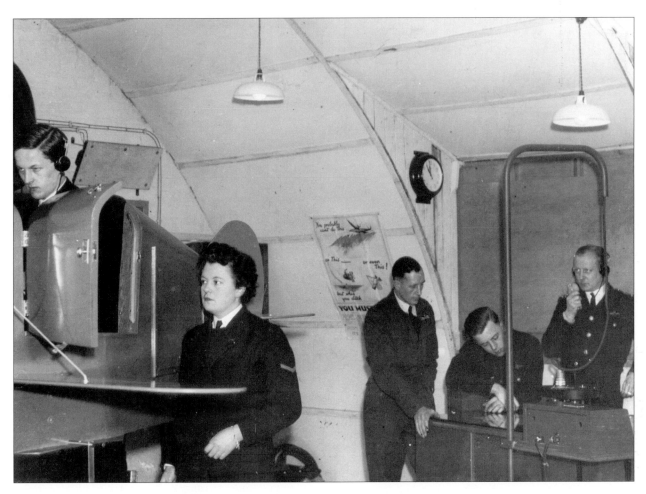

In the Link Trainer, Twatt, 26.01.45; Chris Morrish, Lesley Fowler-Johnson, Ron Heap, Tom Bennett and 'Crem' (talking in mike to Chris). PEMBERTON.

*Very English
landscape in the
Link Trainer
room, Twatt!
26.01.45.* HILL.

*Truck taking pilots of 771 Sqdn. to dispersal for take off, 1944; L. to R. Sub.Lt. Alfred J. Playford, CPO Pilot Frank
Daly, Not Known, Sub.Lt. Pilot.......? (Sub.Lt. Playford later died when his Corsair crashed in Sandwick - see p. 80).*
HASLAM.

Twatt Officers, July 1945 in front of a Boston III
Back Row Sub.Lt. Hoppitt, F/O Ream, Sub.Lts. Barnwell, Treloar, Bennett, Fearnley, F/O Munro, Sub. Lts. Bentley, Jones
Front Row Sub.Lts. Buxton, Scott, Moon, Lts. Mence, Remmington, Linstead, Lt.Cdr. Burke, Lt. Wright-Anderson,
Prentice, F/O Heap, Lt. Middleton, Sub.Lts. Woodhead, Hunt. REMMINGTON.

Swordfish write off near Craigiefield, Kirkwall; pilot switched from gravity to main fuel tanks but unfortunately had
forgotten to check that the main tanks were full before take off; unhurt, he walked away from the wreck! HAMILTON.

Pranged Boulton Paul P.82 Defiant TT.1, DR932 used for fire drill at Twatt. HILL.

Grumman Wildcat IV FN270 which crash landed in a turnip field in Orkney being towed out by the recovery vehicle; see picture overleaf. HAMILTON.

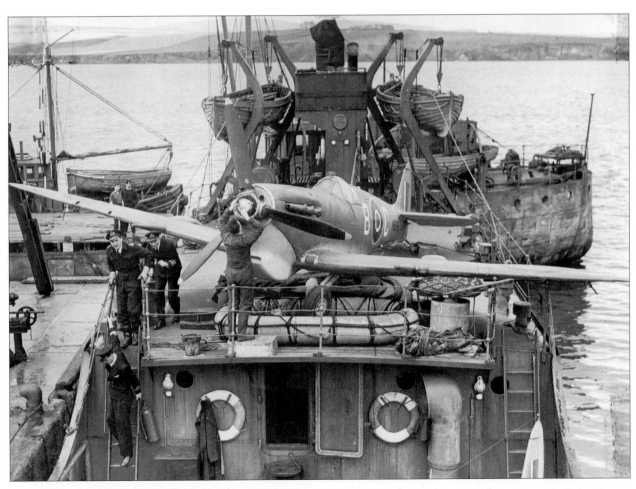

Supermarine Seafire IIc, MB178/179? (884 Sqdn. Victorious) coming back from North Africa being unloaded at Scapa for transport to Hatston Workshops; notice the sand cowl fitted to the front of the aircraft; Lt. Duncan Hamilton at head of stairway and Lt. Mahoney behind; The vessel is believed to be the Crescence which was stationed at Hatston from 1941 - 1943 and at Scapa from 1943 - 1945 for the transport of crashed aircraft. HAMILTON.

Normally civilians were kept well away from crashed aircraft but when a Grumman Martlet came down near Fiold in Westray in April 1943 where there was no Royal Naval recovery vehicle, the help of the local population had to be enlisted! The tractor drivers are Jack Hewison and George Rendall. HAMILTON.

German U-Boats in Loch Eriboll, Sutherland, after surrender, 23.05.45: photographed by aircraft from Twatt. BURKE.

King George V getting ready to hoist up her Walrus. REMMINGTON.

Wren Air Mechanics engaged on routine servicing of a Martinet, Twatt, 10.06.45. PAGE.

Fairey Fulmar in Hatston Workshops. HAMILTON.

Wreckage of Twatt aircraft, Corsair II, JS588 which crashed near Quoyloo on approach to Twatt, on 23 April 1945 at 15.20 hrs. Sub.Lt. Alfred J. Playford, RNVR, killed; buried Norwich Cemetery, Norfolk. HILL.

Grumman Wildcat IV FN270 arrives at the Hatston Workshops on a Bedford low-loader. HAMILTON.

Lift-off; R-4 Sikorsky, Twatt; Lt. Jean-Paul Fournier RN with Senior visiting Wren officer, 6.4.45. FOURNIER.

Helicopter pilot Lt. Jean-Paul Fournier with his technicians in the Petty Officers' Mess at Twatt. FOURNIER.

R-4 Sikorsky helicopter with floats appears to be a trick photograph - both the same machine! HILL.

Twatt R-4 Sikorsky helicopter landing at Rinnigill on the island of Hoy. PRO.

The new Squadron included all of 701, 702, 705, 711, 712, 713, 714, 715, 716, 718 and 720 Flights equipped with Walrus, Seafox and Swordfish. Such an amalgamation created the biggest squadron in the Royal Navy with 65 aircraft. However, unlike the usual Naval Squadrons which normally kept together, the aircraft of 700 Squadron, by their very nature, came together only by chance. These were catapult aircraft embarked on cruisers and battleships and would disembark at Hatston whenever the parent ship was in Scapa Flow. The Squadron was large on paper only but there were occasions when large numbers of the Home Fleet and ships working up for other stations were present in Scapa and at such times, 700 Squadron aircraft were catapulted off to the shore station to avoid damage to the rigging of the aircraft during gunnery practice. Thus, in early 1942, no less than 21 Walrus aircraft, complete with flying and maintenance crews, were mustered at Hatston.

A Headquarters Flight of 700 Squadron, equipped principally with Walrus and later, Sea Otter aircraft was permanently shore based in Orkney. Their duties included Air-Sea Rescue and Anti-Submarine Patrol and in these duties they were joined by Walrus disembarked from capital ships and cruisers. 700 Sqdn. was constantly on call to pick up the crews of ditched aircraft. Sometimes they had to be rescued themselves. In April 1941, Albacore N4155 of 828 Squadron, Hatston, crashed into the sea 50 miles east of Orkney and a Dutch submarine in the vicinity picked up the pilot, the only survivor. A 700 Squadron Walrus was catapulted from HMS *Shropshire* in Scapa Flow to fly the pilot to hospital in Kirkwall and although it rendezvoused successfully with the submarine it could not, because of deteriorating weather, take off again. The solution to this problem presented one of the oddest spectacles of the war. The submarine towed the Walrus to more sheltered waters near Orkney and it took off successfully again! On 25th April 1944, Sea Otter JM761 of 700 Squadron, on a Flight from Abbotsinsch to Twatt plunged into Hoy Sound and, just before the plane sank, the crew were saved by High Speed Rescue launch from Stromness directed from Hatston which had picked up the distress signal. Others were less fortunate. On 24th April 1940, Walrus L2316 on Anti-Submarine Patrol from Hatston, disappeared without trace in the Fair Isle Channel presumably shot down by enemy aircraft which had been reported in the vicinity. On 24th September 1942, in a tragic accident all six members of Walrus L2329 of Twatt Flight and Walrus X9418 of HMS *Sheffield* Flight were killed in a mid-air collision over Scapa Flow. This was one of several mid-air collisions which occurred during the war in Orkney's busy air space. After the publication of the first edition of this book, the author was contacted by the widow of one of these pilots who, for the first time, learned of the exact circumstances and place of her husband's death!

Pilots' and Observers' logs of 700 Squadron record ceaseless hours of Anti-Submarine Patrol. After the catastrophic sinking of HMS *Royal Oak* in the second month of the war, this duty was absolutely vital to protect the comings and goings of the Fleet. Interceptions were rare. G. W. R. Nicholl in *The Supermarine Walrus* records one successful patrol:

> On 10th April 1940, Walrus P5655 (Johnny Groves, pilot, Lt.Cdr A. Fleming, Observer and TAG L/A Smith), attacked a submerged U-boat about ten miles east of the Orkneys. Oil rising to the surface before the attack increased in quantity and A/S trawlers were called to the spot to complete the work, the resultant 'kill' being jointly awarded.

Patrols could be boring in the extreme when U-boats began to give the well defended Orkney waters a wide berth, particularly at the end of the war. Norman Brown, Observer in 700 Squadron, is not proud today of what the crew did to relieve the monotony

> In the absence of enemy submarines, the pilot would obligingly bank low over a basking shark to give the air gunner some practice. I'm ashamed to think of that now, but some terrible things were done in war time. I've seen detachments of the Fleet engage Stack Skerry with 6 inch guns, the shells bursting on the cliff face. Thousands of seabirds must have died. Today we would all hold up our hands in horror at the thought.

Apart from Air-Sea Rescue and Anti-Submarine Patrol work, the squadron also acted as communication channel between ship and shore. Aircraft were catapulted off but, on return, the only way to get back on board was to land beside their ship and to be hoisted on board by crane. This could be an extremely difficult operation in windy Scapa Flow. Bill Larkins, a pilot with 771 Squadron much admired the pilots of 700 Squadron whom he described as 'intrepid airmen who used to fly in amongst the balloon cables in Scapa Flow, to communicate back and forth with their parent ships'. Up to 85 barrage balloons could be flown in Scapa Flow at any one time and presented a nightmarish obstacle to the uninitiated. The balloon area was, of course, out of bounds to all other squadrons, and pilots who transgressed there rarely came out unscathed. A Hurricane of 771 Squadron landed at Twatt minus a wing tip and, more dramatically, Boulton Paul Defiant DR933, lost most of its port wing but, in spite of this, the pilot made a successful belly landing.

700 Sqdn. were expected to operate at all times of day and night and in all weathers. When it was discovered in mid 1943 that 700 Sqdn. pilots had had

no night flying experience, the Admiralty immediately ordered ship-borne aircraft world-wide to carry out night landing practice. At that time most of 700 Sqdn. were based at Twatt and the month was June! Nevertheless pilots did as they were ordered; after 2200 hours they switched on their navigation lights, did circuits and bumps and made the appropriate entry in their Log Books! Meanwhile ground staff would stand outside reading newspapers by natural light!

Aircraft of the Headquarters Flight often had to travel much further afield, frequently to the Faroes, a hazardous journey since these islands were frequently fogbound and in the event of not being able to land, the aircraft did not have enough fuel for the return journey. On March 1st 1944, in a flight lasting more than four hours, a Sea Otter from Twatt flew from Hatston in severe wintry conditions to deliver an urgent consignment to HMS *Victorious* off the Faroes. In the heavy seas, the landing deck was heaving more than forty feet and the pilot, Sub.Lt. Snowdon, with no experience of deck-landing a Sea Otter—which had no arrester hook fitted anyway, wisely chose the landing strip on Faroese soil. A more experienced Swordfish pilot from HMS *Victorious* flew in to collect the vital box.

700 Squadron was based initially at Hatston where, when runways were busy, aircraft had the initial advantage of being able to land in Kirkwall Bay and taxi up the slipway. This was, after all, one of the main reasons why Hatston was chosen as the Royal Navy's first airfield. Circumstances change quickly in wartime and, it was decided that 700 Squadron should join the other non-combatant squadron, 771 squadron at its new base at Twatt and the move was made. 700 Squadron had barely settled in when front-line pilots preparing for *Operation Torch*, the North African landings, spilled over to Twatt since Hatston was unable to cope once again. As a result, in September 1942, 700 Squadron was required to move once more, temporarily, to RAF Grimsetter and 820 and 822 Squadrons took up residence at Twatt. By December 1942, 700 Squadron had returned to Twatt where, for 18 months, they had a busy programme. By this time the Squadron had 63 Walrus aircraft on capital ships, cruisers and shore stations. 18 of these are recorded at Twatt on one occasion. A contributor to the FAA magazine, *Flight Deck*, in December 1945 recalls his time there in 1942 when eight Walrus did a 'balbo across Twatt airfield at nought feet' which he goes on to describe as a 'weird and wonderful sight' as I am sure it was. Any Airshow Committee would pay handsomely to repeat such a performance today!

In addition to its Air Sea Rescue, Anti-Submarine Patrol and Communications roles, 700 Squadron now assumed responsibility for training newly formed Catapult Flights. For pilots and observers, a ten week course, parts of which took place at Donibristle, Dundee and on HMS *Pegasus*, culminated in final training with 'A' Flight at Twatt before joining their ship. More space was required for these developments and, in time, the squadron had its own hangars, accommodation blocks, messes and wardroom built at Quoys on the Twatt airfield.

As time went by and more sophisticated radar was fitted to ships, there was less need for spotter aircraft. The advent of escort carriers and MAC-ships (Merchant Aircraft Carriers) hastened the demise of the Catapult Flights. Headquarters Flight of 700 Squadron, Twatt, continued to perform its roles for a time but finally, on 24th March 1944, the squadron was disbanded and merged with 771 Squadron on the same airfield, a real marriage of convenience. To the variety of aircraft already operated by 771 was added the Walrus and Sea Otter, the latter remaining with that squadron until the end of the war. Former 700 pilots could now gain experience on fighters such as the Hurricane or Corsair or opt for a twin-engined conversion course on Blenheims or Bostons.

The first Royal Air Force squadron to be based in Orkney was No. 254 Squadron equipped with Blenheim IV bombers. This squadron had, in fact, been posted to the new airfield at Sumburgh in Shetland to undertake patrols over coastal shipping, a duty for which, according to its Norse motto, *Fluga, vakta ok ljosta*, to fly, to watch and to strike, it was well equipped to do in this northern setting. However the Squadron had to await the establishment of a Station Headquarters at Sumburgh and had therefore to move in to the RN Air Station at Hatston since RAF Grimsetter was still far from completion. Hatston itself was extremely busy at this time with seven squadrons on station but with the departure of five squadrons on 21st April 1940, the Blenheims of No. 254 Squadron were able to move in next day. As well as shipping protection patrols the squadron assisted in diverting unidentified and neutral shipping into the large Contraband Base which had been established in Kirkwall Bay, just off Hatston. Here, up to 100 merchant vessels would lie impatiently at anchor while Britain considered it had the right to search them for strategic materials bound for Germany. The squadron also undertook reconnaissance duties from Hatston in its brief time there. On 16th May 1940, it finally took up station at Sumburgh but returned briefly to Orkney three years later, on this occasion equipped with Beaufighters. From Skeabrae they conducted an anti-shipping strike off the Norwegian coast.

One whole year after the war with Germany started there was still no permanent RAF presence in Orkney. A small beginning was made however on 15th September 1940 when the first aircraft, a small ex-civil Miles Whitney Straight flown by the

Commanding Officer, Wing Commander C. F. H. Grace arrived at Skeabrae. Though they now had an airfield, such were the demands for the defence of the south of England, that the RAF had unfortunately not one squadron to spare! 804 Squadron of the Royal Navy, Hatston, newly equipped with Grumman Martlets originally intended for the French Air Force, moved in on 10th October 1940. Here they remained until 6th January 1941 when No. 3 Squadron of the Royal Air Force took over.

Altogether 19 RAF squadrons were in residence in Orkney during World War II. It is not necessary to give details of every one of these squadrons for there was little variation in their duties during the war years. Indeed it is not possible to give more than a skeletal outline of the activities of some of these squadrons. It is well known fact that some RAF squadrons active during the war on the British mainland—and indeed beyond—disappeared without leaving one photographic record behind them. Skeabrae was no exception. Only a handful of photographs of RAF aircraft at Skeabrae is known to exist. Apart from a very fine Operational Record in the Public Records Office little is known about the Station apart from what has been gleaned from the memories of servicemen and women who spent some time there. With the help of these notes it is possible, by concentrating on several squadrons to give an idea of the role of Skeabrae in the war years.

No. 3 Squadron was one of the oldest RAF squadrons, being formed as early as May 1912. Equipped with Hurricanes, it was based at Croydon at the outbreak of the war. It had been severely hammered in France and by 23rd May 1940 it found itself in the North of Scotland where it remained for almost a year. It arrived at Skeabrae on 7th January 1941. Desmond Scott, a New Zealander, had just joined No. 3 Squadron as a pilot. His brief impression of Orkney was not favourable. In his book, *One More Hour*, he writes:

> I was so exhausted by the time we reached our destination, I still can't remember where we disembarked at Scapa Flow—Lyness or Kirkwall. All I remember was that it was bitterly cold and snow lay everywhere. Skeabrae was one hell of a place. The two asphalt runways were a luxury for our Hurricanes but everything else was either half finished or surrounded by a sea of mud and slush. Gale force winds would sweep down from the North Sea almost every day, driving the snow into deep drifts and filling the ditches that had been excavated in preparation for the laying of pipes for the station's drainage system . . .
>
> There were no trees on the Orkneys and most of the civilians who were working on the station's complex were from Ireland. The war didn't seem to mean a thing to them and it was not uncommon to see a bunch of them huddled around a coal-fired brazier playing cards. The defence forces guarding the huts

> were the very opposite. If they couldn't find any Huns to shoot at, they gave *us* their full attention. The Navy in Scapa Flow was the worst offender, their motto being to shoot first and to ask questions afterwards.

Due to the draft of all able bodied men into the services, such was the shortage of labour to build airfields that, as Scott points out, hundreds of Irishmen were brought in. When recruitment in Ireland still did not meet the government's expectations, long term prisoners were brought in from jails on the Scottish mainland and 'quarantined' on site at Skeabrae which brought the construction camp workforce up to a total of 800. Initial concern at the introduction of this new element in the workforce proved to be groundless and no difficulties whatsoever were experienced with the new recruits. However hiring drivers for the thirteen road rollers on the site proved exceptionally difficult. Initially only one local, inexperienced driver volunteered for the job and he was required to work from 7 o'clock in the morning until 12 o'clock midnight. At first he was given no lunch break and had to eat his dinner at 1 o'clock in the morning when he got home. When, after some weeks he said, understandably, that he could not carry on, he was fed in the mess!

No. 3 Squadron was in no doubt from the start what its duty was when the pilots were taken to see an almost perfect example of a Ju-88 in a Skeabrae hangar. It had been shot down on Christmas Day 1940 by a Royal Naval Grumman Martlet of 804 Squadron which had been based at Skeabrae pending the arrival of the RAF Squadron. After a very short tour of duty, No. 3 Squadron left on 8th February, the shortest stay of any of the RAF fighter squadrons, indeed much shorter than many of the disembarked Royal Naval squadrons. It was necessary to rotate squadrons between the very active and the quieter stations but it is difficult to understand this short stay when the station was just getting itself going as a fighter base.

The primary function of the RAF fighters at Skeabrae and later, Grimsetter, was to intercept enemy aircraft intruding into British airspace in the North of Scotland. More particularly, its role was to protect Scapa Flow not only from enemy bombers but also from the apparently innocuous reconnaissance aircraft which appeared over the islands with increasing frequency. Other duties included providing escorts for convoys which passed regularly through the Pentland Firth. The Hurricane fighter had a limited endurance and, if the weather was favourable, operated in endless relays from before dawn till after sunset. On clear moonlight nights single patrols would continue and the throaty sound of the solitary Hurricane could be heard in the still Orkney air. The ships of the Home Fleet had also to be escorted to the limit of the fighter's endurance when they left Scapa and on their return. The cruisers of the Northern Patrols, for example HMS *Suffolk*, HMS *Norfolk*, HMS *Birmingham*, HMS *Edinburgh* and HMS *Euryalus* were kept particularly busy.

RAF Skeabrae was regularly used as a training centre for pilots who had recently qualified. The policy of using the remoter stations for training was introduced by Air Chief Marshal Hugh Dowding at the height of the Battle of Britain to give pilots further flying experience. Orkney squadrons would sometimes have as many as ten new pilots! Later on in the war, pilots were trained for overseas postings. The training these pilots received in the defence of Orkney was put to good use defending another island community—Malta. By contrast Orkney was also, as we shall see later, a staging post for pilots who were able to unwind from some of the fiercest air battles of the war.

After the German invasion of Norway in April 1940, the possibility of an invasion of Britain from the north became very real and the possession of

Scapa Flow, the base of the Home Fleet, would have been a severe blow to British morale. Experience had taught the British that in the blitzkriegs which had characterised German progress on the continent of Europe, the destruction of airfields was the first priority. There were four fully operational Air Stations in Orkney by July 1941 and they would be the first to be destroyed; this would be followed by an invasion of the east coast of Orkney supported possibly by airborne troops. The stations themselves were well defended and to test the defences there were several large scale mock invasions of Orkney. By far the largest was *Operation Leapfrog* which took place between 9th and 11th August 1941, doubtless to impress King George VI who was in Orkney at the time. An invasion force of 18,000 troops supported by tanks landed on the south-east of the Orkney Mainland, the main objectives being the seizure of Skeabrae and Twatt aerodromes. Air support was given to the invaders from all aircraft on the islands and also from the Scottish mainland. Hurricanes of No. 253 Squadron carried out attacks

Sea Otter of 700 Sqdn. outside 700 Sqdn. hangars in March 1944, just prior to the disbandment of the squadron
Officers standing in front of engine and cockpit Sub.Lts. James, Astley, Snowdon, Weaver, Cyril Davison, Lt. Bottomley.
Standing in front of aircraft Sub.Lt. Vallely, Lt. 'Happy' Day, Lt.Cdr. Hyde (CO), Sub.Lt. Green, Sub.Lt. Brown
Others On the starboard mainplane, Corp. RAF Bill Mattick, first from the engine on the starboard mainplane, Air
Fitter Frank Kendrick, first from the engine on the port mainplane, Air Fitter George Thain, on Sub. Lt. Brown's right
is Senior TAG Steve Lock, in front of A/C's port float, A.B. Tim ??????, New Zealander and next to him, A.B. 'Joe'
Brain. REMMINGTON.

on the defending troops and provided escort for Blenheims which bombed the aerodromes. Both Air Stations were overwhelmed on the second day. For the Commanding Officer of Twatt it must have been a baptism of fire in more senses than one, his station had been operational for only three weeks! Valuable lessons were learned from such manoeuvres.

By December 1940, the Luftwaffe had called off its daylight offensive in southern England and switched its tactics to the bombing of London by night. The Spitfire and Hurricane squadrons were powerless to intervene and were gradually dispersed throughout Britain to give more general cover. No. 253 Squadron Hurricanes took over the defence of Scapa Flow from No. 3 Squadron on 10th January 1941 and it must have been reassuring for the Station Commander, Wing Commander Lea Cox, to count among the new squadron, veterans of the Battle of Britain. Sometimes the Battle of Britain could be seen re-enacted above Orkney skies when No. 253 Squadron engaged the neighbouring No. 124 Squadron based at Castletown in Caithness in friendly dog-fights! Strange tongues and twangs of the new squadron gave Orcadians a taste of what was to come for practically the only thing these pilots had in common was their Hurricane!

One of the continued unpleasant tasks of the Hurricane pilots was the shepherding of foreign North Atlantic merchantmen into Orkney waters for contraband clearance. General cargo vessels were directed to Kirkwall Bay and oil tankers because of the risk of explosion were required to anchor in Inganess Bay further to the east. The frustration felt by the crews of these vessels as they waited in the long queue was heightened by the danger of being identified in British waters as a British vessel and the consequent risk of U-boat attack for there was no boom protection for them. Such a fate had already befallen the 10,000 ton Danish tanker *Danmark*. The interference and delay was too much for one neutral merchantman who opened fire on a patrolling Skeabrae Hurricane of No. 253 Squadron. The merchantman was never identified or perhaps the British government chose to let the matter rest because of widespread disquiet about the impounding of neutral vessels on the high seas.

The most serious challenge facing the Hurricane pilots and the most frustrating was the appearance, at regular intervals, of high altitude German reconnaissance aircraft which, on fine days, would leave their vapour trails thirty to forty thousand feet above Scapa Flow. The croaking ring of the field telephone, the 'Bandit, scramble' call and the ensuing futile chase left pilots dispirited. There was no way in which a Hurricane could make a successful interception at that altitude. As one officer remarked, 'By the time we got up there, Jerry was back home looking at the prints!' It was perhaps a little comforting for the pilots to know that British reconnaissance aircraft cruised equally contemptuously over German territory.

By this time the Battle of the Atlantic, to the west of Orkney was in full swing. To provide intelligence for the U-Boat commanders, FW200 Condors, capable of a range of 2,200 miles would begin their flight in Bergen or Stavanger and sweep in a broad arc round the west coast of Britain well into the Atlantic. After the fall of France they landed at Bordeaux. Long range Ju-88s also operated reconnaissance patrols from Bergen too, well into the Atlantic. All Atlantic reconnaissance aircraft generally flew to the north of Shetland, well out of harm's way but, with some cloud cover, pilots would risk the short cut through the Fair Isle Channel. On 4th March 1941 three Hurricanes of No. 253 Squadron on patrol intercepted one such Ju-88 and after a brief engagement it crashed into the sea east off Westray. On 6th April 1941 Blue Section of A Flight 253 Sqdn. Skeabrae was scrambled to intercept a Ju-88. Derek Yapp leading in Hurricane V7503 made contact with the aircraft at 20,000 feet and attacked. The starboard engine of the Ju-88 caught fire, the rear gunner ceased firing, the aircraft lost height and was presumed to crash into sea about 10 miles north-east of the station. His own aircraft was damaged in the engagement. His flight was scrambled on the following day, made contact with and chased yet another Ju-88 but it escaped in cloud. Royal Naval as well as Royal Air Force patrols would come across these aircraft sometimes quite unexpectedly and some regrettably did not return to tell of their unexpected encounter. The invaders were rarely picked up by Orkney radars though the radio monitoring services sometimes had a brief forewarning. A typical incident is described by Air Commodore Brown former pilot of No. 253 Squadron at the time

On 11th September 1941, my last day in Orkney and on my last patrol, I was flying a Hurricane on my own to the east of Fair Isle when I was suddenly confronted with a Ju-88 which popped out of the cloud immediately ahead and only a few hundred yards away. Closing in on its port quarter with guns firing I swung round on to its stern. It was a good prolonged burst but, apparently unscathed, the '88 pulled up into the cloud and disappeared. Its presence was reported to sector operations by radio but neither the radars nor the listening service had any trace of it. Back on the ground at Skeabrae I was told there was no doubt I had attacked a twin-engined aircraft but did I know that an RAF Blenheim had been badly shot up and had landed at Sumburgh in Shetland with two of its crew wounded? I was certain that the aircraft had been a Ju-88; I had been so close to it, within a few hundred yards, that the German markings were unmistakable. For about an hour there was strained silence in the

Stack Skerry, used as a target for air bombing and ships' firing practice; no thought could be given to the seabird colonies in those days. PRO.

The cruiser HMS Bermuda catapulting her Walrus, Scapa Flow, 1943. EDWARDS.

Walrus returning to the cruiser HMS Bermuda, Scapa Flow, 1943; note the perilous position of the TAG on the Walrus top wing when waiting to hook up to the crane for recovery. If he overbalanced, the slipstream would take him back into the pusher propeller. EDWARDS.

Defiant DR933/937? Target Tug of 771 Sqdn. hits a barrage balloon cable in Scapa Flow and crash lands; pilot unknown. HAMILTON.

crew caravan. Then the Squadron Commander appeared. In hospital the Blenheim pilot had been told that the Hurricane pilot was very sorry for his error. "What error?" he exclaimed, "what Hurricane squadron? We were shot up by a bloody Ju-88!" No doubt it was the same one. But what if the Blenheim had crashed into the sea and all the crew had been killed?

In common with practically all the squadrons who were resident in Orkney, No. 253 Squadron had its share of accidents and fatalities. On 31st May 1941, Orkney farmer Robbie Taylor was working in one of his fields at Cumlaquoy in Marwick when a Hurricane aircraft began to make a series of power dives off Marwick Head. Robbie formed the impression that the pilot would have difficulty getting out of one power dive. The aircraft disappeared behind the cliffs. There was an explosion, followed by a huge pall of black smoke which, after some time, drifted over his field. Hurricane V7235 crashed at Crustan near Birsay village. This was to be Skeabrae's first fatality and was particularly sad since the pilot was putting on a special display of his flying skills for his local girlfriend who was watching. Two weeks later a fellow pilot was seriously injured when his aircraft crashed near Wasbister in Rousay.

The pilots of No. 253 Squadron and indeed of all squadrons had to see Orkney, its weather and sea in

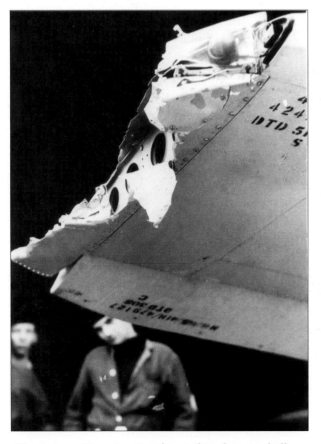

Hurricane minus wing tip after striking barrage balloon cable, Twatt, 18.05.44. Burke.

all their moods. At times battered by wind and rain or blinded by the thickest of Scotch mists and all the attendant anxiety about getting back to base, there were times when the air was crystal clear with unbelievable visibility. The exhilaration felt by some of these young pilots for whom at times war must have seemed a million miles away is expressed beautifully by Brown in his vignette of Orkney *Changing Skies*:

> The most abiding impression of Orkney was a sense of freedom, both in the air and on the ground. Apart from the gun defended area of the Flow the islands presented an extensive, uncluttered and unrestricted aerial playground. Long range aircraft and modern fighters see little of the air and countryside around their bases except fleetingly, when taking off and landing, but Hurricanes, with their limited range and the sea all around Orkney stretching into the distance, were confined to the islands and their adjacent waters except when on operational patrol. For the sole benefit of young fighter pilots, this exclusive flying arena provided, from time to time, huge white cumulus clouds with sharply defined edges and deep caverns through and around which to tailchase, twist, turn, dive vertically down the blossoming faces and climb steeply to loop over their burgeoning tops. It was one of the rare occasions when a pilot could get a perception of height and depth and a surprising realisation that some of the cumulo-nimbus clouds would boil up faster than a Hurricane could climb! At the other end of the aerial scale, at low level, there was the sea rolling in from the Atlantic and offering its broad curling waves with their foaming crests to be skimmed and the breakers to be chased along the deserted curving beaches. There were uninhabited islands over which to practise low level aerobatics with no one to complain and, hopefully, a Squadron Commander blissfully unaware of just how low they were. And if an appreciative audience was required, the lighthouse keepers always seemed to enjoy the show and the unexpected company.

When stationed at Twatt as an Observer with 771 Sqdn. Frank Walker spent much of his time in the air above 20,000 feet doing radar calibration runs for the Home Fleet, frequently looking down at the brilliant white clouds which he described as 'smooth as a sheet on a hospital bed' in startling contrast with the weather at ground level. Sometimes on the other hand the sky was completely cloudless and on 28th June 1943 he recorded in his Log Book that he could see the Hebrides, Wick and Shetland all at the same time!

Is it any wonder that, at the beginning of the war, some volunteer pilots thought they had to pay to join the flying services! On 20th September 1941, No. 253 Squadron moved out to be replaced No. 331 Hurricane Squadron. With its motto *For Norge*, this squadron was made up of Norwegians—35 officers and 178 airmen—213 personnel altogether, under the command of Major Bull. Many of them had had something of the experience of war already, escaping from occupied Norway at the risk of their lives. Among them was pilot Leif Lyssand who writes:

Along with a party of other Norwegians we escaped by boat from occupied Norway. Sailing westwards, just as other harassed Norwegians had done a thousand years before, we made landfall on the island of Sanday in Orkney. Here we received a great welcome. It was my ambition to join the Royal Air Force and become a pilot. In this I was successful. I was even lucky enough after many tests, to qualify as a fighter pilot. I joined No. 331 Squadron which was made up entirely of Norwegians*. Imagine my surprise and delight when I was eventually posted back to the Orkneys. We were stationed at Skeabrae. When my first flight took me over the North Isles of Orkney I saw Sanday far below. When I arrived there some months before, exhausted from my journey and anxious about the future, little did I know that, so soon, my burning ambition would be realised.

* there was at least one Swedish mercenary in this squadron

The Squadron felt very much at home here on old Norwegian soil and, less than three weeks after their arrival, there were emotional scenes at Skeabrae when His Royal Highness, Crown Prince Olaf of Norway and Admiral Reiser Larsen, Officer Commanding the Norwegian Air Force, visited them. 801 Sqdn. pilots joined in the celebrations of the arrival of the Crown Prince as H. E. Duthie writes:

I well remember the visit of the Crown Prince of Norway who brought with him a couple of cases of Aquavit. The evening was spent toasting, with heel clicking, members of the Norwegian Royal Family and the British Royal Family, Winston Churchill, and as there was at least one Swede in the squadron, the Swedish Royal Family—and each other. Towards the end, heel clicking, or even standing, became very difficult!

Sergeant Pilot Ulf Wormdal ('Worm') was artistically inclined and the visit inspired him to design a Squadron Crest, a winged Viking ship floating on clouds, all on a shield of the Norwegian flag. This crest can be seen today on the memorial to this squadron at North Weald in Essex.

To the usual operations carried out by the

700 Sqdn. Maintenance Crews with Walrus and Petrol Bowser outside squadron hangars, Quoys, Twatt, 1943.
Left to Right Air Artificer/4 ?? Joseph (HMS Belfast), Air Fitter C. Gilbert, Air Fitter?? Wilson (HMS Belfast), Ldg.
Air Mechanic G. Edwards, Ldg. Air Mechanic ?? Simmonds, Air Fitter Frank Kendrick, Radio Mechanic Harry
Stephens, Air Mechanic White?, Air Fitter ?? L....(uncertain), Air Mech.? Slater, Air Fitter Gupwell, (in front,
kneeling), Air Fitter J. Hannah. EDWARDS.

Skeabrae squadrons, No. 331 Squadron added air to air firing. A glider was towed up several times to about 4,000 feet and then released over the aerodrome. It came down twisting and turning whilst attacks were made on it. The Squadron were disappointed in their time there to have only two encounters with enemy aircraft despite having frequent scrambles, especially at dawn. Lt. Birkstead suggested a permanent state of readiness by flying dawn and dusk patrols and this became a feature of operations on the station until 10th May 1945 when they were discontinued. In operational flying, No. 331 Squadron had two fatal accidents. On 16th March 1942, Sgt. Pilot Ulf Wormdal spun into the sea, when in combat rehearsal as he tried to follow a Swordfish in its tight turning arc. The other fatality occurred mysteriously during one of the many scrambles to the north of Orkney. 2nd. Lt. Per Svanøe Endresen flying in line astern at 25,000 feet with Lt. Henning Leifseth disappeared without trace although visibility was good. Despite an extensive search no trace was ever found.

With so few opportunities for real action, the Norwegians became restless. To while away the time the Norwegians planned 'invasions' of their homeland and listened eagerly to news from any source. 801 Squadron with Sea Hurricanes spent the period 8th November 1941 until 14th February 1942 at Skeabrae and made great friends with the Norwegians. Some of the 801 Sqdn. pilots had taken part in operations off Norway in HMS *Glorious* in April 1940 when equipped with dive bombing Skuas. Norwegian Harald Meltzer tells of 'George' a pilot in 801 Squadron of the Royal Navy who caused great amusement by relating the following story:

George* had led a Flight of four torpedo carrying aircraft up some fjord in the north of Norway during the campaign there. Visibility was not too good and he found that the mountains on each side of the fjord gradually closed in on him so that he had not enough room in which to turn nor could he go upwards to make a turn since in front of him were mountains at the end of the fjord. The three aircraft that were with him crashed on the mountain sides and the pilots were killed but somehow or other he himself managed to make a safe landing. Eventually he got back to England on a destroyer and made his way to London. In his own leisurely time he rang up the Admiralty to say he was back but he was not perfectly understood by them and he was told, "Oh yes, George, he was killed in Norway." Well George said no more. Here, he thought, was a wonderful opportunity for some free leave. So he rang up his wife who said, "Who is that speaking?" "George," he replied. "George who?" she asked. "Why George," he answered. "Yes, but which George, there are so many Georges?" George said he then hung up the telephone and thought, 'By Jove, here is another chance!' He told us he spent a month in

London having a wonderful time and, finally, getting a bit bored, he went along and reported to the Admiralty for further duties. He had this story well worked up with all the skill of a great raconteur!

* there was in fact no 'George' in 801 Sqdn. at this time; the story probably relates to the adventures of Lt.(A) Jack Welply (known as 'Jacko' or 'The Whelp') [G.L. communication from H. E. (Red) Duthie, 801 Sqdn. pilot]

The British and Norwegian squadrons did have certain communication problems as H. E. Duthie relates:

The executive order to scramble was given to the relevant squadron on the field telephone and this was followed by a green Very fired from the Control Tower to indicate that the runway was clear. In practice, 801 and 331 Squadrons were usually given alternate scrambles though this could be varied according to the serviceability of the aircraft. 801 and 331 Squadrons had dispersals at either end of the main runway and this meant that we sometimes had to take off downwind! But there was an additional hazard for 801 Sqdn. which wasn't in the pilot's handbook! When No. 331 Sqdn. (Norwegian) were given the scramble and therefore had priority, 801 Sqdn. readiness pilots were quite happy to remain huddled round the tortoise stove in the crew room. However when 801 Sqdn. scrambled, things often went rather differently. The reason was this. The Norwegians, all of whom had a personal score to settle with the Germans, were determined not to miss a chance to get even and often acted on the green Very for 801 Sqdn! On a scramble therefore it was not unusual to find a Spitfire, tail up, coming down the runway in the opposite direction! The rule was keep to the left and keep the offside wheel out of the snow or mud at the side of the runway! Sometimes there seemed to be only inches between the wingtips! The Control Tower, when they realised what was happening, would fire a red Very which meant that the runway was not clear but by that time everyone was too committed to do much about it! Why there were not any monumental pile-ups, I will never know! The scramble was fortunately only a section of two aircraft; had it been a Flight scramble I shudder to think of the consequences! If ever taxed on the subject, the Norwegians suddenly lost their command of English! However, on the whole, we got on very well together.
The Norwegians enjoyed their seven months stay in the islands where they had trained hard and learned a lot but the pilots wanted more action and could not disguise their joy when, on 28th they learned that they were to be posted to North Weald in Essex where they were likely to get all the excitement they wanted. On 3rd May 1942 the Squadron moved out and their place was taken by No. 164 Spitfire Squadron.

The constant flying duties of the solitary Skeabrae squadrons placed a considerable strain on

Norman Brown, Observer, Twatt, in front of a Walrus, August 1943. BROWN.

them and during the period when the Norwegians were resident, an additional RAF squadron was brought in to reinforce the RAF presence. No. 132 Squadron with 16 Spitfire IIb's arrived from Peterhead on 15th February 1942 and began to share duties with No. 331. After four months at Skeabrae it transferred to RAF Grimsetter in the East Mainland of Orkney and converted to Vb's. Grimsetter had in fact been open since October 1940 as a satellite of Skeabrae and had been in regular use since then. Though a small station, it was as Fighter Sector Station in 14 Group, operationally very important. Sited on the Deerness Road at a suitably strategic distance from the airfield (and still standing) was the massive RAF Kirkwall Operations Room which controlled the movements of RAF aircraft from the Faroes to Caithness, provided a 'listening service' for bombers operating off Norway and plotted the movements of all aircraft in its sector. Tactically the positioning of the second squadron in the east of Orkney made sense. It was from this direction where the enemy generally came and the five minutes gained by positioning a squadron here could make all the difference between a successful and an unsuccessful interception. Despite the positional advantage, No. 132 Squadron recorded no interceptions. Records of their activities are meagre.

On a training flight off Deerness on 22nd August 1942 Sgt.Pilot Renyard was killed when his Spitfire Vb, BL667 crashed. No. 132 Squadron left Grimsetter on 22nd September 1942.

The arrival of No. 164 Spitfire Squadron at Skeabrae on 4th May 1942 brought yet more strange tongues to the islands. The Squadron had at least one Argentinian pilot and bore the Spanish motto *Firmes Volamos*, firmly we fly, since the money for the squadron had been collected by the Argentine-British. No. 164 had been formed at Peterhead only a few weeks previously and got off to a bad start by losing two aircraft on landing at Skeabrae, Spitfire X4328 landing too close to R7220 and chopping off the tail. Fortunately no casualties were recorded. A similar incident occurred at nearby RNAS Twatt some months later but in severe weather conditions. No. 164 Squadron is remembered in official records for the number of accidents in which it was involved all of which can be probably attributed to inexperience. One pilot, by breaking to the left instead of the right after a mock attack on the Fleet in Scapa Flow went straight between the masts of one of the capital ships and removed all the aerials. Remarkably, he got back to base. The same pilot, coming in low from the Atlantic over the cliffs of Yesnaby shortened his propeller blades by a few inches yet lived to tell the tale! There were other accidents and one casualty. Pilot Officer D. B. Bridger, an Argentinian, was killed when his Spitfire Va P9563 hit a workman's hut in a low pass over the station. In the many patrols carried out by this squadron it had only one partially successful contact with the enemy when a Ju-88 was attacked and damaged to the east of Orkney. The squadron left Orkney on 10th September 1942. In September, No. 132 Squadron at Grimsetter was replaced by No. 129 and on the departure of No. 164 for Peterhead, No. 602 Squadron took over duties at Skeabrae. For No. 602 Squadron this was the first of two periods of residence at Skeabrae. For both squadrons, their stays were uneventful. By early 1943 they had left the islands. To give the squadrons much needed air to air firing practice No. 1494 Fighter Gunnery Flight moved to Skeabrae in early 1943 with target towing Lysanders. In March a most unfortunate incident occurred. To prevent the tail of an aircraft rising when the pilot brought the engine to full power it was normal practice for two aircraftmen to lie on the tail. This was invariably the case with Lysanders since, in the Orkney winds, the Lysander had a tendency to become airborne before the engine started! The pilot of Lysander T1580 mistook a signal and took off with an aircraftman still on the tail. He climbed to 200 feet at which point the aircraftman fell off, the aircraft went out of control and crashed. L/AC A. C. Lane was killed and two of the flying crew were injured. This resulted in one of several courts-martial held at Skeabrae during the war, in two of which, pilots had to stand trial. It is difficult to understand why this accident had to happen at all for an identical incident, fortunately not fatal, had occurred with a Seafire aircraft of 804 Squadron of the Royal Navy at Hatston barely three weeks earlier. The fantastic adventure of this member of the ground crew made the national newspapers and is described in the chapter *The Carrier Men*. The same Gunnery Flight devised a new method of releasing a drogue but due to a misunderstanding between the pilot and the winch operator, the plane flew very low over the station dragging behind it some 1,500 feet of cable. Unfortunately, on the end of this cable was a 5lb. lead weight which passed through the Station at 120 mph., almost demolishing the Armourers' Section. Hitherto, only seaplanes had been known to cast anchor! One wonders what would have happened had the lead weight hooked on anything! Incidents like this were rarely isolated. Although the Royal Navy at nearby Twatt were experts in drogue towing, on one occasion a drogue broke away and the winch which reeled in the cable jammed. Before the TAG could clear the blockage the drogue cable had sped over the Orkney countryside to the great alarm of a farmer—and no doubt the horse—when it passed between the animal and the plough!

Because of the peculiar requirements of the Orkney Stations, there was close liaison between the RAF and the Royal Navy. 801 and 880 Seafire Squadrons disembarked from HMS *Furious* and using lodger facilities at RAF Skeabrae took advantage of the presence of No. 601 Spitfire Squadron of the RAF to get in some valuable dog-fighting practice in early 1944. RAF personnel fitted ground installations into cruisers such as HMS *Suffolk* and HMS *Norfolk* to enable the fighter pilots to communicate directly with the Fleet. Also No. 1476 Ship Recognition Flight, equipped with Ansons was moved to Skeabrae where it remained for more than a year. There was enormous scope in Orkney to give pilots much needed experience in identifying British, Commonwealth and Allied warships. Among the other twin-engined aircraft to visit Skeabrae were the torpedo carrying Beaufighters of No. 254 Squadron based at North Coates in Lincolnshire. They spent a week on the Station at the beginning of April 1943 engaged in anti-shipping strikes off the Norwegian coast.

Is it a mere coincidence that all the RAF squadrons based at Grimsetter appeared to have been funded from Indian sources? No. 132 Squadron had the name *Bombay*, No. 129 was called *Mysore* and had as its badge the *Gunda Bherunda of Mysore*, No.

Sea Otter over Orkney, March 1944. BROWN.

234 was known as *Madras Presidency*. Signals Officer, Mike Walker who was based at Skeabrae from 1942 until 1943 writes that because of problems with the Control Tower at Grimsetter he had to drive a signals truck from Skeabrae to Grimsetter in time for the arrival of No. 132 *Bombay* Squadron. 'An Eastern Potentate was going to give us some money for aircraft but wanted to see a static firing display before he did so and Grimsetter had the only runway that could be used to fire out to sea.'

No. 234 Squadron was the last RAF squadron to be resident at Grimsetter. In the interests of economy and efficiency the RAF moved out and based both squadrons at Skeabrae. It will be recalled that the RAF required only one station in Orkney in the first place, but, by default, ended up with two. The Royal Navy desperately wanted back its own original air station, Skeabrae, but a compromise was reached with the RAF when the Royal Navy assumed control of Grimsetter on 6th July 1943, becoming an independent command on 15th August 1943 when it was commissioned as HMS *Robin*.

Altogether eleven RAF squadrons were based in Orkney during the remainder of the war. In keeping with the cosmopolitan nature of the pilots responsible for the aerial defence of Scapa Flow, these included No. 312 and No. 313 (Czech.), No. 441 (Royal Canadian Air Force), No. 329 (Free French) and No. 451 and No. 453 (Royal Australian Air Force). Operations were routine and differed little from what has already been described but there were, nevertheless, several highlights.

All pilots speak of the fickle nature of the Orkney weather and a good, though sad, illustration of this can be given from a No. 66 Squadron patrol. The Station Diary of Skeabrae records that on 12th March 1943, two Spitfires took off at 10.53 on a sector recce counter clockwise round Orkney. The weather was fine with occasional heavy showers. The last fix on Pilot Officer Donald's aircraft was south of Westray at 11.33. At 11.41 the patrol ran into a severe blizzard and Pilot Officer Donald radioed 'My screen is covered, I can see nothing' and required an immediate fix but because of interference from another transmitter the Control Tower could not give the aircraft its position. Control successfully brought in the other patrolling aircraft the pilot of which reported that, off Birsay, visibility dropped to ten yards. Despite extensive searches by four Walruses, two Lysanders and a Dominie, no trace of Pilot Officer Donald's aircraft was found.

German reconnaissance over Scapa Flow stepped up in early 1943 for the course of the war was turning and Germany feared a renewed attempt at invading Norway from the north. The Station Diary records that on 22nd March 1943 at 17.10, a Ju-88 on reconnaissance flew over Scapa Flow at 34,000 feet. On this occasion visibility was perfect and vapour trails could easily be seen. Guns were fired from the Kirkwall area but the aircraft was travelling at great speed. Warrant Officer Lawson of No. 66 Squadron intercepted this aircraft at 17.15, 20 miles east of Scapa Flow and gave a half second burst at 1,200 yards but the enemy dived into cloud. This is a fairly normal entry to be found in the Operational Record Books of all the northern Fighter Stations. What makes this entry of particular interest is that, much later, the pilot of that German aircraft was interrogated when he crash landed in Britain. Under interrogation he spoke of his operations, including this:

> On 22nd March 1943 I took off from Ålborg (in northern Denmark) for a photographic reconnaissance of Scapa Flow and I returned with film which, in view of the anxiety about the invasion of Norway, was developed and taken immediately to Oberst Rowell and shown to Hitler personally. Thirty six ships were identified. I flew at 36,000 feet above cloudbase and encountered extraordinarily accurate fire. I took evasive action but was followed by the AA fire. Fortunately they slightly underestimated my speed or I could easily have been shot down. When leaving Orkney I was chased for twenty minutes by three fighters and I went into a steep dive but I was followed all the way by the fighters. At 3,500 feet I ran into cloud base and escaped.

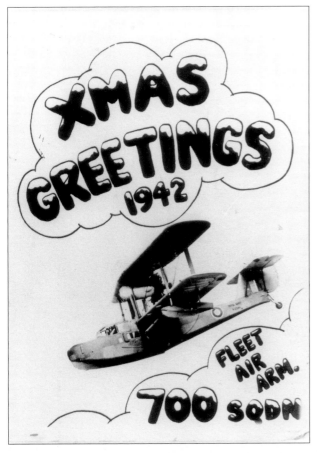

700 Squadron Christmas card sent from Twatt; the aircraft is a Walrus and appears to be W2741. EDWARDS.

The menace of high flying reconnaissance aircraft remained—and they were getting faster. To counter this menace, a specially modified 'high flying' Spitfire was introduced; only a few were ever made and sent to strategic parts of Britain. These were Spitfire VI's and VII's with Rolls-Royce two stage supercharged engines, pressurised cockpit and increased wing-span to cope with the rarified air at 50,000 feet. Two of these truly magnificent flying machines were based at Skeabrae. No. 312 Czech was the first squadron at Skeabrae to be equipped with these Spitfires though there is no record of these aircraft in use by them. A photograph taken sometime between mid-January and mid-February 1944 of a Mk.VII with the markings DU-G and a note to the effect that the Spitfire 'belonged to a previous squadron' clearly identifies it as being attached to the Czech squadron which had aircraft in the DU series. John Sigmund, a member of the servicing echelon of the Czech 312 Sqdn. confirms this when he writes 'I well remember one of our 'A' flight pilots, Antonin Ocelka, going up in one of these planes to about 45,000 feet. He came back telling us that the whole cabin iced up'. It is almost unbelievable that aircraft were flying at this altitude above Orkney in early 1944!

No. 602 Squadron was based at Skeabrae from 18th January 1944 until 9th March 1944. This squadron was known as the *City of Glasgow* Squadron, the money to equip the squadron having been raised in that city and it was appropriate that Glaswegian Ian Blair should distinguish himself in the short time the squadron was based in Orkney. On 20th February he was piloting Spitfire Mk. VII, MD114, DU-G when he intercepted and shot down a long-range Messerschmitt Bf 109 20 miles to the east of Orkney. A fellow pilot in the Squadron was Pierre Clostermann who later in the war became one of France's flying aces and a well-known writer and politician. In his book *The Big Show*, Clostermann, using rather too much writer's licence, gives a graphic account of this incident. He claims he took part in the action and did everything apart from shooting the enemy aircraft down. Squadron pilots know better. At the time of the incident he was actually on the ground! Clostermann does however give an excellent description of a scramble at Skeabrae:

> Jacques and Kelly were 'on readiness' from 1030 hours to 1400 hours. Superb weather but bitterly cold. Not having anything much to do, Ian Blair and I were playing a game of chess. At 12 o'clock everybody went off to lunch but we decided to finish our game. Kelly enviously watched the others going—this cold

Cannon shells being loaded at Skeabrae. HORNE.

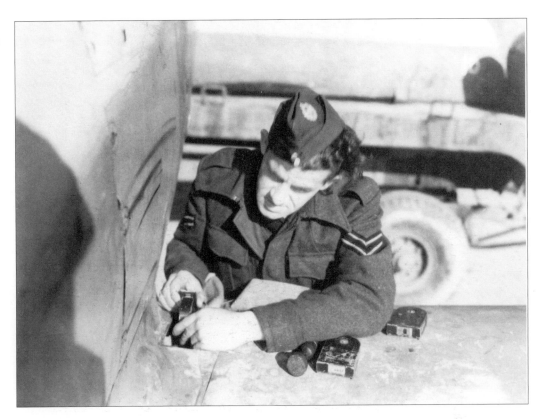

Skeabrae; inserting ciné gun cassettes in a Spitfire wing root fillet; this camera operated automatically when the guns were fired; petrol bowser in background. HORNE.

RAF Skeabrae—refuelling the Spitfire; operating the pump at the back of a petrol bowser. HORNE.

sharpened the appetite and, as usual, he was famishing. We ended up by taking pity on him and offered to take their place. They accepted joyfully for it must be admitted that this high altitude readiness was rather a bind. They went. We slipped on our Mae Wests, put our parachutes and helmets ready in the two Spitfires. 1222 hours.

"Your queen's had it," said Ian.

My queen certainly was cornered but just as he stretched out his hand to take it, the air-raid siren went. In the ensuing turmoil, queens, pawns, rooks, everything, went for six. The fitters rushed into the corridor with a clatter of boots. I dived for the door shouting 'Scramble, scramble!' Ian leapt out of the window. In less than 50 seconds I was installed, strapped in, oxygen switched on and with the engine ticking over. Three white rockets from Control showed that the runway was clear. The ground was frozen so hard that we could safely cut across the grass to get on the runway. At 1223 hours 35 seconds exactly we took off at full throttle and already Control was giving us our first instructions. "Hallo Dalmat Red One, Pandor calling, bandit approaching, B for Baker at Z for Zebra, climb flat out on vector zero, nine, five. Out!" I fumbled inside my boot for my code card which had become mixed up with my maps. I was so clumsy about it that I had to ask Pandor to repeat.

O.K. a Jerry was approaching Scapa Flow at altitude Z—I looked it up on the card. Phew! Z meant 40,000 feet! I set my course, still climbing at full boost. Ian's Spit hovered a few yards away and I could feel his amused eyes on me under the sun goggles. It was a wonderful winter's day—not a trace of cloud in the sky—and the Arctic sun pierced my eyes. I switched on the heating and set the pressure in my cabin.

"Hallo Dalmat Red One. Pandor calling, bandit now over B for Baker. Hurry up!"

"Hallo, Pandor, Dalmat answering, I'm climbing flat out on vector 095, I'm angels R for Roberts.

"What did the controller take us for—rockets? In five minutes we had got to 23,000 feet; not bad going. In the meantime I had been thinking this Jerry must be a reconnaissance aircraft. In this weather he must be able to get perfect photographs. The Fleet's ack-ack couldn't shoot because of us, naturally, and the navy must be cursing. At all costs we had to get that Hun. If we didn't, the Admirals would get us!

Pilot Officer (later Squadron Leader) Blair takes up the story:

There were always pilots ready for action should any unidentified aircraft be picked up by radar. It was 20th February 1944 and Fl/Lt. Bennett and I were on stand by at readiness in the Flight Dispersal Hut. In my experience nothing much ever happened but this day a hurried message came over the Tannoy. 'Scramble enemy aircraft approaching coast'. We took off and climbed full out. I was about 38,000 feet and levelling out when I received the signal 'Dalmat I, bandit ahead'. Sure enough, right ahead were vapour trails. He must have seen me just at that

time for he dived to starboard on a southerly course going all out. I opened up everything I had and went into a power-dive after him. We were now at about 4,000 feet diving hell for leather seaward. My speed was so terrific that I was forced to throttle back to avoid passing what I could clearly see was a long range Messerschmitt Bf 109. I took careful aim and gave him a two second burst with both cannon and .303 machine gun. His starboard wing broke off and flew in the air. There was a crash and a shudder as I collided with some of the falling debris. The Messerschmitt turned over and over and plunged seawards. I saw it burning with a cloud of black oil smoke on the water as I turned to head for base. But my fortune was soon to change. The debris had hit my radiator and my engine was failing. I was still 50 miles off the coast of Orkney and further still from Skeabrae. I thought I might have to bale out but I kept heading westwards. Land appeared to starboard and I reckoned it was Stronsay. I thought I could save the aircraft and myself if I did a belly landing there. I picked a spot and came down. It turned out to be less than ideal for I ploughed through a couple of fences and ended up against a turf wall. I was lucky to get away with a nasty bang in the face—I was certain that I must have at least broken my nose. Climbing out of the cockpit I saw at a short distance away a farmhouse which turned out be the farm of The Hill. There was no one around so I went up to the farmhouse door and knocked. It was opened by someone whom I found out later to be Miss Reid. I told her "I've pancaked in your backyard I need a doctor." Miss Reid was very suspicious; she thought I was a spy. To convince her I wasn't a Messerschmitt pilot I asked her to come and see the plane and its RAF markings! From then on, all was well. A Dr. Pyle arrived and

331 Norwegian Spitfire Crest designed by Ulf Wormdal when he was stationed at Skeabrae. MELTZER.

did a stitching job on site; he told me my nose didn't appear to be broken and apart from the cut I would, at worst, get away with two good black eyes.

Three months later, on 30th May 1944, there was another successful interception from Skeabrae when three enemy aircraft appeared on the Orkney radar screens. No. 118 Squadron were scrambled and identified them as Ju-88s. At 25,000 feet Flight Officer J. J. Parker, an Australian, and Warrant Officer Taylor isolated one and, after a short exchange, the aircraft crashed into the sea. There were no survivors. This was the last successful engagement over Orkney.

With the focus of the war now in Central Europe intrusions into Orkney airspace became fewer and fewer. One type of German aircraft appeared from time to time but, to the great frustration of RAF pilots, was allowed to pass. This was the German meteorological flight, known to the RAF as *Weather Willie*. After the cracking of the Enigma Codes the British made use of the valuable meteorological information which was transmitted regularly back to base from these long Atlantic sorties! To prevent arousing the suspicion of the Germans, squadron pilots were instructed to make mock attacks on these enemy aircraft with short bursts of fire which, of course, invariably missed. At least this did give the Spitfire pilots some degree of satisfaction but one

wonders how this bizarre instruction was understood by the Station Commanders and explained away to the pilots all of whom would have been ignorant of the cracking of the Enigma Codes.

With the change in the direction of the war, the operational work of the RAF diminished. In fact when No. 66 Squadron and No. 234 left Orkney in June 1943, only one squadron, No. 312 replaced them. The remaining squadrons posted at Skeabrae were at times very stretched to cover convoy and patrol work but they remained vigilant—it was all too easy to be jumped on without warning. On 10th March 1945 Fl/Lt. E. W. Martin of No. 441 Sqdn. vanished without trace while on patrol to the south of Scapa. But it was possible to be too vigilant. On 11th June 1944 two Spitfires of No. 118 Squadron on patrol to the east of Orkney came across an unidentified aircraft which did not respond. The pilot of BL718 opened fire and the aircraft crashed into Auskerry Sound. Unfortunately the aircraft was a Mosquito of No. 33 Squadron Leuchars on passage to Sumburgh. One of the crew members was killed. In the subsequent court-martial, the Spitfire pilot was cleared of blame. There were several incidents like this during the war when exhausted pilots forgot to switch on their IFF (Identify Friend or Foe) particularly when the war was in its early stages and nervous fingers were on the trigger. In his book *The Supermarine Walrus*

Handley Page Harrow Transport of No. 271 Squadron flies out after bringing in No. 132 Squadron to Skeabrae on 15 February 1942 from Peterhead. The Harrow was a pre-war bomber converted to a transport by replacing the nose and tail gun turrets by fairings; it could transport 27 service personnel; the village of Dounby is under the tail wing and Hourston Army Camp to the right; photograph taken by Roc of 771 Sqdn. Twatt. FAA.

VA Spitfires of No. 164 Squadron on dispersal at Skeabrae with eight machine gun armament, sometime between May and September 1942 (R. E. G. Sherward via C. H. Thomas) in David Smith 'Action Stations'.
SHERWARD.

G. W. R. Nicholl tells of pilot Johnny Groves flying the Queen Wren on a recruiting drive from Hatston to Sumburgh in Walrus L2239 on a murky November day in 1939. There was an extremely strong head wind inducing a navigational error and it was with some relief that the pilot eventually saw Sumburgh Head, albeit passing distantly on the port side. He resolved to land at Sullom Voe. His relief was short lived for in the sky ahead black smoke puffs showed that he was under fire from the cruiser HMS *Carlisle* anchored in the voe. Giving the Queen Wren the assurance that a bit of ground to air firing practice was underway, Groves quickly fired off his Very pistol with the correct recognition stars of the day and the firing from the cruiser stopped. All went well with the landing in the voe and the cruiser sent its pinnace to the Walrus. However the coxswain had no knowledge of its distinguished passenger and Pilot Groves must have cursed for him when coming alongside the aircraft he shouted, 'Cor, sir, laugh? They thought you was a Jerry!'

The Royal Navy almost brought down one of its own Skuas coming in to Hatston after a report had been received of enemy aircraft approaching. On 31st March 1940 a day when many enemy reconnaissance patrols passed over Orkney, a warship fired at a Hurricane of No. 605 Squadron from Wick passing over Scapa Flow even though it was flying at a height of only 1,200 feet! A month

Equipment Store personnel, Skeabrae 1943; of the WAAFS in the middle row, the second on the left is L.A.C.W. E. M. Dunnett, first WAAF at Skeabrae; to the left of the WAAFS is ?? Ball and to the right,?? Smalley; WAAF Officer Southern in front row. DUNNETT.

Father Christmas, Sqdn/Ldr Ramsden, visits Skeabrae, 1943. HORNE.

High Flying Spitfire MD114 FVII in pen at Skeabrae sometime after 5.03.44; special modifications enable this aircraft to be used at high altitude against enemy reconnaissance aircraft; such modifications included pointed wing tips, four bladed propeller, high altitude Merlin engine with six ejector exhausts each side, retractable tail wheel and broad chord pointed-top rudder. BLAIR.

Pilot Fl/Lt. Ken Souter RAF, relaxes at the Bay of Skaill, May 1945; Fl/Lt. Souter was finally based at RNAS Twatt, one of a number of RAF personnel attached to RNAS stations in Orkney. PEMBERTON.

Vicky Luker with Roger Bush, Pilot Officer 611 Sqdn. Skeabrae, Christmas, 1943. HORNE.

"That's the fourth time this week he's done that; he used to be a Spitfire pilot". HOLDEN.

later the cruisers HMS *Arethusa* and HMS *Galatea* out of Scapa opened fire on Red Section Hurricanes of No. 43 Squadron also based at Wick. On 25th November 1940 Hurricanes of No. 3 Squadron, by this time based at Castletown just before their move to Skeabrae, were on Scapa patrol and intercepted what they believed to be a captured Whitley and shot it down. The aircraft crash landed at Wick and none of the crew was injured. This was fortunate as the aircraft was a genuine RAF Whitley from Kinloss.

By early 1945, even if war related activity appeared to be winding down in Orkney, Orcadians were dramatically reminded of the never ending conflict across the North Sea when, on 31st March a giant Liberator B-24 of the United States Air Force crashed near Walliwall Quarry outside Kirkwall. The sole survivor was the Co-Pilot, Lt. Pulrang. The mission was so secretive that even today details are sketchy. Apparently it had been based at Harrington in Bedfordshire and had flown from its advanced base at Kinloss with a complement of Norwegian commandos all of whom, including the pilot, were killed. Rumour got around that it had been brought down by friendly fire but an investigation into the crash revealed engine failure.

With more experienced pilots, better aircraft and communications, there were few fatalities among the RAF squadrons at Skeabrae towards the end of the war but the Orkney weather and topography sometimes proved master. On 6th April 1945 Capitaine Sassard of No. 329 Squadron Free French Air Force failed to clear the top of mist covered Skelday Hill in Birsay as he took off on dawn patrol.

The Squadron Diary solemnly records his funeral ceremony in Kirkwall on 10th April.

By contrast there were great celebrations at Skeabrae on 8th May—even the WAAFs had a free pint of beer with their mid-day meal. There was no work in the afternoon so that everyone could have an opportunity to hear Winston Churchill's speech which was relayed over the Tannoy at 3pm. In the evening a dance for all ranks was held. Celebrations went on next day, there was a free film show in camp in the evening and more entertainment for, by coincidence, the Gordon Highlanders' concert party was visiting the Station that night. First Officer Foster-Barham writes of her Twatt Wrens:

> A very successful party was held in the Skogar Barn on VE night. I arranged for cakes trifles, jellies, sandwiches and eight barrels of beer to be freely available to everyone! I broke all rules and let the Senior Officers' Mess entertain the Wrens, watched carefully by Chiefs and Petty Officers as drinks much stronger than beer were being handed out!

On 10th May dawn and dusk patrols at Skeabrae were discontinued, presumably because none of No. 329 Free French Squadron was fit to get up! One week later, on 17th May, readiness state came to an end. By 24th July, at Twatt, the whole of 771 Squadron with its 51 aircraft had moved out and, three days later, 603 Squadron Spitfires left Skeabrae for Turnhouse. On the last day of July 1945, 846 Sqdn. Avengers, the last frontline squadron to be based in Orkney took wing for Crail in Fife and the Orkney skies resounded once more only to the cry of the gull and the sough of the wind.

Patrolling aircraft looks down on Q Class destroyer HMS Quiberon off Orkney, 1944; cliffs of Hoy in background. EDWARDS.

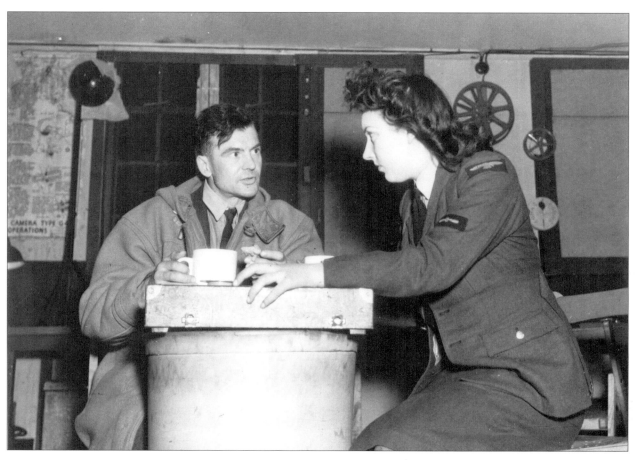

Drama rehearsal at Skeabrae for 'Gaslight' by Patrick Hamilton; Frederick Peisley, who later had a number of film and television roles, with WAAF Vivian Marwood. HORNE.

WAAFS and WRENS at Skeabrae, March 1944, before the Twatt Wrens were accommodated at Skogar, Twatt; these Wrens were mostly R/T operators who worked at the Fighter Direction Centre at Hesta Geo, Birsay. WRENS include, Left to Right, Back Row Paula West (Met.), Nin MacDonald-Smith, unknown, Sue Farrant, unknown, Jean Moar (an Orcadian), unknown. Fourth Row Prue Webber Front Row Bobby David (parachute packer), Tilly Peel, Rachel Murray-Bisset. TAYLOR.

Chapter Five

The Carrier Men

On 27th August 1939, the aircraft carrier HMS *Ark Royal* entered Orkney waters and disembarked the Skuas of 800 Squadron of the Royal Navy, the first front-line squadron to touch down at the new Royal Naval Air Station at Hatston. During Hatston's short but busy life another 71 squadrons of the Royal Navy and six squadrons of the United States Navy were to disembark there. The squadrons came and went according to the movements of their parent carrier; on average the accumulative total for each Royal Naval squadron was ten weeks but this varied from the 4 days spent at Hatston by 1842 Squadron in August 1944 to the 80 weeks spent by 804 Squadron between November 1939 and May 1944. 804 Squadron was not however initially a disembarked squadron; it was formed at Hatston in September 1940 as a front-line squadron with the specific task of defending Scapa Flow until this role was taken over by the Royal Air Force.

In the beginning all carrier squadrons disembarked at Hatston airfield but as the war progressed and Scapa Flow became busier Hatston was unable to cater for the needs of all carriers. There were, on occasions, ten carriers in Scapa, all with different requirements, and other air stations as they became available on the Mainland of Orkney, coped with the overflow from Hatston. Between June and September 1940, there were, at times, no less than 8 squadrons with more than 100 aircraft based at Hatston, far beyond the capacity of the station. By 10th October RAF Skeabrae was operational and 804 Squadron with its Sea Gladiators moved there from Hatston. Altogether 10 squadrons or detachments of squadrons of Royal Navy aircraft had lodger facilities at Skeabrae during the war. By June 1941 Twatt was able to accommodate front line aircraft; the first resident visitors were 812 Squadron with Swordfish which also moved in from Hatston. The large numbers of aircraft in 700 and 771 Squadrons meant that Twatt was rarely in a position to offer facilities to disembarked carrier planes but despite this, Twatt handled 15 front line squadron disembarkations. In October 1942 RAF Grimsetter had to accept 700 Squadron of the Royal Navy while Hatston, Twatt and Skeabrae stations trained front line squadrons for the *Operation Torch* landings in North Africa. As explained elsewhere, Grimsetter was eventually transferred to the Royal Navy to ease pressure on Hatston and before the war was over, 21 front line squadrons had used the airfield.

After the sinking of HMS *Royal Oak* on 14th October 1939, most of the Home Fleet dispersed and after 16th October when HMS *Ark Royal* disembarked 816 Squadron for one day at Hatston, aircraft carriers did not use Scapa Flow or embark aircraft from Hatston for six months until the defences had been reinforced. After the German invasion of Norway on 9th April, the strategic importance of Scapa Flow assumed a new significance. In April and May, as explained in the chapter *In the Front Line*, shore based aircraft attacked enemy positions but with the arrival of the carriers HMS *Glorious* and HMS *Ark Royal* in April, a pattern of combat was established which continued intermittently until the end of the war. Fighter support was badly needed over Norway where the flush-deck carrier HMS *Furious* had taken up position. Initially equipped with two Swordfish squadrons, 816 and 818, but no fighters, *Furious* had been damaged by enemy bombing and now with only eight serviceable aircraft left, had to return to Britain for urgent repairs.

Arriving off Scapa on 22nd April 1940, *Glorious* disembarked her 823 Swordfish Squadron, taking on board 803 Squadron Skuas and 804 Squadron Sea Gladiators from Hatston. The carrier already had on board 18 Gladiators of No. 263 Squadron RAF which were being ferried to Norway. Meanwhile 800 Squadron and 801 Squadron Skuas, also from Hatston, joined *Ark Royal*. On 23rd April, with cruiser and destroyer support, *Glorious* and *Ark Royal* sailed from Scapa, heading east to Norway on *Operation D.X.* which had several aims, most importantly to give aerial support to the ground troops between Trondheim and Åndalsnes. Even before they left, the crews had a good idea of what was in store for them. Five days earlier, Hatston Skua pilots had found themselves powerless to stop the persistent bombing of the cruiser HMS *Suffolk* on passage from Norway to Orkney. Now, for all to see, the cruiser lay beached and severely battered at Longhope in Scapa Flow, having struggled across the North Sea, latterly with no steering gear.

Altogether HMS *Ark Royal* and HMS *Furious* had on board 21 Swordfish, 29 Skuas, 5 Rocs and 18 Sea Gladiators of the Royal Navy and 18 Gladiators of the Royal Air Force. On paper, it was quite a formidable aerial armament. But things did not go well on the Norwegian operations. The RAF Gladiators were destroyed by the Luftwaffe shortly after they landed in Norway; HMS *Glorious* lost five Skuas and eventually only four were operational. These transferred to *Ark Royal* and on 27th April, only four days after leaving Scapa, she set sail again for Orkney to embark more aircraft. The carrier was held up in Orkney because of bad weather which prevented the aircraft flying on but by 1st May she had rejoined the Task Force. *Glorious* arrived to find that central Norway around Namsos was being evacuated and the carriers were immediately caught up in determined Luftwaffe action. Despite heavy bombing of the British warships, no vessels suffered a direct hit and only one Skua was lost in intensive aerial combat. Some surprise was expressed at this by the British pilots because the naval gunners, with so little experience, had great difficulty in distinguishing between friend and foe and fortunately their fire was highly inaccurate!

At the end of the day, it was considered that the risk to the warships was too great in relation to what they were able to do to support the ground troops and the carrier force withdrew, heading back once more for Scapa Flow. HMS *Ark Royal* returned on 6th May and covered the naval bombardment of Narvik.

Miraculously she escaped the heavy bombing encountered by the British support vessels but Bill Lucy, CO of 803 Squadron who had planned the *Königsberg* raid from Hatston was killed along with his Observer Hanson when driving off attacks by Heinkel 111s. *Glorious* sailed from Greenock on 14th May to ferry No. 46 Squadron Hurricanes of the RAF to Norway and HMS *Furious* joined her with No. 263 Gladiator Squadron which had just been brought up to strength. All three carriers met off the Norwegian coast on 18th May, the first time they had been together. The weather was so bad, that it wasn't until 21st May that *Furious* was able to land her Gladiators; even so two of the Gladiators and the guiding Swordfish crashed into a mountain on the approach to Bardufoss, to the north of Narvik. It was decided not to land the Hurricanes in these circumstances and the three carriers set off for Scapa once more. On the return trip to Norway, the Hurricanes were finally flown off *Glorious* to Bardufoss, on 26th May, two weeks after being embarked. On that very same day, the British suffered an enormous blow when the cruiser HMS *Curlew*, equipped with sophisticated radar for anti-aircraft defence, was sunk near Narvik. All did not go well for *Glorious* either; a disagreement between the Captain and the Commander (Flying) about the wisdom of mounting a particular operation led to the return of *Glorious* to Scapa Flow and the transference of the Commander (Flying) to the *Dunluce Castle* on his way to a court-martial.

On 31st May, *Glorious* and *Ark Royal* left Scapa and turned into the Pentland Firth bound for the last time for Norway from where all 25,000 allied troops

Swordfish being loaded with aerial mines at Hatston 1941; centre left probably V4631; this Swordfish was made by Blackburn and nicknamed 'Blackfish'. FANCOURT.

were to be finally evacuated. *Ark Royal* re-embarked 800 and 803 Squadrons from Hatston to provide fighter cover for the troops. *Glorious* already had 802 Squadron Gladiators and six Swordfish of 823 Squadron aboard but primarily for her own protection since it was to be her duty to ferry back to Scapa the remaining aircraft of No. 263 Gladiator Squadrons of the Royal Air Force which had done such outstanding work after they had been landed at Bardufoss. As for the Hurricanes, it was considered impossible to land them on a carrier; they would have to be abandoned. However when *Glorious* was off Norway the bold plan was devised of attempting to bring back the Hurricanes too. In a brilliant display of flying, both Gladiator and Hurricane squadrons were successfully embarked. The evacuation of Norway went perfectly to plan and by midnight on 9/10th June, the flotilla was on the move westwards, some to Scapa, some to the Clyde. The story of the fate of HMS *Glorious* is well known. Accompanied by only two destroyers, HMS *Ardent* and HMS *Acasta,* she detached herself from the rest of the Fleet and headed for Scapa. On the way she was intercepted by the German battleships *Scharnhorst* and *Gneisenau* and, along with her accompanying destroyers, *Glorious* was sunk with the loss in total of more than 1,500 lives. Sadly the RAF Gladiators and Hurricanes which had been so skilfully flown on in the evacuation by pilots with no experience of deck landings and whose aircraft had no arrester gear, were lost too. The *Scharnhorst* had been damaged in the encounter and sailed south to Kiel for repairs. As *Scharnhorst* was on her way south on 21st June, 821 and 823 Squadrons from Hatston made a revenge torpedo attack on her but to no avail; one squadron aircraft was lost. Three days later another torpedo attack was made by 823 Squadron against destroyers and transports off the Norwegian coast but again with limited success.

As for *Glorious'* Commander (Flying), he was still awaiting his fate in Scapa Flow. With the Captain of *Glorious* lost, there was no prosecution and, in fact no court-martial ever took place. This was nevertheless a most unsatisfactory state of affairs and the Commander spent many of the post war years setting the record straight and successfully clearing his name. Thus ended the Norwegian campaign. For six weeks there had been intensive carrier activity in Scapa Flow now the focus of the war in Europe was to shift south and for a time there was only sporadic carrier activity in Scapa Flow. HMS *Furious* appeared in Scapa in July and 825 Swordfish Squadron flew to Hatston for several days, returning again in September when both 825 and 816 Squadrons were disembarked after an attack on shipping in Trondheim harbour in which five of 816 Squadron Swordfish were lost. After participation in the North African landings in

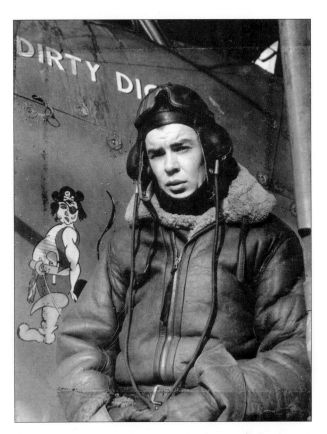

Swordfish Pilot, Sub.Lt. (A) D. Howden, 819 Sqdn., Hatston, 11th March, 1942; two days later on a navigation exercise in bad weather west of Orkney, Howden and his TAG disappeared without trace.
HAMILTON.

October, *Furious* returned to the base of the Home Fleet at Scapa and 801 Squadron disembarked on several occasions at Hatston after taking part in convoy patrols. Another quiet six months passed at Scapa until the new Norwegian offensives began again and the big carriers returned once more. These Norway offensives began with the arrival at Hatston from Donibristle on 24th March 1941 of 828 Albacore Squadron. Its local role was anti-submarine patrol work but extensive torpedo training also took place in preparation for an attack on enemy shipping in Norway. In May 1941, the new Vickers-Armstrong carrier, HMS *Victorious* entered Scapa. She was not yet fully worked up, carrying only a few fighters and torpedo bombers for her own protection and had on board crated Hurricanes bound for the Middle East. With the danger of *Bismarck* and *Prinz Eugen* breaking out into the Atlantic her sailing plans were shelved and from Hatston she embarked 825 Squadron Swordfish recently arrived from Campbeltown. The Squadron Leader was Lt.Cdr. (A) Eugene Esmonde (later to win a posthumous Victoria Cross for his Squadron's attempt at preventing the German warships *Scharnhorst, Gneisenau* and *Prinz Eugen* passing through the English Channel). *Victorious* sailed from Scapa on 22nd May when it was learned that *Bismarck* had escaped into the

HMS Victorious steaming off Orkney in 1941 when the squadrons were working up; note the black wind baffle up front; the aircraft on deck are Albacores with a solitary Fairey Fulmar of 809 Squadron on the stern. COOPER.

An Albacore leaves the flight deck of HMS Victorious in Scapa Flow. IWM.

Atlantic. Her own fighter squadrons, Fulmars of 809 Squadron from St. Merryn in Cornwall attempted to join her but were forced to return because of bad weather. On 24th May Swordfish of 825 Squadron launched a torpedo attack on *Bismarck* scoring one hit and forcing the vessel to reduce her speed. Running short of fuel, *Victorious* had to withdraw and leave the chase to HMS *Ark Royal* which moved up from Gibraltar. The outcome of *Ark Royal's* intervention is well known. The *Bismarck* was crippled by a torpedo attack by 818 and 810 Squadron Swordfish which damaged her rudder and she was eventually sunk by battleships of the Royal Navy.

One Albacore was lost in a dummy torpedo attack when it plunged into the sea near Sanday on 2nd May 1941 killing the Observer and, a few days later another was written off after it made an emergency landing at Hatston. The Squadron's first break came on 23rd May when, after a month's training it flew to Sumburgh to strike at *Bismarck* near Bergen. The operation was cancelled (fortunately in the opinion of the Station Commander) when it was learned that the enemy battleship had left her anchorage and was heading for the Atlantic. Finally, on 2nd July, after 13 weeks' training, the squadron flew on to *Victorious* which,

had entered Scapa triumphantly after the *Bismarck* operation. Meanwhile 809 Fulmar Squadron, fresh from St. Merryn, had spent three weeks at Hatston. They too joined *Victorious* along with 827 Squadron Albacores which had just arrived from Machrihanish. *Victorious* was joined by *Furious* in Scapa Flow and, from the new airfield at Twatt 812 Squadron Swordfish flew on. Clearly, a big operation was underway.

The aim of the operation was to offer some help to the Soviet Union which had been invaded in June 1941 and the plan was to attack the German forces in Northern Norway and Northern Russia. The strike took place on 30th July; 812 Squadron Swordfish and 817 Squadron Albacores from *Furious* were to attack Petsamo while 827 and 828 Squadron Albacores from *Victorious* headed for Kirkenes. The whole operation which, almost unbelievably, took place in broad daylight, was a disaster. John Cooper was a young pilot with 809 Squadron Fulmars whose duty was to provide CAP (Combat Air Patrol) for the Albacore Squadrons from *Victorious*. He had spent a very pleasant three weeks at Hatston before he flew on. His personal account gives some idea of the shortcomings of the mission:

The Home Fleet, under the command of Admiral

'Tex' Van Epps, 809 Sqdn. pilot of Fulmar N4026 makes his first landing on an aircraft carrier, HMS Victorious off Scapa; his radio transmitter was on and his comments were noted! COOPER.

Wake-Walker flying his flag in the cruiser HMS *Devonshire* arrived at Scapa after working up in the North Atlantic and Icelandic waters. 809 Squadron landed on *Victorious* off Orkney. For most of us it was a hair-raising event because we had received very little Dummy Deck Landing Training at Yeovilton. We hadn't even seen an aircraft carrier let alone land on one! Fortunately we all managed with the exception of American fellow pilot 'Tex' Van Epps. He had left his radio on in error and we all heard, first hand, his feelings as his aircraft swung to port and ended up half over the side!

The next shock came on our first take off. To enable the pilots to take off at 20 second intervals the engines were all started at once. Pilots who took off last had to make their way through the whirling and dangerous confusion of propellers and slipstream to reach their aircraft—at least such pilots had the consolation that they had the longest deck run! Fine judgement was required if the ship was rolling and pitching. The few Dummy Deck Landings we had done could not convey to us how, in a gale, a carrier's deck could rise and fall 70 feet!

Our first engagement with the enemy was on the borders of northern Soviet Union. The Kirkenes/Petsamo operation has been well documented. I think that if I were to say anything, it would be so derogatory of those who planned the operation that it might cause embarrassment, mainly because the orders to attack Petsamo and Kirkenes were directed to be carried out in broad daylight, about 50 miles to the north of the two northern ports, with German spotter aircraft in sight above the Fleet. These aircraft were, of course reporting our every move and I know of nobody who took part in the attack on Kirkenes, the target allocated to HMS *Victorious*, who did not think that the order to fly off and attack, invited heavy resistance and casualties. For 809 Squadron, it was the first operation since our formation and most of us were very young and inexperienced. We flew south towards Kirkenes in line abreast and the first I knew of anything amiss was when I saw someone to our right bale out of a burning plane and descend towards the sea by parachute. We were in fact being attacked by Messerschmitt 109s and 110s which had been sitting up sun awaiting our arrival—and they had had plenty of notice! I broke away from the formation and dived with a vague idea of giving some protection to the Albacores. Through the Gosport tube, a voice said, "Don't let's be over enthusiastic sir". It was L/A Frank Gilder, my Telegraphist Air Gunner. Poor Frank, he had no gun and was not a navigator—I'm not quite sure what his role was but he soon found one and proved an invaluable help as a spotter of enemy fighters. I had a rear view mirror but Frank had a wider view of aircraft attacking us from the rear and kept up a running commentary and countdown until the optimum moment to turn. The Fulmar, though large and not very fast, was a manoeuvrable aeroplane and could out-turn the 109s and 110's. When Frank called out "Zero!", I would slam down the wheels and flaps and turn as tightly

as possible. The German fighter would whizz past at speed in a wider turning circle.

Being on the receiving end of these attacks, made it almost impossible to protect the Albacores below us which, laden with torpedoes and labouring into a strong head wind were making slow progress towards Kirkenes from which, incidentally, most ships had already fled! The Albacores were sitting ducks for the 109s and 110s; it was distressing to see the Germans running their bullets or cannon shells through the water behind them, passing forward through the body and kicking up the sea in front of them. After a confused period of dog-fighting with glimpses of friendly and enemy aircraft, sea and coastline during which I fired my guns if and when I could, we found ourselves alone and undamaged. Land-based German pilots never liked flying far out to sea and, after we had flown north for a while, we were lucky enough to spot a solitary Albacore below us, lucky because we knew it would be carrying a navigator and we had a good chance of getting back to *Victorious*. This we did and, dispensing with an approach circuit as we had used so much fuel in the dog-fighting, we landed on but only just; our engine cut out after we had taxied over the crash barrier. When I reported to the Flying Bridge, Commander Flying asked how many of our aircraft were flying out behind me. He was in tears when I said, "None, sir". No fewer than 11 of our 20 Albacores had been lost together with 2 Fulmars. Some of those who made it back to the ship contained dead or wounded crewmen. On the evening of the attack, or maybe a little later when the Fleet had withdrawn to Spitzbergen, Admiral Wake-Walker came on board and addressed the aircrews in the Wardroom. His intention was to boost morale by pointing out that, in spite of losses, the operation had succeeded in showing the Russians (who had just entered the war) that we were supporting them. However the pilots and observers were so angry about the mishandling of the operation that they received what he had to say in stony silence. The atmosphere was both eerie and embarrassing and he had no course but to withdraw.

I was awarded a DSC for my part in the operation. This was, of course, an honour, but, to be candid, any one of the 809 Squadron pilots would have merited it. A dispirited Fleet sailed back again to Scapa where the carriers disembarked what remained of their squadrons.

While HMS *Furious* took part in a Malta convoy, HMS *Victorious* continued to use Scapa Flow to mount attacks on shipping off the Norwegian coast and, from time to time military targets ashore. In August *Victorious* took part in operations in the Barents Sea and in October attacks were made on the Bodø area of Norway. At other times she escorted North Russian convoys, intermittently landing her squadrons at Hatston or Twatt. John Cooper again gives a vivid description of life aboard a carrier in a convoy:

The squadron stayed in *Victorious* for many months, often escorting Atlantic and Russian convoys. This involved flying endless patrols and attacking any German long-distance aircraft shadowing and reporting our position to U-boats. Among these aircraft were the BV138s which were so big we called them 'Odeon Cinemas'! Some hundreds of ships of all sizes would form convoys which would, of course, travel at the speed of the slowest. If any small ship started making smoke and falling further and further behind, we in our fighters would go back to say 'Goodbye', flying past the bridge at sea-level to give them a wave. Such stragglers were easy prey for U-boats.

Flying from a carrier in convoy was extremely tiring, both physically and mentally. Naval pilots and other aircrew have generally agreed that, in the war-time Fleet Air Arm, one was either very bored or very frightened. Life for us as fighter pilots was certainly tiring because of the limited number of aircraft; on *Victorious* there was only one fighter squadron consisting of 12 Fairey Fulmars. We were seldom given more than five minutes notice to get into an aeroplane and fly it off the deck and that was in all kinds of weather. When there was no actual operation going on, we had a minimum of two pilots sitting in an aircraft on deck ready to fly off within 60 seconds of any alarm or emergency. If the sea was very rough, the aircraft would be mounted on a catapult with the other waiting to take its place. In addition to this, four pilots would be in the Ready Room, fully clothed in their flying gear ready to man their aircraft if required. The squadron's remaining pilots would be resting down below or in the Wardroom and would be expected to be ready to fly in less than five minutes. We used to think that our lot in carriers was worse than that of our fellow pilots in the RAF because when they landed, they could relax or go to the local pub with their wives or sweethearts whereas we returned to a bouncy ship, couldn't sleep in our cabins if they were below the waterline and didn't see a girl for months!

In *Victorious* and no doubt in all warships, one of the major strains was the Tannoy communications system through which all orders were transmitted and announcements made. Although 99% of these concerned only ship routine, the other 1% would be an alarm call to Action Stations. Then aircrews among others would drop everything they were doing, wherever they were, and join in a mad rush to man their aircraft. When the Tannoy was switched on therefore, we would all get very tense until our minds and muscles were relaxed by some innocuous announcement such as 'Fatigue party fall in on the foc'sle'. For some odd reason, after fifty years I remember 'Open Royal Marines bathroom' which always seemed to occur at night, I don't know why! Over very long periods, with the system operating night and day, nerves could become frayed. I know of some pilots, observers and gunners in *Victorious* who were 'shovelled ashore with twitch' as we termed it because of this continuous strain which had nothing to do at all with enemy action but rather

with this ceaseless, frustrated anticipation. The actual one in a hundred Action Stations alarm was very noisy. I think it consisted of intermittent blasts on a klaxon followed by an announcement by the Captain.

Victorious could stay at sea for a very long period of time and it was seldom that we got any shore leave at home or went ashore in New York when we escorted convoys westward to the United States. On arrival we would swing around a buoy or steam round the Hudson Light or perhaps head directly to an Icelandic fjord to join a convoy going back to Britain. This endless movement could be very disorientating especially for the hundreds of crew who lived for most of the time below the water line. It used to be amusing for us to see a deck hatch open, an old string vest pop out, the bearer have a sniff of the Arctic air and disappear. That was possibly the first time he had surfaced for months and probably would have no idea whether he was off New York, Murmansk or Spitzbergen. The perpetual daylight in the Arctic summer and indeed in Orkney to some extent, often confused us tired pilots too. I have experienced the peculiar feeling of looking at my watch while playing poker in the Ready Room and not knowing whether it was one o'clock in the morning or in the afternoon.

When we were at sea for very long periods we often ran out of fresh fruit and vegetables and made do with rice balls instead of potatoes. Once our supply of alcohol almost ran out. I recall one tragic period when an evil looking purple liqueur was the only drink available in the Wardroom bar. Of course the majority of pilots drank very little or not at all because they were never off duty in operational waters and could be called upon to fly at short notice. Alcohol combined with carrier take-offs and landings made a very bad cocktail as some tragically found out.

Living for long periods in such conditions, it is little wonder that the front line crews let their hair down when they disembarked to Orkney airfields. After a series of such convoy operations, 809 Squadron was disembarked to Twatt on 26th October 1941. The officers' mess at that time was a Nissen hut and officers have memories of having to lift their feet to get to the bar—their first target—because the wind was blowing so strongly that it was lifting the linoleum off the floor! The Station Commander was thrown into a circular static water tank that night and high spirits were still not defused by Christmas. In this pastoral scene the Station Commander had been able to fatten some geese, no doubt for Christmas Wardroom festivities, but on 23rd December a messenger reported that his geese had 'flown'. Indeed they had; with his revolver, a New Zealand pilot of 809 Squadron had brought their lives to a premature end and fellow pilots were all required to carry a goose on their laps when they flew off to HMS *Victorious* on 23rd December! One might infer

Two Fairey Fulmars from Hatston flying in formation. HAMILTON.

809 Sqdn. pilots in the Wardroom of Victorious after flying from Twatt on Christmas Eve, 1941; before take-off one of them with his revolver had shot and killed the Commander's geese; all the geese were brought back on board in the aircraft on the pilots' laps! John Cooper is under the light; Tony Garland is here somewhere too. COOPER.

that the Station Commander was not very popular but this isn't true; a correspondent describes him as 'a good sort' but he must have found it difficult to forgive the final prank.

Immersion in a circular static water tank seemed to have been the culmination of the night's festivities on a number of occasions, the victim usually being a high ranking officer who entered into the spirit of things or, sometimes, a more risky adventure, a superior officer who had not respected the norms of the Wardroom. An Army officer who commanded a local brigade and who had appeared more than once in the Wardroom at Twatt in full peace-time mess kit did not endear himself to the carrier men, especially when he made advances to a Senior Officer's very attractive daughter. He was given a 'naval' experience when he was deposited in the static water tank which happened to be conveniently placed just outside the Officers' Mess. When he returned to his transport, he found that his tyres had been deflated. This was too much for the Commanding Officer who immediately closed the bar for two weeks. Imagine the anguish of front-line pilots newly arrived only to find the bar was closed! Fortunately the Commanding Officer was a humane man and invited them up in groups to his cabin for drinks!

Squadrons disembarked at Hatston had their moments too. John Laing, a Swordfish pilot at Hatston in the early years of the station and later CO of 835 Squadron cannot remember anyone ever being bored. They made their own entertainment. 'The parties in the wardroom were no doubt extremely wild on occasions—the Commander Frankie Howie danced so energetically on the wardroom table that he fell through all that expensive polished woodwork'!

Duncan Hamilton, the celebrated Jaguar racing driver of the '50s, was Senior Air Engineer at Hatston and saw many squadrons come and go. In his book *Touch Wood* which deals for the most part with his racing career, he devotes a chapter to his experiences at Hatston. Here he describes getting caught up with high spirited young pilots and observers:

> We lived at a tremendous pace; it is impossible to explain some of the crazy things we did. They just seemed natural at the time. We loved to compete against one another. One visiting officer was able to lick the red hot side of a mess stove without burning his tongue. Another who attempted the feat was unable to eat or drink for several days. The unfortunate officer, trying to explain to the Captain why he could not speak properly, or appealing to the M.O. for assistance, was thought to be funny. The inability of one side to understand why it was necessary to lick a red hot stove and the inability of the other to explain why it appeared to be a good idea at the time, created just the situation we enjoyed.

On 23rd February 1942 HMS *Victorious* disembarked 817 and 832 torpedo squadrons at Hatston for a little over a week and they had a busy training programme which was just as well for they were soon to be put to the test. *Victorious* sailed again from Scapa Flow on 4th March and rendezvoused with Convoy PQ12 which had sailed from Reykjavik three days earlier. On 7th March it was learned that the German battle cruiser *Tirpitz*, based at Trondheim, was in the Atlantic and, having failed to intercept the convoy, was returning to Vestfjord. On 9th March 832 Squadron Albacores sighted the enemy and the squadron diary records the subsequent engagement:

> . . . visibility was anything up to 30 miles. Cloud base was at 4,000 feet. The squadron started to climb and soon we were above the clouds with the *Tirpitz* about 15 miles away. We were guided on to the target by ASV but at 09.20hrs the first sub-flight 4A, 4B and 4C dived to the attack with the enemy on its starboard bow below. As soon as the first sub-flight came out of the clouds, the enemy opened fire and they encountered heavy flak during the dive. They dropped on the port bow at approximately 1,000 yds. with the *Tirpitz* turning towards them. The second third and fourth sub-flights then dived to the attack just after the first sub-flight had successfully turned away . . . the enemy put the wheel hard over to starboard and appeared to avoid all torpedoes. The target was thickly obscured by smoke and it is doubtful that a hit would have been seen. During the attack 4P was hit and crashed into the sea. One aircraft of 817 Squadron was also hit, set on fire and likewise crashed. We set course for the carrier and landed on at 10.30hrs.

The torpedoes missed the target and *Tirpitz* escaped to the safety of Vestfjord. The last opportunity for the Fleet Air Arm to confront this battle cruiser on the open sea had been lost. She did not venture out again when carriers were in the convoy in case she suffered the same fate as the *Bismarck*. Damaged by heavy seas, HMS *Victorious* had to be withdrawn at the end of March for a short refit. Disembarking her 809 Squadron Fulmars at Twatt she sailed south, her place being taken by the carrier USS *Wasp*.

Wasp sailed for Britain on 26th March 1942 with Task Force 39 in the company of the battleship USS *Washington*, two heavy cruisers and six destroyers, to reinforce the Home Fleet of the Royal Navy. Commanded by Rear Admiral John W. Wilcox in *Washington*, the Task Force got off to an inauspicious start when, during a severe Atlantic storm, Admiral Wilcox was swept overboard and drowned. Rear Admiral Robert C. Giffen assumed command in USS *Wichita*. The Task Force was met off Orkney on 3rd April by a force based around the light cruiser HMS *Edinburgh*. No sooner had *Wasp*

USS Wasp at anchor, 1942; she joined the British Home Fleet at Scapa in May 1942 and disembarked all her aircraft at Hatston for five weeks.
FANCOURT.

First British aircraft to land on an American carrier; Capt. H. St. J. Fancourt of RNAS Hatston in a Sea Gladiator.
FANCOURT.

arrived in Scapa Flow than the Captain received orders to take part in a most unusual mission. Although attached to the Home Fleet, *Wasp's* first assignment was to go to Malta which was being hammered by enemy bombing and on the point of submission. Air Vice-Marshal Lloyd wrote 'Malta's need is for Spitfires, Spitfires and more Spitfires.' He sent a distinguished pilot, Wing Commander Gracie, back to Britain to tell the authorities at first hand what the situation was like. As a result, Winston Churchill sent a message to President Roosevelt. Spitfires were indeed available in Britain, but there were no British carriers seaworthy at that time with the capability of carrying and flying them off. Churchill wrote 'Air attack on Malta is very heavy. There are now in Sicily about 400 German and 200 Italian fighters and bombers. . . . would you be willing to allow your carrier *Wasp* to do one of these [air ferry] trips, provided details are satisfactorily agreed between the Naval Staffs? With her broad lifts, capacity and length, we estimate that *Wasp* could take fifty or more Spitfires . . .' Roosevelt signalled back 'Admiral King will advise Admiral Poland that *Wasp* is at your disposal as you request.' This operation involving *Wasp* meant that British planes would be flying off a US aircraft carrier and the *Wasp* herself would be the first American warship to enter the European theatre of war on what amounted to a combat mission. The first piece of history was in fact made by Capt. H. St. John Fancourt, CO of Hatston who flew aboard *Wasp* in his Gloster Gladiator, the first British serviceman to land on an American carrier.

To make room for the 47 Supermarine Spitfires which were to be embarked at King George Dock in Glasgow, *Wasp* disembarked part of her well-trained Air Group 7 at Hatston. Three squadrons of aircraft flew to Hatston—Douglas Devastator torpedo planes and Vought Vindicator dive bombers as well as a Grumman Duck, a single float biplane. She retained a squadron of 11 Grumman F4F-4 Wildcat fighters to cover the Malta operation. Duncan Hamilton recalls the arrival of the Americans at Hatston.

> . . . we were summoned to the Captain's quarters where we were given the exciting and unexpected news that the American fleet would be arriving the following day. We had a tremendous rush getting the hangars, squadron offices and so on ready for them and had to work through the night. However when their first aircraft from the great carrier USS *Wasp* flew in, we were ready to receive them. They flew in close formation, a most impressive sight. No sooner had they landed than their wings folded up and they parked themselves in tightly packed groups. It was a fine technical exercise, perfectly performed; yet we knew to our cost that such limited dispersal of aircraft was no longer feasible. One or two well placed bombs and a whole squadron could be wiped

out. I had seen aircraft burn in rows like that when the Luftwaffe had bombed Lee-on-Solent. These American pilots were very experienced airmen; I believe I am right in saying that none of them had less than twelve hundred hours flying to his credit. That night I had my first introduction to the great American game of crap and played on until the early hours. The American fleet is a 'dry' fleet and some of these fellows had not had a drink for weeks. As a result there were many casualties. When Shea and I went down to the landing stage (where launches waited to take them back to their ships) to see them off, their departure looked like an evacuation after defeat. The unsteady walk and green face was much in evidence and the choppy sea was a formidable obstacle to be crossed before their friendly bunks could be reached. Watching the launches as they approached the ships, it appeared that many officers were leaning over the side as if looking for fish. If the local fish had any sense they gave those launches a wide berth that morning.

The *Wasp* stayed in the Flow for six days during which time her aircraft did a mock attack on Hatston aerodrome for Admiral Giffen. Ken Baylis, Air Fitter at Hatston at that time writes:

> Whilst the USS *Wasp* was in Scapa Flow, they put on a show of attacking the aerodrome for Admiral Giffen. I was detailed that afternoon to start up and see off an RAF Spitfire flown in from Skeabrae by a Sergeant Pilot [of No. 132 Squadron G.L.]. I had a grandstand view as I was on the apron with the RAF Spitfire and saw the Wildcats come in just over the hangars with the Devastators a little higher coming from another direction. At the same time the Vindicators came screaming down with wheels and diving brakes lowered. When the American show was over the RAF pilot took off and I returned the trolley accumulator. By this time the Yankee ground crews were starting to go for tea. Suddenly the Spitfire came over our heads at hangar top level and proceeded to give a superb display of aerobatics, finishing with victory rolls all along the runway. One Yank asked me what the aircraft was and I was delighted to say, just casually, "Oh it's an RAF Spitfire, nothing unusual," but inside I was really proud of that Sergeant. I swear he was there on purpose just to show the flag. The fact was that we rarely saw RAF planes so I feel it was more than a coincidence that he was there that afternoon.

The American Squadron Commanders at Hatston were Lt.Cdrs. Eldridge and Turner and Lts. Rooney and Romberg. The squadrons trained intensively while based at Hatston. On 26th April the Devastators took part in an exercise with No. 86 Squadron RAF based at Skitten in Caithness and some landed there. The American squadrons worked closely with the Royal Navy though not always successfully. Duncan Hamilton describes his experiences when flying with one of the American squadrons:

The Americans were always training and we flew with them whenever we could. They had many casualties some flew into high ground, others out to sea on the wrong compass reciprocal and on to Norway where the German fighters got them or they ran out of fuel trying to get back when they realised their mistake. They found flying in and around Scotland a new experience and took some time to adapt themselves. One day Galley and I were flying with their 54th Pursuit Squadron commanded by Lt.Cdr. Turner. In the exercise the Squadron was to dive-bomb an imaginary enemy submarine.
We took off and flew in close formation for about an hour. Both Galley and I knew how hazardous flying could be in this part of the world and hoped that we would not dive-bomb through cloud. We hoped in vain for suddenly Turner fired his guns—the signal that he was about to dive—wheeled over and dived through the cloud below him, followed by some thirty-five to forty aircraft. A microphone attached to a gun ring in front of me no longer hung down but stayed suspended at right angles. In other words the rate of our descent was equal to the gravitational pull of the earth. I became alarmed; not only was there another plane no more than thirty feet behind us but cloud as thick as this might end on top of a mountain. Suddenly we broke cloud and my fears were confirmed for over on our starboard side was an ominous looking mountain. Fortunately the sea was on our port side and we had some two thousand feet in which to come out of our dive. As we skimmed along over the water, everyone realised that if Turner had been a little starboard of where he was when we broke cloud, the whole squadron would have gone into that mountain. As the pilot of my plane put it, "This is not like flying in Arizona."

Incidentally we never saw anything of the submarine we were supposed to dive-bomb though apparently it waited for us all afternoon. The Americans were quick to realise that flying conditions around Britain were not to be trifled with.

The five weeks' hard training in Orkney skies no doubt paid dividends. In mid-May USS *Wasp* was withdrawn from the Home Fleet and sailed for the South Pacific. On 7th August 1942, USS *Wasp* took up station off Guadalcanal and Eldridge and Romberg's Squadrons lifted off to lead the American invasion.

After her short refit, HMS *Victorious* returned to the Home Fleet and to Scapa where she continued for the most part on North Atlantic convoy duty but at the end of July she was required to join *Operation Pedestal*, a Malta convoy, and on 4th August 1942 a new class of carrier, HMS *Avenger* appeared in Scapa Flow to take over the North Atlantic convoy patrols. *Avenger* was the first of the so-called Escort Carriers to enter service with the Royal Navy; they were all simple conversions of merchant hulls, had wooden decks and one hangar. She had on board 802 and 883 Sea Hurricane Squadrons and a Flight of 825 Swordfish. *Avenger's* aircraft spent a month working up in Scapa and the carrier finally set sail on 3rd September to join Convoy PQ18 off Iceland. Nine days later the carrier pilots were involved in fierce air battles with enemy aircraft in a series of massed torpedo attacks on the merchant ships. Five enemy aircraft were destroyed and 21 damaged. Unfortunately four Sea Hurricanes were also lost,

On right, Capt. Reeves commanding USS Wasp with Capt. Fancourt, CO, RNAS Hatston. FANCOURT.

three brought down in error by fire from the merchant ships. After this brilliant intervention in the North Atlantic *Avenger* was joined in Scapa by HMS *Furious* in preparation for the invasion of North Africa in November 1942. In addition to her 823 and 824 Albacore Squadrons, *Furious* had on board 807 Squadron recently equipped with 12 Seafire IIc's, the first time these aircraft had been seen in Orkney. The Orkney skies were to see many more of them in the months to come.

Operation Torch, the code name for the North African landings, caused a considerable stir in and around Scapa Flow for it was here where the huge carrier Task Force was assembled. In September fourteen different squadrons (including the RAF) could be counted at airfields in Orkney. Eight Royal Naval squadrons used Hatston during this month, two Royal Naval squadrons had to use lodger facilities at RAF Skeabrae and to enable 820 and 822 Squadrons to disembark, the Headquarters Flight of resident 700 Squadron of the Royal Navy was required to move to RAF Grimsetter. Extensive training went on in the skies over Scapa. In one such exercise to the west of the island of Hoy, 807 Squadron lost its first Seafire when, in a fighter attack, the pilot over-corrected a spin.

By October HMS *Victorious* joined the Task Force at Scapa having miraculously survived fierce enemy action in the Malta convoy, *Operation Pedestal*, during which the carrier HMS *Eagle* was sunk. The carriers HMS *Biter* and HMS *Formidable* completed this impressive armada which altogether had on board 103 fighters and 50 strike aircraft, many of these being airborne at the same time. By 21st October the Task Force had sailed and Scapa Flow was empty. On the way south, the carriers HMS *Argus* and HMS *Dasher* joined the Fleet and as it approached the Moroccan coast it was met by five aircraft carriers of the American Atlantic Fleet, USS *Ranger*, USS *Sangamon*, USS *Chenango*, USS *Suwanee*, and USS *Santee* with, in all, another 136 aircraft embarked. The largest of these carriers, USS *Ranger* was later to become a familiar sight in Orkney waters. *Operation Torch* was a huge success, giving the allies a foothold in North Africa, the only tragedy to mar the mission being the loss of the carrier HMS *Avenger* to torpedoes from U-115 near the end of the operation on 15th November. There were only 17 survivors. Reported missing was John Lane, brother of Dick Lane, the first operator of Hesta Geo Fighter Direction Centre in Birsay. Their brother was Allen Lane, founder of Penguin Press,

US Naval Airmen and planes at HMS Sparrowhawk, Hatston: US crews with Devastator torpedo bombers fallen in for inspection in front of their machines, April 1942; Vindicator bomber in background. IWM.

US pilots at Hatston watching some of their machines in flight; the aircraft behind is a Vindicator which was called Chesapeake in Britain; April 1942. IWM.

hence the call sign 'Penguin' chosen by Dick for the Centre.

After *Operation Torch*, HMS *Victorious* arrived in Scapa and discharged some of her damaged 884 Squadron Seafires to Hatston for repair. She then left for a short refit, after which she sailed westwards to join the United States Navy for operations in the South Pacific and HMS *Furious* joined the Home Fleet in January 1943 to replace her. In the same month extensive training began in Orkney for the next operation, the landings in Italy, exercises for which were to go on for six months. Royal Naval squadrons flew in from all parts of Britain for training in the wide open Orkney skies; 880 and 899 Squadron Seafires and 817 Squadron Albacores due to see action in HMS *Indomitable* and the 878 and 890 Martlets and 894 Seafires bound ultimately for HMS *Illustrious*.

Meanwhile Russian convoy patrol work continued. On 26th February the carrier HMS *Dasher* entered Scapa Flow badly damaged after running into a severe Atlantic storm on her way to join up with Convoy JW53 en route from Iceland; many of her aircraft had also been rendered unserviceable. She disembarked 816 Squadron and a detachment of 837 Swordfish and 804 Sea Hurricanes squadrons.

Mike Crosley was one of the 804 Squadron pilots. He describes the hectic scene at Hatston on his arrival:

> [We] . . . flew north to Hatston which was crowded with fighters (there were 7 squadrons there at the time G.L.) including some new Seafire squadrons working up for *Illustrious* and *Formidable**. We watched them taxying round the narrow perimeter track, unable to see ahead without swinging their long noses from side to side. Sometimes they overdid it, running onto the grass and up-ending in a drainage hole. They were doing their deck landing practice somewhere in the North Sea. They were very impatient when we on the runway kept them waiting. They suffered badly from overheating particularly when taxying downwind—and they would start waving frantically from their cockpits at Air Traffic Control to let them take off before they boiled. We had already seen one of them take off in a cloud of steam.
> * more probably *Indomitable* G.L.

The Seafires were in fact doing deck landing practice on HMS *Furious* probably somewhere off Deerness. During these exercises an Air Mechanic of 894 Squadron had a most terrifying experience. It was customary for ratings to lie over the tail of an aircraft to keep it down while the pilot revved up to full power. It was also normal practice for them to remove themselves before the aircraft started moving! A very strong wind was blowing down *Furious'* deck and a snowstorm had just begun as she turned into the wind. The pilot came to full revs and one of the ratings jumped off; the pilot assumed that both men had left the tailplane and so he took off. The wind strength, the slipstream and the noise of the engine combined to make the aircraft movement imperceptible to the tail-borne rating. There was no means by which the deck party could communicate with the pilot and the aircraft set course for Hatston. Leading Air Mechanic James Overed takes up the story:

Sea Hurricane II landing on board a carrier off Orkney; possibly HMS Avenger. HAMILTON.

> I had my eyes closed but on opening them I saw to my horror that the carrier was below and astern and that we were just passing over the top of a cruiser underneath. I hung on like glue . . . I thought of my wife and daughter . . . I thought my number was up. I was tempted to let go when I saw the cruiser for he might rescue me if he was watching but decided to hang on. After about 15 minutes or so I heard a reduction in engine revs and I prepared for a crash landing, not knowing where I was. The runway (at Hatston) was white with snow so I thought he was crashing in a field so I pulled my legs up in order not to have them trapped under the fuselage. After landing I did not remember anything more until I came to inside the ambulance. I was told afterwards that the pilot removed me and placed me upon the snow and covered me with his flying coat and put his Mae West under my head for a pillow . . . Next morning the pilot visited me in hospital and though I was too full of admiration for his skill to speak, he said, "Good show, jolly good show!"

When James Overed joined the Squadron he probably hadn't thought too deeply about its motto *Capable of anything anywhere*! It was said that the

fitter was so cold that all the way to hospital he had to be kept in the same shape without bending him! Both the pilot and air mechanic had done a magnificent job, bringing themselves and their aircraft down safely. As mentioned earlier, less fortunate was the aircraftman holding down the tail of a RAF Lysander at Skeabrae. He was carried to a height of 200 feet, fell off and was killed. The pilot failed to gain control of the aircraft and crashed injuring two of the crew. These were not isolated incidents. James Boyd, an Air Mechanic Armourer, also had an unofficial trip ashore to Hatston from HMS *Furious* on 3rd January 1944 when a Seafire pilot of 801 Squadron believed he had an all-clear signal!

In the busy training period leading up to the invasion of Italy, four Seafires were lost in Orkney, two in a mid-air collision. Two Grumman Martlets also crashed in the islands, running out of fuel after they had lost their way in low cloud. As far as the Italian landings was concerned, from the point of view of the Fleet Air Arm, it was a qualified success. HMS *Indomitable* was crippled by one torpedo dropped by a lone Ju-88 which escaped unharmed. With the capitulation of the Italian Navy in September 1943, there was little need for a carrier force in the Mediterranean. HMS *Formidable* returned to the Home Fleet at the end of 1943 and HMS *Illustrious* headed for the Indian Ocean; it was to be late summer 1944 before carriers reappeared in the Mediterranean.

On 13th July 1943, a new bird arrived at Hatston. 12 Grumman Avenger I's of 845 Squadron flew in from

A cartoonist on board the carrier records the unscheduled flight of Overed!"

Date/Duration

1

2

3

4   0.45   bombing, Bogue method from 5,000 ft.

   2.00   A/S bombing followed by A.L.T. on HM ships

   0.35   A/S bombing, Woodwick range

5

6   0.50   homed by DF method from Stack Skerry area

7   1.15   attack on HM cruiser dropped torpedo runner

8   1.45   attacks on HMS *Duke of York*

   1.55   homed by W/T to Wick and back by R/T

   2.00   night exercise 100 miles out to sea good W/T contact

9   0.40   A/S bombing, Bogue method

   0.45   A/S bombing from 5,000 ft. two direct hits

10   0.50   air firing cross overhead exercise 180 rounds zero hits

11   1.55   torpedo and dive bomb attacks on Stack Skerry

   1.00   attack on HM ships by formation of 16 aircraft

12   0.35   bombing, Bogue method at Woodwick Range

   0.35   air firing cross overhead exercise 200 rounds zero hits

13   1.25   A.L.T. formation of 17 aircraft attacking enemy ships

14

15   0.55   bombing from 3,500 feet dropping sticks of two

16   0.55   radar exercise homed on submarine and small drifter

   1.30   night exercise attempted attack on HMS *Gambia* got lost in snow storm homed on D/F

17   0.50   astern defence exercise range 400 yds. 4 hits

   0.35   dropped four sticks of two bombs

18

19   1.05   homed on submarine range approx. 5 miles

20

21

22   0.35   A/S bombing of towed water target

   1.45   Naval Exercise W/T OK returned early rough weather

23   1.00   air firing fired turret into sea R/T OK

24

25   0.25   A/S bombing putrid weather

   0.25   A/S bombing down to 100 feet

26   1.10   14 aircraft attack on HMS *Duke of York*

27   1.15   night flying attempted attack on HMS *King George V* and HMS *Howe* with 8 aircraft

28

29   0.30   A/S bombing on Woodwick Range

   0.20   A/S bombing; stick of two moving water target

30

Squadron Commanders of USS Wasp who served under Capt. Fancourt at Hatston; L-R, Lt. Romberg, Lt.Cmdr Eldridge, Lt.Cmdr. Turner, Lt. Rooney. FANCOURT.

HMS *Chaser* after their journey across the Atlantic. They were joined soon after by 846 Squadron Avengers and both squadrons became familiar sights in Orkney skies when they embarked on extensive training and evaluation exercises which, in the case of 845 Squadron, went on for six months. The intensity of the programme can be seen from the Log Book of Sub.Lt. Burrenston in November 1943. Notice the entries 'rough weather', 'putrid weather' and 'got lost in snowstorm' all characteristic of Orkney weather at this time of year. In the latter case he was fortunate to be able to home on D/F, unlike Lts. Wiren and Brett of 878 Sqdn. Hatston who, five months earlier in dense fog, were unable to pick up the signal and crashed in the West Mainland of Orkney. Sub.Lt. Burrenston was soon to see action in the Far East when, operating from HMS *Illustrious* and in conjunction with Navy units from USS *Saratoga*, his squadron attacked the Japanese naval base at Surabaja on 19th May 1944. Sadly his luck ran out on 29th January 1945 when he was shot down by the Japanese in the attack on the oil refineries at Palembang. He survived the crash but he and his TAG were executed by the Japanese on 11th March 1945 along with 11 other British Flying Officers.

In Norwegian waters meanwhile, there had been little Fleet Air Arm activity. Only HMS *Furious* had been available and, with her limited endurance, only restricted operations had been possible. However, in August 1943 the Americans returned once more to Scapa Flow. USS *Ranger* of the American Atlantic Fleet, had been loaned to the Home Fleet while the HMS *Illustrious* was engaged in supporting the landings in Italy. USS *Ranger* entered Scapa Flow on 19th August 1943. The oldest purpose built carrier in the American Navy, launched in 1933, she was still a

formidable fighting force and set out to prove it. Her 71 aircraft of Air Group 41 consisting of Dauntless dive bombers, Avengers and Wildcats, disembarked to airfields in Orkney—Hatston, as before and also Twatt where 15 TBF-1 Avengers landed. Air to air firing exercises were conducted between 771 Squadron Fleet Requirements Unit at Twatt and American Air Group 4 Wildcat Squadron (Fighting 4th). Extensive training in Orkney culminated in a surprise strike on Bodø in Norway on 4th October 1943 when a harbour full of shipping came under attack. American Dauntless bombers and Avenger torpedo bombers sank or damaged ten enemy ships for the loss of three aircraft. USS *Ranger* returned to Scapa Flow on 6th October and patrolled with the British Navy in waters reaching to Iceland. She sailed from Hvalfjord in Iceland on 26th November 1943 to rejoin the American Navy.

At the beginning of 1944, the Royal Navy began to step up activity in Norwegian waters. While attempting to intercept a convoy, the *Scharnhorst* had been sunk by HMS *Duke of York* on Boxing Day 1943 and now the continued presence of the battle cruiser *Tirpitz* in Kaafjord and the prospect of yet another break out into the Atlantic led to a Fleet Air Arm plan to destroy this warship in her base. Preparations had been made in early 1943 to do this when *Tirpitz* was in Altenfjord. A planned torpedo attack on the warship at night by Swordfish squadrons was abandoned however when the carrier HMS *Dasher*, which was scheduled to take part in the operation, blew up in the Firth of Clyde on 27th March 1943.

Scapa Flow was assembly point for *Operation Tungsten* which comprised six aircraft carriers with 153 aircraft embarked and with supporting warships.

All the preparatory work for this operation was done in the north of Scotland. Loch Eriboll in Sutherlandshire was chosen as a dummy range because of its resemblance to Kaafjord and here a mock battleship was marked out on an island in the sea loch. HMS *Furious* disembarked her 827 and 830 Barracuda Squadrons and 801 Seafire Squadron to Hatston in December 1943 for initial training and, the following month, 831 Barracuda Squadron arrived. 880 Squadron Seafires arrived in February at Skeabrae and in March 1834 Squadron Corsairs flew in to Grimsetter. It was the first time Corsairs had been seen in the islands. The squadrons had to fly from Hatston to Loch Eriboll for training and on 23rd March a most unfortunate incident occurred when 827 and 830 Squadron Barracudas, flying in misty conditions, ran into shellfire from a battleship firing at a drogue towed by 771 Squadron from Twatt. By some miracle there were no casualties and the crews were given a foretaste of what they were to experience in Norway.

Operation Tungsten on 3rd April 1944 was the most successful of the Fleet Air Arm attacks on the *Tirpitz*. The battle cruiser was badly damaged and put out of action for three months and the Arctic convoys were able to have a brief respite. When the Fleet returned to Scapa on 6th April no less than seven squadrons disembarked, mainly from the Escort Carriers HMS *Emperor*, HMS *Striker*, HMS *Fencer*, HMS *Pursuer* and HMS *Searcher*. *Emperor's* Hellcats landed at Hatston; these aircraft had not been seen in Orkney before.

These raids on Norway were in part the contribution of the Royal Navy to *Operation Fortitude North*, a deception sustained mainly by false radio signals to delude the enemy into thinking that the invasion of Europe was to come from Norway. Training continued and, in one exercise on 20th April, the crew of Barracuda DP983 had a narrow escape. In a gale gusting to 80 mph, 830 Squadron flew off from Hatston to join HMS *Furious* in Scapa Flow. TAG Allan Thomson writes:

> We were on a circuit at about 400' awaiting our turn to land on when there was a severe jolt followed by a tremendous vibration from the engine. Smoke floats were jumping out over their retaining catches and even the transmitter/receiver swung forward on its hinges as the whole airframe shuddered. We were in for a ditching. In a few seconds we hit the water. With full fuel tanks we would sink in 40 seconds. I jumped out on the fuselage, saw that the others were in the water then grabbed the life raft that was already ballooning alongside. Not a moment too soon for the aircraft nose dipped and she slowly disappeared below the storm waves. We fired off a couple of distress signals and finally a drifter came alongside but a combination of raging sea and her speed made the rescue attempt impossible. Fortunately a 40 foot pinnace from HMS *Rodney*

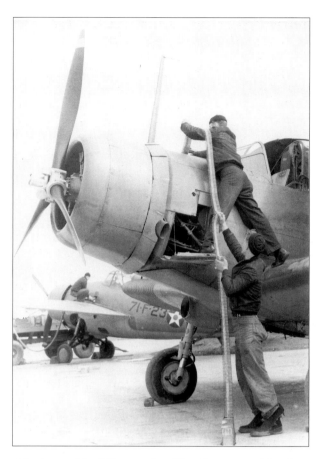

Members of the US groundstaff loading ammunition into a Devastator torpedo bomber at Hatston; in the background a Wildcat is being refuelled from a petrol bowser. IWM.

was able to connect although it was only with great difficulty that we got aboard. I remember some of the seamen stripped off their sweaters so that we could get out of our soaked gear. Only then did we learn what had happened to us. Balloon Command had signalled that all barrage balloons were down in Scapa Flow but in fact some could not be winched in because of the gale and we had struck a barrage balloon cable! Had the balloon cable been armed I wouldn't be writing this now!

On 19th April HMS *Activity* and HMS *Fencer* accompanied by twenty one other vessels left Scapa Flow for the Soviet Union, this escort force being required to bring back 45 merchant ships of Convoy RA59 from Kola Inlet. The ships were nominally empty but advantage was taken to transport back to Scapa Flow over 2,000 Soviet sailors who were to crew the battleship HMS *Royal Sovereign* after its transfer to the Soviet Union. On board HMS *Fencer* were Admiral Levchenko and his staff. The return convoy was constantly harassed by enemy submarines and during one encounter a merchant ship with a large complement of Soviet sailors on board was sunk. *Fencer's* 842 Wildcat and Swordfish squadron were nevertheless credited with the destruction of three enemy submarines. There was no rest for *Fencer*; she was immediately ordered south to cover *Operation Overlord*, the Normandy landings.

In May HMS *Victorious* arrived in Scapa Flow and when bad weather restricted operations off the Norwegian coast, King George VI took the opportunity to visit the Fleet in Scapa Flow. He went aboard many of the ships including the carriers HMS *Searcher* and HMS *Victorious*. The latter put to sea flying the Royal Standard and the King watched with interest as 28 Corsairs of 1834 and 1836 Squadrons and 21 Barracudas of 827 and 829 Squadrons took off from her flight deck and landed on.

In June 1944 an extraordinary thing happened at RNAS Hatston. This busy station which had been packed with fighters since the outbreak of war found itself abandoned. The answer was simple. With the Normandy landings in progress many Royal Naval squadrons were moved to RAF bases on the south coast of England and Orkney based squadrons created diversionary attacks on Norwegian shipping. From 10th June until 13th June there were no aircraft at Hatston and for the Station Commander, these must have been blissful days! The relief was short lived. By 8th July 1944 there were seven squadrons on the station—that meant over 90 aircraft—and the Fireflies of 1770 Squadron which had earlier experienced three months hard training at Hatston were required to move out to nearby Grimsetter. The reason for this concentration of aircraft was another planned attack on *Tirpitz*. *Operation Mascot* as it was called brought the new carrier HMS *Indefatigable* into Scapa as well as HMS *Formidable* and HMS *Furious*. By 14th July the carriers had embarked all their aircraft including 1770 Squadron Fireflies which were to see action for the first time. On the way to HMS *Formidable* from Hatston, Corsair pilot Lt. Hewetson of 1841 Squadron crashed on the Hoy Hills and a whole week passed before the wreckage was found. For the second time in a month, Hatston was left empty, on this occasion for four days! *Operation Mascot* took place on 17th July; unfortunately the attacking aircraft found their quarry enveloped in a smoke screen and the mission was aborted. But the Fleet Air Arm was persistent. The carriers returned to Scapa and training went on. In August there were five squadrons of Barracuda torpedo bombers based in Orkney and the Seafire and Wildcat squadrons there were joined by 18 Corsairs of 1842 Squadron. The British Escort Carrier HMS *Trumpeter* and the Canadian manned HMS *Nabob* joined the Carrier Fleet HMS *Furious*, HMS *Formidable* and HMS *Indefatigable* in Scapa Flow for *Operation Goodwood* which was to take place at the end of August 1944. These five carriers had altogether 167 aircraft embarked! When we consider that there were five shore based squadrons in Orkney at that time (including 771 Squadron which alone could muster 35 aircraft) there would have been well over 300 aircraft in the Scapa area. *Operation Goodwood* had only limited success. Eleven aircraft were lost and on 26th August HMS *Nabob*, after 1,100 miles of steaming, limped into Scapa after being hit by a torpedo which had torn a hole fifty feet by forty feet in her thin hull. The US built frigate HMS *Bickerton* was less fortunate; she too was torpedoed and had to be scuttled off Norway. It fell to RAF Lancasters of No. 9 and 617 Squadrons with 12,000 lb. *Tallboy* bombs finally to dispose of the *Tirpitz* at Tromsø on 12th November 1944.

The aged HMS *Furious* took part in only one more operation—minelaying in the Leads off the coast of Norway in mid September. She was then withdrawn from service with the Home Fleet and placed in reserve. Her place was taken by the new carrier HMS *Implacable*; although her keel had been laid down in 1939 she had had so many modifications on the basis of carrier performance in action that she was only now operational. Arriving in Scapa in October she immediately embarked further squadrons for some highly successful strikes off the Norwegian coast accompanied by HMS *Fencer*, HMS *Pursuer* and HMS *Trumpeter*. Lt. Cdr. (A) Mike Crosley was by this time commanding 880 Seafire Squadron. They flew on to HMS *Implacable* from Skeabrae on 8th November 1944. In his book *They gave me a Seafire*, he describes this experience:

Implacable had originally been designed to take only a little more than half the 78 aircraft that she would shortly have to accommodate in her two hangars. No guns or other impedimenta had been removed to compensate for the extra space now taken up to be the extra hangar. With 500 extra crew, she was grossly overcrowded. When 880 and 801 with 828 (18 Barracudas) and 1771 (12 Fireflies) arrived, the squadron's ratings had to take pot luck with the left over messdecks. The initial result was that most of our squadron were having to sling their hammocks in the passageways. These were in use day and night and our men were being bumped by people trying to get by and were losing their sleep. Many of the more junior officers in the ship had to 'treble up'. As all of us (A) RNVR boys were most junior of all, we got a particularly poor choice. I had the deepest, noisiest and least ventilated cabin the builders could have devised. It was three decks down and out over the starboard outer screw. Still it was at least mine own and there was plenty of room to spread out. Another mission on 21st November was abandoned after the carrier was caught in severe gales and 880 squadron was happy to get back to Skeabrae where Christmas preparations were already underway.

We now had to be allowed some time for Christmas leave. In order to make our unexpected arrival home more welcome, we decided that we would each take a turkey with us on the journey south. Dougy Yate, whose father ran a chain of East

One of Nicolas Horne's photographs—not taken in Orkney but a common occurrence in Orkney nevertheless— holding down the tailplane while the pilot warms up for take-off; X4333 is a photo- reconnaissance Spitfire PRV from No. 1 Photographic Unit RAF Benson. HORNE.

Avenger, 845 Sqdn. at Hatston. FAA.

Aircrew of 846 Sqdn, Hatston Orkney; the aircraft in the background is an Avenger. FAA.

London butcher shops, knew all about turkeys and he came round on the squadron BSA motorbike and side-car to visit the crofters on the islands. The crofters would then parade their turkeys, either in the farmyard or in the kitchen, depending on the weather. Dougy would pick the ones he liked, diving on the poor birds before they knew what was coming. Our cabins at Skeabrae were full of feathers for the next few days as Dougy organised a squadron plucking party.

It is comforting to learn that their Christmas birds were obtained legitimately in contrast to the 809 Squadron Fulmar pilots who had left Twatt two years earlier with the Commander (Flying)'s geese on their laps!

In January at the smaller and normally quiet RNAS Grimsetter, there were two Seafire squadrons based—801 and 880, both of which had 24 aircraft. In addition 881 Squadron with 20 Wildcats were based there. Fortunately for much of the time some of the Wildcats were detached to HMS *Premier* and HMS *Trumpeter* since the station could not have coped with 68 aircraft! Both 801 and 880 Squadrons

were bound for the Pacific and though the war in Europe was near a close, there was no respite for these squadrons. Mike Crosley again:

> Norman (Goodfellow), Dougy (Yate) and I had had much experience in 804 in manoeuvring fighter formations easily in the air. All that was necessary for us now was to use this formation and method of manoeuvre to position our Seafires for a *simultaneous* dive on ground targets so that the strafing attack could be completed in 20 seconds and before the enemy gunners could remove their fingers. Up to 16 of our Seafires would dive simultaneously from three different directions and the enemy would not know which to aim at. After careful thought we worked it out that 16 Seafires diving at once would have only one sixteenth of the gunners firing at each Seafire for one sixteenth of the time! In theory we would therefore have about 60 to 100 times less chance of being shot down. Our formation dive from at least three different directions would also reduce the time taken to reform afterwards and so save fuel.
>
> We practised these coordinated attacks with radio silence on every 'target' we could find, islands in the middle of Scottish lochs, various ships with prior

permission and our own airfields and dispersals. At times our aircraft crossed over each other in the pullout of the dives. Of course there was bound to be danger from our own shells when we used our guns instead of the camera guns. However we reckoned that the risks from this were slight compared with the risks of coming down singly to zero feet on an airfield well alerted and defended by 200 guns or more.

With HMS *Implacable* capable of flying off at least 50 aircraft in one strike—more than two British carriers worth heretofore—constant deck-landing practice was essential. We aimed at 20 second deck-landing intervals. While we were at Grimsetter we had all 48 Seafires in the air at once.

The standard of flying of these two large squadrons was extremely high; during their nine weeks training in Orkney there was only one fatality and that was caused through a freak accident. Midshipman Ian Penfold's glove caught in the cockpit hood as he slid it forward on take off. His vision was obstructed at a vital moment and he lost control of his aircraft. On 15th March HMS *Implacable*, left her moorings at Scapa. On board

were 1771 Firefly Squadron and 828 Squadron Avengers, both squadrons having earlier spent over a month in training at Hatston. Off Orkney 801 and 880 Seafire squadrons flew on; they were bound for the Pacific Ocean and another war.

For the remaining months of 1945 it was the Escort Carriers HMS *Campania*, HMS *Nairana*, HMS *Puncher*, HMS *Premier*, HMS *Trumpeter*, HMS *Queen*, HMS *Vindex* and HMS *Searcher* which frequented Scapa Flow. Their aircraft were engaged in minelaying and bombing operations on the Norwegian coast to hold up the German convoys but, as the months passed, targets were getting fewer and fewer. The last raid and one of the most successful took place on 4th May 1945, only four days before VE day when 44 aircraft from three Escort Carriers attacked Kilbotn U-boat supply base, destroying the depot ship and sinking a U-boat. The last war-time carrier to enter Scapa Flow was the Escort Carrier HMS *Premier* which arrived two days after VE Day and disembarked 856 Squadron Avengers. The last of the carrier men, nine Avengers of 846 Squadron left Twatt on 31st July for Crail in Fife.

846 Sqdn. Hatston Avengers at rest at the end of the day: 1944. HOWES.

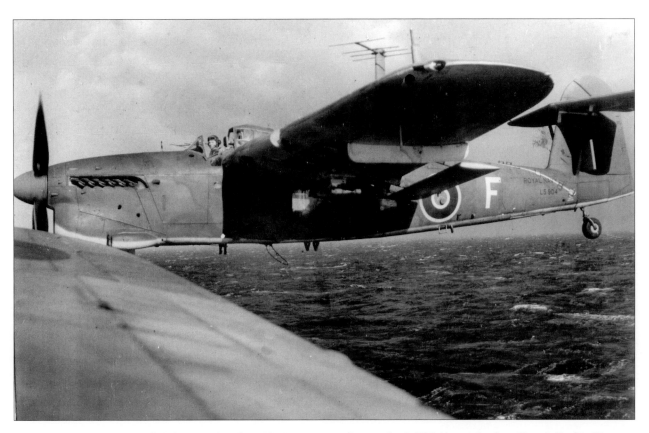

Barracuda II, LS904 off Orkney, 5 October, 1944; note aerial—standard ASV (Air to Surface Vessel) Radar. HILL.

HMS Searcher, based at Scapa with 882 Sqdn. Martlets embarked. COOPER.

Barracuda pilot at Hatston, 830 or 831 Sqdn. 1943: name unknown. HAMILTON.

882 Sqdn. Martlets taking off from HMS Searcher off Orkney; the smoke is coming from Searcher's exhausts which are located on the side of the vessel. COOPER.

Captain Davies, HMS Searcher, with Commander Flying, Scapa Flow. COOPER.

King George VI arrives on board HMS Victorious at Scapa, May 1944. COOPER.

King George VI talks to John Cooper, CO 882 Sqdn., on HMS Searcher in Scapa. COOPER.

HMS Tracker in convoy off Orkney with Avengers embarked August 1944. HILL.

The cruiser HMS Kent and HMS Implacable in Scapa Flow, July 1944. FAA.

Photo-reconnaissance Spitfire PRV or earlier recognisable by its one-piece windscreen and riveted-on bulges in sides of hood; perhaps used as a training aircraft at Skeabrae; the pilot is believed to be Lt. (A) Bill Griffith of 801 Sqdn.
HORNE.

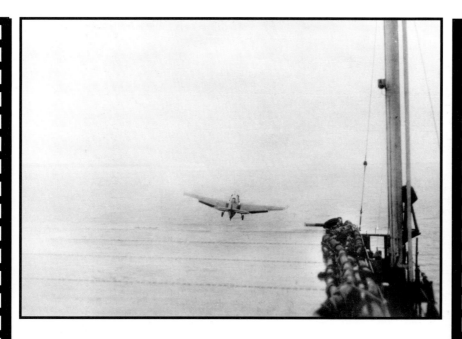

Avenger JZ159 'C' of 846 Sqdn. takes off for Hatston from HMS Trumpeter in Scapa Flow on 24 August, 1944 for compass swinging. Pilot Sub.Lt. Thomas, Observer unknown, Air-Gunner David Heath, Air Mechanic Arthur Jacobs. The wind is too light and the aircraft fails to gain height. HOWES.

The Avenger pancakes in Scapa Flow. HOWES.

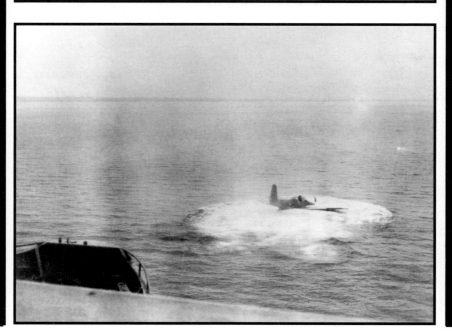

Remarkably, the Avenger floats; bow of HMS Trumpeter in the foreground. HOWES.

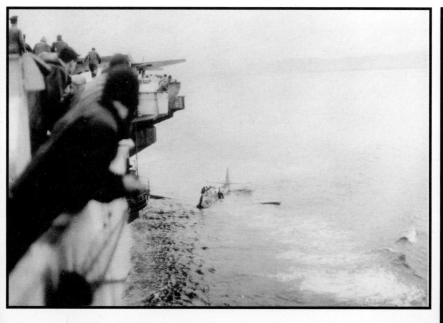

The crew scramble out as the aircraft drifts towards the stern of the carrier. HOWES.

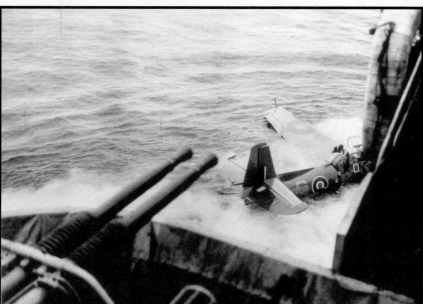

Air Mechanic Jacobs can be seen grasping the hatchway near the roundel and the turret housing; Air Gunner David Heath on the wing. HOWES.

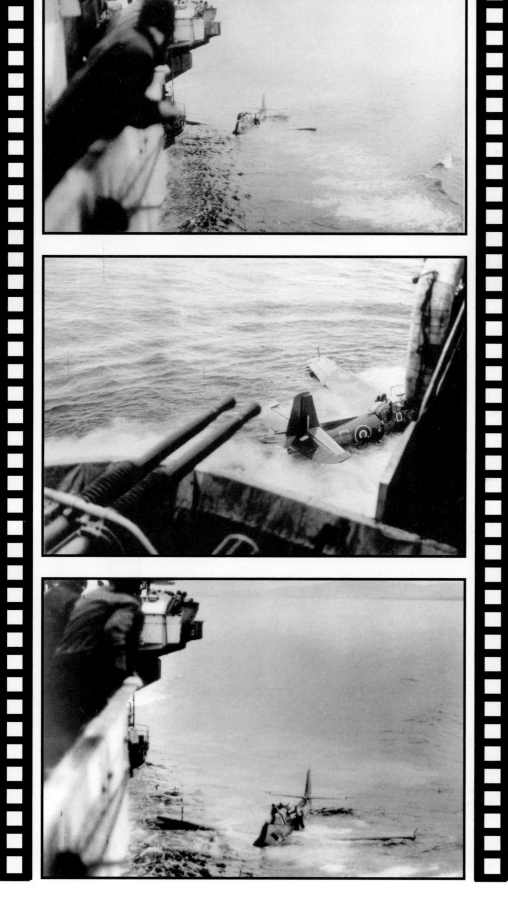

Air Gunner Heath standing on the port wing, Pilot, Observer and Air Mechanic on the starboard side. HOWES.

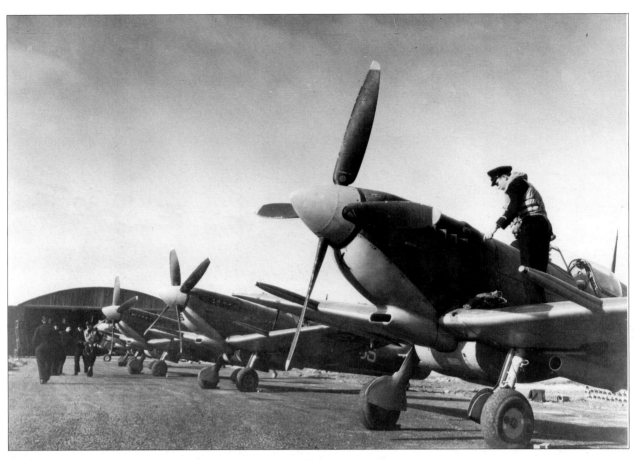

Seafire IIIs of 801 Sqdn. at Skeabrae, ashore from HMS Implacable, December 1944; note the extended chin intakes with tropical filters; underneath overload fuel tanks for extending range can also be seen. HORNE.

801 Sqdn. and 880 Sqdn. aboard HMS Implacable with Seafire IIIs, Scapa Flow, 26.11.44 before leaving for Norway when they ran into a hurricane. Left to Right Paddy Seigne 880, Peter Arkell 880, Bill Griffith 801, Dicky Dankaster (or Doug Richardson?) 880, Harry Norcott 801, Denis Kirby 880, Stuart Jewers, CO 801. HORNE.

Fleet Air Arm pilots, 801 Sqdn. Skeabrae, disembarked from HMS Implacable, December 1944. HORNE.
Left to right: Norman Goodfellow, Senior Pilot, Neville Turnbull (New Zealander), David Crabtree, Dennis Kirby, Ken Boardman*, Pat Patullo#, Peter Arkell, Doug Richardson, Bob Simpson.
* ran out of fuel on third wave off, April 1945, off west coast of Australia; ditched behind Implacable, got out of Seafire and then believed taken by a shark   # shot down off Japan

882 Sqdn. pilots in Ready Room of HMS Searcher; John Cooper, CO of the squadron is briefing his men before an operation in Norway; during this operation, the officer on the extreme right, 'Gladys' Pearson, was shot down and captured; John Cotching, the pilot whose head only appears, was shot down and killed. COOPER.

'Divisions' at Scapa Flow; march past on HMS Vindex to Rear Admiral Cunningham Graham, March, 1945; to the rear is a Swordfish III with radome between the undercarriage legs. FAA.

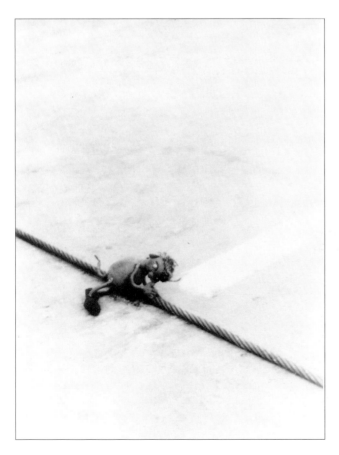

Landing accidents on aircraft carriers were common; barrier crashes were frequently caused by gremlins which held down the arrester wires! HMS Vindex, Scapa Flow, 1944. FAA.

898 Sqdn. on board HMS Searcher off Scapa Flow; Left to Right, Back Row: Unknown, Unknown, Rod Harrison, CO Dickie Henderson, Dick Shepherd, D. Farthing, Duff (New Zealander). Front row: Unknown, Paine, Court St. George, Unknown, Sharp who survived three crashes into the sea only to be killed later on. COOPER.

HMS Premier in Scapa Flow, 26 September 1944 with 856 Squadron embarked; it consisted of 9 Grumman Avenger torpedo bombers and 3 Grumman Martlet (Wildcat) Fighters; they were engaged in anti-submarine patrols, Norwegian coastal bombing, minelaying and Murmansk convoy support; arrived in Scapa two days after VE day and the squadron was disbanded. FAULKNER.

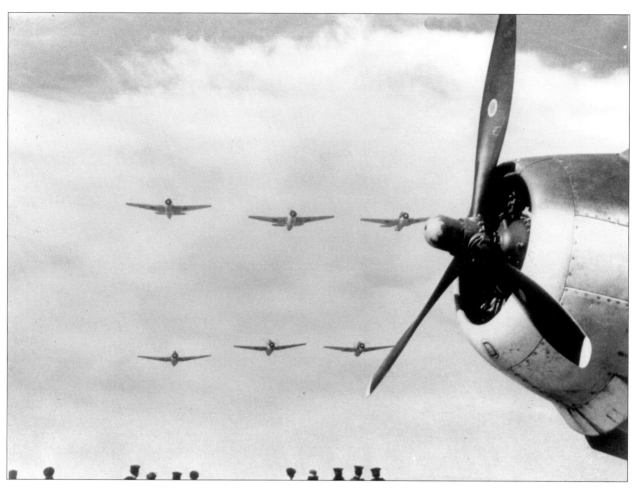

846 Squadron leaving Hatston for Twatt, 1 August 1945. HOWES.

Chapter Six

A Posting to Orkney

There were many ways for servicemen and women to arrive in Orkney during the war. None emulated the arrival of the German balloonists Distler and Jördens who, as early as 1910, made the epic flight from Augsburg to Kirkwall mentioned in page 18. In November 1941, 801 Sqdn. flew twelve Sea Hurricanes from St. Merryn in Cornwall to Skeabrae in 4 hours and 40 minutes which at that time was considered a record for single seater fighters flying in formation. When squadrons were posted to Orkney it was important that the ground crews arrived as soon as possible. For RAF crews the normal journey was by train to Peterhead where they embarked on a Handley Page Harrow of 271 Sqdn. John Sigmund wrote to say that the ground staff of Czech 312 Sqdn., of which he was a member, flew in a Harrow directly from Churchstanton in Somerset to Skeabrae, the journey lasting six hours. It would be wrong to assume that all those attached to the flying services arrived by air. Perhaps the strangest wartime arrival was Leif Lyssand, a Norwegian airman who escaped from occupied Norway and, after a 200 mile journey, made landfall with other compatriots on the island of Sanday in a small boat. Leif became a Spitfire pilot in No. 331 Squadron and, by sheer coincidence, was posted back to Orkney!

Pilots, Naval Observers and TAGs usually flew in with their squadron from shore stations or from carriers. It was normal practice to fly off the carrier before it entered Scapa Flow since the ship had to head into the wind to assist take-off. Ratings attached to the squadron were usually transferred to a lighter in Scapa Flow and from thence to the pier at St. Mary's in the parish of Holm or to Scapa Pier which was nearer Hatston. The official chronicler of RNAS Hatston writes:

> Scapa Pier is a venue that will linger for long in the memories of squadron personnel embarking or disembarking with stores and personal baggage at short notice at all hours of the day and night, usually in the rain.

When aircrew were joining a new squadron at any of the military airfields in Orkney, they were required like anyone else to make the long journey by train usually to Thurso. Lt. Keith Remmington, 771 Squadron pilot was posted from Freetown in Sierra Leone to Twatt! He writes:

> I can well remember the journey north—anything but comfortable—I travelled on the daily troop train known as the Jellicoe which left Euston at 10 o'clock. It was very full and the only refreshment on board was a canteen car run by the Salvation Army. The train was due in at Perth at 20.30 and fortunately it arrived on time which allowed us to have a meal in the Station Hotel. If you arrived after 21.00 you were unlucky. From Perth there were two trains, one leaving at 22.30 with the Army, Air Force and Women's Services, the latter were locked in their carriages, no doubt to protect the poor men. The Naval train departed at 23.00 and we arrived at Thurso at 7 o'clock the next morning and transport took us to the Royal Hotel for breakfast and then on to Scrabster where the *Earl of Zetland* was waiting for us. An uneventful crossing to Stromness followed and I subsequently realised how lucky I had been after some more lively crossings on later occasions. Transport then conveyed us to Twatt having been travelling then for a full 24 hours.

The train described by Keith Remmington, the famous 'Jellicoe' was run specially for the services. It was often sarcastically referred to as the Jellicoe Express, because of the time it took to make the journey! This troop train had its origin in World War I and the nickname Jellicoe had stuck. On 16th April 1940 the Perth to Thurso leg of this service was re-inaugurated and later, with the movements of vast numbers of military personnel northwards, two Jellicoe trains had to run daily, one 'pure Jellicoe' for naval personnel, the other an Army/RAF Jellicoe running half an hour earlier. Normally this journey was long enough and bad enough but, in February 1941, in a severe snowstorm, the Inverness to Thurso leg of the journey took four days to cover 120 miles! Even after a reasonable rail journey north there was still the prospect of being delayed for a day or more at Thurso if the weather was too bad for the ferry to cross to Orkney. Sometimes the ferry was held up for other reasons. Twatt Wren Mary Treby remembers arriving at Thurso in May 1944 and getting no further for some time:

In my instructions I was told to report to the Wrennery in Thurso for breakfast before crossing the Pentland Firth to Stromness where I would be met with transport. I duly made my way to the Wrennery which I discovered was opposite the small station. I promptly reported to the regulating Petty Officer only to be told that after breakfast I wouldn't be allowed to make the crossing for some time. The reason given was that the King and many important people were having a conference on board the Flagship in Scapa Flow. I was told to remain in the Wrennery in case a signal came to say that I could cross. I was confined indoors until just before 4 p.m. and I was standing by the window looking out when suddenly there appeared an old fashioned Rolls Royce with the Royal Standard flying in the breeze. It drew to a halt outside the railway station and out smartly stepped our beloved King dressed in Naval uniform. Within a very short time a signal came through to say that I could now make the crossing to Orkney. I quickly gathered my belongings and made my way to the quayside where I boarded the *St. Ola*. I cannot remember exactly the time we sailed but I do remember that it was a very rough crossing; there were only a few civilians on board and I was the only representative of the services.

Inga Marchant, a Grimsetter WAAF, reminds us of the work undertaken by the voluntary services as the train wound its way through the Highlands.

Very many stations had groups of local women who gave us delicious scones and sometimes even shortbread. When on a tour of the Highlands forty years later, sometime in the 1980s, we stopped at Helmsdale. There I was able to thank once again one of those wonderful ladies.

She recalls a particularly interesting journey in which she found a 'stowaway' on board the train:

My most uncomfortable journey was sitting on a toilet seat nursing the baby of a very determined wife who, not having heard from her husband for some time, had somehow got herself on board to confront him. I often wonder whether she ever caught up with him. As for her journey, it was quite unauthorised which was why she was hiding in the toilet.

Muriel Wears, another Twatt Wren describes her arrival at Stromness:

I arrived as an urgent replacement and of course, as usual, in the Services, nobody knew I was coming! I looked a very sorry sight sitting on a box of kippers at Stromness, absolutely dejected. I had been sick all the way over, my hair which was very long at the time, had all come straggling out of my little round hat and I was rather like a pea-green colour. Eventually a three ton truck arrived to take me up to Twatt. It was driven by a sergeant in the Marines. He told me to get in the front with him and put my luggage in the back which I did and when I settled down in the front, he started patting my knee and saying "How about coming to the camp dance with

me tonight?" My first thought was, "Gosh they must be short of women up here because I was looking the most miserable little wreck you've ever seen!"

On 18th January 1944, No. 602 Squadron arrived at Skeabrae from Detling in Kent. It appears that the pilots were taking over aircraft left by a previous squadron and so the whole squadron was to be moved directly by Transport Command. England was enveloped in fog and a decision was made to move the squadron by rail instead to Aberdeen. From there trucks would take them to RAF Peterhead from where huge Harrow transports would take them to Skeabrae. In the Station Diary of Skeabrae, is a copy of the note sent to No. 217 Squadron Transport Command, Doncaster requesting *8,000 lbs. lift at am 18th January to emplane 602 Squadron Peterhead to Skeabrae.* Pierre Clostermann was a No. 602 Squadron pilot and in his book, *The Big Show*, he gives an account of the journey north:

We piled our luggage into the lorries and went and had lunch at the 'Star' in Maidstone where we found Jimmy Rankin and Yule. A few last rounds of drinks, promises . . . As usual I was cluttered up with a mass of belongings—mandoline, Irvin jacket, etc. Luckily Jacques was there to help.
On the way through London we dropped in, in a body—24 pilots—at the 'C————', a very swanky and exclusive club in Soho. After half an hour, the manager, fearing for his interior decoration and seeing the alarm of his immaculately dressed clientele, came and asked us to move on. A few well chosen arguments, including the transfer of his magnificent white carnation to Ken's buttonhole and a threat of public debagging, were enough to calm him down. From 6 to 9.30 (our train was at 10.20) we drank hard—whisky, beer, whisky. By 9.30 we were bottled and singing our squadron ditties. 'I belong to Glasgow' followed 'Pistol Packing Momma' and 'Gentille Alouette' and gradually we embarked on the more lurid terms of our repertoire. Our fellow guests began to feel embarrassed, to blush, and some of them even discretely made themselves scarce. Robson climbed up on a table, upset a few bottles and we began to intone in chorus 602's war cry:
'One, two, three, four, five!'
'Six, hooooo! Twooooooo!'
At that point the captain very nicely reminded us that we had a train to catch. It was just as well he did, for, as we were getting up, the proprietor burst in escorted by two policemen and half a dozen MPs (Military Police). After a few minutes of confused explanations we succeeded in getting rid of them and surged down the Piccadilly Circus underground. A civilian permitted himself an out-of-place remark about 'those good-for-nothing RAF blokes'. Robson and Bob Courly inserted his umbrella into the moving staircase which jammed with a terrifying din. We took a compartment by storm, the passengers regarding us with a mixture of incredulity

and horror and finally we found ourselves at King's Cross.

We piled our luggage on the electric trolleys. Carpenter took over the controls and embarked on an epic dash along the platforms crowded with travellers, the warning bell going full-blast. It was such a riot that the stationmaster took a hand in person, followed by an imposing escort of military police. An unwise move on his part for, within a minute or two, his beautiful cap, covered with gold braid, had mysteriously found its way into Tommy's suitcase. This cap now figures among the Flight's most valued trophies, together with a London policeman's helmet, a Canadian general's beret and a Panzer Grenadier colonel's forage cap, brought back from Dieppe by Bill Loud.

The platforms were swarming with people and what with the blackout, it was hard to find our way about. However we did eventually succeed in finding our reserved compartment at the door of which, an MP and a railway official were mounting guard. Our Pullman was divided in two, with a communicating door. The other half was occupied by No. 129 Squadron from Hornchurch, also going 'on rest'. We soon made friends. A terrific racket again, everyone singing, bottles flying. Round about 2 am, we organised a rugger match, but it fizzled out for lack of players. By 3 o'clock, everyone was asleep, on the seats, under the tables, on the carpet in the gangway, even in the luggage racks.

18th January 1944: It was a pitiful squadron which emerged from the train at Aberdeen at about 5 o'clock in the morning. Dishevelled, unshaven, covered with soot, our mouths like the bottom of a parrot's cage, we first had to unload our luggage and manhandle it over to the lorries and buses taking us to Peterhead. Then we embarked in two gigantic Harrow transports, piling our luggage in the fuselages. I noticed that each one of us unobtrusively sat down on his parachute bag. Some clot began repeating the story of how a Harrow had been shot down on this trip by a Ju-88 a few weeks earlier[*]. During the take-off we all clenched our teeth but when we were airborne, we heaved a sigh of relief and began to crack a few jokes. Not for long! The air was far from calm and the machine began to pitch and toss, shaken by air pockets. The laughs soon gave way to a mood of profound gloom. This pathological state was not unconnected with the state of our stomachs which had not yet recovered from the corrosive mixture of beer and whisky. Every pilot held his head in his hands, his elbows on his knees and nobody thought of admiring the beautiful snow covered country over which we were passing. We reeled out of the Harrow at Skeabrae in Orkney with dry throats and asleep on our feet. We wished the Station Commander would go to hell as he did his utmost to make us welcome in a charming little speech which we had to listen to standing in the open under the piercing blasts of the wind.

Skeabrae in winter might just as well be the North Pole. God knows what maniac at Air Ministry had the bright idea of setting up a fighter base in those god-forsaken islands. A few hours' daylight in the twenty-four; occasionally a gleam of sun pierces the wan clouds, disperses the Arctic mist and reveals a desolate countryside, windswept rock emerging from the thick snow.

[*] There is no record of this but on 30th December 1944 a Harrow of No. 271 Sqdn. en route Peterhead-Skeabrae with equipment and personnel of 441 Sqdn. Royal Canadian Airforce was bounced by Ju-88s.

It was mid January after all! Although Orkney is normally fortunate in getting very little snow, during the war years there were some very heavy falls which created considerable problems on the airfields. During one of these snowfalls a Naval Message which must surely rank as one of the funniest wartime Naval communications, was sent from Hatston. It read, 'Snow clearing equipment has been found under snowdrift'! A very touching winter story is told by Norman Mills, attached to 823 Squadron at Hatston. The squadron was moving south but first he had to dig his Swordfish out of a snowdrift. To his great surprise he found a sheep buried but still alive. Trying to extricate the sheep he was astounded to come across a little kitten tucked up cosily in its fleece! The sheep ran away and there was little time to solve the problem of the kitten which had to take flight with the squadron. It was adopted as the family cat and lived to the age of twelve but to the last remained as wild as the Orkney winter!

No matter what season they experienced Orkney, many servicemen expressed sentiments similar to Pierre Clostermann. This is typified in that well known poem based on an Australian original:

The Bloody Orkneys *

This bloody town's a bloody cuss—
No bloody trains, no bloody bus,
And no one cares for bloody us—
In bloody Orkney.

The bloody roads are bloody bad,
The bloody folks are bloody mad,
They'd make the brightest bloody sad,
In bloody Orkney.

All bloody clouds and bloody rains,
No bloody kerbs, no bloody drains,
The Council's got no bloody brains,
In bloody Orkney.

Everything's so bloody dear
A bloody bob for bloody beer
And is it good?—no bloody fear,
In bloody Orkney.

The bloody 'flicks' are bloody old,
The bloody seats are bloody cold,
You can't get in for bloody gold
In bloody Orkney.

The bloody dances make you smile,
The bloody band is bloody vile,
It only cramps your bloody style,
In bloody Orkney

No bloody sport, no bloody games,
No bloody fun, the bloody dames
Won't even give their bloody names
In bloody Orkney.

Best bloody place is bloody bed
With bloody ice on bloody head
You might as well be bloody dead
In bloody Orkney.

This poem is attributed to 'Captain Hamish Blair' but apparently no one by this name and rank ever served in the Armed Services in Orkney!

Orcadians were furious at the publication of this scurrilous verse and Kirkwall man, Sydney Leitch, hit back. Here are some verses:

This bloody war's a bloody cuss
For what it's brought to bloody us
Is bloody trouble, bloody fuss
In peaceful Orkney.

The so-called soldiers bloody Gay+
On two and bloody six a day
Their bloody looks keep Huns away
From peaceful Orkney.

Supercilious bloody Wrens
Can't even push their bloody pens
And strut about like bloody hens
All over Orkney . . .

+the reference is to the Gordon Highlanders who manned critical communication centres in the islands and whose nickname was the 'Gay Gordons'.

Sydney was not being truthful about the poor welcome the service personnel received. Jean Williams, a Fighter Direction WAAF based in Kirkwall spoke for all servicemen and women when she wrote, 'I remember especially how the people welcomed us; we must have been an intrusion on their lives but they never showed it.'

An unknown serviceman, accustomed to defending the islands in another sense, rose to defend them in verse:

The Blessed Orkneys

I read a most distressing verse,
In accents 'bloody' and so terse
That I produce one the reverse
Of this, our Orkney.

It is a shame—I do not know 'im,
The author of that vile poem,
For I would dearly love to show 'im,
A lovely Orkney.

Blossoms with their edges creaming,
Daffodils in thousands teeming,
Caused all through the Gulf Stream streaming,
To fair Orkney.

We came up here with naught to lose,
For pleasure there is much to choose,
Especially if you want to booze,
In Flowing Orkney.

The Royal Hotel—a perfect bar,
If you ever want a jar,
On Saturdays, remote, afar,
In silent Orkney.

I watch the Walrus and the Skua,
Over Scapa Flow so sure,
If they flew low they would be fewer,
In well-armed Orkney.

If you are on dancing bent,
The ATS and WRENS and WAAFS are lent,
Sometimes no chaperons are sent,
In trusting Orkney.

We came up here, we understood,
To fight, to die, to shed our blood,
Even if it's mixed with mud
In driest Orkney.

The troops on Burray, Hoy and Flotta,
Go to Kirkwall for a spot'er
Recreation and what not'er
In gayest Orkney.

My seven days' leave I almost spurn,
With all those wasted hours to burn,
Before the moment of return
To blessed Orkney.

Anon

To the pilots, the weather meant everything and pilots' logs for the winter seasons are sprinkled with 'diabolical', 'putrid', 'foul', in reference to the weather. In *About Tern*, the magazine of HMS *Tern*, Twatt, the writer asked, 'What have Orkney and the opera *Madame Butterfly* in common?' Answer—one fine day! It would be true to say that everyone found it difficult to adjust to the high winds so frequently experienced in Orkney. Harald Meltzer, pilot with No. 331 Norwegian Squadron describes the weather of March 1942:

> . . . there were at least twenty days in March on which the wind blew hard. There were periods of five, six or seven days when the wind blew a gale without stopping. The draughts would come tearing in through every crack and crevice but we had learned the art of keeping warm by putting on enough clothes and keeping fires going well in our rooms. The wind would make a roaring noise in the chimney pipe day and night; still we could sleep all right in spite of it. A 100 m.p.h. gale would often shake our little hut so much that we would lie in bed and almost believe we should be airborne any moment!

And airborne they did become on some occasions. The official historian of Hatston writes of conditions in the autumn of 1939:

> Accommodation, during what turned out to be a

windy autumn, continued to be a major problem. Huts were slow to arrive and tents were still in use until about the end of November; mud was everywhere and, despite precautions, tents, partially completed huts and hangars suffered damage from the most severe winter experienced in Orkney for the past 25 years. It was a matter of departmental pride that the Meteorological Hydrogen Balloon Filling Tent was the last to become airborne.

John Cooper, 809 Squadron Fulmar pilot, was intrigued by the most unusual natural phenomenon he observed in the officers' mess at RNAS Twatt. When the wind blew strongly it would sweep under the hut and lift the linoleum right off the floor! The strong winds would create such a powerful draught in the chimney of the cast iron heating stoves that they would become red hot! Is it little wonder then that we find recorded in the official history of Lyness the sober fact that Royal Naval establishments in Orkney consumed three quarters of a million tons of coal in the five years, May 1940 - May 1945!

There were others who loved what they saw and wrote very movingly of their impressions of Orkney. 'Cyclops' Brown, Hurricane pilot with No. 253 Squadron moved from a round of:

> . . . weekend and evening tennis parties, cricket, golf, country clubs, ice-skating at Purley and Streatham and at the Queen's Club, a wide choice of good

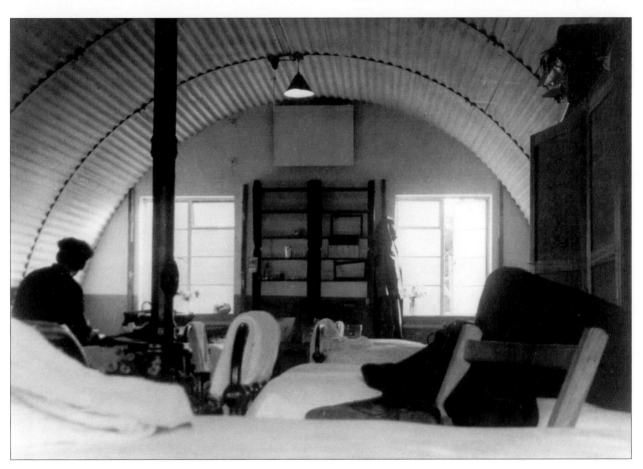

Officers' accommodation at Bryameadow, Twatt. HILL.

restaurants and pubs, and, for the more adventurous, some of the London clubs and shows were still open, and only a taxi ride back home. And then, suddenly, the squadron found its self on an apparently bare, windswept island. What on earth had Orkney to offer compared with all that?. . . there were some people who took to the place almost from the start and for many men with an urban background it began to grow on them as an acquired taste, to be explored, experienced and then savoured. A Czechoslovak sergeant pilot of No. 253 Squadron was overheard to remark to a Norwegian pilot officer "It certainly beats Prague!"

The pilots were the most privileged. In the first instance they had probably flown in to Orkney and then, from the air, were soon familiar with the islands and their surrounding seas as a complete entity and, if they so wished, were able to take an intimate look at the wilder, deserted places and otherwise inaccessible bird and marine life. Many among the transitory population came to enjoy this new scene, at least in retrospect and even those who never took to Orkney and regarded Skeabrae as yet another dreadful hutted RAF camp would have acknowledged that at least it was different.

Jack Holden was a Leading Stoker in the Royal Navy. As he said, he 'joined the Navy and never went to sea', the whole of his service life was spent at RNAS Twatt! His first impression of Orkney was not good but gradually he saw the islands in a new light:

> I can't find a word suitable for the winter of 1942 - 1943. It rained and it blew and when it got fed up of that it blew and it rained. I hated with all my heart this bleak island and its flaying wind. The Spring of 1943 was one of these rare years when winter departs as if cut off with a knife. The island, so it seemed to me, was transformed overnight. The land was carpeted with wild flowers, trout leaped in the lochs, birds were everywhere. I looked at it all, "Well it's not such a bad place after all," I said to myself. Hatred had turned to a cautious liking and as the year progressed, that liking turned to love, a love so deep that it embraced every stick, stone and sprig of heather and went into every fibre of my being and has remained with me to this day. I have never been outside the British Isles but I know there is nowhere else on earth for me. This is the land for which I was born and here, one day, I will be buried. I can ask for no more than that. Much of the transition from hatred to love of Orkney was due to the Moars of Howe in Birsay, a family with whom I had become very friendly. Every off-duty day I was never in the camp, I was with them, working in the fields, shooting, trout fishing or sea fishing. The fishing in Orkney in war time was superb. Many a time we rowed home in the endless daylight of summer with a boatload of cod or haddock under the magnificent cliffs of Marwick Head. The air above us was filled with thousands of wheeling seabirds, razorbills, guillemots, puffins, kittiwakes. I would walk back to

> camp in the early hours and it seemed that the corncrake rasped in every meadow and the corn buntings jingled on every fence. As I write this it all comes back so vividly. Orkney was, to me, a land of endless wonder. Long winter nights (I had an all-night pass) were spent yarning indoors under the light of the Tilley lamp. It became 'my home' and 'my family' and so it has remained to this day. The old folk have, alas, gone now as old folk must, Mother, Father, Grandad, Auntie Jessie, Uncle Bill, all gone now. They lie at rest in a lovely little cemetery near the sea in Birsay. When I am that way, I go in and look at the headstones. My mind goes back to the years when we were all together. I have a feeling, it can be no more than a feeling, that they know I am here and are as happy as I am. We are, in a sense, all together again.

After the war Jack moved from Kent and took up residence in Orkney. When stationed at Twatt he used his artistic skills to produce for the station magazine many funny cartoons, some of which are included in this book. In retirement his water colours of birds gained him fame, some of these paintings being highly prized now by those who bought them. His last wish, to be buried in Orkney, became reality in 1988.

The accommodation and facilities at the stations improved enormously as the war progressed so what the service personnel found when they arrived depended on when they came to Orkney. Despite the fact that Hatston was the Royal Navy's first purpose built station, conditions were rather grim at the beginning as the official history of Hatston points out:

> When war was declared, the runways were nearly complete but only two hangars had been erected; suitable accommodation for aircrews, maintenance ratings and personnel operating the ancillary services were non-existent; the only house in the vicinity, Grainayre and Scott's House being already earmarked for offices and stores. Billets were found nearby in houses, hotels, the Drill Hall and Kirkwall Public Library as well as a few even in the prison! The overflow lived under canvas, the weather at this time being, providentially, warm and dry. . . . Kirkwall Bay was busier with traffic than it had ever been; the piers were totally inadequate to receive the hundreds of tons of goods to be unloaded; ships had sometimes to sail without discharging their full cargoes with the result that while Orkney was in despair for roofing material to complete their huts, Lerwick had a superabundance of roofs but no floors or windows or vice versa. . . . In the spring and summer of 1940, work on the station continued at top pressure and conditions steadily improved although lack of fresh fruit and vegetables resulted in a case considered to be due to lack of Vitamin C; the patient who had been on the station for nine months, was treated for scurvy with large doses of orange juice and made a rapid recovery. This incident

Can this really be Orkney? On a beautiful summer's day Twatt Wrens Celia Green and Mary Kiddie gather wild lupins on Yonbell, the hill above RNAS Twatt; 'I shall never forget the wildness of Orkney, the beautiful colourings of the sea and the hills, the glorious blue lupins. The hardships one forgets, the beauty, never'. (Jean Maliphant née Jamieson or Cawkell?). PEMBERTON.

resulted in fresh fruit and vegetables being flown up from Donibristle and there was no recurrence of the trouble. The Wardroom was ready for occupation in October, thus releasing other hut accommodation for ratings but the quarters for Wrens [who arrived at the beginning of 1940 G.L.] were not completed until about a year later.

Local man, Ned Spence was contracted to unload and transport these hut sections:

> A great, massive boat came into Stromness from America with huts for Hatston and we had to cart them too. There was no Ferry Road then and we had difficulty coming through that narrow bit there at Flett the Butchers. When we were loading them we had to watch and make sure that the load wasn't wider than that bit of street.

Very wet weather prevailed in Orkney in early 1940 and the construction sites became seas of mud. Ashes from the ubiquitous cast iron heating stoves were used to make paths and keep the quarters reasonably tidy. Station staff had a difficult job creating reasonable conditions for the new arrivals. In his book, *"It's Really Quite Safe"*, Hank Rotherham explains how some of these problems were overcome at Hatston:

> Our Paymaster-Commander was a Welshman by the name of Ivor Dummer. He was a superb scrounger and had managed to acquire from liners being converted to troopships, pictures and furniture which would otherwise have been thrown out. These were used to fit our otherwise stark Mess and cabins. The dentist doubled as wine secretary and he kept us well supplied even when London was tightly rationed. He did this by bartering such things as eggs and lobster which were readily available in the Orkneys but very hard to come by on the mainland. Wine merchants seemed to be most obliging in finding stock in the furthest recesses of their cellars when offered either of these commodities. By common consent, a small bomb shelter was dedicated to the safety of the wine—it being thought it was well worth running some personal risk in the event of an air raid rather than face the greater perils of drought.

When the first party of Royal Naval personnel arrived at Twatt in March 1941, they had similar problems to face. A small croft served as a galley and dining hall while the Administration Block housed the Wardroom, officers' sleeping quarters, general offices, Naval stores, SPO office and sickbay! By June 1941 when Cdr. Rotherham assumed command a ratings' dining hall had been built which doubled up as sleeping accommodation. As for Skeabrae, it was in such a state when the first RAF party arrived in September 1940 that 50% had to be sent on leave! In October the Officers' Mess was still at Holodyke House in Harray, about two miles away! The Station Diary records:

> officers have to be billeted out; the men however do their best to settle in in a very sporting and cheerful manner with little grousing and make the best of a somewhat uncomfortable situation.

New arrivals at Twatt were highly amused by the name which has vulgar associations in English. Some ratings used the address T.W.A.T.T. to avoid embarrassment hoping that their families would see this as merely another Royal Naval abbreviation! The station actually lay in the district of Isbister and should have been given this name but it apparently took its name from the nearest Post Office. The Orkney placename 'Twatt' stems from the perfectly innocent Old Norse word *þveit*, meaning a 'clearing'! When slit trenches were dug round the camp perimeter, these were referred to amusingly as the 'Chastity Belt'. The first Station Commander, Commander Hank Rotherham capitalised on the name of his station and visiting dignitaries were presented with a fine scroll which gave them the *Freedom of Twatt*. Designed by rhymster Lt.Cdr. Archie Fleming and artist Royal Marine Major Bertie Bass, it caused much hilarity. It is not on record whether this freedom was bestowed on His Majesty, King George VI, when he visited the station in March 1943!

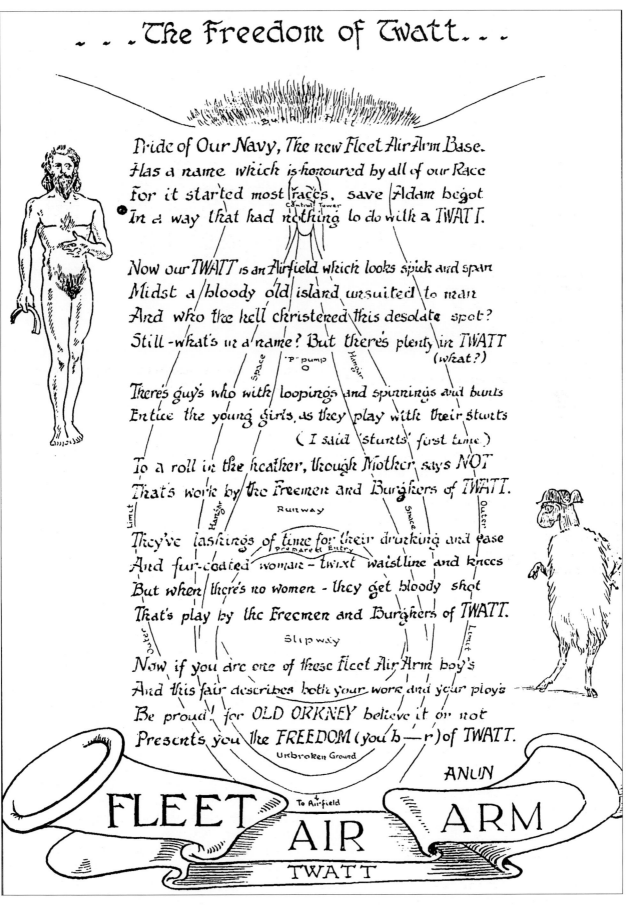

...The Freedom of Twatt...

Pride of Our Navy, The new Fleet Air Arm Base.
Has a name which is honoured by all of our Race
For it started most races, save Adam begot
In a way that had nothing to do with a TWATT.

Now our TWATT is an Airfield which looks spick and span
Midst a bloody old island unsuited to man
And who the hell christened this desolate spot?
Still - what's in a name? But there's plenty in TWATT
(what?)

There's guy's who with loopings and spinnings and burts
Entice the young girls as they play with their stunts
(I said 'stunts' first time)
To a roll in the heather, though Mother says NOT
That's work by the Freemen and Burghers of TWATT.

They've lashings of time for their drinking and ease
And fur-coated woman - twixt waistline and knees
But when there's no women - they get bloody shot
That's play by the Freemen and Burghers of TWATT.

Now if you are one of these Fleet Air Arm boy's
And this fair describes both your work and your ploys
Be proud! for OLD ORKNEY believe it or not
Presents you the FREEDOM (you b——r) of TWATT.

ANUN

FLEET AIR ARM
TWATT

The Freedom of Twatt; an honour bestowed on all male Twatt officers and visiting male dignitaries in the early days of the station; the drawing is attributed to Major Bertie Bass who was in charge of a Royal Marine detachment on HMS Devonshire. ROTHERHAM.

At Hatston; on the occasion of the visit of King George VI; the C/O with his Wren officer staff; third from the left, Mrs. Rumbelow-Pierce; second from the left, Honor Pryde, second from the right, Mrs. 'Puckiz' Finch-Noyes, extreme right, Margaret Baikie, Hall of Tankerness; Captain H. St. John (Fanny) Fancourt; Albacore aircraft in background. BODEN.

Twatt officers and Wrens celebrate the 21st birthday of Rachel Murray-Bissett at a picnic among the sand dunes at Aikerness in Evie; note the gramophone! Left to right Len Page, Rachel Murray-Bissett, Keith Remmington, Muriel Wears, Helen Wilson. REMMINGTON.

Skogar Wardroom party, Twatt, December 1944; Graham Peacock, Freddy Watts, side view of Peter Cornish, Lt.Cdr. Dobson, back of Joe Mence, side view of Alan Moore, 'Crem', Cdr. Jackson, W. D. Bundy, Elizabeth Wright. PEMBERTON.

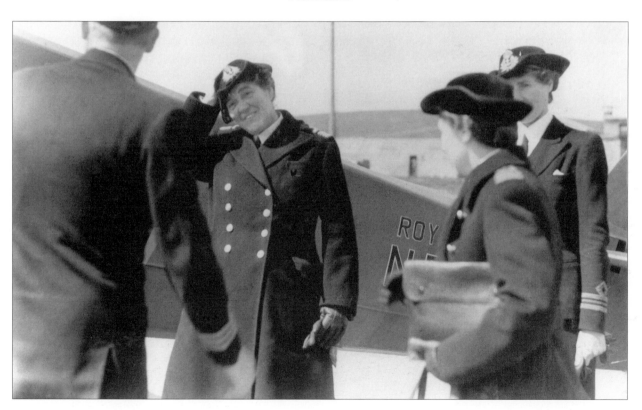

Arrival of the Queen Wren, Dame Vera Laughton-Matthews at Twatt, 10.06.45; Captain Jackson, Dame Vera, her secretary and I/O Foster-Barham; Dame Vera was the author of 'Blue Tapestry', the story of the Wrens. PEMBERTON.

Royal Naval personnel were particularly pleased to find Wrens well represented in Orkney. When, at the outbreak of war, the Queen Wren, Dame Vera Laughton-Mathews proposed that Wrens be immediately despatched to Orkney to release men for other duties, the suggestion was scoffed at. She protested, 'My girls have it up here you know.' 'It doesn't matter where your girls have it,' said an Admiral, 'my boys will find it!' So the story is told by ex-Fleet Air Arm officers! But the Admiralty came very quickly round to thinking along the lines of the Queen Wren. Before 1939 was out, there were already Wrens at Lyness, the Headquarters of the Home Fleet and at its peak the Station could boast 615 Wrens. RNAS Hatston received its first Wrens in early 1940 and eventually had a complement of 265. On 13th April 1943 WAAFs arrived at Skeabrae but clearly they had been anticipated earlier as an amusing story related by 'Red' Duthie of 801 Squadron reveals:

When we arrived at Skeabrae, the resident Flying Control Officer was an ageing Fl/ Lt. (he must have been at least 40 years old!) called Montgomery who claimed that he and half a dozen others had been sent up to commission the aerodrome. He told us the following story about the early days of the station. They had been living in the most spartan conditions for many weeks when a Bristol Bombay appeared out of the blue, landed, offloaded two large packing cases beside the runway, taxied back and took off again. Monty, who had been elsewhere at the time, returned to find his staff and most of the contractors gathered round the cases in eager anticipation. What could it be? Food? Blankets? Warm clothing? A crowbar was borrowed from the contractors and the cases prised open on the spot. The contents were found to be packets of sanitary towels supplied by the Nuffield Foundation. The nearest servicewomen at that time were Wrens at Hatston, fourteen miles away!

Wrens did not appear at Twatt until late 1943. There were only six initially and they had to share accommodation with the WAAFs at Skeabrae. At Grimsetter there was also a small complement of WAAFs towards the end of the war. The location of the camps for the Wrens and WAAFs produced considerable debate. Lady Cholmondeley arrived from London and insisted that the Wrennery be a mile or two away from RNAS Hatston but, fortunately, her visit coincided with a snowstorm and she immediately saw that, with little transport available, the plan was impracticable. The Wrennery was built directly opposite RNAS Hatston, though with a main road between them and, eventually, the fences were breached so that a station gate faced the Wrennery gate! At Skeabrae the WAAF camp was situated in a small enclosure some miles away from the station and as Mike Walker, a Signals Officer there at the time says 'Security there was

considerably tighter than round Scapa Flow.' By 1944 very fine Wrens quarters had been built within the perimeter of RNAS Twatt providing accommodation for 7 officers and over 350 other ranks. The Wren First Officer Mary Foster-Barham nevertheless had to fight to have the seven foot high softwire fence which was being erected round the Wrennery removed! Despite this progressive move the Wrens were very closely chaperoned there.

Wrens and WAAFs were not the only women to be found on the Orkney airfields. Keith Remmington, 771 Squadron pilot describes the excitement of a new arrival at Twatt:

. . . the Corsair was a bit of a brute. It was especially difficult on the ground because of its long nose and taxying was always a problem. I shall always remember the first one being delivered to us. When it taxied in to dispersal, we all gathered round full of interest and some apprehension. The cockpit hood slid back and, to our astonishment, out got a petite American lady pilot. We were amazed that someone so small and so attractive could handle such an ugly looking brute of an aircraft. When asked what it was like to fly she replied "It sure is a hot ship. You fan her in at 95 knots and when you cut the throttle, she sure does stop flying." I think that was a pretty fair description of the aeroplane!

The woman was of course a member of Air Transport Auxiliary which employed a number of American women pilots. This is the only record of an American woman pilot in Orkney but, considering the vast numbers of new aircraft which arrived, she was probably one of many. Experienced pilots found these young ladies intriguing and there was a sneaking admiration for them and their skill in handling powerful military aircraft. Mike Crosley speaks of quite a bit of banter among the pilots of 801 Squadron when the new Seafire LIII's were delivered to Skeabrae in December 1944 by the ladies of ATA:

Dougy (Yate) was wondering how they managed at 5 'g'. He reckoned their bra straps would part. He invented a new type with a cantilever system of weights and pulleys which was self compensating. The Mark II version used more sophistication still— solenoids and rheostats to arrange constant uplift at all 'g' loadings from minus -2 to +8!

As far as women on the stations are concerned we must not forget the ubiquitous NAAFI girls. Catherine Mair was in the NAAFI at Twatt:

I was met at Stromness by a Mrs. Lindsay, a very formidable lady who later was very nice to a homesick Scot. As mobile canteen driver, I was pretty much my own boss. I also became a very popular girl if only for my 'cup of char and a wad'. I was 'Jock' or 'Lofty' to them being 4' 11½"! It was my duty to supply 'Stand Easy' (tea breaks) morning and afternoon and even through the night sometimes. A cup of tea was 2d. and that was for any size of cup! One day a bright spark brought along a 2lb. tomato tin as a cup! When a matelot was broke I sometimes let them write his name on the slate which I had fixed to the roof of the van. I was only let down once as far as payment was concerned and by a fellow Scot too! He ran up a bill a bit higher than most (the boys knew I had to clear the money out of my own pocket). Unfortunately the Scot boasted in the bar that I could whistle for my money. The upshot of that was, a sailor with a very black eye came to the van with an apology and cleared his debt. I never knew who gave him the black eye but he got no more credit.

I got to know the area very well and when a sailor was going home I was often asked to get something to take with them so I became very well known at the surrounding steadings and farms as I always managed to find butter, cheese, eggs and sometimes even a chicken for them. There was also a NAAFI at the RAF station at Skeabrae nearby and there was great rivalry between the Skeabrae NAAFI driver and myself. We always tried to see who could reach the NAAFI bakery in Stromness first in the morning to get the best cakes for our boys. Most of the matelots at Twatt were English and Eccles cakes were in great demand. I always made sure I had a good supply of them!

By 1944, new arrivals found large and busy stations. There were over 400 permanent staff at Hatston. When seven squadrons and their ground crews were disembarked, there were certainly times when there were more than 1,000 men on the Station assisted by more than 200 Wrens. The station had a very fine cinema-cum-theatre and a very active theatrical group. Originally run by Hatston test pilot, Lt. Shea Simmonds, this role was later assumed by Met. Officer Lt. Donald Hewlett who was later to become well known on stage and on television. In the early days of the war, before Hatston was fully established, servicemen and women were welcomed wholeheartedly by Kirkwall Amateur Dramatic Group. In Chapter 3 we described how their performance of 'Tilly of Bloomsbury' did not stop even for an air raid!

Twatt and Skeabrae also had fine cinemas. From the Twatt magazine *About Tern** we learn something of the large part played by the cinema in the lives of the men and women on station:

There are so many different things which go to make *The Orcadia* one of the best cinemas in the islands. Naturally, most of our patrons consider only the 3d., 4d. or 6d. that they pay for some kind of seat and then if the film comes up to their expectations, they go away feeling very pleased about the whole thing. While on the subject of seats, it may surprise you to know that well over 100,000 people have paid cash to see the 317 big performances that have been exhibited in the last twelve months. This does not include such performances as special instructional films, ENSA's dances or the three special children's matinées.

The box-office record in *The Orcadia* is held by *This is the Army* which drew a crowd of 1171, closely followed by *Mutiny on the Bounty* with 1167. *Song of Bernadette* came third with 1133+. It may interest the officers to know that more of them attended the *Song of Bernadette* than any other show. The average weekly takings for a film show is between £20 and £25 out of which 15gns. is deducted to pay for the lease of the films. Films are supplied by the Royal Naval Film Corporation.

* the station was known as HMS Tern; for those with no military knowledge, the clever title of the magazine is a pun on 'About Turn', an order given in marching.
+there were, on average, five cinema shows per week.

As these figures show, Twatt, by this time was a very large establishment. Living quarters offered accommodation for 173 officers and 965 other ranks. The new Wrens' camp on station had accommodation for 7 officers and 357 ratings. It is doubtful whether the Station ever reached its full complement; the official Station history talks of 150 Wrens on site. Towards the end of the war a fully equipped hospital offering X-Ray facilities and catering for the whole Station was built adjacent to the Wrens' quarters. The story is told that the only operation in the theatre was conducted on the Commander's dog. Found chasing sheep, an irate farmer had discharged his shotgun at it but the pellets were skilfully removed by a naval surgeon!

Frank Walker of 771 Sqdn. has a vivid memory of an impressive ceremony which took place when he was stationed there in the summer of 1943. This was the opening of a new chapel dedicated to St. Magnus. He wrote:

The chapel was an ordinary size standard Nissen hut only distinguishable from the outside by having a cross on the end wall above the roof level and by being kept in a smart painted condition. I cannot recall the inside but I suppose it was like a standard size dormitory hut with a central door at one end leading to a short corridor between two rooms, store and office, with the rest open. There would be seating on benches for about a hundred. It was consecrated by the Bishop of Orkney and Aberdeen and we cleared lower deck so that there were far more people than could get inside and the ceremony was held in the open. It was a fine windy day with occasional light showers. The Bishop was in full vestments with staff, mitre, and a fine green and red cope embroidered with gold wire. He had a powerful voice (he needed it) and stood on a small grassy knoll with blue sky and a few low dark clouds behind him. With the wind blowing his vestments, he was the most impressive bishop I have seen. The Viking undertones called to mind Magnus the Martyr himself.

The Bishop of Aberdeen at the dedication of the St. Magnus Chapel at RNAS Twatt.

Perhaps the most extraordinary thing to happen in the history of the Royal Navy occurred at RNAS Twatt. A baby boy was born on the 'ship'! A Wren Petty Officer who had just been drafted in became very ill one night and caused great consternation among the younger Wrens. Twatt Wren Muriel Wears gives the inside story:

> In the middle of the night the Petty Officer started moaning and some of the girls went in to see what was wrong with her. She complained of terrible pains in her stomach so they got her an extra hot water bottle, some more blankets and gave her a good stiff dose of Andrews Liver Salts. Despite this she kept on making an awful lot of noise and moaning so two of the girls decided they would have to go and get the Duty Wren Officer because, by this time the whole hut was not only awake but very concerned. The officer arrived quickly, took one look at the patient and exclaimed "My God, she's having a baby!" That really shows how young and innocent we all were. The girls in the cabin were quite shocked! The Petty Officer was transported to the Sick Bay where a young doctor safely delivered a bouncing baby boy. The birth was duly entered in the ship's log! Later in the day some of us were going to Stromness and begged a lift from the Station

ambulance. The girls spoke of their adventure during the night. "I know all about it", said Dr. McCaskey, "I was there! Frankly", he went on, "I was a bit apprehensive—I'd never delivered a baby before and I didn't expect that to be one of my duties on a Naval Air Station!"

First Wren Officer Mary Foster-Barham wrote to say that this was one of only two Wrens who were pregnant on station in her time there and she was amused by the fact that in both cases the men came asking for help as the girls would not marry them!

On 4th April 1941, the Skeabrae Literary and Debating Society discussed the motion *It is possible to be happy though in Skeabrae*! The motion was carried by 24 votes to 12! By any standards Skeabrae was a large and busy Station. Even at the time the motion was discussed there were 550 service personnel on site plus one Hurricane Squadron and its servicing echelon which could have counted for at least another 150. The WAAFs were still to arrive and by 1944 there were occasions when four squadrons of aircraft were based here. As the outcome of the debate suggested, Skeabrae does seem to have been a happy station. It featured a well organised social life. The camp had its own cinema

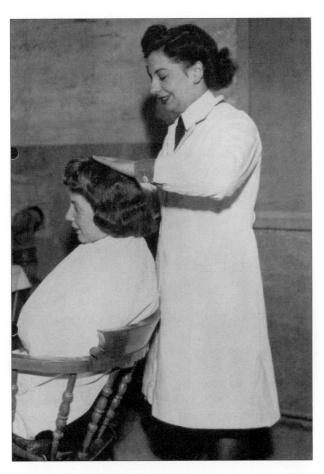

*Mary Treby (née Rogers), Wren Hairdresser, Twatt, 1945;
Wren Lily ? seated.* TREBY.

in 1942 and later a well equipped gymnasium was added; the Commanding Officer was proud to record in the Station Diary that there were classes in German and French, choral and dramatic societies, music club and facilities for every sport including squash.

Among the two and a half thousand flying personnel regularly stationed in Orkney, one could expect to find quite a few artists such as rating Jack Holden to whom we have already referred. Many spent time drawing cartoons, sketching, decorating their quarters or even their aircraft! Regrettably most of this artwork has been lost. However we do have photographs of squadron mascots drawn on the fuselages of 809 Squadron Fulmar aircraft at Hatston by Ken Frazer, one of the ground staff there. Ulf Wormdal designed a crest for 331 Squadron, a copy of which is included elsewhere in the book. 'Crusty' Pye speaks of the 880 Squadron crest which was designed when the squadron was stationed in Orkney. There was much debate about the motto, one suggestion being *Semper in Excretum* which regrettably had to be rejected, squadron pilots being of the opinion that it would not meet with the approval of the Lords of the Admiralty! They had to be content with *Surgentes Vim Aquarimus*. The crest was carved out of solid mahogany by one of the

ground staff at Grimsetter and this original still exists today in Canada.

In common with all the larger military camps in Britain, the Fleet Air Arm and Royal Navy were entertained regularly by ENSA concert parties. The huge garrisons stationed in Orkney attracted the very best in the world of entertainment and a veritable galaxy of stars came and went to Orkney during the war years. H. E. Duthie, 801 Sqdn. pilot at Twatt recalls:

> . . . the pièce de résistance was a visit from the full Central Band of the RAF. The performance was given in a corrugated iron shed which I imagine must have been some sort of village hall at one time (the Sandwick Hall G.L.). It was packed to the doors and I remember having to sit sideways on my chair to avoid the slide of one of the trombones. The officers of course had the front seats and most of us were stone deaf for days afterwards. The noise was phenomenal but I am still reminded whenever I hear 'Chatanooga Choo Choo'!

Tommy Handley recorded one of his ITMA shows from Twatt, a BBC recording which is still available on cassette! Gracie Fields visited twice; other stars included John Mills, Bernard Miles, Gertrude Lawrence, George Formby and Terry Thomas. Leslie Henson the comedian was a popular entertainer and when he appeared in the Garrison Theatre on the island of Flotta, King George VI was in the audience. Yehudi Menuhin accompanied by Marcel Gazelle, the Belgian pianist, played at both Hatston and Twatt and made a tour of the warships in Scapa Flow, staying overnight in HMS *Duke of York*. He corresponded with the author about this experience: 'It was most exciting to be among those wonderful men and feel that very British amalgam of men, sea and ships. On my trip back to the Orkney Mainland, I had to board a destroyer in dense fog and I was landed on an abandoned shore at the northern-most tip of Scapa where I boarded a waiting car on the slope behind the beach. I shall never forget that; it was almost unreal'.

Much of the entertainment had to be provided by the forces themselves. Despite the vast distance from the nearest brewery, there never seemed to be a shortage of beer and beer brought out the best in the many natural entertainers. Dancing on top of the highly polished table tops in the mess was a popular past-time but on one occasion at Hatston strong oak table could not cope with the weight of the entertainers and in the resultant crash the table was reduced to matchwood! When Lt. Donald Hewlett was posted to Hatston he was surprised to notice as he lay in his bunk that there was a bullet hole in the ceiling. He told me that he often wondered how this had happened. Correspondence from an officer stationed at Hatston before Donald's time may help to answer that question:

> The many Antipodeans did their very best to keep everyone's spirits high, like the Australian ballet dancer attached to 700 Squadron who did a *pas de deux* and in a dramatic crescendo discharged his revolver through the cabin roof!

All kinds of activities were encouraged by the Station Commanders. Hatston counted an experienced pigman among the staff and what began as a small hobby soon grew into a commercial undertaking! There were 100 pigs on Station at one point fed on swill from the kitchens! Commander (Flying) at Twatt kept geese and a Squadron Commander happily cared for his plot of radishes on the same station. A garden competition was held annually at Skeabrae. Lt. Shea Simmonds kept at Hatston a pet Shetland pony which developed a great liking for beer and would wander into the Junior Officers' Mess for a noggin. On one occasion, it inadvertently got itself into the Senior Wardroom much to the alarm of a visiting Admiral who registered a very strong complaint to the Station Commander when the pony stood on his foot apparently because no beer was forthcoming! The owner of the beast and his totally innocent fellow officer had their mess bills stopped for a month. All ranks were allowed to keep dogs at Skeabrae. 2nd. Lt. Per Svanøe Endresen, pilot with No. 331 Squadron Norwegians at Skeabrae, kept his dog in his room. Fellow pilot Harald Meltzer wasn't amused at first:

> (Per Svanøe) moved in with a dog—a damned dog I called it at first because it had long shaggy hair (front and back looked alike!) and smelled terribly. Mud, hairs and smell were spread all over the room and I complained bitterly—but only at first. In a few days, James washed the dog and, after I had recovered from the first shaking of water over my bed, the hair, mud and smell problem was resolved. The dog was called 'Fury' but I never saw him show any. He seemed to get some of James' spirit for he was always pattering about quite happily.
> [Sadly James later disappeared without trace while on patrol at 25,000 feet north of Orkney]

At Hatston there were even sufficient dogs on station at one time to permit a Dog Show! Lt. Duncan Hamilton had a small spaniel there which he called 'Lucky'. He had returned from leave to Hatston sitting in the nose of an unheated Boston bomber with 'Lucky' on his knee wrapped in an Irvin jacket. 'Lucky' sat happily in the corner of his office until, one day when left alone for a short time, he started, out of boredom, to chew up some papers.

Unfortunately the papers were the assembly instructions for crated American fighters about to be built and transferred to a waiting convoy in Scapa Flow. The story goes that the Fleet, unaware of this act of canine sabotage, waited until further copies were flown in via Iceland!

Sometimes airmen, especially pilots, were able to enjoy themselves during the course of their duties too! There was no Air Traffic Control in Orkney and, when on non-operational flying and out of sight of the station, the powerful engine of the fighter and the freedom of the Orkney skies often tempted the pilot to test not only his own skill and the capabilities of the machine but sometimes the sufferance of any crew present! Passing between the Old Man of Hoy and the cliff face was something of an initiation test for young pilots. Shortly after arriving in Orkney, Skeabrae pilot 'Cyclops' Brown of No. 253 Squadron made a fast pass through the gap in his Hurricane and congratulating himself on his achievement banked his aircraft sharply round only to see to his great surprise three Royal Navy Skuas follow him through! Less fortunate was an Albacore pilot ferrying an aircraft from Ayr. Apparently caught in violent unpredictable turbulence and updraughts along the cliff face, the aircraft struck the Old Man of Hoy and crashed on the Hoy Hills. Only recently some of this Albacore has been salvaged and used to complete the only surviving example of this aircraft which is held in the Fleet Air Arm Museum at Yeovilton in Somerset.

It was one thing for a pilot flying solo to attempt this feat but it was another thing for the pilot to subject his Observer or TAG to such an experience. Even a lumbering Walrus of 700 Squadron with Sub.Lt. Lawrence at the helm and Norman Brown as Observer completed this dangerous manoeuvre. Dick Stark, 771 TAG at Twatt writes:

> Some pilots made you feel very confident in their ability to fly the aircraft, others were jittery. At the other extreme were wild fellows who at the end of an exercise would do all kinds of tricks probably just for a Wardroom boast. Once we came back from an exercise in the Pentland Firth so close to the cliffs of Hoy that the aircraft was getting thrown around with the turbulence and I was violently sick. It was the only time I was ever airsick. Twice I made the journey home between the Old Man of Hoy and the cliff. That was a dangerous manoeuvre but many pilots tested their skill in that narrow gap. Everyone knows that part of the main road between Kirkwall and Stromness was closed to traffic to become the main runway at Hatston. On one occasion we actually landed on a main road which was still in use! I think the pilot probably did it for a dare. We were flying parallel to the Evie road, the pilot had a good look to see that there was no traffic and down we went! Of course we didn't stop—we just carried on and took off again.

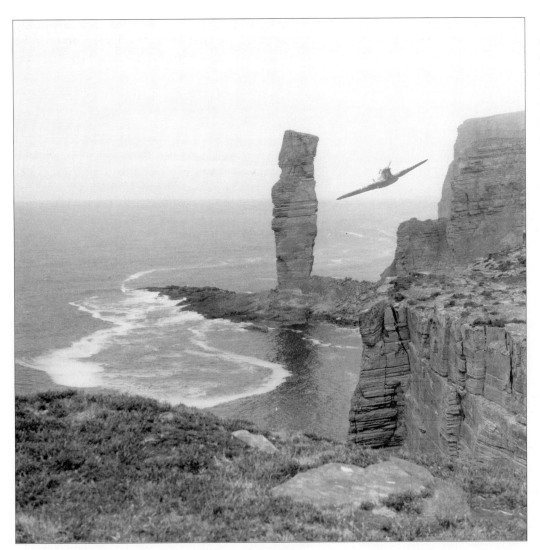

Tom Halhead was a TAG with 771 Squadron based at Hatston. On 21st February 1941 he was detailed to fly in a Hawker Henley with Midshipman Peter Twiss as pilot. He wasn't to know at that time that Midshipman Twiss had the makings of a test pilot. Tom describes the experience:

The wind was such on that day that we took off over Kirkwall Harbour. We got to the end of the runway at a terrific rate of knots, wheels up at a height of a few feet and the next thing I remember seeing were the seagulls leaving the tops of the masts of the fishing vessels, I would say—hastily. I suppose this was to be expected, the trouble was that I, instead of observing this from above, happened to be looking up at them!

Pilot Twiss pulled the stick back and vertically upwards we shot to about 3,000 feet where we did a sort of roll off the top and headed overland to a RAF station which was nearing completion at Skeabrae. Here we did every sort of show-off manoeuvre in the book and clewed up making all sorts of passes at the Control Tower. There was some RAF bod out on top shaking his fist at us in anger; he looked really annoyed. I reminded the pilot we were supposed to be doing a height finding exercise for the Army Ack-Ack units. His reply was some kind of mumbo-

jumbo and up into the sky we went to about 20,000 feet. It was a bit cold up there so down we came in rolls, dives, twists and turns—you name it, we did it! I had not done any aerobatics ever before and, after an hour of it, I was beginning to feel really groggy. I told the pilot this but got no let-up. I recall sending a message to the Army that our height was 8,000 feet and then I was violently sick somewhere over Scapa Flow and away went my teeth! I felt so rotten, I didn't care a hoot! However our time was up not long after this and we came back to Hatston where, of course, everyone considered it to be a huge joke, including the CO who was very decent about it and got me fixed up with a new set of false teeth in no time at all. Initiation? I was never airsick again.

Wing Commander Lea Cox, Station Commander at Skeabrae, did show his anger at this brash intrusion from RNAS Hatston but he let it pass. Captain 'Fanny' Fancourt, Commanding Officer of Hatston was most displeased when the RAF hit back with its own Hurricane shortly afterwards:

Flying a Hurricane to the north of Kirkwall one day led, inadvertently, to my only direct contact with Hatston and its commander. I was minding my own business when, suddenly, out of the clouds, pounced a stubby little Martlet naval fighter. Clearly its pilot wanted to play. Then followed a hectic dog-fight, screaming tight turns, vapour streaming from the wing tip vortices in ribbons, flick half rolls and the dangerous, therefore forbidden head-on attacks. As always in such affairs the tourney got lower and lower and both pilots were oblivious that it had shifted to the centre of Captain Fancourt's airfield and around his hangars. The Martlet pulled up, waggled its wings, lowered its wheels and went in to land. I returned to Skeabrae but I found to my surprise that, awaiting me, was the Squadron Commander. "The Captain of Hatston wishes to see you tomorrow," he said. "At what time?" I asked. "He will see you when you get there. You are going to walk—all eighteen miles—and no lifts." I was dismissed. To get there at a reasonable time the following day I decided to set off at midnight. About eleven hours later I dusted off my battered shoes, straightened out my crumpled best blue jacket and entered the Captain's office. As an introduction I was told that, in normal circumstances, I would have been interviewed with the other offender but he had turned out to be a distinguished naval officer much senior to me and the Captain was not going to let the Air Force see and hear him receive an old fashioned dressing down which he, assuredly, was about to be given. I was then informed that neither the Fleet Air Arm, nor the Royal Air Force nor the Luftwaffe was going to be allowed to create mayhem over Captain Fancourt's Royal Naval Air Station. If I, as a Royal Air Force fighter pilot, was so fond of violent manoeuvres at low level I would be sent to sea for a month in a destroyer. I was wished good-day and told to have a pleasant walk back to Skeabrae.

['Cyclops' Brown was the Hurricane pilot; the 'distinguished Senior Naval Officer' could only have been Lt.Cdr. J. M. Wintour, CO of the ill-fated 802 Squadron, at that time based at Hatston. The original 802 Squadron went down with HMS Glorious on 8th June 1940; it was reformed at Hatston on 21st November 1940 with 12 Martlets. In September 1941, the squadron embarked in HMS Audacity on a Gibraltar convoy and in an engagement on this trip the CO was shot down. Subsequently HMS Audacity was torpedoed and the whole squadron lost again. G.L.]

From time to time in the early years of the war there were officially planned attacks on Hatston by Skeabrae pilots to test the air defences there. Sometimes the combat must have been frightenly close for on one occasion in late 1941 Nigel Fisher in a Sea Hurricane of 801 Squadron landed back at Skeabrae with bits of aerials from Hatston Control Tower dangling from his tail wheel!

On 22nd March 1943 German photographic intelligence identified 36 ships in Scapa Flow and

Watchkeepers of Ark Royal Cabin off duty, Twatt. Back Row: Paula Edwards, Janet Renton, L/Wren Helen Wilson, Nan Chisholm, unknown, Hilda Smith. Front Row: Doreen Campbell, Margaret Mitchell, unknown, Rosemary Gornall. REMMINGTON.

Cathy Mair (née McKenzie) and Elizabeth Sinclair, two NAAFI girls at Twatt. MAIR.

'Stand-easy', coffee break on the squadron; Air Mechanics of 771 Sqdn. Twatt, at the main camp, 1944; L/A Mechanic John Shedden; Wren Jean Wenham; Wren Ruby Heymans; Air Mechanic Ted Lambeth. HEYMANS.

The auditorium; the ex-cinema seats were specially flown up by the Nuffield Services organisation. HORNE.

Hatston Show: The Importance of being Earnest. HEWLETT.

they feared an imminent invasion of Norway. John Cooper, was First Lieutenant of 881 Squadron Martlets based at Hatston between March and August 1943. The Squadron trained hard for what came to be a mock invasion of Norway code-named *Operation Tindall*. Mock enemy counter moves were also rehearsed. John Cooper volunteered for one of these defence exercises as a respite from aerial combat. He became overnight one of several German saboteurs dropped by parachute over The Mainland of Orkney with a brief to 'enter Hatston Air Station and blow up aircraft, vehicles and military installations'. They were permitted to commandeer any military vehicle and any piece of military equipment to achieve their aim and 'blowing up' was defined as 'placing a sabotage sticker on' an aircraft or piece of equipment. Volunteers were dressed in plain blue sweaters and trousers and allowed nothing in their pockets except one coin to telephone for help if necessary. Three days were allowed for the task during which time the 'saboteurs' were not permitted to speak English.

What appeared initially to be a lot of fun transpired to be rather a dangerous assignment. It wasn't possible to tell the civilian population about the exercise and anyone not in military dress, unable to speak English and snooping about an Orkney farmyard was extremely likely to have both barrels of a shotgun discharged in his direction. (Orcadians would not assume he was a spy or even if he was they would be more concerned that he was stealing eggs!) If he did succeed in walking unobtrusively over the open Orkney countryside (a difficult exercise since the only cover offered for the most part would be fencing posts) he was still likely to be torn apart by the guard dogs at Hatston or dispatched by a nervous Marine guarding the perimeter fence. John Cooper describes what really happened:

On my first exercise I found myself alone beside a road at two o'clock in the morning somewhere on the Mainland of Orkney while the Naval van which had dropped me off drove off in the semi-darkness to scatter my fellow saboteurs. Although dropped blind from the van, I had a good idea of where I was because I was very fond of Orkney by then and had seen every inch of the islands, large and small, from the air. I took to the heather and moorland and, over very rough going, worked my way slowly towards (I hoped) the East. Sometime after dawn, in true Hollywood style, a long line of little figures,

Kirkwall Arts Club, Club Room, 1944; this club was founded by Lt. Donald Hewlett, a Royal Naval Met. Officer at Hatston in October 1943; Dame Sybil Thorndyke was one of the first speakers and Sir John Geilgud was the club patron. HEWLETT.

HATSTON EMPIRE

DONALD HEWLETT

PRESENTS

"Robinson Crusoe"

"ORKNEY HERALD" OFFICE.

The Hatston Pantomime was a great success! Lt. David Corkhill, 819 Sqdn. Hatston is the 'Army' officer on the right! HORNE.

presumably soldiers, appeared on the distant skyline and I speeded up my progress. After some time I could see that another lone figure was moving away from the beaters on a course converging with mine. After stalking each other for a while this turned out to be a fellow spy and together we managed to avoid the search party without being spotted.

Around midday Jack (I have forgotten his second name for we had not met before) and I found ourselves in the parish of Stenness lying in good cover at the back of the Standing Stones Hotel which was being used for the accommodation of very senior officers of, I presume, all three services. At that time of day, the area at the back of the hotel was deserted; there was just one official Naval car used no doubt for the transport of Senior Naval officers, invitingly parked in a small yard out of sight of the kitchens. After some discussion Jack and I decided that, if we could get possession of the car and perhaps some coats and hats from the hotel, we might be able to bluff our way into Hatston, through the Main Gate, rather than get stuck on the perimeter barbed wire and be eaten by Alsatians. I discovered that I had a small comb I had forgotten about in my shirt pocket and conceived the idea of starting the car with one of its teeth. Accordingly I crawled

across the yard while Jack kept watch and, finding the car door unlocked, managed to get the engine going after an agonising fiddle.

Still unobserved, Jack joined me and took the wheel, turning the car round to be poised for a racing approach round the corner of the building to the front door. This we arranged he would do after slowly counting up to ten and meanwhile I strolled around to the front door and into the foyer. To my joy, I saw in a side passage, an impressive array of highly decorated naval greatcoats and hats hanging from pegs among sundry other exalted garments. I therefore grabbed an Admiral's coat and hat and was about to grab another when, down the stairs, came a formidable lady who had manageress written all over her. She let out a series of loud yells just as Jack screeched to the front door with the passenger door open for my immediate embarkation. I bowed silently to the lady, rushed out to the car and we shot off down the Kirkwall road circumnavigating a Naval Commander who tried to stop us and who, we learned later, would have shot at us had he been armed since the Standing Stones Hotel officers had not been warned of the exercise. In fact, this omission was to our advantage since those at the hotel were unaware that we might make for Hatston and did not therefore telephone a warning of our possible arrival. As it was, Jack tore along the Kirkwall road while I tore the lining out of my captured hat (which was too small for me) and got into the greatcoat. I laid my sleeve along the window, turned up my collar to conceal my age (I was 25) and crammed the hat over my eyes. I was certainly flaunting some impressive scrambled egg. There was a pipe in the pocket and that came in handy too.

As Jack and I sped towards Hatston, we agreed that he was dressed just a bit informally for an Admiral's driver even if his navy blue sweater and trousers were unremarkable, so when we neared the Air station, we drew into the kerb beside an unsuspecting and small matelot who stiffened and stood rigid to attention when he saw the weight of gold braid on my sleeve and hat. Beckoning him slightly nearer (Admirals are often deaf), I reached out and, murmuring "Guten morgen mein Freund", removed his cap and we shot off to Hatston. I must confess that I am not entirely certain that this last little twist in my story actually happened but the intention was certainly there and it certainly should have been done. In any event, why spoil a good wartime story for a hap'orth of tar!

Jack and I swept through the Main Gate of the Air Station past the armed guards, slowly enough for them to take note of the seniority of the distinguished passenger but just fast enough for them to be unable to hear clearly my smiling response (in medieval Polish) to their challenge! Fortunately they did not shoot at us and we were able to drive, with pomp and ceremony all round the Air Station slapping our 'bomb' stickers on everything in sight. Nobody was around as everybody was busy catching spies trying to get in over the wire. We finished up in the Wardroom with all officers rising sharply to their feet when we entered!

There was, of course, a considerable celebration of our success but I was later carpeted by the Commanding Officer of the Station who told me that Junior Officers did not further their long term naval careers by mutilating Admirals' caps*. However Jack and I received a note of congratulation from our victim and a little parcel containing a broken comb which he had found in the greatcoat pocket.

Mutilating an Admiral's cap was in no way a bar to promotion. John Cooper was appointed CO of 882 Wildcat Squadron shortly afterwards!

In the early days of the war before the stations had become properly organised, victualling arrangements were haphazard. Despite the fact that Orkney produced the finest beef, Skeabrae initially flew in all its food supplies from Wick! H. E. Duthie of 801 Squadron recalls these trying times:

Other memories are, for days on end, living on a diet of tinned corned beef and swede! It seemed at the time that the station was totally reliant for food on an elderly DH86 supplying it from Wick. The pilot of this aircraft did marvels and arrived on days when even the seagulls were grounded. However there were long periods when the wind was in the 60s and 70s and cloud base between ten and twenty feet.

Then the supplies stopped coming! During these periods, a typical day's menu would read:

Breakfast - corned beef and swede fritters
Lunch - fried slices of corned beef with mashed swede
Dinner - corned beef stew with diced swede

The permutations showed a vivid imagination but always around the same two constituents. It was a number of years after Skeabrae before I could look a helping of swede in the face again.

Latterly, service men and service women were generally of the opinion that food on the Orkney stations could not be equalled. Beef production has, for many years been the main farming activity in Orkney and after these initial difficulties, Stations were victualled from local sources wherever possible. Astonishingly, in a county famous for its egg production, the cooks made much use of dried eggs—especially for other ranks.

In this respect Jack Holden writes amusingly of the Twatt galley:

Those who served in the Navy will remember that the Service was steeped in tradition—what Nelson did then must be done now and for evermore! At 12.30 mid-day every Saturday, Nelson must have eaten corned beef, so we had it! One dish that

Leading Wren Sonia Thorpe (née Morrison) and Wren Jessie Haldane in the Electrical Workshop, Twatt, 10 June 1944.
THORPE.

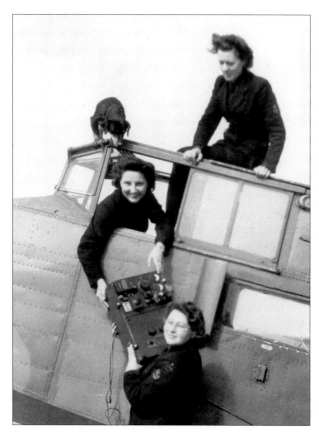

Ann Parker, Audrey Smith, Bulgie and George on Walrus; dogs such as George were frequently kept on RNAS and RAF Stations in Orkney. RNAS Hatston even had a Dog Show on one occasion! Twatt, March, 1944. PEMBERTON.

Paula West, 'Met' Wren, sending up balloon to test wind speed, Twatt, 14 April, 1944. PEMBERTON.

Nelson couldn't have had was reconstituted egg. I understand that dehydrated egg powder was manufactured in America and sent from America by well-meaning Yanks. Had the U-Boats concentrated on sinking egg ships instead of tankers and munitions, they would have earned the eternal gratitude of the Royal Navy. As it was, vast consignments of the stuff got here and, as far as I could make out, authority considered that, since the Navy had conveyed it here, the Navy could eat it. Egg powder, when it got into the hands of galley cooks, was lovingly mixed with last week's washing up water, then stirred and churned until it looked and tasted like sludge from the Nile estuary. 'Hands to breakfast' blared the Tannoy. Eager matelots rushed to the galley, up went the hatch. "What are we on?" asked the first arrivals. "Ersatz egg", cook would reply, always wearing a long suffering expression of "Don't blame me—I didn't lay the bloody eggs," when this dish was served. The effect on the queue was astounding. Ninety per cent promptly vanished back to the various huts where we all had a private stock of eggs, bacon and farmhouse cheese easily obtainable from the islanders. Those who had spent all their akkers on booze in the NAAFI and had no stock were out of luck—either they ate it or they went without. One stoney broke warrior in our mess, having breakfasted on ersatz egg, came and sat on my bunk. "You know Jack", he said, "if we put that

bloody stuff inside bloody bombs and dropped it on the bloody Germans, the bloody war would be over in a week." I must say that I was inclined to agree with him.

Real eggs were extremely rare in Britain during the war but were plentiful in Orkney. King George VI visited Orkney on 9th August 1941, and when he flew south he carried a box of eggs under his arm for the Queen! 'Egging' was a popular pastime among Station personnel. Norwegian Harald Meltzer paints a delightful picture of an evening at Skeabrae:

> . . . we slept two to a room with the exception of the Commanding Officer and the Flight Commander. It would be quite cosy for, with a good fire in the small stove, the room could become surprisingly warm. Then we would sit and smoke or read and talk with friends. Quite often, one of us had either a bottle of Aquavit or whisky, and another would have fresh farm eggs. So, with some sugar from the Mess and a bowl and whisk, we made eggedosis in the evening. What luxury among such desolation.

Eggs were purchased to take back home and eggs were even sent by post in special boxes! Chief P/O Pilot Eric Haslam of 771 Squadron at Twatt writes that the Station Commander allowed pilots the use of a 10 cwt. truck to go round the farms for eggs. But all kinds of transport were used. Skeabrae pilot Pierre Clostermann ranged far and wide looking for eggs:

> Jacques and I organised an egg round. Using the little Tiger Moth attached to the station, we raided the archipelago twice a week, landing near the farms and snaffling all the eggs. At the end of a fortnight of eggs for breakfast, lunch, tea *and* dinner, the very sight of an egg made our gorges rise. Ken even made out that feathers were growing down his back.

By 1945 a more sophisticated means of transport was used at Twatt—the Station helicopters—but Orkney farmers were not too keen on them landing in their back yard! True the slipstream from the rotors made a good job of sweeping up the farm courtyard but tended to sweep up the hens too and badly affected egg production! Another great delicacy savoured by the men and women on the stations was lobster which at that time could be purchased for 5/- (25p.) Twatt and Skeabrae men could, with a little skill and some local knowledge, catch their own lobsters off the rocks at Marwick. The Station Magister from Hatston did a regular shuttle service to the island of Stronsay for lobsters! Hank Rotherham describes an encounter with some Orkney fishermen:

> One of the few boat outings in which I took part happened when the crew of our small motor launch—an old private pleasure launch which bore the name of HMS *Sparrowhawk*—suggested that they take us out fishing, the crew being local fishermen in the Navy. So they prepared and then took us out along the coast, lining up leading marks. Then, when satisfied, they dropped the end of a long line with hundreds of baited hooks and buoyed the end. The line was laid out then, carefully following leading marks until the whole line was laid when they buoyed that end. Then we rushed back and pulled up the first end and on most hooks there was a haddock but, after a bit, dogfish also found the line and we started to get up whole fish, half fish and simply heads, backbones and tails! We were about to throw these useless bits over the side when our crew produced a box and insisted on this being filled. Why we wondered? But then, on the way home, we sighted a lobster boat and closed it and traded those bits of fish for lobsters. They were short of bait so we returned to the Station with plenty of fish for all and lobsters for a feast for ourselves and our friends. A beautiful day and, indeed it had been a lovely day. I should add that, by having a vessel in the water bearing the name of our Station, HMS *Sparrowhawk*, our men were qualified for ship's tobacco and their rum ration!

On the Air Stations men and women of all ranks rubbed shoulders with visiting dignitaries. King George VI visited Orkney five times; on one occasion there were three kings on warships in Scapa Flow. Apart from King George VI, King Håkon VII of

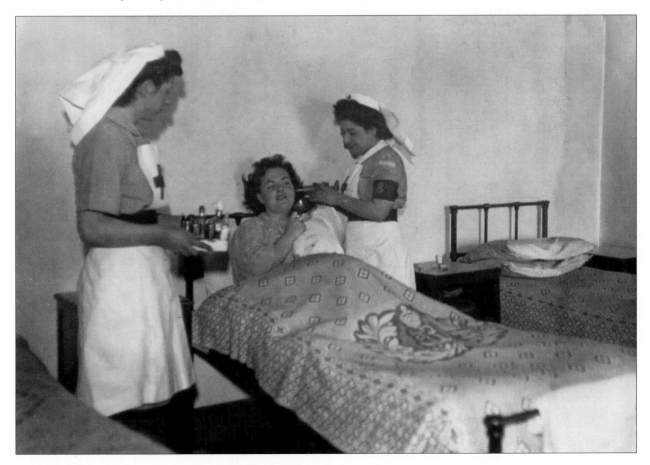

Sick Bay, Twatt, 10.06.45; Nurses Sheila Reed and May Stoddart attending Sylvia Winstanley. PEMBERTON.

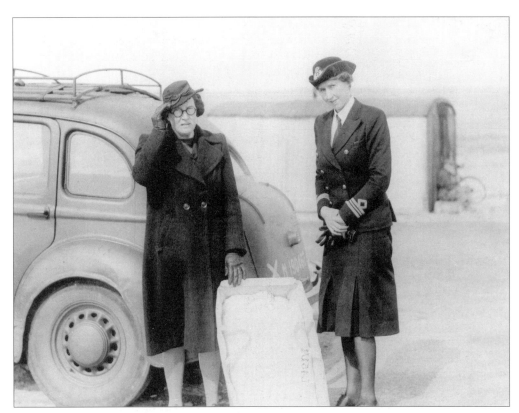

A Wren Petty Officer, one of two Wrens who gave birth to a child when on Station at HMS Tern, Twatt. She is seen here with Wren First Officer, Mary Foster-Barham and the new, very young member of the ship's company: Mary Foster-Barham later married Robert Barton, DFC, CO of Skeabrae who had served with No. 249 Sqdn. in the Battle of Britain and Malta; one of many marriages among service personnel in Orkney. HILL.

Nicolas Horne running the Skeabrae Music Club; all the records in the background have returned to Orkney and are now in possession of BBC Radio Orkney. HORNE.

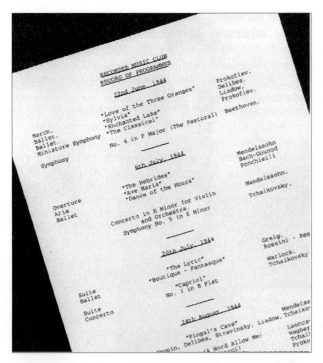

RECORDED MUSIC CLUB
RECORD OF PROGRAMMES

22nd June. 1944.

March.	"Love of the Three Oranges."	Prokofiev.
Ballet.	"Sylvia"	Delibes.
Ballet.	"Enchanted Lake"	Liadow.
Miniature Symphony	"The Classical"	Prokofiev.
Symphony	No. 6 in F Major (The Pastoral)	Beethoven.

6th July. 1944.

Overture	"The Hebrides"	Mendelssohn
Aria	"Ave Maria"	Bach-Gounod
Ballet	"Dance of the Hours"	Ponchielli
	Concerto in E Minor for Violin and Orchestra.	Mendelssohn.
	Symphony No. 5 in E Minor	Tchaikovsky.

20th July. 1944.

Suite	"The Lyric"	Greig.
Ballet	"Boutique - Fantasque"	Rossini - Res
	"Capriol"	Warlock.
Suite	No. 1 in B Flat	Tchaikovsky
Concerto		Mendelss

24th August. 1944.

"Fingal's Cave"	Mendelss
Delibes, Stravinsky, Liadow, Tchaiko	Leonca
(A Word Allow Me)	Wagner
(...)	Tchai
	Proko

Programme planned for Recorded Music Club, RAF Skeabrae, June-August 1944; it is interesting to see German music represented; the BBC played German music during the war but all German songs and operas had to be sung in English! HORNE.

Norway was there and King George II of the Hellenes. Other members of Royal families included HRH The Duke of Kent who came to Hatston and HRH Crown Prince Olaf of Norway and HRH Prince Bernhard of the Netherlands who spent some time at RAF Skeabrae. Churchill visited Orkney at least four times. Senior military figures moved shuttle-like between Orkney and London. Admirals and Generals were a common sight in the islands. Admiral Ramsay who planned the Naval side of the D-Day operations visited Hatston. General Montgomery also included Hatston in his exhausting morale boosting tour of Britain before D-Day when he was able to address more than one million men and women. He covered the British mainland by special train but, for the Orkney leg, he travelled in a Dakota of the United States Air Force. This was the only occasion that he addressed personnel on a Royal Naval Air Station. Other visiting Generals included Sir Alan Brooke and Sir Freddie Pile. Air Chief Marshal Sir W. Sholto Douglas was rather fond of Orkney and paid four visits to Skeabrae. At least four other Air Marshals visited this Station during the war. Foreign visitors included Admiral Kharlamoff, Deputy Chief of the Russian Naval Staff who inspected Skeabrae. Among civilian dignitaries were A. V. Alexander, First Lord of the Admiralty, who naturally had to make many calls on Orkney. Rev. Tubby Clayton, founder of the Toc H in Ypres during World War I lived near Skeabrae during World War II and was a frequent and warmly welcomed visitor there and at all other stations.

A secret visit was made to Hatston during the war by the American Ambassador to Britain who arrived from London. His mission was to meet Averell Harriman the US special envoy to the Soviet Union who, between 28th September and 4th October 1941, took part in the delicate negotiations at the Moscow Conference on the beginnings of the convoy system to the Soviet Union. Harriman flew from Murmansk to Hatston and found his arrival there more difficult than the Conference. Capt. Herbert St. John Fancourt, Commanding Officer at Hatston was there with the Ambassador when the aircraft, after its mammoth flight, appeared over Hatston:

I remember one incident of international importance at Hatston that nearly ended in disaster. The United States envoy to the Soviet Union, Mr. Harriman, returned by Catalina flying boat from Murmansk to report after a high-powered meeting with the Russians. It was a very long flight with Hatston the first stop. The American ambassador to Britain came up from London to meet Mr. Harriman. We stood on the slip at Hatston and watched the Catalina coming in to Kirkwall Bay. I think the pilot was dead beat for he made three or four extremely dangerous attempts to land, having to put his engines on again and roaring over our heads—almost between the hangars. We were not in W/T touch so could not tell him to land in the outer bay. However he did eventually land and all was well. The American ambassador said to me "I guess the President would not have been too happy if the best we could do was to ask him to send a wreath"!

By contrast many servicemen and women made close and lasting friendships with the local islanders. Norman Brown, Observer with 700 Squadron remembers how his free time was spent:

It was for me a great pleasure to get inside the Orkney farm houses and experience the genuine warmth of Orkney folk. Sometimes I walked over the hills to Housegarth in Sandwick for I became very friendly with the Linklaters. I can still see Maggie baking at the big table in what is now their sitting room. Jackie was just a boy then but even so he could play tunes on his little melodeon. I couldn't imagine at the time that our adopted holiday home was to be Appiehouse just down the road from them. I also became very friendly with the Spences at Norton. What a fine old man Willie Spence was. We visited him every time we returned to Orkney on holiday. Latterly he was in the Eastbank Hospital and after the usual delightful conversation I said that we would have to be on our way. "But we'll be back again next year and we'll come and see you", I hastily added. But Willie must have had some kind of premonition for he replied wryly, "Yi'll mibbe no ken me address next time though." He died shortly afterwards.

Arthur (Tiny) Small, a Radio Operator at Twatt recalls his associations:

We made some very good friends when my wife and I were stationed in Orkney, among them Miss Jean Matches and her sister and brother who lived at Gorn in Sandwick and we used to visit them regularly. I always looked forward so much to Sunday afternoon there. Miss Matches used to be able to find four leaf clovers so easily in one little patch of her field and in my little book I still have a four leaf clover that she gave me all these years ago for luck. We needed all the luck we could get at that time. We kept in touch with her for a number of years and it was quite a blow when someone wrote to say she had died for that was the end of our close contact with Orkney. I still have at least two letters she wrote to us. One telling us of an exceptional summer they had in 1946. She says that July and August had cloudless skies and eventually the water ran out. The cattle needed the drink as well as the humans. She told me that they had to go across to Twatt airfield which still had a supply from the Loch of Boardhouse. She says in her letter that there were queues of people and vehicles waiting to load up with water. After spending three years in Orkney I found it hard to believe that the islands could have a water shortage!

TAG Dick Stark of 771 Squadron did not, in the circumstances, expect to find the natives quite so friendly:

My lasting impression is of the friendliness of the local people in these troubled times. I got to know one family particularly well and that happened by chance. When a drogue was dropped from an aircraft we had strict instructions to release it over the airfield. Occasionally it didn't work out that way. I had to retrieve one of mine from Lower Linklater farm where I had been forced to ditch it. Expecting to be severely upbraided by the farmer for this unwarranted intrusion on his property we were astonished to find ourselves welcomed most warmly. Not only that—we were invited back over and over again. There was always something on the table there for us. We repaid their kindnesses by helping them sometimes with their farmwork. One Christmas I went down there with two of my shipmates and helped them pluck all their turkeys. On 5th March 1943 I was very seriously ill in Kirkwall hospital after our Boulton Paul Defiant crashed into the Bay of Firth. The pilot was killed. My parents were flown up from Nottingham to be at my bedside. My Orcadian friends didn't forget me. Do you know these folks were so kind that, when they heard that I had had a bad accident and that I couldn't eat solid food, they sent some chickens into the hospital so that the staff could make soup for me! And when we went home on leave we always carried a box of eggs. They were worth their weight in gold!

Jack Holden describes the Orkney table:

One day, after working in the fields, we went in to tea. An Orkney table in war-time had to be seen to be believed. It groaned under the weight of goodies. Mounds of farm butter, cheese, eggs, bannocks,

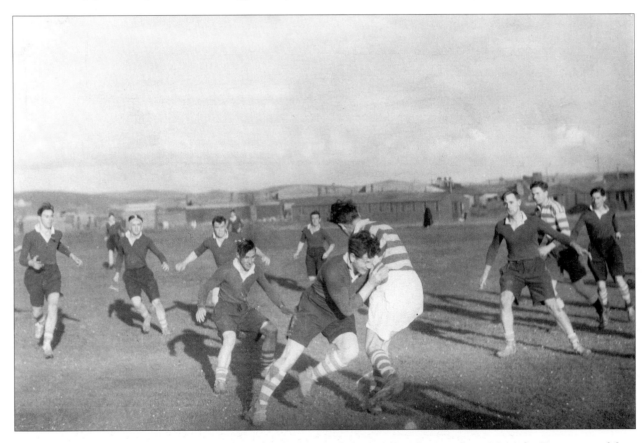

Rugby at Twatt, 1944; RNAS Twatt in hooped jerseys v. RNAS Grimsetter; the score was 36 - 3 for Twatt, two of the tries for Twatt being scored by Trevor Dole. REMMINGTON.

sowan scones, pancakes and that item of Orkney fare that I could never manage—oatcakes. The ingredients (if anyone is interested) are: two parts shore grit, one part cement and a spoonful of latex to bind the lot together. On the table that day were two items that I had never seen before—seagulls' eggs and boiled limpets. I viewed these two gustatory delights with suspicion but my friends were tucking in happily. Oh well—when in Rome. I tucked in also. Over the centuries Orcadian stomachs must have become inured to the devastating effects of gulls' eggs and limpets. Mine wasn't. Half an hour later I nearly died on the farm midden heap. When in Rome it is not always wise to do as the Romans do.

Airmen and women of all ranks based at Skeabrae and Twatt vividly remember the delight of visiting Janet Cooper who kept a small tearoom at The Palace in Birsay. Tea here was often the culmination of a long coastal walk. It was a favourite meeting place for the service personnel of both sexes, fraternisation within the camp perimeter being severely frowned upon. Many a match was made in these surroundings. Lt. Keith Remmington writes:

> . . . we would walk to Birsay and have tea provided by two charming ladies in a private house. I can still recall seeing the cake-stands piled high with lovely scones, baps, cakes etc. and we were encouraged to eat as much as we could. Also included in the price was a boiled egg for a total cost of 1/3 or 1/6 if the tea included two boiled eggs. We really both enjoyed these visits and considering the distance to walk, the teas must have been very good indeed.

For all serviceman and women there came a time to head south again, 'going down the line' as it was

Capt. H. St. J. Fancourt, CO, RNAS Hatston with rather a cold looking Gracie Fields at Hatston, 1941. WYLES.

ENSA Show visits Hatston; comedian Leslie Henson in centre (short and balding with glasses); tall officer behind him is Shea Simmonds, Hatston test pilot who was in charge of recreation at that time. HEWLETT.

popularly known. It would only be fair to say that, for many this was their happiest day! Whether going on leave or to another posting, some were lucky enough to be able to fly south either with the Air Ferry based on Jersey Airlines or with Scottish Airways. Royal Marine pilot Richard Partridge was amused by the experience of flying to Inverness in a de Havilland Dominie:

> These Dominie trips always used to amuse me because, if the pilot had a full load of passengers, about seven or eight I think, he used to taxi out to the end of the duty runway, and when in position for take-off, he would turn around and casually ask the rear four passengers to come forward and kneel in the passageway just behind him so that it would be easier for him to get the aircraft tail up when taking off. Of course, as soon as airborne, the four passengers returned to their seats.

There was great rivalry between Air Ferry and Scottish Airways. Air Ferry crews wore naval uniform and prided themselves in being able to fly in such diabolical weather conditions that no military aircraft would dare take off. Commander Hank

SKOGAR WARDROOM. R.N.A.S. TWATT.

BOXING DAY 1944.

297 BEERS.

42 RUMS.

3 DEPTH CHARGES.

3 JUGS MILK.

This is to certify that the above was consumed by the following gentlemen On the occasion of the induction of Nobby Clark as An Honorary Member of the R.A.F.

Guvnor Reed   Nobby Clark   Graham Peacock
Grandpop Rudhall   Tom Bennett   Kipper Herrington
Johnny Treloar   Curly Hares   Ian Houghton
Ken Souter   Pete Cornish   Johnny Ream

[Cabaret is included in the above.]

Jive by Juke Box Kemington and his phonograph.

Man is not drunk who from the floor
doth rise and ask for more,
But drunk is he who helpless lies
without the strength to ever rise.

Boxing Day 1944; copy of certificates of liquid consumed on this day; presented to certain gentlemen at Twatt on the occasion of the induction of Lt. Nobby Clark, RNVR, as an Honorary Member of the RAF! Handwork by Wren Rachel Murray-Bisset, a student of Duncan of Jordanstone School of Art, Dundee; REMMINGTON.

Rotherham, Executive officer at Hatston recalls witnessing this:

> I saw a Rapide taxi out to the runway with four men holding the wingtips in 50 knot winds. With the aircraft lined up into wind, the pilot would signal to let go and the aircraft would take off, going virtually straight up.

Crossing the Pentland Firth by ferry and the long train journey to the south of England was a fearsome prospect for all service personnel. Many describe how horribly sick they were on the Pentland Firth with its strong winds and sweeping tides. Despite their fears there was only one recorded tragedy in the war years when an Air Fitter, George Marley, leaned against a gate which had not been properly closed and fell into the sea. A prolonged and, sadly, fruitless search ensued. Lt.Cdr. Molyneux, CO of 771 Squadron hated the journey so much that, when going on leave he used to borrow 771 Squadron Maryland bomber to fly to his home in Sussex. He conveniently parked it at a nearby RAF Station where he had a very good Polish friend! For the lower ranks, no such luxury. Eleanor Robertson, a WAAF stationed at Grimsetter gives an account of a typical departure. Everyone was deliriously happy— at least for some time:

> I won't forget leaving Orkney. It was so rough the boat didn't sail so we had to return to the camp and left the following day. Not being much of a sailor I found a bunk before the boat sailed but a lot of the girls went up on deck for a great sing-song. But there was still a tremendous swell on the sea and it wasn't long before they all joined me down below and were being as sick as I was.

Two servicemen going on leave from Hatston were fortunate to get a lift from an aircraft flying from Hatston to Inverness. To their surprise they were then whisked down through Scotland at an alarming rate. Trains were diverted to help them in their progress and staff cars eagerly awaited their arrival at every stop. They could not believe their good fortune. It was only much later that they were told they had been mistaken for two messengers carrying secret codes from an operation off Norway. The messengers had failed to catch the Orkney aircraft and it had not been possible in the time available to change all the specially made transport arrangements!

Sometimes others from the lower deck succeeded in getting air transport home but for some it ended in tragedy. Sam Sephton was a rating at Twatt and was going home on leave:

> In the autumn of 1944 twenty-two of us going on leave had a chance of a flight to Doncaster in a Handley Page Harrow troop carrier or store carrier which was returning empty. All went well on take off; the flight was bumpy and uncomfortable for

there were no seats but we settled down. Some slept, others chatted. Suddenly and with no warning, there was a hellish explosion. I must have blacked out and came to, thinking I had been dreaming for I was lying on a piece of rough moorland. Then I realised that some of my shipmates were lying round me all looking rather dazed, some bleeding from facial injuries, others moaning. There was a smell of engine oil in the air and I looked up in disbelief to see our plane a total mass of twisted green metal lying about twenty yards away. The plane had hit a hill top. I was lucky; I had only a small cut over my left eye. One of my cabin mates, Rating Fred Burton, was dead but most of my shipmates and the crew were very lucky too; they were all scattered round the hillside and only a few had broken legs and arms. It seemed incredible that all but one of us survived the impact.

But life on the stations could be hazardous too. Cora de Looze, a NAAFI girl at Hatston had a narrow escape when she failed to notice Control Tower signal and drove her van across the duty runway in the path of an incoming fighter. She was severely upbraided by the Commanding Officer. In a similar incident at Twatt, a truck-load of ratings went straight across the runway when a Boston bomber was taking off. Rating Lewis who was the only one to witness the perilous situation, shouted to his cabin-mates and threw himself off the vehicle. The pilot of the Boston did a quick wheels up, cleared the truck and, fortunately, his aircraft did not stall. Tragically, Lewis, who had alerted his cabin mates, was killed in his heavy fall on the tarmac.

On VE Day there were only three full squadrons left in the whole of Orkney. All ranks, including WAAFs had a free pint of beer with their lunch at Skeabrae, the afternoon was free and everyone listened with interest to Churchill's speech which was relayed over the Tannoy. A dance for all ranks was held in the evening. At Twatt, all flying was cancelled and the ship's company assembled in *The Orcadia* cinema for an address by the Commanding Officer, Commander E. S. Jackson. The Fleet Air Arm magazine *Flight Deck* records that:

> . . . after that the fun began in earnest. The canteens were well patronised and the Chiefs and Petty Officers went up to the Wardroom for a noggin. After lunch, those still on their feet indulged in two soccer matches, England v. Scotland and Wales v. Ireland and also Married v. Unmarried. The results aren't recorded; the official chronicler was one who took his celebrations seriously.

Although flying was cancelled, official station duties still had to be carried out however inefficiently but the top brass humanely turned a blind eye. Twatt Wren Beryl Turner writes:

> I was in the Control Tower as a teleprinter operator along with a sailor named Walter and a Chief Petty Officer who mysteriously disappeared shortly after we came on duty. Feeling sorry for the two of us who were left, friends brought in lots of food and drink of which Walter partook freely. Unfortunately the Captain arrived at midnight. I was quite sober and said "Good evening, sir." My duty colleague, Walter, stood to attention wavering and the Captain asked him, "Where is the Chief Petty Officer?" "Gone to see the Captain, sir", was the reply, whereupon he slumped at the Captain's feet. The Captain looked down at him, looked at me, uttered a mild, "Carry on!" and disappeared. With the wisdom of hindsight he probably meant, "What a carry on"!

The Ship's Log for Hatston and Grimsetter have not survived. The last entry in the Operations Book of Skeabrae is 29th June so we have no means of telling how VJ Day was spent at Skeabrae. At Twatt, NAAFI girl Catherine Mair records:

> That night everything that could burn was taken up Yonbell, the nearest hill, to make a bonfire. I was coerced into taking the van up as far as I could with refreshments. It was quite a night! After that, the camp wound down until there were only 500 men left, then the NAAFI had to go too. I seem to remember we hung on waiting for the last plane to leave. There was some drama - for the last plane to leave Twatt had engine trouble and when it did go it only just made it to the other side of the Pentland Firth.

By early 1946 all the war-time postings to Orkney had left. Jack Holden has the last word:

> In January 1946 came the news that we were to go to Eastleigh, Southampton, pending demob. I went to the farm for what I thought would be the last time. To say goodbye to this family that I had come to love so much was a heartbreaking business. I am a very emotional man and easily moved to tears. When the final moment came, I could not speak. I hope I never have to go through that again. I walked back to the camp. When I reached the top of the hill, I turned and looked back at the silhouette of the farm, clearly visible against the backcloth of the sea. That farm had been my home for three years and emotion crowded upon emotion. I turned away and walked silently back to camp. The world had gone flat and empty. Next day the boat sailed. I stayed down in the hold; I did not want to see Orkney fade into the distance as I wanted no repetition of that sad, sad yesterday.

When the visitor looks at the Orkney landscape today there may be scant reminders of the effect that the war had on the islands but a closer look will show that many of the houses have a uniform shape determined by the design of the war-time servicemen and servicewomen's huts around which they were built! There were thousands of these wooden huts scattered round the islands. Some were in poor shape at the end of the war, were of little value and could

Lt. Duncan Hamilton in Irvin jacket on the beach at Hatston with Lt. Shea Simmonds, dog 'Lucky' and the workshop Jeep. HAMILTON.

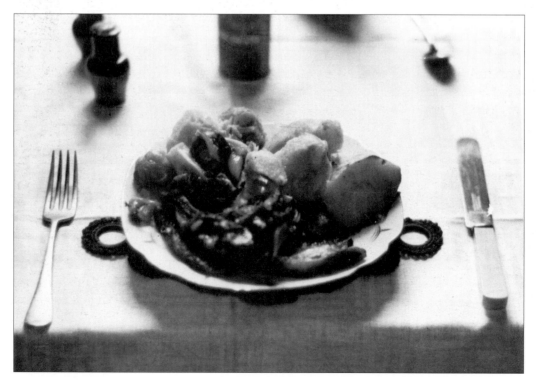

Lunch at RAF Skeabrae; when the Station finally got underway there were few complaints about the high standard of food for the main meals. HORNE.

John Cooper, CO, 882 Sqdn., Hatston; notice the graffiti on the Mae West; in some instances such art work could be rather risqué! COOPER.

In the dining hall, Skeabrae, Christmas, 1943; Flight Officer Skerman is at the end of the table with the box; others in the photograph are Baker CO, Cpl. Ashton, Cpl. Gonnery, Peggy Borrer, May Burus, Jean Forsyth, Marion Hunter, Cpl. Edwards, Vera ?Hohnran, Pauline Castle, Rae Ada Royal, Gladys Perry, Kay Hall, Dorothy Nicoll, Dowie. HORNE.

What are the Twatt Wrens cooking up in the galley? HILL.

King George VI inspects Hatston personnel. FAA.

Field-Marshall Montgomery on a morale boosting visit to Orkney takes the salute at Hatston, after arriving in an American C-47 (Dakota), May 1944; on the extreme right of the party is Capt. Geoffrey Gowlland, Commanding Officer, Hatston; an inscription on the back of this photograph, obviously written by RN staff reads 'What a dreadful salute but what can you expect from a pongo?!' CONDOR.

Admiral Ramsay, who later commanded the naval forces in the Normandy Landings, in a Walrus of 700 Sqdn; he was killed in a plane crash on 2nd January 1945 on his way to meet Field Marshal Montogomery in Brussels. HAMILTON.

Beechcraft Expeditor HD760 arrives at Twatt with unidentified dignitary, possibly Brendan Bracken, First Lord of the Admiralty; late 1944, early 1945. HILL.

Geological expedition in Orkney; on left, Rev. 'Tubby' Clayton, founder of Toc H movement; on right Lt. Donald Hewlett, Hatston; centre possibly a minister? HEWLETT.

Tait of Dounby jack up a hut, ready for transport by road to another site as a new home! Left to right: Alfie Tait, James Kirkness, ??, Freddie Tait, Billy Merriman.

be bought for a few pounds. One enterprising Orcadian who decided to earn some additional income bought such a hut and spent his winter evenings chopping it up into firewood for sale. However when there were complaints that his sticks would not burn he did some investigation only to find to his great dismay that the hut he had bought had been fireproofed! Many of the huts on the other hand were made from finest Oregon pine and commanded a good price. With the return of servicemen at the end of the war and the great housing shortage, the huts were bought, dismantled into sections and transported to a new building site. Even the plasterboard was removed and recycled. As a young boy I remember one of my bedroom walls had a fine painting of a Hurricane bursting through the clouds in an impressive power-dive! A local contractor, Alfie Tait of Dounby, was able to dispense with hut dismantling completely and move them on a low loader to a new site.

Living in such huts which were not designed for northern latitudes, Orkney families in the beginning had to put up with the same privations experienced by the servicemen and servicewomen. Winds howled through the weatherboarding and for those who had bought War Department linoleum to cover the wooden floors, they found too that in a strong gale the underfloor draught would make the linoleum 'hover' and create a peculiar sensation when walking! Those who had bought huts with bombproof glass with a wire mesh embedded in it could not even perform that much loved Orkney activity—looking out of the window! There were compensations for this nevertheless. Cheap, high-powered, military binoculars became readily available and when one such pair was brought into the Antiques Road Show in Orkney in recent years, the interviewer asked, 'Does everyone in Orkney have such binoculars?' 'Oh yaas,' came the reply, 'fur we spy on each ither'!

The inadequacy of such homes for permanent living became all too clear in the severe winter of 1947 when, with no insulation, the occupants found that overcoats had to be worn sitting round a blazing fire; the best place was in bed with, at their feet, several hot bricks (salvaged from a camp)! In the morning when they reluctantly arose they found their false teeth frozen in the jam jar! More insulation was needed. For this reason many of these huts were encased in concrete blocks and roofed over with asbestos sheeting—and so some of them remain today. In most cases the old wooden hut has been stripped out, the interior rebuilt with proper insulation and a new roof added. In some cases a second storey has been built but always the shape has been determined by the foundation size of the old war-time hut!

It would be perhaps true to say that in Orkney more than in any other part of Britain there was enormous rapport between the service personnel and the local people. What made this possible was the relentless pursuit of eggs! An initial tentative knock on the farmhouse door often led to return visits and the inevitable invitation to join the family. At the tender age of eight and towards the end of the war, I cycled to Breckan in Dounby with my mother to see Davina and Jimmy Miller, old friends and neighbours when we had lived at Guithe. We had not been there very long until the door opened and in walked a stranger. He wore an Air Force great-coat,

Moorside, Stenness, where the author spent his early childhood, originally an army hut, but later enclosed in concrete blocks to give extra warmth.

Moorside as it is today shows little sign of its humble origin.

spoke in a strange accent and said that he had come to see if Davina had any eggs. Some banter was exchanged between him and his hostess for some time as he stood with his back to the open peat fire. After a while Davina said, 'Mercy, tak aff thee coat an sit doon,' an invitation which he found so amusing that he repeated it several times during the course of the afternoon and in this way the phrase and the memory of the visit became imprinted on my young mind. My mother told me later that the visitor was an Australian airman and with the help of records I now know that he must have been attached to No. 451 Squadron stationed at Skeabrae in May and June of 1945 and I would have been eight years old.

When elderly Orcadians of a winter evening sit and tell stories as they have been accustomed to do since the saga days, they recall some of the amusing incidents of the war years. There was for instance a tug of war between a farmer and some children for possession of a drogue which had fallen from a Royal Naval Target Towing aircraft near Oxtro School in Birsay. The children on their way home from school had spotted the drogue fall into a field and had rushed to get it and collect the £3 reward. The farmer on whose land it fell had other ideas and wanted the reward himself. When other children seeing what was going on rushed to their friends aid, the combined forces were too much for the farmer who, with many unprintable oaths, conceded defeat!.

An elderly gentleman from Deerness who was rather deaf had the habit of driving his old bull-nose Morris slowly in the middle of the road. He had just passed the gate of Grimsetter RAF Station on his way to Kirkwall when a senior RAF officer in a staff car pulled out of the gateway at high speed heading in the same direction. Soon he attempted to overtake the car ahead, but try as he might, with much horn blowing, he could not get past. When Mr. Laughton's car finally came to a halt in a Kirkwall street and he emerged, an angry officer jumped out, red-faced, and accosted him, 'Don't you know there is a bloody war on and I'm in a hurry—I have followed you for two miles and I couldn't get past you.' Mr. Laughton listened to the tirade and took the pipe out of his mouth.

'Weel,' he said, 'yi'll just hiv tae get a faster car.'

Centre: Janet Cooper's tearoom at the Palace, Birsay, a favourite haunt of servicemen and women during the war . . .
'and when the occasion allowed, not to mention the weather, we would walk to Birsay and have tea provided by two
charming ladies in a private house. I can still recall seeing the cake-stands piled high with lovely scones, baps, cakes
etc., and we were encouraged to eat as much as we could. Also included in the price was a boiled egg for the total cost
of 1/3 or 1/6 if the tea included two boiled eggs'. (Lt. Keith Remmington, RNVR, 771 Sqdn. Pilot, Twatt). MARWICK.

Many of the tales relate to dialect misunderstandings. The Londoner who asked for soda was surprised to see a stick of solder placed on the counter for him. The pronunciation of 'solder' in Orkney dialect is very similar to Cockney 'soda'! When a smart RAF officer with immaculately trimmed red moustache enquired in pukka tones in a Stromness shop whether he might have two torch batteries, he was rather nonplussed by the shopkeeper's query, 'Whit size is thee plicko?' Orcadians always called a torch by this strange name!

When, in the early stages of the development of RNAS Hatston, one of the Executive Branch of RNAS Hatston enquired about the location of the nearest dump, he was instructed by the Local Council that all waste should be transported to the Peedie Sea (a small sea loch to the west of Kirkwall, dialect 'peedie' meaning 'small'). Such an instruction went down the chain of command until finally the ratings assigned to the task of waste disposal, and by now accustomed to living in a world of abbreviations, enquired innocently on what part of the station they could find the P.D.C.!

We made a light hearted reference earlier to the Orcadian's fondness for looking out of the window.

Could this have its origin in the war years when Orcadians were asked to keep a close look out for spies? Perhaps this knowledge helps us to understand why, when Spitfire pilot Ian Blair crash landed in Stronsay on 20th February 1943 after a successful dual with a Messerschmitt and knocked on the door of the farm of The Hill in Stronsay with blood pouring from his nose, Miss Reid challenged him with the words, 'You're a spy!' Poor Ian had to show her the roundels on his plane before she believed him!

There are a hundred and seven references to the wind in this book which demonstrates that, to the southerner, the strength of the wind and its effects is one of the most enduring memories of life in Orkney. As was said elsewhere, three quarters of a million tons of coal were burned in Royal Naval establishments in Orkney between the years 1940 and 1945! There is no record of coal consumption in RAF and Army camps but it would be safe to say that the figure quoted could easily be multiplied by a factor of two. Such high coal consumption meant that chimneys had to be swept frequently. At Hatston a civilian was called in to sweep a poor venting chimney. It was a windy day when he arrived. He sealed off the fireplace, climbed to the roof-top and, as was the custom at that time placed in the flue a large metal ball which he began to haul up and down. However the ball had been inadvertently placed in the chimney of the top secret Cypher Room the fireplace of which had not been sealed. Suddenly the occupants found themselves, their equipment and papers engulfed in clouds of soot. A black faced Wren ran out and shouted at the top of her voice to the sweep but the wind was blowing so strongly he could not hear her and carried on until he had done a thorough job. The outcome is not known!

During the war years when Orkney still had a simple farming economy it was quite common to tether the milking cow near the farmhouse. A serviceman newly arrived in the islands was writing home as a fierce storm raged outside. Looking out through the cabin window he saw such an animal for the first time. He wrote:

'Mother, you can't imagine how strong the wind blows up here. My hut is tied down in case it blows away. There's a farm next door and looking out through the window I can see that the farmers even tie down their cows.'

Memories sometimes go back to the 1st World War. The reader will know perhaps that one of the most tragic events of that war occurred in 1916 when HMS *Hampshire* struck a mine off Orkney. Field-Marshal Lord Kitchener and all the many advisers who were accompanying him on his mission to Russia were lost. A headline in one of the national dailies declared, 'Kitchener and his staff lost out of Scapa Flow'. An elderly gentleman reading the headline remarked that he could understand the concern about the loss of such a great man but why was such a fuss being made about his walking stick!

No doubt some of these tales were fireside creations but the following story again from World War I relates to a believable misunderstanding. Two naval officers were walking out to Scapa Pier and happened to pass a farmer repairing a broken down wall. By way of conversation one of them remarked to the farmer, 'I hope none of our chaps is responsible for that!' 'Oh no!' the farmer replied cheerily, 'it's the kye (i.e. cattle), sir.' As they walked on he was amused to hear one say to the other, 'How the hell could that wall have been knocked down by the Kaiser?'

Many of the friendships formed between service personnel and Orcadians during the war still continue even though now it is often with the second generation. Jean Williams from Nottingham was a WAAF stationed at Kirkwall Fighter Control Centre and she wrote to say the WAAFs' tour of duty was for nine months but she didn't know of any WAAF in 'Ops' who did not volunteer for a second tour, despite the fact that about 95% of the 'Ops' WAAFs came from the south of England! Is it little wonder then that so many have returned time and time again, some to settle happily in the islands in their retirement years.

Sadly, for many young men, Orkney was not their chosen resting place but 'fur them thit wir ta'en,' as old folk in the islands would say, may this book perpetuate their memory.

Lt.Comm. Molyneux, CO, 771 Sqdn., Twatt. MOLYNEUX.

Advertisement in the Hatston Chronicle, the Air Station's newspaper, encouraging servicemen and women to fly to and from the islands. HALHEAD.

Hatston remembers its association with the Fleet Air Arm.
Above: A memorial erected by the Royal British Legion, Kirkwall to those who lost their lives
Below: Roads on Hatston Industrial Estate recall the name of the station, HMS Sparrowhawk, and the names of Fleet Air Arm aircraft.

Chapter Seven

Epilogue: the Return

The war is over and the Churchill Barriers are formally opened to civilian traffic. BALFOUR BEATTY.

The WAAF

Route forms are notoriously erratic documents, taking liberties with time and space but even the hardened R.T.O. was surprised when he saw mine.

"Glasgow to Birmingham via Kirkwall, Orkney. Lumme! Are you ENSA?", he asked. I explained that I was a WAAF in the process of being demobbed and that anyway I'd like to see Orkney again, and why quibble at a few hundred miles at the expense of the Air Force?

"Just as you like; don't forget the eggs," he shouted after me.

I had left Orkney shortly after VE Day when it was still a garrison. Army camps and aerodromes ringed the islands and Scapa Flow was busy with the movements of the Fleet to the Pacific. As soon as the Dominie in which, surprisingly, I was the only passenger, flew low over the Mainland I noticed changes. The Flow was empty. Not even the drifters which, for six years, had run a shuttle service between the Fleet and Kirkwall, steamed across the water. The islands from the plane, a relief map in brown and green, looked deserted. There was little traffic on the roads and the causeways which landlocked the Flow stretched white and empty from island to island.

Arrived in Orkney I had nothing to do but wait for permission to go to Birmingham so I spent my time in nostalgic excursions. Like most sentimental journeys, they were not a success. The island seemed covered with deserted camps. Nissen huts are never decorative but, cleaned and inhabited they have a homely quality. Decaying in an isolation of peat and heather, they presented a scene of dereliction. One Ack-Ack site, famed for its hot punch on cold dance nights, had been converted into a ramshackle smallholding. A black cow peered from the sergeant's mess and hens roosted on the cookhouse shelves.

In Orkney the weather knows no happy mean. There are calm days when sea and sky are luminous with a blue rarely seen outside albums of Swiss views. There are other days when the wind reaches speeds of 60 mph, sea mists swirl over the hills and it rains horizontally. I chose one of those gusty days to visit Stenness, an inland loch famous for the size of its trout. I had visualised myself rowing on the calm water, recapturing the essence of summer days. Instead, cold and bedraggled, I stood in the doorway of the inevitable Nissen hut. A courteous voice interrupted my reverie.

"You would like a lift into Kirkwall?"

An army truck, crowded with soldiers had stopped. I climbed up thankfully and was settled snugly on to a pile of sacks, a greatcoat with a Polish flash round my shoulders. Poles were an innovation. "How do you like Orkney?", I asked. There was babel.

"Siberia. It could be no worse."

" Why are we here? We do nothing. Here we sit and the wind—it blows—and the rain . . ."

"The Government. It does not know what to do with us. We are—how you say—on the shelf."

I tried to cheer them by describing the luxuriance of the Orkney summer when primroses, wild lupins and spotted orchids all bloom together and night becomes a short twilight. But, looking out on the waste of mist and heather, they were not impressed.

"Anyway, flowers do not help when you are somebody's mistake."

This was something that had changed. During the war, however much we might grumble at the wind and the isolation, the ships safely riding at anchor in Scapa Flow, gave us some sense of purpose. These Poles had nothing but the feeling that they were an embarrassment sent 'out of sight, out of mind'+.

That evening, an egg-box under each arm, I walked out to visit my friends who lived in a croft built only a few yards above the high-tide mark. Mrs. I. was gathering in the hens who had been picking along the beach all day. She greeted me very calmly.

"So you have come back. We're glad to have you. Come inside. I'll boil you an egg."

While I ate the egg, flanked by scone spread with Orkney butter and Orkney cheese, she told me the news of the farm. They had a new make of incubator and another cow, an Ayrshire this time. Their eldest son had come back from the Navy so they were beginning to reclaim some of the moor. A few days ago, two young seals had been washed almost to their door. About two feet long, with white fur. Yes, they had been put back. Her daughters returned from work sparkling with their five mile ride.

"There's a dance on at the Hall* tonight, you'd better come," they told me.

The Hall, a grey stone house of many sharply angled wings was approached through the farmyard but leading to a blank wall at the back was a parody of an avenue of stunted pine and fir. Across the cobbled court was a walled graveyard whose grey tombs were lit by two hurricane lamps hanging above the barn door. We climbed up the wooden staircase and watched a dance that might have been described by Hardy. Two fiddlers, one of them most patriarchally whiskered, swayed on a platform at the end of the barn which was intermittently lit by oil lamps set in sconces set in the wall. The dancers moved in and out of the shadows to the wail of a Highland Schottische. The dance ended—and there were the men, navy suited and solemn, sitting with their hands on their knees, while opposite, in a long row, sat the girls. The fiddlers, joined this time by an elderly woman pianist, struck up 'Two Little Girls in Blue'. There was momentary confusion as the line of men, almost without breaking, slid across the room. Then everybody was turning rhythmically in an old-fashioned waltz.

On my way to Birmingham I remembered that dance. I need not have worried because Orkney was changing. She had scarcely done that in a hundred years. She was simply sloughing her alien war-time skin.

* the Hall of Tankerness

+after the war a detachment of the 25th Infantry Battalion, Polish Army, was based temporarily at the large Hillside Camp near Quindry in South Ronaldsay.

(from The Times, May 1946; signed I.M.; the writer, Inga Marchant, contacted the author after the publication of the 1st Edition. G.L.)

My wife and I came back to visit Orkney forty years after I had left. It looked such a different place. Everywhere looked prosperous, so much of the land had been cultivated, even Yonbell, the hill behind Twatt, was covered in lush grass. We took the car on to one of the runways and I went over to two farmers near the old squash courts and asked if we could walk around.

"Yes", came the reply, "we only graze the land but you can go where you want."

"And can we walk up Yonbell?"

"Why do you want to go up there?" they asked.

"Well I used to work up there at the DF Hut during the war."

"You used to work up there?", one of them remarked in astonishment, "there were only three men ever allowed up there during the war; I was only a boy at the time but I can still remember the name of one of them—Tiny Small he was called."

I couldn't believe my ears! Imagine that 100,000 servicemen and women passed through Orkney during the war and I return after 40 years to find that somebody remembers me! You can't imagine the feelings it brought back. I found out that the man I was talking to was Tom Johnston of Bryameadow. I couldn't honestly say that I remembered Tom but he told me that when he was about eleven or so I would pat him on the head and ask him to help me carry some batteries up the hill! We spent a lovely evening with Tom and his wife and we swopped a lot of yarns. He could remember men that I couldn't!

I told Tom how I could remember the two little ponies that always seemed to stand in the same corner of a field whatever the weather. They often had thick sleet and snow on their backs in winter. This field lay on the route to the DF Hut and, as you can imagine, after three years, these ponies really got to know us and we always had found time to talk to them. In the end we really believed that they could understand what we said to them and I think we also believed that we could understand all their little whinnies and gestures!

Before we left the old airfield I was determined to visit the Control Tower which, at that time, was under sentence of death. I was determined to force my way in through the piles of muck. It was all pitch black; there were strange noises inside, birds beating a hasty retreat and angry at my entrance but as I told them 'I was here before you!' It was upsetting to see the building in such a state. Of course as a PCB it wasn't just a Control Tower, it was a communications centre and it had all sorts of office staff inside—met. office and staff, little telephone and exchange. I looked into all the rooms but didn't go up the ladder from the WT office to the Control Tower—it looked a bit dangerous but the structure looked quite sound and I thought 'What a shame to destroy it'. I felt very happy when I learned later that it was to be saved.

Arthur (Tiny) Small,
1985

Summer 1990: Lynx MK.3 (CTS) of 700L Squadron, Portland, pays a nostalgic visit to Twatt Airfield, the proving ground of the Royal Navy's first operational helicopters and where the original 700 Squadron disbanded in March 1944. JOHNSTON.

Postscript: the author tells of a series of remarkable coincidences

I want to begin at the farm of Binscarth near Finstown in Orkney. On the morning of 4th June 1943, there was some excitement at the breakfast table. During the night mother had been awakened by an unusual sound, not like an explosion. She got up and looked out; it was 3 a.m., faint summer light, but there was nothing to be seen—a thick North Sea fog 'tae the door' as they say in Orkney. Just before breakfast my brother David had come in from the farm to say that a plane had crashed near Stymilders. Of course we all wanted to rush up and see it before we went to school but mother soon dispelled that idea.

'You wouldn't be allowed anywhere near it, there will be guards there and you will get shot if you go near it', so that ended that!

We had just arrived home from school when we saw the familiar dark blue RN truck drive slowly past our garden gate. On the low loader behind it were the remains of a crashed aircraft. We dashed inside and asked if we could now go and see where it had crashed. Permission was granted and we set off. I was amazed to find that they had cut Hobbister's fencing wire to get to the plane! There was nothing to be seen apart from a few bits of twisted green metal and tyre marks where a crane had been working. We went home disappointed.

Forty years later I was doing an archaeology project with some local children. Now archaeology is all about digging and it is rather a frustrating project to undertake with children because digging is forbidden on scheduled sites. We had previously dug up an old farm kitchen midden and classified everything we had unearthed. What could we do on this occasion? I remembered reading a book on a new amateur activity popular in the south of England—aircraft archaeology. Extraordinary finds had been made in the marshlands of East Anglia. 'Why don't we dig up a bit of that aircraft that crashed when I was a boy?' I thought to myself. I spoke to John Kemp of Hobbister who was very willing for us to search his land. A pupil brought along a metal detector and we hadn't scanned the peaty moor for very long until we got the tell-tale signal of metal underneath. Then the excitement of digging started. Imagine the glow in the children's eyes when up came a piece of aircraft frame. This was real archaeology!

Now the questions started. What type of plane was it? Who was the pilot? Why did it crash? All I could say at the time was what I had heard when I was little. The pilot was a New Zealander; it was one of three aircraft which had taken off from a carrier in Scapa Flow. There had been a spy on board and he had made the aircraft crash. It was a good story but

what were the facts I wondered? To answer this question we wrote to the Admiralty. I received the reply that regrettably many of the Fleet Air Arm records were destroyed after the war and it would never be possible to answer such questions so the children had to be content with my version.

I was a member of the Birsay Community Council in Orkney for a number of years and at one of their meetings in 1987 a well known local farmer told the Committee that the very next day an army demolition squad was going to blow up the Control Tower of Twatt Royal Naval Air Station. He felt that this should not go ahead since it was now of considerable historical interest. The committee agreed that there should be a stay of execution and the Chairman asked for a volunteer to approach Orkney Islands Council. Since I was on holiday I volunteered and the next day I approached the Chief Executive directly. He gave me a sympathetic hearing and the Tower was saved. The Community Council expressed their appreciation but felt that, having preserved the Tower, there was a duty to find out something about it. This task fell to me once more and it was in this way that I became absorbed in a subject about which I knew absolutely nothing. The outcome was the publication of this book.

Some people have strange hobbies. Living in Ross-shire is a gentleman who, for many years had been collecting from all kinds of sources details of aircraft which crashed in Scotland during the war. I was able to send him information on 50 Orkney crashes and by way of gratitude he forwarded details of a number of crashes of which I had no record. I was particularly intrigued by one record, a Grumman Martlet IV, Serial Number FN288 of 878 Squadron Hatston which had crashed west of Finstown on 4th June 1943. The pilot was Lonsdale Wiren of the Royal New Zealand Naval Volunteer Reserve. A corner of the jigsaw was beginning to get filled in.

One day Tom Johnston of the farm of Bryameadow near the former Royal Naval Air Station at Twatt was fencing when a tourist approached him and asked if he could get his permission to climb the hill known as Yonbell behind the farm.

'Yes, that's OK,' said Tom, 'but why would anyone want to do that?'

'I spent most of the war in a little hut up there,' replied the visitor.

'Then you must be Tiny Small,' said Tom. The man was almost moved to tears that someone, after forty years, still remembered his name.

'I was a young boy at that time,' said Tom, 'and used to carry your batteries up to your hut'!

So an old friendship was renewed and through an

introduction I came by chance on some more information. It happened in this way.

Tiny was reminiscing about his days as a Radio Operator on Yonbell.

I have in my possession copies of reports I had to make after two aircraft crashed and the pilots were killed. The date of the report is 4th June 1943. We, the HF/DF operators, weren't usually called upon to give bearings or homings to Hatston or Skeabrae although we could have done so with no difficulty. I don't think either station had HF/DF. Some aircraft were in difficulties and it was a case of getting to the top of Yonbell very quickly. I was able to give bearings for one aircraft. I was told that there were three airborne but I was able to make contact with only one. Its call-sign was Newport Blue Three and I am pleased to say that I got him in safely to Skeabrae. The other two aircraft were lost before we set watch. We were called at 2.50 am. I was obviously in bed at that time and I had to get up and make my way up to the DF hut and I set watch about 3.05 am. I don't know how I got up there so quickly! Not only was the hillside rough, it was also covered with man-made obstacles. It was quite light at that time of the year and although it was so early the visibility was quite good—just a bit of sea fog. I knew there would be an enquiry into the loss of the aircraft so for several weeks I carefully measured my walks from the mess to the DF Hut to account for the time lag between being called and setting watch. When I went to the Court of Inquiry, lots of people were called to give evidence and I was asked at the time by one of the questioning officers about the distance I had to cover. When I told him that it was 1500 yards he said, 'How do you know that?' I replied that I had paced it out every day since the incident. The officers laughed and I couldn't understand that for it was a serious business to me.

When on holiday I met in Somerset a gentleman who was surprised to learn that I came from Orkney.

'Where in Orkney?' he asked.

'Originally from Finstown,' I replied.

'Know it very well,' he said, 'still the same lady in the Pomona Inn?! I was Senior Aircraft Engineer at Hatston. It was my job to organise the assembly of aircraft there and repair damaged ones; by God there weren't half some crashes in the Orkneys. I remember going to one just west of the Finstown Gap. Three Grumman Martlets were despatched on a night exercise; they should never have been sent out, they ran into a fog bank and couldn't get back to base. They got one down at Skeabrae but the others just circled till they ran out of petrol. One crashed just west of Finstown and the other in Harray. It was a terrible blunder; there was a big inquiry into it.'

I had been speaking to Duncan Hamilton who in the 50s and 60s became a well-known racing driver. I told him that I had lived at Binscarth as a small child and he was amazed at the coincidence.

Michael Harvey, a pilot with 881 Sqdn. Martlets at Hatston came across a copy of *Sky Over Scapa* and wrote to say how much he had enjoyed it. I noticed that he would have been at Hatston at the same time as Lonsdale Wiren and I wrote to ask whether he could remember him. He could not remember the name but he certainly could recall two New Zealand pilots in 878 Sqdn. on the station at the time who were 'notable characters and close companions'. Their party piece was to perform a Maori war dance late at night in the mess. Sand from the fire buckets was strewn on the floor and the dance was performed in a near naked state. If the WREN bar steward was still around she would close the bar and beat a hasty retreat! There was no doubt in his mind that Lonsdale Wiren was one of them as the following story indicates.

In August 1943 Michael was posted to 890 Sqdn. and joined HMS *Illustrious* for the Salerno landings. Sometime later a fellow pilot who had met the survivor of the night flying exercise and who had learned at first hand of the cause of the accident described what had happened. Lonsdale Wiren and he, a fellow New Zealander, were formating on the leader Lt. (A) Stanley Brett. While turning and with no warning they ran into a bank of cloud. He put his machine into a steep climb and reached 16,000 feet before coming out. Of course since it was mid-summer in Orkney there was plenty of light and though he scanned this way and that he could see no trace of his companions. Below him was a carpet of cloud extending as far as the eye could see. After some time and to his great relief he picked up a radio signal and was eventually directed to the airfield at Skeabrae where he made a safe but somewhat scary landing. Later he learned of the fate of the others.

One day a letter arrived postmarked 'Wellington, New Zealand'. Someone had handed Trevor Wiren a copy of the Fleet Air Arm Magazine and he had found in it an article written by me about his brother who was killed in an air crash in Orkney. He thought he would write and tell me something about him. I couldn't believe it! Trevor wrote:

Lonsdale Wiren was born in Wellington, New Zealand in September 1916. He was the eldest of a family of four, brother Trevor being born in 1919, sister Vera in 1922 and sister Patricia in 1930. He was well built, physically very strong and a great sportsman. He was in the first eleven cricket and the first fifteen rugby at college. The family loved him. He was a little different from the rest of them, a bit of a tear-away and a real dare devil. He was a good son and a great brother to me and my sisters though he was rather irresponsible, living for the day while I, the quieter, looked forward rather more. His intentions were always good but it was usually I who fed the chooks and mowed the grass and cut the firewood. This is the kind of guy he was. In our teenage days Dale went for a holiday with some friends and some days later I couldn't find my pair of shoes. On his return he said that he didn't think I would need them! He was just too nice to get cross with! I idolized him. He didn't have much time for things academic and no job seemed to offer him the adventure after which he craved. He became very unsettled and, by the age of 23, still had not found his niche in life.

In September 1939, at the outbreak of war he took himself down to the recruiting office in Wellington and returned to surprise his family by saying that he had volunteered for the Navy. He hoped he would pass his naval pilot's test and get some real thrills. War was for him the ultimate adventure. He qualified as a pilot and took to flying like a duck to water. Like Lonsdale (or 'Dale' as we called him) I also volunteered for service during the war and was attached to the Royal Navy. I met up with him in London in 1943. Typically Dale, he wanted to borrow my Burberry coat for the night. Of course I loaned him it but the night turned into a week and no one in the NZ Forces Club knew where he was. So there I was in London with no coat and no money to buy another either. The coat was returned gracefully and with a 'Thanks Trev' accompanied by a look in his eye as if to say 'well I kept it a bit longer but I don't suppose you needed it anyway'. I couldn't bring myself to tell him that I had been tearing my hair out for a week! In London Dale told me how much he loved flying and the service. I was so pleased to learn that, at last, he had found his niche in life.

I was in Malta when the news of Dale's death reached me and naturally I was very upset. I thought of the family too. My mother was already a widow at the age of 43, with two daughters aged 21 and 13 with only a small allowance from our meagre services pay and a widow's pension. How would she take this blow? I thought deeply about Dale. At least he had died doing what he loved. Although his last flight was fatal I am sure that he would have been feeling philosophical about things when the realisation came that he would not be landing safely. I later returned to Britain after the Sicilian invasion and while on leave I took the opportunity to visit Orkney. The padre at Hatston took me to St. Olaf's Cemetery. I found it very peaceful with an austere beauty. I was pleased I had made the effort.

The jigsaw was complete but by this time my pupils had passed on and I had retired from teaching. It's a pity that they hadn't been able to hear the true story.

One day in Somerset there was a knock at the door. There stood two strangers.

'You won't know me,' said the older, 'my name's Trevor Wiren and this is my son Dale. Do our names mean anything to you?'

It almost brought tears to my eyes. We had a very long talk. Before they left I said to Dale, 'I've got a little present for you and from a cupboard I took down a small piece of green airframe. On it was stamped the date '1943'.

Aircraft Crash Records
Orkney

I sometimes feel that, if I could stop the paperwork caused by accidents, I could then stop the accidents which caused this paper work which now prevents me stopping accidents
[seen in a Commander (Flying)'s office]

World War I

1914

Date	Aircraft	Base/Sqdn.	Details
?.08.14	Henry Farman Seaplane 129		Arrived Scapa; subsequently crashed into sea; details unknown.
21.11.14	Sopwith Bat Flying Boat No. 1; 38		Scapa Flow; destroyed in a gale.

1915

Date	Aircraft	Base/Sqdn.	Details
	No Information		

1916

Date	Aircraft	Base/Sqdn.	Details
23.10.16	Sopwith Schneider Seaplane 3798		Forced landing in sea near Scapa Flow after taking off from HMS *Campania*.
24.10.16	Short Seaplane Type 184 9075		Crashed on take off after forced landing, Scapa Flow.

1917

Date	Aircraft	Base/Sqdn.	Details
12.02.17	Short Seaplane Type 184 9069		Crashed on take off after forced landing Scapa Flow.
20.05.17	Short Seaplane Type 184 9078?		Capsized and sank, Scapa Flow; from HMS *Campania*.
10.08.17	Sopwith Pup		Five days after making the first ever successful landing on a vessel, Sqd. Commander Edwin Dunning was drowned in Scapa Flow when his aircraft went over the side of HMS *Furious* when his engine stalled as he attempted to abort the landing.
16.10.17	Short Seaplane Type 184 N1271		Crashed into sea east off Pentland? Skerries.

1918

Date	Aircraft	Base/Sqdn.	Details
03.08.18	Sopwith Camel 2F-1 N6636		Crashed Kirkwall Bay.
30.09.18	Felixtowe F-3 Flying Boat N4412	F Flight	Crashed and wrecked near Kirkwall.

World War II

Date	Aircraft	Base/Sqdn.	Details
?.09.39	Walrus Aircraft Catapult Sqdn. L2180 L2191 other unknown	HMS *Southampton* HMS *Newcastle* HMS *Glasgow* 712 Sqdn.	When Sqdn.Cmdr. Lt.Cdr. E. H. Shattock led his four aircraft in an impressive 'balbo' across Scapa Flow they were caught in a sudden 50mph. gale which sprang up without warning; three landed at Stromness severely damaged.
20.09.39	Ju-88	KG30	Crashed off Hoy.
12.10.39	Ju-88 4D+EK	Luftwaffe	Shot down over Scapa Flow by AA and crashed Pegal Burn, Hoy: Uffz. Ambrosius survived: OB/Lt. Flaemig, Pilot; Uffz. Attenburger; Obergfr. G. F. R. Faust, Air Gunner killed.
17.10.39	Ju-88	Luftwaffe	Crashed in sea between Hoy and Stroma; shot down by shore AA during dive bombing attacks on HMS *Iron Duke* with three other Ju-88s.
10.12.39	Ju-88	4D+EK	Shot down Scapa Flow.
27.12.39	Avro Anson I K6280	Wick 269 Sqdn.	Engine failure; ditched east of Orkney.
28.12.39	Sea Gladiator N5504	Hatston 804 Sqdn.	Mid-air collision in formation; aircraft became uncontrollable; Pilot Lt.Cdr. J. C. Cockburn baled out at 6,000 feet and landed safely.

Date	Aircraft	Base/Sqdn.	Details
04.01.40	Dornier Do-17		Crashed into sea off Copinsay.
09.01.40	Swordfish ?	Hatston 771 Sqdn.	Took off downwind at Hatston towards Sea Gladiator waiting at end of runway; Swordfish got airborne but hit Sea Gladiator which was a write-off; crew abandoned Swordfish 6 miles from Hatston. Sea Gladiator Pilot, P/O G. W. Peacock. (*photographic record of Peacock in a Twatt Hurricane over Scapa*)
09.01.40	Sea Gladiator N5506	Hatston 804 Sqdn.	See above.
11.01.40	Skua II ?	Hatston 803 Sqdn.	The squadron transferred to Wick on this day; before/on departure this Skua spun in off turn at 500', Tor Ness, Stronsay; Midshipman (A) John W. D. Barr (HMS *Merlin*) died in hospital at Kirkwall, buried New Romney, Kent: L/A Ginger Uren, age 22 killed; buried Plymouth Old Cemetery.
08.03.40	Ju-88	Luftwaffe 2/KG30	Shot down by F/O Dutton, Hurricane, 111 Sqdn., Wick, 40 miles east of Orkney.
16.03.40	Aircraft	Luftwaffe	Crashed in sea, Scapa Flow.
18.03.40	Rapide DH82 G-AFEY	Scottish Airways	Crashed Kirkwall.
02.04.40	Ju-88 ?	Luftwaffe	Shot down by AA on raid on Burray and Hoy; in sea?
07.04.40	Skua II L3025	Hatston 800 Sqdn.	Reconnaissance, Hatston-Bergen, diverted to Sumburgh on return because of contrary wind; made emergency landing on airfield officially closed due to waterlogging; engine torn off and aircraft a write-off; Capt. R. T. Partridge RM, O.K.; returned to base by Swordfish from Hatston.
08.04.40	He111, H-3 1H+FM	Luftwaffe 4/KG26	Ditched 9 miles SSE of Copinsay Lighthouse after combat with F/O J. Edmunds in Hurricane of 43 Sqdn.
09.04.40	Skua II L2948	Hatston 800 Sqdn.	Stalled and crashed in sea on turn landing on HMS *Glorious* when joining up for convoy work: P/O Pilot W. E. Chinn, age 23 killed, buried St. Olaf's, Plot 1, Grave 24: N/A A T. G. L. Burgess age 20 killed: buried St. Olaf's, Plot 1, Grave 26.
10.04.40	Do-17 ?	Luftwaffe	Fired at off Copinsay by Sub.Lt. Fell and P/O Peacock, 804 Sqdn., Hatston: believed to have crashed into sea after distress call indicating leaking petrol tank.
10.04.40	Heinkel III P (or H?)	Luftwaffe	Shot down by Hurricanes of 43 Sqdn., Wick, 10 miles east of Burray; three crew members survived; this aircraft and the one above were two of seven bombers brought down on the same day.
20.04.40	Skua II L2999	Hatston 800 Sqdn.	Crashed between Lerwick and Orkney on a reconnaissance flight, 59 81' N, 019' W: Midshipman (A) Pilot John R. Crossley, age 19 killed: P/O (A) M. Hall age 23, killed: on Lee-on-Solent Memorial.
21.04.40	Gloster Gladiator II N5624	Hatston 804 Sqdn.	Crashed into sea after engine failure attempting to land on HMS *Glorious* when squadron flew from Hatston.
22.04.40	Skua II	Hatston 800 Sqdn.	Crashed into sea landing on HMS *Ark Royal*: pilot picked up.
24.04.40	Walrus L2316	Hatston 700 Sqdn.	Missing on A/S patrol: crashed in Fair Isle Channel: enemy aircraft in vicinity: Pilot P/O (A) C. L. Smeathers killed: Midshipman (A) Paul L. Furbe age 19 killed: N/A C. E. Adams, HMS *Edinburgh*, age 20 killed.
15.05.40	Do-8G ?	Luftwaffe 1/KO/FLGR 406	Shot down by Skuas of 801 Sqdn., Hatston, east of Orkney.

18.05.40	Swordfish I ?	Hatston 823 Sqdn	Forced landing in sea with engine trouble: Sub.Lt. (A) Harald D. Mourilyan, N/A Roy Parkinson age 21 both drowned.
31.05.40	Tutor 1 K3305	Wick Station Fight	Ditched in Pentland Firth.
31.05.40	Sea Gladiator ?	Hatston 804 Sqdn.	Spun at Hatston from 400' while on training flight; Sgt. Sturgess killed.
19.06.40	Reliant X8521 (formerly G-AEYZ)	1STT	Forced landing in Sanday.
08.07.40	Henley III ?	Hatston 771 Sqdn.	Ran off Hatston runway into Swordfish on take off: Swordfish a write-off.
08.07.40	Swordfish ?	Hatston 770/771 Sqdn.	See above
14.08.40	Gloster Sea Gladiator II N2277	Hatston 804 Sqdn.	Blown into Ops. Block at Hatston by severe gale and bent its rear severely; repaired but see 02.12.43.
19.09.40	Vega Gull W9378 (formerly G-AETF)	Hatston Flight	Brakes locked and wheels failed to grip on grass on landing at Hatston: hit wall: write-off.
22.09.40	Swordfish I L7635	Hatston 821 Sqdn.	Forced landing in sea on A/S patrol, 60 8' N, 3 23' W: Sub.Lt. Frederick C. Saunders age 21 *Ark Royal*, lost: Sub.Lt. Derek J. T. Marcus, Observer, age 21, HMS *Sparrowhawk* lost, body washed ashore Sanday 4-6.11.40, buried Lady Churchyard, Sanday: N/A G. H. Gaynon killed, body recovered Stronsay, buried St. Olaf's Plot 2, Grave 6.
26.09.40	Magister I T9679	Castletown Station Flight	Crash landed on HMS *Furious* in Scapa Flow.
26.10.40	Swordfish I L2794	Hatston 821 Sqdn.	Took off Sumburgh on A/S patrol; landed with engine trouble, took off again, crashed in sea within 4 miles Quendale Bay, Shetland, 12.35 pm: Pilot Midshipman (A) Richard T. Chambers RNVR age 19 HMS *Sparrowhawk* killed: body washed up Lerwick 02.11.40: buried Lerwick New Cemetery, Terrace 11, Grave 14: Sub.Lt. Peter B. Laycock, age 19, HMS *Sparrowhawk*, Observer, MPK: N/A B. F. A Brewster, age 20 killed: buried Lerwick New Cemetery, Terrace 11, Grave 15.
??.10.40	Martlet BJ508	Hatston 804 Sqdn.	Believed to be a write-off at Hatston sometime between 07.10.40 and 27.10.40.
28.10.40	Martlet I BJ568	Skeabrae 804 Sqdn.	Transferring to Skeabrae, swung on take off and crashed at Hatston: in attempting to avoid B Flight Hangar: stalled and hit a mound: Pilot Midshipman (A) Birrell slightly injured.
17.11.40	Martlet I BJ?	Skeabrae 804 Sqdn.	Being delivered from Hatston, flew into ground in landing circuit: Pilot Sleigh injured.
20.11.40	Walrus L2257	Hatston 700 Sqdn.	Capsized at Sullom Voe, Shetland: N/A D. W. Charnock, age 21, killed.
03.12.40	Sea Gladiator ?	Skeabrae 804 Sqdn.	Struck Martlet I in take off; former burst into flames: 2 injured: Pilot Sub.Lt. (A) Gunn baled out after pulling parachute rip cord and virtually knocked himself out!
03.12.40	Martlet I ?	Skeabrae 804 Sqdn.	See above: Pilot Hutchison.
25.12.40	Ju-88 4N+AL W/R 7122	Luftwaffe 3(F) 22 SOLA	Shot down near Flotterston, Sandwick by Martlet I piloted by Lt L. V. Carver and Sub.Lt. T. R. V. Parke from Skeabrae at 2.05 pm: Lt K. Schipp, Fw. H. Schreiber, Uffz. J. Spörtl and Obergefr. K. Rotter taken prisoner: first kill of war by UK pilot in US aircraft: aircraft salvaged complete by 15.02.41 and stored in hangar at Skeabrae for some time. (*photographic record*)

1941

Date	Aircraft	Base/Sqdn.	Details
02.01.41	Hudson P5147	Wick 269 Sqdn.	Swung on take off on icy runway (Skeabrae?): hit rut and undercarriage collapsed: port wing engine and undercarriage badly damaged.
09.01.41	Hurricane IIA/IIB	Skeabrae 3 Sqdn.	Overshot and overturned on landing after extra long flight: Sub.Lt. A. N. Cole concussed; details uncertain: 3 Sqdn. RAF was at Skeabrae at this time but unlikely to have had naval pilot.
13.01.41	Hurricane R4076	Skeabrae 3 Sqdn.	Landed with drift after extra long flight: ran off runway and into mud: undercarriage collapsed: Pilot Officer A. I. Miller OK: aircraft repaired.
24.01.41	Sea Gladiator ?	Skitten 804 Sqdn.	Crashed on take off (Skeabrae?): Pilot Eyres.
05.02.41	Swordfish I V4296	Campbeltown 828 Sqdn.	Crashed into Kirkwall Bay.
04.03.41	Ju-88 A6+CH	Luftwaffe 1(F) 120	Crashed in sea 1 mile east of Westray Firth? at 2.35 pm after combat with three Hurricanes of 253 Sqdn. Skeabrae.
19.03.41	Hudson I N7310	Wick 220 Sqdn.	Flew into Hoy Hills in cloud: 4 killed: army sentry on guard duty at wreck died of exposure.
01.04.41	Albacore I N4172	Hatston 828 Sqdn.	U-boat search off Cape Wrath: found nothing: on return to base, ran into snowstorm, radio failed, crash landed Whiten Head, Tongue, Sutherland: TAG P/O Polmeer slightly injured: Pilot Lt.Cdr. Leon Cubitt and Observer Sub.Lt. Goodger OK: wreckage recovered and aircraft rebuilt: can now be seen in FAA Museum, Yeovilton, Somerset.
0?.04.41	Albacore I N4155	Hatston 828 Sqdn.	Crashed into sea 50 miles east of Orkney; pilot picked up by Dutch submarine was only survivor: Walrus P5178 from HMS *Shropshire* in Scapa Flow landed beside submarine to collect survivor but because of heavy swell could not take off: towed by submarine to shelter of Orkney waters!

Date	Aircraft	Base/Sqdn.	Details
06.04.41	Ju-88 ?	Luftwaffe	Blue Section, 253 Sqdn. Skeabrae led by Pilot Derek Yapp in Hurricane V7503 intercepted this aircraft at 20,000 feet, attacked and starboard engine caught fire; rear gunner ceased firing: aircraft believed to have crashed into sea; V7503 damaged in engagement.
28.04.41	Hurricane V6929	Skeabrae 253 Sqdn.	Undershot and stalled on approach: repaired: Sgt. Pilot T. R. Bromhall.
02.05.41	Albacore I	Hatston 828 Sqdn.	Sub.Lt. Stanley W. Everett, RNVR, Observer, age 21, killed North Sound during dummy torpedo attacks.
12.05.41	Walrus ?	HMS *Quebec*	Ditched due to engine failure en route Donibristle - Scapa Flow to join HMS *Quebec*: pilot unknown: passengers Vice Admiral (Destroyers) Hamilton and Senior Army Officers.
14.05.41	Albacore I L...	Hatston 828 Sqdn.	Crashed Hatston after emergency landing: crew, Bellairs and Paton OK.
31.05.41	Hurricane I V7235	Skeabrae 253 Sqdn.	Crashed in flames 1.25 miles south-west of Crustan, Birsay: Sgt. Pilot H. M. Cox, RAF, killed: first fatal accident at Skeabrae.
12.06.41	Hurricane I P3383	Skeabrae 253 Sqdn.	Crashed 2 miles east of Wasbister, Rousay at 16.03: Sgt. Pilot Read, RAF seriously injured.
02.07.41	Fulmar II N4026	Hatston 809 Sqdn.	Ended up half over side of HMS *Furious* landing on when off Orkney: Pilot Sub.Lt. 'Tex' Van Epps OK. (*photographic record*)
04.07.41	Hurricane I V6673	Skeabrae 253 Sqdn.	Crashed near Skeabrae airfield on final at 16.30: write-off.
12.07.41	Fulmar	809 Sqdn.	Crashed into sea attempting to land on HMS *Victorious*.
29.08.41	Hurricane IIB Z5042	Castletown 124 Sqdn.	Crashed half mile west of Skeabrae airfield at 11.45: Sgt. Pilot J. M. Harris killed.
24.09.41	Spitfire	Castletown 124 Sqdn.	On flotsam patrol, flew into ground near Rendall, 5 miles north of Finstown: Sgt. Pilot R. F. C. Pauley RCAF killed: buried Sandwick.
10.10.41	Hurricane IIB	Skeabrae 331 Sqdn. (Norwegian)	Forced landing at Brough Head, Birsay; pilot uninjured.
05.12.41	Sea Hurricane IB Z4835	Skeabrae 801 Sqdn.	Operational scramble to identify unknown aircraft (returning Catalina had forgotten to switch on IFF!): propeller went into coarse pitch, stalled, crashed into henhouse to east of airfield perimeter; aircraft broke in two behind cockpit: write-off: Sub.Lt. H. Duthie RNZVR escaped with slight cut on chin!
03.12.41	Sea Hurricane IB AF981	Hatston 1st. Line Reserve	Overturned on landing at Twatt: Pilot Cdr. H. C. Ranald spent some time trapped in cockpit until crane arrived from Hatston.
12.12.41	Roc I L3186	Hatston 771 Sqdn.	Crashed on height finding exercise at sea: Pilot Sub.Lt. Jack Tattersfield, RNVR, killed: L/A G. Hall (Wee Geordie) died 13.12.41.
?? ?? 41	Spitfire	Skeabrae 331 Sqdn. (Norwegian)	Lt. James Endresen flying in line astern at 25,000 feet with Lt. Henning Leifseth disappeared without trace to the north of Orkney although visibility was good; despite an extensive search no trace was found.

1942

Date	Aircraft	Base/Sqdn.	Details
10.01.42	Spitfire V B P8729 (call sign 'Green')	Skeabrae 331 Sqdn. (Norwegian)	Forced landing near Cleat, St. Ola, ex ops: write off: Lt Hvinden OK.
13.01.42	Swordfish P4222	Hatston 771 Sqdn.	Forced landing in Eday due to low cloud: Pilot Sub.Lt. Norris and TAG Richard Stark OK. Lt Noel Goddard arrived from Hatston to fly off plane: landed at Hatston minus tail wheel which had caught on fence on take off.
24.02.42	Spitfire Mk.II P8580	Skeabrae 132 Sqdn.	Swung off runway at Skeabrae into soft earth and overturned.
13.03.42	Swordfish I	Hatston 819 Sqdn.	Sub.Lt. (A) D. Howden RNZVR, Sub.Lt. Cameron and TAG lost in bad weather on navigation exercise west of Orkney: intensive search revealed no trace.
15.03.42	Albacore I N4176/4B	Crail 833 Sqdn.	Undercarriage collapsed on landing at Hatston from HMS *Victorious*: write-off: Sub.Lt. (A) K. Smith OK but lost off HMS *Victorious* 08.04.43: buried Oatu Cemetery, Honolulu.
16.03.42	Spitfire IIa P7759	Skeabrae 331 Sqdn. (Norwegian)	Sgt. Pilot Ulf Wormdal killed; spun into the sea 3 miles west of Brough of Birsay when in combat rehearsal trying to follow a Swordfish in its tight turning arc.
01.04.42	Swordfish II W5889	Hatston 833 Sqdn.	North Sound, Orkney, 12.15 pm.: ALT against HMS *Atmah*; during get away aircraft flew into water, bounced off, climbed steeply to 600' before stalling and diving vertically into sea: Sub.Lt. (A) A. Edward Iveson, RNVR, HMS *Jackdaw*, age 21, Leading Photog. (A) Sydney V. Horne F/MX57545, age 23, HMS *Sparrowhawk* both missing, presumed killed: on Lee-on-Solent Memorial.
02.04.42	Swordfish II W5924	Hatston ex 833 Sqdn.	Aircraft being ferried to Crail by RNAS Donibristle: wreckage seen in Pentland Firth: cause of crash unknown: Sub.Lt. (A) Harold Shaw, RNVR, age 21, HMS *Merlin*, 782 Sqdn. and two soldiers going on leave, QMS J. Gallagher, RAOC and Sgt. Drummond missing, presumed killed.
04.05.42	Spitfire I X4328	Skeabrae 164 Sqdn.	Landed too close on arriving at Skeabrae from Peterhead: chopped tail off R7220: squadron's first day in Orkney.
04.05.42	Spitfire VA R7220	Skeabrae 164 Sqdn.	See above.

31.05.42	Spitfire VA/VB ?	Skeabrae 132/164 Sqdn.	Forced landing in Auskerry after getting lost: no further details.
11.06.42	Swordfish I ?	Hatston 835 Sqdn.	Hit obstacle on edge of runway on landing from Lee: Lt Shirley-Smith OK.
15.06.42	Spitfire VA R7267	Skeabrae 164 Sqdn.	Crashed at Dounby due to faulty controls (could turn only to port): plane turned over on its back on impact and pilot thrown out through canopy which had been opened in an abortive attempt to bale out: Pilot F/L. Dowling trapped under wreckage and rescued only slightly bruised: aircraft a write-off.
26.06.42	Albacore I BF592	Evanton Aircraft Repair Yard	Aircraft being ferried Evanton-Hatston in poor visibility and with cloud base at 500' hit Old Man of Hoy and crashed Mel Fea 11.55 am.: aircraft burnt out: body of Pilot Sub.Lt. (A) James Leggat RNVR, HMS *Merlin* found Rackwick and buried at sea: on Lee-on-Solent Memorial.
30.06.42	Skua II L2951	Twatt 771 Sqdn.	Taxying, swung into hole: X-X damage: Lt George F. Clarke RCNVR, OK.
30.06.42	Defiant TTI ?	Twatt 771 Sqdn.	Landed without tail wheel after striking obstacle on take off: pilot, OK but lost 18.09.45, age 30, on maintenance flying, HMS *Nutchatch* .
08.07.42	Spitfire VA P8706	Skeabrae 164 Sqdn.	Crashed on approach to Skeabrae.
09.07.42	Skua II L2883	Twatt 771 Sqdn.	Hit balloon cable and crashed into Scapa Flow killing Pilot Lt (A) Noel J. Cornes, RNVR, age 27 and L/A A. G. Jones, age 19 (buried St. Olaf's Cemetery, Plot 2, Grave 20/26).
13.07.42	Swordfish V4593	Hatston 825 Sqdn.	At Woodwick bombing range: failed to recover from dive: all crew killed; Pilot Sub.Lt. (A) James H. Wood RNVR, age 21 buried St. Olaf's (funeral 16.07.42), Plot 22, Grave 22: L/A (A) J. G. Bowick and Airman R. W. Doakin.
13.07.42	Maryland AR717	Twatt 771 Sqdn.	Port undercarriage locking gear failed: write-off?; Pilot Lt.Cdr. C. M. Davies: *(photographic record).*
23.07.42	Albacore I ?	Hatston 817 Sqdn.	Crashed in North Sound: L/A A. G. W. Howard killed: on Lee-on-Solent Memorial: no other casualties reported.
22.08.42	Spitfire VB BL667	Sumburgh 132 Sqdn.	Crashed on training flight off Deerness: Sgt. Pilot Reynard killed.
23.08.42	Spitfire VA P9563	Skeabrae 164 Sqdn.	Crashed at Skeabrae on training flight: wing-tip caught workman's hut during low flying practice: Pilot Officer D. B. Bridger (Argentinian) killed. [NB 164 Squadron was called the British-Argentine Squadron].
27.08.42	Skua I L3026	Twatt 771 Sqdn.	Spun in off steep turn from 300' and crashed Houton Head: crew of two killed: Pilot Peter K. W. Nias, RNVR, age 20, buried St. Olaf's, Plot 33, Grave 2: L/A Alfred L. Fletcher, age 29, buried St. Olaf's Plot 33, Grave 2.
16.09.42	Albacore I N4155	HMS *Indomitable* 827 Sqdn.	Ditched 13 miles west of Brough of Birsay; serial number must be wrong (see ?.4.41); base also wrong since 827 Sqdn. was at Machrihanish at this time.
18.09.42	Roc L3177	Twatt 771 Sqdn.	Engine failure in Pentland Firth: ditched off Hoy: L/Photographer Spiller and L/A Benjamin Bassett both killed: Pilot Sub.Lt. W. C. Larkins picked up by destroyer HMS *Tanaside*.
18.09.42	Seafire IIc MA976	Hatston 807 Sqdn.	Fell into sea after over-correction of spin during fighter attack: sank, leaving no trace: Sub.Lt. (A) Alfred G. Harvey, RNVR. lost: on Lee-on-Solent Memorial.
24.09.42	Walrus I L2329	Twatt 700 Sqdn.	Mid-air collision in Pentland Firth: Pilot Sub.Lt. (A) Maurice G. Clyde, RNVR, Sub.Lt. (A) A. Ernest Hardwick, Observer, L/A Charles P. Penn-Simkins, age 20, all killed: on Lee-on-Solent Memorial.
24.09.42	Walrus X9481	HMS *Sheffield* 700 Sqdn. Flight	Mid-air collision with above: Pilot Lt (A) Neil S. Mackenzie, RNVR: Observer Sub.Lt. (A) Peter J. Wheatley, age 20: L/A Frederick J. P. Payne, all killed.
12.10.42	Seafire MB121	Skeabrae 884 Sqdn.	Barrier crash in HMS *Victorious* after deck landing trials in preparation for North African landings: damaged propeller; transported by lighter to Scapa, hence to Hatston. *(photographic record)*.
17.10.42	Spitfire VB AD478	Grimsetter 129 Sqdn.	Pilot dazzled by floodlight on landing at Grimsetter: off runway and overturned: write off.
21.10.42	Spitfire VI BS436	Skeabrae 602 Sqdn.	Swung off runway at Skeabrae into cross-wind and overturned in soft ground.
28.10.42	Roc I L3187	Twatt 771 Sqdn.	Off runway and tipped on nose: crew unknown.
11.11.42	Spitfire V ?	Grimsetter 129 Sqdn.	Ditched off Eday: Pilot Officer Dixon picked up: OK.
12.11.42	Spitfire V ?	Grimsetter 129 Sqdn.	Stalled on landing and undercarriage leg collapsed: Pilot Sgt N. A. Rushmere.
27.11.42	Roc I L3104	Twatt 771 Sqdn.	Belly landing when undercarriage would not lower: Pilot Sub.Lt. A. R. Duff.
15.12.42	Sea Hurricane I Z7089	Twatt 771 Sqdn.	Ex workshops, Hatston: dived into Peedie Sea from 600': Lt (A) Thomas N. Bush RNZVR, age 27, killed: buried St. Olaf's, Plot 33, Grave 1.

Date	Aircraft	Base/Sqdn.	Details
05.01.43	Defiant DR885	Twatt 771 Sqdn.	Undercarriage collapsed on landing: Pilot Sub.Lt. W. C. Larkins OK.
20.01.43	Spitfire VB BL253	Hatston 899 Sqdn.	Dived into sea whilst circling airfield, 500 yds. north of Hatston: Sub.Lt. (A) Douglas L. F. Barber, RNVR, age 20, killed: buried St. Olaf's, Plot 33, Grave 9.
03.02.43	Spitfire BS442	Grimsetter 234 Sqdn.	Swung on landing and nosed over: Pilot Sgt R. W. Shepherd OK.
03.02.43	Seafire IB MB362	Hatston 880 Sqdn.	On camera gun attacks near Woodwick Bombing Range, Evie: collided with another Seafire at 6,000': Sub.Lt. (A) Lloyd H. Johnson RNZVR, age 21, killed: buried St. Olaf's, Plot 33, Grave 11.
03.02.43	Seafire MB369	Hatston 880 Sqdn.	Mid-air collision: see above: Sub.Lt. (A) Anthony C. Smalley RNVR, age 23, killed: buried St. Olaf's, Plot 23, Grave 9.
13.02.43	Blackburn Roc I L3085	Twatt 771 Sqdn.	Ditched off Orkney.
05.03.43	Seafire IB ?	HMS *Furious* 801 Sqdn.	Pilot Lt (A) David Wilkinson landed at Hatston with L/A (Armourer) James Edward Overed on the tailplane: aircraft had taken off from HMS *Furious* off Deerness and pilot was unaware that the airman was still holding down the tail: after a 15 minute flight in wintry conditions Overed quickly recovered in hospital (compare 30.03.43)
05.03.43	Defiant I DR937	Twatt 771 Sqdn.	Crashed in Wide Firth due to engine failure: Pilot Sub.Lt. Jack Patterson RNZNVR missing, presumed killed: L/A Richard Stark seriously injured.
11.03.43	Henley L3309	Twatt 771 Sqdn.	In bad visibility two aircraft made an identical approach to Twatt: at 300' the propeller of the higher aircraft, a Roc, cut off the tail of the lower, a Henley, Pilot Sub.Lt. (A) Ted Gilbert, RNZNVR: both aircraft crashed: L/A A. P. W. Molony was badly injured: flown to a hospital ship thence to Aberdeen. (*photographic record*)
11.03.43	Roc I ?	Twatt 771 Sqdn.	Collided with Henley (see above): Pilot Lt. Thackera RN. (*photographic record*)
12.03.43	Spitfire V W3321	Skeabrae 66 Sqdn.	Pilot Officer Donald took off from Skeabrae at 10.53 am on a sector reconnaissance, counter-clockwise round Orkney: caught in a snow storm south of Westray; last message 'My screen is covered, I can see nothing.' Extensive search by 4 Walruses, 2 Lysanders and a Dominie found no trace.
16.03.43	Spitfire V ?	Skeabrae 66 Sqdn.	Fighter evasion exercise: tried to follow a Swordfish (771 Sqdn?) in a tight turn: flick stalled into sea: no further details.
30.03.43	Lysander III T1580	Skeabrae 1494 FG Flight	Took off 9.43 am with L/Ac L. C. A. Lane on tail: climbed to 200': L/Ac Lane fell off and was killed: pilot lost control and aircraft crashed: 2 crew injured: pilot (name withheld) court-martialled (compare 05.03.43).
08.04.43	Defiant TT.1 DR937	Twatt 771 Sqdn.	Hit barrage balloon cable in Scapa Flow and lost wing tip: crash landed: pilot unknown. (*photographic record*)
08.05.43	Skua II ? D	Twatt 771 Sqdn.	Crashed near Twatt: engine torn from mountings: no other details. (*photographic record*)
22.05.43	Spitfire VB AB537	Skeabrae 66 Sqdn.	Crashed on take off on training flight Skeabrae due to engine failure: Pilot F/Sgt A. Hill OK: aircraft a write-off.
23.05.43	Martlet IV ?	Hatston 878 Sqdn.	Belly landed between Fiold and Berriedale, Westray: pilot OK: transported to Pierowall thence by boat to Kirkwall for repair at Hatston Workshops. (*photographic record*)
28.05.43	Roc I L3170	Twatt 771 Sqdn.	Crashed near what appears to be Harray Loch: no further details. (*photographic record*)
04.06.43	Martlet IV FN288	Hatston 878 Sqdn.	One of three Martlets which took off from Hatston at 2.45 am on a night flying exercise and flew into low cloud: Twatt HF/DF operator ran half a mile at 3 o'clock in the morning to the transmitter on Yonbell in a desperate attempt to get the aircraft down: one landed safely at Skeabrae: FN288 crashed 400 yds. to north of Stymilders in Stenness: Lt (A) Lonsdale H. Wiren, RNZNVR, age 26, killed: buried St. Olaf's Plot 33, Grave 4 (see below).
04.06.43	Martlet IV FN248	Hatston 878 Sqdn.	One of three Martlets (see above): crashed Huntscarth, Harray and burst into flames setting fire to the hillside: Lt (A) Stanley G. Brett, RNVR, age 24, killed: buried St. Olaf's, Plot 33, Grave 15.
07.06.43	Roc I L3098	Twatt 771 Sqdn.	Pilot Sub.Lt. (A) A. D. Fyffe, RNZNVR, failed to ensure undercarriage locked down for landing and it collapsed: probably a write-off.
14.06.43	Chesapeake I ?	Twatt 771 Sqdn.	Crash landed due to engine failure: Pilot Sub.Lt. Hunter and TAG J. B. Griffin OK.
15.06.43	Seafire IIC MB255	HMS *Indomitable* 880 or 899 Sqdn.	Aircraft ditched in sea alongside ship and sank: cause unknown: Sub.Lt. (A) Robert A. Lawson, RNZNVR, age 20 lost: on Lee-on-Solent Memorial.
21.06.43	Walrus II X9467	Twatt 771 Sqdn.	Starboard wheel collapsed on landing: Pilot Sub.Lt. Williams and Observer N. Brown OK.
03.07.43	Chesapeake I ? 'G'	Twatt 771 Sqdn.	Crashed near Twatt due to engine failure: Pilot Sub.Lt. Mence and TAG J. B. Griffin OK.
27.07.43	Seafire IIC MB187	HMS *Illustrious* 894 Sqdn.	On Fighter Direction exercise, crashed in sea 9 miles west of Rora Head: Pilot Sub.Lt. (A) Robert W. D. Forbes, RNZNVR, age 24, missing, presumed killed.
??.07.43	Boston Havoc ?	Twatt 771 Sqdn.	Crashed at Twatt: details unknown. (*photographic record*)
26.08.43	Skua II L2927	Twatt 771 Sqdn	Ditched off Orkney.

21.09.43	Seafire IIC LR682	Hatston Reserve	Hit obstruction: undercarriage collapsed: write-off: Pilot D. G. Dick, RNVR.
09.10.43	Avenger I (TBF-1) FN787	Hatston 845 Sqdn.	Spun into sea off Old Man of Hoy, 10.05 am from 4,500' after collision with Seafire during Fighter Evasion exercise: Pilot Sub.Lt. Peter C. A. Heath, RNVR, Observer Sub.Lt. Kenneth W. Richter, age 23, P/O TAG Gavin Rough (Jock), age 25, missing, presumed killed: all on Lee-on-Solent Memorial.
09.10.43	Seafire IB ?	Skeabrae 801 Sqdn.	Collision with Avenger above: no casualties reported.
22.10.43	Roc I 'A' L3159	Twatt 771 Sqdn.	Crashed on South Ronaldsay: crew cut free by Italian prisoners of war: Pilot Sub.Lt. Chadwick, TAG D. J. Cole and Midshipman passenger cut free by Italian Prisoners of War!
29.10.43	Roc I 'G' ?	Twatt 771 Sqdn.	Brake failure: overshot runway on landing returning from Army AACE: Pilot Sub.Lt. Reid and TAG J. B. Griffin OK.
??.10.43	Seafire IB ?	Skeabrae 801 Sqdn.	Landed on NW/SE runway with faulty undercarriage: slewed to port striking and very seriously injuring Air fitter standing well to side of runway: pilot OK.
??.10.43	Boston Havoc T8B	Twatt 771 Sqdn.	Landed at Twatt with front wheel unlocked: ran along runway on nose: Pilot Sub.Lt. Mence and crew OK.
16.11.43	Grumman Avenger IC TBF FN899	Hatston 832 Sqdn.	Ditched near Hatston.
22.11.43	Beaufighter TF.XLX415	Wick 144 Sqdn.	Ditched 8 miles NE of Stronsay: 282 Sqdn. Wick located wreck at 2.30pm: Pilot F/Sgt P. G. Fletcher lost: high speed launch picked up Navigator F/Sgt H. I. Shepherd.
02.12.43	Gloster Sea Gladiator N2277	Twatt 771 Sqdn.	Crashed 2 miles SW of Rora Head: Walrus from Twatt picked up survivor.
09.12.43	Barracuda II DP927	Hatston 830 Sqdn.	Aircraft burst into flames and dived into sea from 3,000' during dive bombing attacks with live bombs on Ramma Stacks, Shetland: Pilot Sub.Lt. (A) Roy D. West, RNVR, age 22 killed, body recovered, buried Lerwick New Cemetery, Terrace 11, Grave 21: Observer Sub.Lt. (A) James Brown RNVR, age 20 and L/A Edward W. Kelly, age 21 lost: on Lee-on-Solent Memorial.
18.12.43	Spitfire MB765	Skeabrae 453 Sqdn. (Australian)	Engine caught fire: belly landed Deerness; Pilot F/Sgt Scott, RAAF.
18.12.43	Supermarine Seafire L.IIC/III NN329	HMS *Stalker* 880 Sqdn.	Ditched in sea near Grimsetter; salvaged and repaired but crashed two years later killing the pilot (see 13.02.45).
18.12.43	Oxford Mk. I HN600	Fraserburgh 14(P) AFU	Crash landed on Auskerry after getting lost: Pilot Sgt Franks on seeing unfamiliar lighthouse keeper's uniform thought he was in Germany and addressed lighthouse keeper as 'Kamerad'! Pilot lifted off by lifeboat 27.12.43: aircraft pounded to pieces by sea.
??.??.43	Walrus ?	Twatt 700 Sqdn.	Forced landing with engine trouble in shallow Isbister Loch, Birsay; anchored overnight; next day aircraft dragged to road where wheels were lowered, wings folded and transported back by low loader to station.

1944

Date	Aircraft	Base/Sqdn.	Details
24.01.44	Martinet TT.1 MS615	Twatt 771 Sqdn.	Pilot believed he had engine trouble: aborted take-off: aircraft went on to nose: write-off.
25.01.44	Ju-88 ?	Luftwaffe	Shot down by Bofors gun on Hoy.
28.01.44	Spitfire VB MB828	Skeabrae 602 Sqdn.	Landing ex-ops, caught by gust of wind and tipped on nose: Pilot Fl/Lt J. O. Carpenter OK.
20.02.44	Spitfire VII MD114	Skeabrae 602 Sqdn.	Crashed in Stronsay due to debris from Bf109 which Pilot Officer Ian Blair had just shot down: aircraft salvaged, repaired and saw further service certainly until 24.11.48.
22.02.44	Messerschmitt Bf109	Luftwaffe	Shot down by Pilot Officer Ian Blair, 602 Sqdn. 50 miles east of Stronsay: no survivors.
07.03.44	Spitfire VB BL686	Skeabrae 602 Sqdn.	Crashed on Shapinsay: F/O Oliver OK: aircraft salvaged and saw further service until March 1945.
07.03.44	Spitfire VA EP767	Skeabrae 602 Sqdn.	Problem with undercarriage; forced to belly land in front of Skeabrae Control Tower after night flying exercise: 2nd Lt P. F. Clostermann OK; aircraft repaired and saw service until June 1947.
27.03.44	Wildcat V JV350	HMS *Fencer* 842 Sqdn.	Landed upside down on top of another aircraft when embarking on HMS *Fencer* to take part in *Operation Tungsten*: damage done to both aircraft.
30.03.44	Skua II ?	Twatt 771 Sqdn.	Ferrying two Air Mechanics to Castletown, skidded on landing in a snowstorm: off runway and tipped on to propeller: P/O Pilot E. Haslam and passengers OK.
11.04.44	Blenheim IV V6173	Twatt 771 Sqdn.	Oil leak in engine: trip aborted: undercarriage collapsed on touch down and aircraft swung violently to starboard ending up off runway: Pilot Lt.Cdr. Cyril Burke and Co-Pilot W. (Bill) Larkins OK. (*photographic record*)
19.04.44	Swordfish II ?	HMS *Fencer* 842 Sqdn.	Crashed on deck while landing to take part in return of Convoy RA59 from Kola Inlet; repaired.
20.04.44	Barracuda II DP983	HMS *Furious* 830 Sqdn.	Struck barrage balloon cable and crashed into Scapa Flow; crew rescued.

25.04.44	Sea Otter I JM761	Twatt 771 Sqdn.	From Abbotsinsch to Twatt, forced landing in Hoy Sound due to engine failure: Pilot Lt. Reid: Observer Sub.Lt. W. N. Brown: Gunnery officer passenger (who because of seniority took command of the ditched aircraft!): rescued by High Speed Launch before plane sank.
26.04.44	Skua I L2951	Twatt 771 Sqdn.	Forced landing in sea 6 miles west of Stromness: Pilot Sub.Lt. Louis F. Weatherall RNZNVR, age 22, killed: buried St. Olaf's, Plot 33, Grave 8: L/A TAG Derrick Read, age 19, killed: body sank during recovery.
01.05.44	Martinet TT.1 ?	Twatt 771 Sqdn.	Spun into ground, Rousay: Walrus X9586 Twatt, Pilot C P O Crozer and Observer N. Brown flew out to investigate: Pilot P/O (A) G. H. Abbott, age 20, killed: buried St. Olaf's Plot 33, Grave 10: L/A TAG A. S. Boar, age 20 killed: buried Plot 33, Grave 19.
09.05.44	Oxford I BG555	Skeabrae 598 Sqdn.	Crashed in Scapa Flow east of Cava on Army Co-operative Exercise: Pilot W/O D. S. McGregor, Fl. Mechanic LAC H. E. Haywood, passenger Fl/Lt W. O. Helm all missing, presumed killed.
11.05.44	Hurricane IIB PG483	Twatt 771 Sqdn.	After exercising with HMS *Nelson* and HMS *Argonaut*, crashed on landing at Twatt due to ground loop: Pilot P/O Haslam OK.
12.05.44	Blenheim IV V6285?	Twatt 771 Sqdn.	Off runway and on its nose in the mud. (*photographic record*)
23.05.44	Martinet TT.1 MS684	Twatt 771 Sqdn.	Write-off: no further details.
30.05.44	Ju-88	Luftwaffe	Shot down at 25,000' by Spitfires of 118 Sqdn. Skeabrae, Pilots F/O J. J. Parker (Australian) and W/O Taylor: no survivors.
06.04.44 - 06.06.44	Wildcat V ?	Hatston 882 Sqdn.	Landing at Hatston through cloud cover Pilot Lt. W. (Bill) Edney RNZNVR, disappeared without trace.
10.06.44	Vickers Warwick I BV417	Wick 281 Sqdn.	Returning from search for missing Catalina at 62 22' N, 02 01' E, ditched in Scapa Flow due lack of pressure in starboard engine: Pilot Officer J. A. Murray and crew OK.
11.06.44	Mosquito FB.VI HR133-N	Leuchars 33 Sqdn.	Shot down by two 118 Sqdn. Skeabrae Spitfires, BL718 and BM423 into Auskerry Sound very close to Stronsay: one crew member of Mosquito killed: Pilot of BL718 (name withheld) cleared by court martial.
17.06.44	Barracuda II BV922	HMS *Furious* 827 Sqdn.	Forced landing in Scapa Flow due supercharger or valve gear failure: three crew picked up including Lt George Cockburn-Yorke, perhaps the only naval officer to ditch wearing mess kit!
05.07.44	Hellcat I ?	Hatston 1840 Sqdn.	Crashed at Grimsetter: no further details.
11.07.44	Corsair JT461	HMS *Formidable* 1841 Sqdn.	Took off from Hatston, 11.40 am en route to HMS *Formidable*: crashed on Hoy: wreckage discovered only one week later: Pilot Lt. (A) Edward de E. Hewetson, RNZNVR, buried Lyness RN Cemetery, Hoy, Plot H, north border, Grave 6.
14.07.44	Martinet TT.1 ?	Twatt 771 sqdn.	Engine failure on take off with 32 ft. winged target in tow: ditched in Isbister Loch; Pilot P/O Eric Haslam concussed and flown to hospital ship: P/O Scougall OK.
08.08.44	Seafire F.III LR819	Skeabrae 880 Sqdn.	Struck contractor's car parked near perimeter track, Skeabrae: damage XI-S: Pilot Sub.Lt. Penfold OK but lost 10.03.45.
14.08.44	Martinet TT.I ?	Twatt 771 Sqdn.	Aircraft struck mast of dockyard drifter and crashed into Scapa Flow: Pilot P/O (A) Keith Foster killed: buried St. Olaf's Plot 33, Grave 13: TAG L/A Donald R. Griffiths, age 19 killed: buried Plot 33, Grave 21. (*photographic record of pilot*)
22.08.44	Barracuda II MD647	Hatston 814 Sqdn.	Engine failure at 20' on take off at Hatston: belly-landed: write-off: Pilot Lt (A) D. M. Bell OK.
23.08.44	Tiger Moth NL699	Skeabrae 313 Sqdn. (Czech.)	Caught by gust of wind as it took off from emergency landing ground on Stronsay: stalled and crashed: Pilot F/Sgt Hallatt OK.
24.08.44	Grumman Avenger I Y155	HMS *Trumpeter* 846 Sqdn.	Took off from Scapa Flow for compass swinging at Hatston: did not gain height: crashed into sea and sank in 90 seconds: not recovered: Pilot Sub.Lt. Thomas, A/G David Heath, A/M Arthur Jacobs and Observer (name unknown) OK.
17.09.44	Fairey Firefly DT946	HMS *Indefatigable* 1770 Sqdn.	Crashed after take off from HMS *Indefatigable*, Orkney.
09.10.44	Ju-88 ?	Luftwaffe	Shot down 80 miles ENE of Herma Ness by 611 Sqdn. Skeabrae (flying from Sumburgh?)
16.10.44	Grumman Avenger I 'F'	HMS *Fencer* 852 Sqdn.	Stalled and crashed into sea on take-off from HMS *Fencer* for A/S patrol on return to Scapa Flow from minelaying and shipping strike Årumsund Fjord, Norway: Sub.Lt. (A) A. S. Watson, Sub.Lt. (A) F. Bromilow and P/O Aitken all picked up by dinghy from HMS *Scorpion*.
17.10.44	Short S.25 Sunderland II T9088	4-OTU	Missing off Orkney.
22.10.44	Blenheim IV V6251 T8U	Twatt 771 Sqdn.	Tyre burst on landing: aircraft tipped on nose: Pilot Lt (A) Keith Remmington, RNVR, P/O W. Jones OK.
16.11.44	Catalina IVA JX264	Sullom Voe 210 Sqdn.	Flew into sea off Orkney: no other details known.
02.12.44	Wildcat VI JV751	HMS *Trumpeter* 846 Sqdn.	Crashed over port side of carrier off Orkney: Sub.Lt. (A) A. E. Ames RNVR.
03.12.44	Firefly I DV122 'J'	HMS *Implacable* 1771 Sqdn.	Crash landed at Hatston on Dummy Deck landings when undercarriage was retracted in error after landing: Sub.Lt. W. R. Blatchley RNVR, OK.

1945

Date	Aircraft	Base/Sqdn.	Details
01.01.45	Liberator GR.V FL949Y	Tain 331 Sqdn.	Failed to heed high ground warning: crashed near Rora Head, Hoy: all eight Czech crew killed: buried Tain.
08.01.45	Spitfire VC EE772	Skeabrae 441 Sqdn. (Canadian)	Turned off Skeabrae runway after landing and high wind tipped aircraft on to nose.
13.02.45	Supermarine Seafire III NN329	Grimsetter 880 Sqdn.	Pilot's glove caught in cockpit hood on take-off, obstructing vision: crashed, killing Pilot Midshipman Ian Penfold: buried St. Olaf's.
??.02.45	Avenger I ?	Hatston 856 Sqdn.	Overturned in cross-wind landing at Hatston; 4 crew OK including WREN passenger in turret!
??.02.45	Sikorsky R-4 Hoverfly	Twatt 771 Sqdn.	Slewed round on take-off and tail rotor struck a parked Blenheim: both aircraft badly damaged: helicopter a write-off but reconstructed at Twatt for pilot/technician instruction purposes.
04.03.45	Sikorsky R-4B Hoverfly KK971	Twatt 771 Sqdn.	Forced landing off Hoy; sank at mooring.
10.03.45	Spitfire ?	Skeabrae 441 Sqdn. (Canadian)	Fl/Lt E. W. Martin on an exercise disappeared south of Orkney: extensive search revealed nothing: pilot presumed killed.
21.03.45	Seafire F.III LR856	Non-operational Ex 880 Sqdn?	Being ferried to Donibristle (from Grimsetter); pilot flew into low cloud, struck hillside and burst into flames half mile west of Settiscarth in Firth: Sub.Lt. Isaac G. Cohen RNVR, HMS *Merlin* killed: buried Willesden Jewish Cemetery, London.
31.03.45	Liberator B-24-H-CF 42-50331	Harrington (Beds.) 331 Sqdn.	One of several B-24 aircraft using Kinloss as an advanced base for operations against Norway; emergency forced landing due to engine failure; crashed Walliwall west of Kirkwall and burst into flames: Co-Pilot Peter Pulrang baled out at low altitude and survived: Pilot Henry Polansky, six crew and six Norwegian commandos killed.
??.04.45	Reliant I FB542	Twatt 771 Sqdn.	Crashed at Twatt: Pilot Alec Gray, passengers Alex Surgenor and Wren Mary Kiddie, photographer, Twatt, unhurt.
06.04.45	Spitfire LF.IX TB914	Skeabrae 329 Sqdn. (Free French)	On dawn patrol crashed in mist at 500' on Skelday Hill, Birsay at 6.36 am, four minutes after take-off; Pilot Capitaine Sassard, Free French, killed: buried St. Olaf's Cemetery 10.04.45.
19.04.45	Martinet TT.1 MS632	Twatt 771 Sqdn.	Undercarriage collapsed on landing: write-off.
23.04.45	Corsair JS588	Twatt 771 Sqdn.	Non operational: hit hillside near Quoyloo, Sandwick and disintegrated: Sub.Lt. (A) Alfred G. Playford RNVR, killed: buried Norwich Cemetery, Norfolk. (*photographic records*)
27.04.45	Avenger II JZ400	Hatston 853 Sqdn.	Arrester hook pulled out after catching No. 1 wire on embarking HMS *Queen* in Scapa Flow: ran into parked squadron aircraft and caused much damage.
01.06.45	Dominie II NR795	Skeabrae Station Flight	Hit Nissen hut, Millfield Camp, Stromness: Sgt. Dennis, Sgt W. F. Colborne and Cpl. N. C. Brimmicombe all killed: Pilot Fl/O T. G. R. Roe died of injuries in Kirkwall.

Aviation War Diary

ORKNEY

1939 - 1945

Introduction

This diary was compiled to assist the author in writing *Sky Over Scapa 1939 - 1945* and is a book in itself. It was not initially intended for publication but at the request of several enthusiasts who became aware of the diary after a copy was placed in the Orkney Library, a modest 50 spirally bound copies were produced for sale. With the publication of this new edition of *Sky Over Scapa 1939 - 1945* the opportunity has been taken to include the diary so that it can become more widely available. The diary details on a daily basis movements of squadrons and flights of Fleet Air Arm and Royal Air Force aircraft to and from Orkney during World War II and gives a dramatic impression of the high degree of activity at the military airfields on the islands. The information at the base of the monthly sheet gives details of the aircraft operated by each squadron, the station/carrier from which the squadrons arrived and to which they departed.

There were altogether 89 squadrons of aircraft based in Orkney during the war years. 13 front-line squadrons of Royal Naval aircraft spent more than five months on the islands which gives a good idea of the amount of training that was undertaken. Of the 19 squadrons of RAF aircraft, six of them spent more than six months. 1944 was the busiest year when there were, on average, 13 squadrons based in the islands every month. February 1943 however holds the record; in that exceptional month there were 16 squadrons based in Orkney. In the summary which follows it can be seen that the island squadrons operated 37 types of aircraft during the war years. These statistics do not take into account all the aircraft which visited Orkney, bringing in supplies, distinguished visitors, or temporarily diverted because of bad weather. The Brewster Buffalo was evaluated at Hatston; American squadrons stationed here brought the Grumman Duck; the Handley Page Harrow and Catalina were frequent visitors to Orkney. Such aircraft do not appear in official records but the reader will find frequent reference to them in the book.

Twenty six Royal Naval aircraft carriers disembarked aircraft to, or received aircraft from, Orkney airfields. The highest number of aircraft carriers recorded in Scapa Flow at any one time was 10. For some of these such as *Glorious*, *Audacity* and *Avenger* and USS *Wasp*, their last voyage from the islands ended in disaster. A number of carriers e.g. *Vindex* and *Illustrious* used the naval base without disembarking aircraft to shore stations. United States Navy *Wasp* and *Ranger* not only used Scapa as a base but also disembarked squadrons for training. Such disembarkation and embarkation usually took place outside Scapa Flow to give the carrier an opportunity to head into the wind at speed but sometimes, in strong winds, this could be attempted in the safety of Scapa Flow itself.

Operational squadron arrived in Orkney from a number of stations the length and breadth of Britain. The speed at which some of these squadrons moved, even in the early years of the war, is remarkable. A detachment of Sea Hurricanes of 801 squadron which left St. Merryn in Cornwall on 8th November via West Freugh and Arbroath took 4 hours 40 minutes to complete the journey to Skeabrae! How envious must have been the poor infantryman who trundled north for two days on the troop train Jellicoe and then had to face the rigours of the Pentland Firth. Altogether 47 stations despatched aircraft to, or received aircraft from, Orkney stations. Many of these stations are well known today e.g. Abbotsinsch (Glasgow Airport), Turnhouse (Edinburgh Airport), or Yeovilton, still a Royal Naval Air Station, but of some, such as Charlton Horethorne or Zeals, there is no trace. To guide the reader, the location of all these stations is given.

The complex movement of squadrons in war-time is mind-boggling. Is what we see in these pages part of some grand design or merely the result of pragmatic decisions made by the exigencies of war? Probably a little of both as can be seen from the June 1944 page of the diary where we note that anything capable of flying has been moved south to back up the Normandy invasion. Pilots of 845 Squadron Avengers on the other hand who spent six months hard training in Orkney skies in 1943 and 1944 were convinced that the Admiralty had forgotten about them!

Much of the material in this war diary has been pooled from Ray Sturtivant's *Squadrons of the Fleet Air Arm* and James Halley's *Squadrons of the RAF*. The writer owes a sincere debt of gratitude to both these researchers.

Military Aircraft

Based in Orkney,

1939-1945

Albacore	March 1941 - April 1943
Anson	December 1942 - June 1943
Avenger	July 1943 - July 1945
Barracuda	January 1943 - April 1945
Blenheim	April 1940 - May 1945
Boston	September 1944 - July 1945
Chesapeake	May 1942 - April 1944
Corsair	August 1944 - July 1945
Defiant	June 1942 - August 1943
Dominie	August 1944 - August 1945
Expeditor	August 1944 - July 1945
Firefly	December 1943 - September 1945
Fulmar	June 1941 - October 1942
Havoc	December 1942 - September 1944
Hellcat	April 1944 - September 1945
Helldiver	October 1944 - November 1944
Henley	October 1939 - August 1943
Hoverfly	January 1945 - July 1945
Hurricane	January 1941 - April 1945
Kingfisher	February 1942 - January 1943
Martinet	August 1943 - July 1945
Martlet	September 1940 - November 1943
Maryland	October 1940 - September 1944
Roc	August 1939 - May 1944
Sea Fox	January 1940 - September 1942
Sea Gladiator	September 1939 - June 1944
Sea Otter	December 1942 - July 1945
Sea Hurricane	July 1941 - June 1944
Seafire	September 1942 - July 1945
Skua	August 1939 - April 1944
Spitfire	November 1941 - July 1945
Swordfish	August 1939 - June 1944
Traveller	August 1944 - September 1944
Walrus	November 1939 - June 1944
Whitney Straight	December 1940 - January 1941
Wildcat	February 1943 - June 1945

Aircraft Carriers

disembarking squadrons to and/or embarking squadrons from,

Orkney Airfields,

1939 - 1945

Royal Navy

Argus	April 1941 - June 1943
Ark Royal	August 1939 - June 1940
Audacity	September 1941
Avenger	July 1942 - October 1942
Biter	February 1943
Campania	January 1945 - March 1945
Chaser	February 1944
Dasher	February 1943
Emperor	April 1944 - May 1944
Fencer	April 1944 - June 1944
Formidable	October 1942 - November 1944
Furious	May 1940 - October 1944
Glorious	April 1940
Implacable	October 1944 - March 1945
Indefatigable	May 1944 - September 1944
Indomitable	October 1941
Khedive	May 1944
Nabob	August 1944
Nairana	January 1945 - February 1945
Premier	September 1944 - May 1945
Puncher	February 1945 - April 1945
Pursuer	April 1944 - March 1945
Queen	March 1945 - April 1945
Searcher	April 1944 - April 1945
Striker	April 1944 - July 1944
Trumpeter	August 1944 - April 1945
Victorious	May 1941 - June 1944

United States Navy

Ranger	September 1943
Wasp	April 1941 - May 1941

Air Stations

from which squadrons arrived and to which they departed

Abbotsinsch	Strathclyde; transferred to Royal Navy from RAF; now Glasgow Airport
Arbroath	Tayside; RN Air Station
Ayr	Strathclyde; originally RAF Station transferring latterly to Royal Navy
Banff	Grampian; RAF Station
Bircham Newton	Norfolk; RAF Station
Campbeltown	Strathclyde; RN Air Station
Castletown	Highland; RAF Station
Charlton Horethorne	Somerset; originally RAF Station; later transferred to Royal Navy
Churchstanton	Somerset; RAF Station
Crail	Fife; RN Air Station
Detling	Kent; RAF Station
Donibristle	Fife; RN Air Station affectionately known as 'Donny Bee'
Drem	Lothian; RAF Station
Dunino	Fife; originally RAF Station, transferred later to Royal Navy
Dyce	Grampian; RAF Station; now Aberdeen Airport
Eglinton	Northern Ireland; originally RAF Station; transferred to Royal Navy
Evanton	Highland; originally RAF Station; transferred later to Royal Navy
Fearn	Highland; originally RAF Station; transferred to Royal Navy
Gosport	Hampshire; RAF Station
Harrowbeer	Devon; RAF Station
Hawkinge	Kent; RAF Station
Ibsley	Hampshire; RAF Station
Lasham	Hampshire; RAF Station
Leconfield	Humberside; RAF Station
Lee	Hampshire; RN Air Station
Lympne	Kent; RN Air Station at beginning of war, it was soon transferred to RAF
Machrihanish	Strathclyde; RN Air Station
Martlesham Heath	Suffolk; RAF Station
Maydown	Northern Ireland; originally RAF Station; later transferred to Royal Navy
North Coates	Lincolnshire; RAF Station
Perranporth	Cornwall; RAF Station
Peterhead	Grampian; RAF Station
Skitten	Highland; RAF Station
St. Eval	Cornwall; RAF Station
St. Merryn	Cornwall; RN Air Station
Stornoway	Western Isles; RAF Station
Stretton	Lancashire; RN Air Station
Sumburgh	Shetland; RAF Station
Tain	Highland; RAF Station
Thorney Island	Sussex; RAF Station
Turnhouse	Lothian; RAF Station; present day Edinburgh Airport
West Freugh	Dumfries and Galloway; RAF Station
West Raynham	Norfolk; RAF Station
Wick	Highland; RAF Station
Worthy Down	Hampshire; transferred to Royal Navy from RAF in April 1945
Yeovilton	Somerset; RN Air Station
Zeals	Wiltshire

N.B Detachments are underlined

1939 August

	Hatston								Grimsetter				Twatt				Skeabrae		
1																			
2																			
3																			
4																			
5																			
6																			
7																			
8																			
9																			
10																			
11																			
12																			
13																			
14																			
15																			
16																			
17																			
18																			
19																			
20																			
21																			
22																			
23																			
24																			
25																			
26	771																		
27	771	800																	
28	771	800																	
29	771	800																	
30	771	800																	
31	771	800																	

771 Swordfish (from Evanton)

800 Skua II, Roc I (from Ark Royal)

1939 September

	Hatston									Grimsetter				Twatt				Skeabrae		
1	771																			
2	771																			
3	771																			
4	771																			
5	771																			
6	771																			
7	771																			
8	771																			
9	771																			
10	771																			
11	771	810																		
12	771	810																		
13	771	810																		
14	771																			
15	771																			
16	771																			
17	771																			
18	771																			
19	771																			
20	771																			
21	771	818																		
22	771	818																		
23	771																			
24	771																			
25	771																			
26	771																			
27	771	810	821																	
28	771	810	821																	
29	771	810																		
30	771	810																		

771 *Swordfish*

810 *Swordfish I (from Ark Royal)*

818 *Swordfish I (from Ark Royal)*

821 *Swordfish I (from Ark Royal)*

1939 October

	Hatston									Grimsetter				Twatt				Skeabrae		
1	771	803	818	810																
2	771	803	818																	
3	771	803	818																	
4	771	803	818																	
5	771	803	818																	
6	771	803	818																	
7	771	803	818																	
8	771	803	818																	
9	771	803	818																	
10	771	803	818																	
11	771	803	818																	
12	771	803	818																	
13	771	803	818																	
14	771	803	818																	
15	771	803	818																	
16	771	803	818																	
17	771	803	818	816																
18	771	803	818																	
19	771	803	818																	
20	771	803	818																	
21	771	803	818																	
22	771	803	818																	
23	771	803	818																	
24	771	803	818																	
25	771	803	818																	
26	771	803	818																	
27	771	803	818																	
28	771	803	818																	
29	771	803	818																	
30	771	803	818																	
31	771	803	818																	

771 *Swordfish, Henley III*

803 *Skua II, Roc I (from Ark Royal)*

810 *Swordfish I (from Ark Royal)*

816 *Swordfish I (Ark Royal)*

818 *Swordfish I (from Ark Royal)*

1939 November

	Hatston								Grimsetter				Twatt				Skeabrae			
1	771	818																		
2	771	818																		
3	771	818																		
4	771	818																		
5	771	818																		
6	771	818																		
7	771	818																		
8	771	818																		
9	771	818																		
10	771	818																		
11	771	818																		
12	771	818																		
13	771	818																		
14	771	818																		
15	771	818																		
16	771	818																		
17	771	818																		
18	771	818																		
19	771	818																		
20	771	818																		
21	771	818																		
22	771	818																		
23	771	818																		
24	771	818																		
25	771	818	769																	
26	771	818	769																	
27	771	818	769																	
28	771	818	769																	
29	771	818	769																	
30	771	818	804																	

769 Sea Gladiator

771 Swordfish, Henley III, Walrus

804 Sea Gladiator formed at Hatston as a shore based fighter squadron from a nucleus of the 4 Sea Gladiators of 769 Squadron based there.

818 Swordfish I

1939 December

	Hatston									Grimsetter					Twatt					Skeabrae			
1	771	818	804																					
2	771	818	804																					
3	771	818	804																					
4	771	818	804																					
5	771	818	804																					
6	771	818	804																					
7	771	818	804																					
8	771	818	804	803																				
9	771	818	804	803																				
10	771	818	804	803																				
11	771	818	804	803																				
12	771	818	804	803																				
13	771	818	804	803																				
14	771	818	804	803																				
15	771	818	804	803																				
16	771	818	804	803																				
17	771	818	804	803																				
18	771		804	803																				
19	771		804	803																				
20	771		804	803																				
21	771		804	803																				
22	771		804	803																				
23	771		804	803																				
24	771		804	803																				
25	771		804	803																				
26	771		804	803																				
27	771		804	803																				
28	771		804	803																				
29	771		804	803																				
30	771		804	803																				
31	771		804	803																				

771 Swordfish, Henley III, Walrus

803 Skua II, Roc I (from Ark Royal)

804 Sea Gladiator

818 Swordfish I (to Abbotsinsch)

1940 January

	Hatston								Grimsetter				Twatt				Skeabrae		
1	771		804	803															
2	771		804	803															
3	771		804	803															
4	771		804	803															
5	771		804	803															
6	771		804	803															
7	771		804	803															
8	771		804	803															
9	771		804	803															
10	771		804	803															
11	771		804																
12	771		804																
13	771		804																
14	771		804																
15	771		804																
16	771		804																
17	771		804																
18	771		804																
19	771		804																
20	771		804																
21	771	700	804																
22	771	700	804																
23	771	700	804																
24	771	700	804																
25	771	700	804																
26	771	700	804																
27	771	700	804																
28	771	700	804																
29	771	700	804																
30	771	700	804																
31	771	700	804																

700 Walrus, Swordfish I/SP, Seafox I (formed at Hatston by amalgamating the 700 Series of Catapult Flights)

771 Swordfish, Henley III, Walrus I

803 Skua II, Roc I (to Wick)

804 Sea Gladiator

	Hatston								Grimsetter			Twatt			Skeabrae		
1	700	771	804														
2	700	771	804														
3	700	771	804														
4	700	771	804														
5	700	771	804														
6	700	771	804														
7	700	771	804														
8	700	771	804														
9	700	771	804														
10	700	771	804	803													
11	700	771	804	803													
12	700	771	804	803													
13	700	771	804	803													
14	700	771	804	803													
15	700	771	804	803	800												
16	700	771	804	803	800												
17	700	771	804	803	800												
18	700	771	804	803	800												
19	700	771	804	803	800												
20	700	771	804	803	800												
21	700	771	804	803	800												
22	700	771	804	803	800												
23	700	771	804	803	800												
24	700	771	804	803	800												
25	700	771	804	803	800												
26	700	771	804	803	800												
27	700	771	804	803	800												
28	700	771	804	803	800												
29	700	771	804	803	800												

700 *Walrus, Swordfish I/SP, Seafox I*

771 *Swordfish, Henley III, Walrus*

800 *Skua II (from Ark Royal)*

803 *Skua II, Roc I (from Wick)*

804 *Sea Gladiator*

1940 March

	Hatston							Grimsetter				Twatt				Skeabrae		
1	770	771	804	800	803													
2	770	771	804	800	803													
3	770	771	804	800	803													
4	770	771	804	800	803													
5	770	771	804	800	803													
6	770	771	804	800	803													
7	770	771	804	800	803													
8	770	771	804	800	803													
9	770	771	804	800	803													
10	770	771	804	800	803													
11	770	771	804	800	803													
12	770	771	804	800	803													
13	770	771	804	800	803													
14	770	771	804	800	803													
15	770	771	804	800	803													
16	770	771	804	800	803													
17	770	771	804	800	803													
18	770	771	804	800	803													
19	770	771	804	800	803													
20	770	771	804	800	803													
21	770	771	804	800	803													
22	770	771	804	800	803													
23	770	771	804	800	803													
24	770	771	804	800	803													
25	770	771	804	800	803													
26	770	771	804	800	803													
27	770	771	804	800	803													
28	770	771	804	800	803	806												
29	770	771	804	800	803	806												
30	770	771	804	800	803	806												
31	770	771	804	800	803													

700 Walrus, Swordfish I/SP, Seafox I

771 Swordfish, Henley III

800 Skua II

803 Skua II, Roc I

804 Sea Gladiator

806 Skua II, Roc I (from Worthy Down to West Freugh)

1940 April

	Hatston								Grimsetter			Twatt			Skeabrae			
1	770	771	804	800	803													
2	770	771	804	800	803													
3	770	771	804	800	803													
4	770	771	804	800	803													
5	770	771	804	800	803													
6	770	771	804	800	803													
7	770	771	804	800	803													
8	770	771	804	800	803													
9	770	771	804	800	803													
10	770	771	804	800	803													
11	770	771	804	800	803													
12	770	771	804	800	803	801												
13	770	771	804	800	803	801												
14	770	771	804	800	803	801												
15	770	771	804	800	803	801												
16	770	771	804	800	803	801												
17	770	771	804	800	803	801												
18	770	771	804	800	803	801	823											
19	770	771	804	800	803	801	823											
20	770	771	804	800	803	801	823											
21	770	771	804	800	803		823											
22	770	771						254										
23	770	771						254										
24	770	771						254										
25	770	771						254										
26	770	771						254										
27	770	771						254										
28	770	771			803			254										
29	770	771			803			254										
30	770	771			803			254										
31	770	771	820		803			254										

700 Walrus, Swordfish I/SP, Seafox I

771 Swordfish, Skua II, Roc I, Henley III

800 Skua II (to Ark Royal)

801 Skua II (from Evanton to Hatston to Ark Royal)

803 Skua II, Roc I (to Glorious)

804 Sea Gladiator (to Glorious)

820 Swordfish I (from Ark Royal)

823 Swordfish I (from Glorious to Evanton)

254 Blenheim IV (from Bircham Newton)

1940 May

	Hatston								Grimsetter			Twatt				Skeabrae		
1	700	771	820	806	803	254												
2	700	771	820	806	803	254												
3	700	771	820	806		254												
4	700	771		806		254												
5	700	771		806		254												
6	700	771		806		254												
7	700	771		806		254												
8	700	771		806		254												
9	700	771		806		254												
10	700	771		806		254												
11	700	771		806		254												
12	700	771		806		254												
13	700	771		806		254												
14	700	771	823	806		254												
15	700	771	823	806	_801_	254												
16	700	771	823	806	_801_													
17	700	771	823	806	_801_													
18	700	771	823	806	_801_													
19	700	771	823	806	_801_													
20	700	771	823	806	_801_													
21	700	771	823	806														
22	700	771	823															
23	700	771	823			804												
24	700	771	823			804												
25	700	771	823	800	803	804												
26	700	771	823	800	803	804												
27	700	771	823	800	803	804												
28	700	771	823	800	803	804												
29	700	771	823	800	803	804												
30	700	771	823	800	803	804												
31	700	771	823			804												

700 *Walrus, Swordfish I/SP, Seafox I*

771 *Swordfish, Skua II, Roc I, Henley III*

800 *Skua II, Roc I (from Ark Royal)*

801 *Skua II (Furious)*

803 *Skua II (to Ark Royal)*

804 *Sea Gladiator (from Furious)*

806 *Skua II (from West Freugh)*

820 *Swordfish I (to Ark Royal)*

823 *Swordfish I (from Evanton)*

254 *Blenheim IV (to Sumburgh)*

1940 June

	Hatston								Grimsetter			Twatt			Skeabrae			
1	700	771	821	823	804													
2	700	771	821	823	804													
3	700	771	821	823	804													
4	700	771	821	823	804													
5	700	771	821	823	804													
6	700	771	821	823	804													
7	700	771	821	823	804													
8	700	771	821	823	804													
9	700	771	821	823	804													
10	700	771	821	823	804													
11	700	771	821	823	804													
12	700	771	821	823	804													
13	700	771	821	823	804													
14	700	771	821	823	804	800	701	803										
15	700	771	821	823	804	800	701	803										
16	700	771	821	823	804			803										
17	700	771	821	823	804													
18	700	771	821	823	804													
19	700	771	821	823	804													
20	700	771	821	823	804													
21	700	771	821	823	804													
22	700	771	821	823	804													
23	700	771	821	823	804	801												
24	700	771	821	823	804	801												
25	700	771	821	823	804	801												
26	700	771	821	823	804	801												
27	700	771	821	823	804	801												
28	700	771	821	823	804	801												
29	700	771	821	823	804	801												
30	700	771	821	823	804	801												

700 *Walrus, Swordfish I/SP, Seafox I*

701 *Walrus (from Ark Royal to Donibristle)*

771 *Swordfish, Skua II, Roc I, Henley III*

800 *Skua II (Ark Royal)*

801 *Skua II, Roc I (from Detling to Furious)*

803 *Skua II (Ark Royal)*

804 *Sea Gladiator*

821 *Swordfish I (from Evanton)*

823 *Swordfish I*

1940 July

	Hatston							Grimsetter			Twatt				Skeabrae		
1	700	771	821	823	801		804										
2	700	771	821	823	801		804										
3	700	771	821	823	801		804										
4	700	771	821	823	801		804										
5	700	771	821	823	801		804										
6	700	771	821	823	801		804										
7	700	771	821	823	801		804										
8	700	771	821	823	801		804										
9	700	771	821	823	801		804										
10	700	771	821	823	801		804										
11	700	771	821	823	801		804										
12	700	771	821	823	801		804										
13	700	771	821	823	801		804										
14	700	771	821	823	801		804										
15	700	771	821	823	801		804										
16	700	771	821	823	801		804										
17	700	771	821	823	801		804										
18	700	771	821	823	801		804										
19	700	771	821	823	801		804										
20	700	771	821	823	801		804										
21	700	771	821	823	801		804										
22	700	771	821	823	801		804										
23	700	771	821	823	801		804										
24	700	771	821	823	801		804										
25	700	771	821	823	801		804										
26	700	771	821	823	801	825	804										
27	700	771	821	823	801	825	804										
28	700	771	821	823	801	825	804										
29	700	771	821	823	801	825	804										
30	700	771	821	823	801	825	804										
31	700	771	821	823	801		804										

700 *Walrus, Swordfish I/SP, Seafox I*

771 *Swordfish, Skua II, Roc I, Henley III*

801 *Skua II*

804 *Sea Gladiator*

821 *Swordfish I*

823 *Swordfish I*

825 *Swordfish I (Furious)*

1940 August

	Hatston							Grimsetter		Twatt		Skeabrae		
1	700	771	821	823	801		804							
2	700	771	821	823	801		804							
3	700	771	821	823	801		804							
4	700	771	821	823	801		804							
5	700	771	821	823	801		804							
6	700	771	821	823	801		804							
7	700	771	821	823	801		804							
8	700	771	821	823	801		804							
9	700	771	821	823	801		804							
10	700	771	821	823	801		804							
11	700	771	821	823	801		804							
12	700	771	821	823	801		804							
13	700	771	821	823	801		804							
14	700	771	821	823	801		804							
15	700	771	821	823	801		804							
16	700	771	821	823	801		804							
17	700	771	821	823	801		804							
18	700	771	821	823	801		804							
19	700	771	821	823	801		804							
20	700	771	821	823	801		804							
21	700	771	821	823	801		804							
22	700	771	821	823	801		804							
23	700	771	821	823	801	825	804							
24	700	771	821	823	801	825	804							
25	700	771	821	823	801	825	804							
26	700	771	821	823	801	825	804							
27	700	771	821	823	801	825	804							
28	700	771	821	823	801	825	804							
29	700	771	821	823	801	825	804							
30	700	771	821	823	801	825	804							
31	700	771	821	823	801	825	804							

700 *Walrus, Swordfish I S/P, Seafox I*

771 *Swordfish, Skua II, Roc I, Henley III*

801 *Skua II*

804 *Sea Gladiator*

821 *Swordfish I*

823 *Swordfish I*

825 *Swordfish I (from Furious)*

	Hatston								Grimsetter			Twatt			Skeabrae		
1	700	771	821	823	801	825	804										
2	700	771	821	823	801	825	804										
3	700	771	821	823	801	825	804										
4	700	771	821	823	801	825	804										
5	700	771	821	823	801		804										
6	700	771	821	823	801		804										
7	700	771	821	823	801		804										
8	700	771	821	823	801		804										
9	700	771	821	823	801		804										
10	700	771	821	823	801		804										
11	700	771	821	823	801		804										
12	700	771	821	823			804										
13	700	771	821	823			804	816									
14	700	771	821	823			804	816									
15	700	771	821	823			804	816							0		
16	700	771	821	823			804	816									
17	700	771	821	823			804	816									
18	700	771	821	823			804	816									
19	700	771	821	823			804	816									
20	700	771	821	823			804										
21	700	771	821	823			804										
22	700	771	821	823	801		804										
23	700	771	821	823	801		804										
24	700	771	821	823	801	825	804										
25	700	771	821	823	801	825	804	816									
26	700	771	821	823	801	825	804	816									
27	700	771	821	823	801	825	804	816									
28	700	771	821	823	801	825	804										
29	700	771	821	823	801	825	804										
30	700	771	821	823	801	825	804										

700 Walrus, Swordfish I S/P, Seafox I

771 Swordfish, Skua II, Roc I, Henley III

801 Skua II

804 Sea Gladiator

816 Swordfish I (Furious)

821 Swordfish I

823 Swordfish I

825 Swordfish I (to Furious)

1940 October

	Hatston								Grimsetter		Twatt			Skeabrae			
1	700	771	821	823	801	804											
2	700	771	821	823	801	804											
3	700	771	821	823	801	804											
4	700	771	821	823	801	804											
5	700	771	821	823	801	804											
6	700	771	821	823	801	804	816										
7	700	771	821	823	801	804											
8	700	771	821	823	801	804											
9	700	771	821	823	801	804											
10	700	771	821	823	801									804			
11	700	771	821	823										804			
12	700	771	821	823										804			
13	700	771	821	823										804			
14	700	771	821	823										804			
15	700	771	821	823										804			
16	700	771	821	823										804			
17	700	771	821	823										804			
18	700	771	821	823										804			
19	700	771	821	823	801	804											
20	700	771	821	823	801	804											
21	700	771	821	823	801	804											
22	700	771	821	823	801	804											
23	700	771	821	823	801	804											
24	700	771	821	823	801	804											
25	700	771	821	823	801	804											
26	700	771	821	823	801	804											
27	700	771	821	823	801	804											
28	700	771	821	823	801									804			
29	700	771	821	823	801									804			
30	700	771	821	823	801									804			
31	700	771	821	823	801									804			

700 *Walrus, Swordfish I S/P, Seafox I*

771 *Swordfish, Skua II, Roc I, Henley III, Maryland*

801 *Skua II (Furious)*

804 *Martlet I*

816 *Swordfish I (transit, Furious to Campbeltown)*

821 *Swordfish I*

823 *Swordfish I*

1940 November

	Hatston								Grimsetter			Twatt			Skeabrae			
1	700	771	821	823	801										804			
2	700	771	821	823	801										804			
3	700	771	821	823	801										804			
4	700	771	821	823	801										804			
5	700	771	821	823	801										804			
6	700	771	821	823	801										804			
7	700	771	821	823	801										804			
8	700	771	821	823	801										804			
9	700	771	821	823											804			
10	700	771	821	823											804			
11	700	771	821	823											804			
12	700	771	821	823											804			
13	700	771	821	823											804			
14	700	771	821	823											804			
15	700	771	821	823											804			
16	700	771	821	823											804			
17	700	771	821	823											804			
18	700	771	821	823											804			
19	700	771	821	823											804			
20	700	771	821	823											804			
21	700	771	821	823	801										804			
22	700	771	821	823	801										804			
23	700	771	821	823	801										804			
24	700	771	821	823	801										804			
25	700	771	821	823	801										804			
26	700	771	821	823	801										804			
27	700	771	821	823	801										804			
28	700	771	821	823	801										804			
29	700	771	821	823	801										804			
30	700	771	821	823	801										804			
31																		

700 *Walrus, Swordfish I S/P, Seafox I*

771 *Swordfish, Skua II, Roc I, Henley III, Maryland*

801 *Skua II (to Furious)*

802 *12 x Martlet I (formed at Hatston)*

804 *Martlet I*

821 *Swordfish I*

823 *Swordfish I*

1940 December

	Hatston								Grimsetter				Twatt				Skeabrae			
1	700	771	821	823	802												804			
2	700	771		823	802												804			
3	700	771		823	802												804			
4	700	771			802												804			
5	700	771			802												804			
6	700	771			802												804			
7	700	771			802												804			
8	700	771			802												804			
9	700	771															804			
10	700	771															804			
11	700	771															804			
12	700	771															804			
13	700	771															804			
14	700	771	801														804			
15	700	771	801														804			
16	700	771	801														804			
17	700	771	801														804			
18	700	771	801														804			
19	700	771	801														804			
20	700	771	801														804			
21	700	771	801														804			
22	700	771	801														804			
23	700	771	801														804			
24	700	771	801														804			
25	700	771	801														804			
26	700	771	801														804			
27	700	771	801														804			
28	700	771	801														804			
29	700	771	801														804			
30	700	771	801														804			
31	700	771	801														804			

700 Walrus, Swordfish I S/P, Seafox I

771 Swordfish, Skua II, Roc I, Henley III, Maryland

801 Skua II

802 Martlet I (to Donibristle)

804 Whitney Straight, Sea Gladiator, Martlet I

821 Swordfish I (disbanded: replaced by X Flight: to Donibristle)

823 Swordfish I (disbanded)

1941 January

	Hatston								Grimsetter			Twatt			Skeabrae			
1	700	771	801												804			
2	700	771	801												804			
3	700	771	801												804			
4	700	771	801												804			
5	700	771	801												804			
6	700	771	801												804			
7	700	771	801												3			
8	700	771	801												3			
9	700	771	801												3			
10	700	771	801												3			
11	700	771	801												3			
12	700	771	801												3			
13	700	771	801												3			
14	700	771	801												3			
15	700	771	801												3			
16	700	771	801												3			
17	700	771													3			
18	700	771													3			
19	700	771													3			
20	700	771													3			
21	700	771													3			
22	700	771													3			
23	700	771													3			
24	700	771													3			
25	700	771													3			
26	700	771													3			
27	700	771													3			
28	700	771													3			
29	700	771													3			
30	700	771													3			
31	700	771													3			

700 *Walrus, Swordfish I S/P, Seafox I*

771 *Swordfish, Skua II, Roc I, Henley III, Maryland*

801 *Skua II (to St. Merryn)*

804 *Sea Gladiator, Whitney Straight, Martlet I (to Skitten)*

3 *Hurricane IIA, IIB (from Castletown)*

1941 February

	Hatston							Grimsetter			Twatt			Skeabrae			
1	700	771												3			
2	700	771												3			
3	700	771												3			
4	700	771												3			
5	700	771												3			
6	700	771	801											3			
7	700	771	801											3			
8	700	771	801											3			
9	700	771	801											3			
10	700	771	801											253			
11	700	771	801											253			
12	700	771	801											253			
13	700	771	801											253			
14	700	771												253			
15	700	771												253			
16	700	771												253			
17	700	771												253			
18	700	771												253			
19	700	771												253			
20	700	771												253			
21	700	771												253			
22	700	771												253			
23	700	771												253			
24	700	771												253			
25	700	771												253			
26	700	771												253			
27	700	771												253			
28	700	771												253			

700 *Walrus, Swordfish I S/P, Seafox I*

771 *Swordfish, Skua II, Roc I, Henley III, Maryland*

801 *Skua II (from St. Eval to Donibristle)*

  3 *Hurricane IIA, IIB (to Castletown)*

253 *Hurricane I (from Leconfield)*

1941 March

	Hatston								Grimsetter			Twatt			Skeabrae			
1	700	771													253			
2	700	771													253			
3	700	771													253			
4	700	771													253			
5	700	771													253			
6	700	771													253			
7	700	771													253			
8	700	771													253			
9	700	771													253			
10	700	771													253			
11	700	771													253			
12	700	771													253			
13	700	771													253			
14	700	771													253			
15	700	771													253			
16	700	771													253			
17	700	771													253			
18	700	771													253			
19	700	771													253			
20	700	771													253			
21	700	771													253			
22	700	771													253			
23	700	771													253			
24	700	771	828												253			
25	700	771	828												253			
26	700	771	828												253			
27	700	771	828												253			
28	700	771	828												253			
29	700	771	828												253			
30	700	771	828												253			
31	700	771	828												253			

700 Walrus, Swordfish I S/P, Seafox I

771 Swordfish, Skua II, Roc I, Henley III, Maryland

828 Albacore I (from Donibristle)

253 Hurricane I

1941 April

	Hatston									Grimsetter			Twatt			Skeabrae			
1	700	771	828													253			
2	700	771	828													253			
3	700	771	828													253			
4	700	771	828													253			
5	700	771	828													253			
6	700	771	828													253			
7	700	771	828													253			
8	700	771	828													253			
9	700	771	828													253			
10	700	771	828													253			
11	700	771	828													253			
12	700	771	828													253			
13	700	771	828													253			
14	700	771	828													253			
15	700	771	828													253			
16	700	771	828													253			
17	700	771	828													253			
18	700	771	828													253			
19	700	771	828													253			
20	700	771	828													253			
21	700	771	828	812												253			
22	700	771	828	812												253			
23	700	771	828	812												253			
24	700	771	828	812												253			
25	700	771	828	812												253			
26	700	771	828	812												253			
27	700	771	828	812												253			
28	700	771	828	812												253			
29	700	771	828	812												253			
30	700	771	828	812												253			
31	700	771	828	812												253			

700 *Walrus, Swordfish I S/P, Seafox I*

771 *Swordfish, Skua II, Roc I, Henley III, Maryland, Blenheim I*

812 *Swordfish I (from Argus)*

828 *Albacore I*

253 *Hurricane I*

1941 May

	Hatston									Grimsetter			Twatt			Skeabrae			
1	700	771	828	812												253*			
2	700	771	828	812												253			
3	700	771	828	812												253			
4	700	771	828	812												253			
5	700	771	828	812												253			
6	700	771	828	812												253			
7	700	771	828	812												253			
8	700	771	828	812												253			
9	700	771	828	812												253			
10	700	771	828	812												253			
11	700	771	828	812												253			
12	700	771	828	812												253			
13	700	771	828	812												253			
14	700	771	828	812												253			
15	700	771	828	812												253			
16	700	771	828	812												253			
17	700	771	828	812	825											253			
18	700	771	828	812	825											253			
19	700	771	828	812												253			
20	700	771	828	812												253			
21	700	771	828	812												253			
22	700	771	828	812												253			
23	700	771		812												253			
24	700	771	828	812												253			
25	700	771	828	812												253			
26	700	771	828	812												253			
27	700	771	828	812												253			
28	700	771	828	812												253			
29	700	771	828	812												253			
30	700	771	828	812												253			
31	700	771	828	812												253			

700 *Walrus, Swordfish I S/P, Seafox I*

771 *Swordfish, Skua II, Roc I, Maryland, Henley III, Blenheim I, Albacore*

812 *Swordfish I*

825 *Swordfish I (from Campbeltown to Victorious)*

828 *Albacore I (to Sumburgh to intercept the Bismarck; recalled to Hatston)*

253 *Hurricane I*

* unknown number of extra squadrons drafted in to Skeabrae when Intelligence reported large build up of German troops and equipment in Norway indicating invasion of Northern Britain imminent: in the event the troop concentrations moved east for the invasion of Russia.

	Hatston								Grimsetter			Twatt			Skeabrae			
1	700	771	828	812											253			
2	700	771	828	812											253			
3	700	771	828	812											253			
4	700	771	828	812											253			
5	700	771	828	812											253			
6	700	771	828	812											253			
7	700	771	828	812											253			
8	700	771	828	812											253			
9	700	771	828	812											253			
10	700	771	828	812	809										253			
11	700	771	828	812	809										253			
12	700	771	828	812	809										253			
13	700	771	828	812	809										253			
14	700	771	828	812	809										253			
15	700	771	828	812	809										253			
16	700	771	828	812	809										253			
17	700	771	828	812	809										253			
18	700	771	828	812	809										253			
19	700	771	828	812	809										253			
20	700	771	828	812	809										253			
21	700	771	828	812	809										253			
22	700	771	828	812	809										253			
23	700	771	828	812	809										253			
24	700	771	828	812	809										253			
25	700	771	828		809										253			
26	700	771	828		809								812		253			
27	700	771	828		809								812		253			
28	700	771	828		809								812		253			
29	700	771	828		809								812		253			
30	700	771	828		809								812		253			
31	700	771	828		809								812		253			

700 *Walrus, Swordfish I S/P, Seafox I*

771 *Swordfish, Skua II, Roc I, Maryland, Henley III, Blenheim I*

809 *12 x Fulmar II (from St. Merryn)*

812 *Swordfish I*

828 *Albacore I*

253 *Hurricane I*

1941 July

	Hatston					Grimsetter	Twatt	Skeabrae
1	700	771	828	827	809		812	253
2	700	771					812	253
3	700	771					812	253
4	700	771					812	253
5	700	771					812	253
6	700	771					812	253
7	700	771					812	253
8	700	771					812	253
9	700	771					812	253
10	700	771					812	253
11	700	771					812	253
12	700	771					812	253
13	700	771					812	253
14	700	771					812	253
15	700	771					812	253
16	700	771	821				812	253
17	700	771	821					253
18	700	771	821					253
19	700	771	821					253
20	700	771	821				880	253
21	700	771	821					253
22	700	771	821					253
23	700	771	821					253
24	700	771	821					253
25	700	771	821					253
26	700	771	821					253
27	700	771	821					253
28	700	771	821				818	253
29	700	771	821				818	253
30	700	771	821				818	253
31	700	771	821				818	253

700 *Walrus, Swordfish I S/P, Seafox I*

771 *Swordfish, Skua II, Roc I, Maryland, Henley III, Blenheim I*

809 *Fulmar II (to Victorious)*

812 *Swordfish (to Furious)*

818 *9 x Swordfish I (from Arbroath)*

821 *Swordfish I (from Detling)*

827 *Albacore I (to Victorious)*

828 *Albacore I (to Victorious)*

880 *Sea Hurricane 1a (from Yeovilton to Furious)*

253 *Hurricane IIA,IIB*

	Hatston									Grimsetter			Twatt				Skeabrae			
1	700	771	821										818				253			
2	700	771	821										818				253			
3	700	771	821										818				253			
4	700	771	821										818				253			
5	700	771	821										818				253			
6	700	771	821										818				253			
7	700	771	821		809	817							818				253			
8	700	771	821	827	809	817							818				253			
9	700	771	821	827	809	817							818				253	310		
10	700	771	821	827	809	817							818				253	310		
11	700	771	821	827	809	817							818				253			
12	700	771	812	827	809	817							818				253			
13	700	771	812	827	809	817							818				253			
14	700	771	812	827	809								818	880			253			
15	700	771	812	827	809								818	880			253			
16	700	771	812	827	809								818	880			253			
17	700	771	812	827	809								818	880			253			
18	700	771	812	827	809								818	880			253			
19	700	771	812	827	809								818	880			253			
20	700	771	812	827	809								818	880			253			
21	700	771	812	827	809								818	880			253			
22	700	771	812	827									818	880			253			
23	700	771	812	827									818	880			253			
24	700	771		827									818	880			253			
25	700	771		827									818	880	802		253			
26	700	771		827									818	880	802		253			
27	700	771		827									818	880	802		253			
28	700	771		827									818	880	802		253			
29	700	771		827									818	880	802		253			
30	700	771		827									818	880	802		253			
31	700	771		827									818	880	802		253			

700 *Walrus, Swordfish I S/P, Seafox I*

771 *Swordfish, Skua II, Roc I, Maryland, Henley III, Blenheim I*

802 *Martlet I, Martlet III (from Machrihanish)*

809 *Fulmar II (from Victorious to Victorious)*

812 *9 x Swordfish I (from Furious to Furious)*

817 *Albacore I (from Furious to Victorious)*

818 *Swordfish I (to Machrihanish)*

821 *Swordfish I (from Hatston to Twatt)*

827 *Albacore I (from Victorious)*

880 *Sea Hurricane Ib (from St.Merryn*

253 *Hurricane IIA, IIB*

310 *Hurricane IIA (Czech.) - based at Dyce: escort for HM King George VI*

1941 September

	Hatston									Grimsetter			Twatt				Skeabrae			
1	700	771		827									821	880	802		253			
2	700	771		827									821	880	802		253			
3	700	771	809	827									821	880	802		253			
4	700	771	809	827									821	880	802		253			
5	700	771	809	827									821	880	802		253			
6	700	771	809	827									821	880	802		253			
7	700	771	809	827									821	880	802		253			
8	700	771	809	827									821	880	802		253			
9	700	771	809	827									821	880	802		253			
10	700	771	809	827									821	880			253			
11	700	771	809	827									821	880			253			
12	700	771	809	827									821	880			253			
13	700	771	809	827									821	880			253			
14	700	771	809	827									821	880			253			
15	700	771	809	827									821				253			
16	700	771	809	827									821				253			
17	700	771	809	827									821				253			
18	700	771	809	827									821				253			
19	700	771	809	827									821				253			
20	700	771	809	827									821	832			331			
21	700	771	809	827									821	832			331			
22	700	771	809	827									821	832			331			
23	700	771	809	827									821	832			331			
24	700	771		827									821				331			
25	700	771		827									821				331			
26	700	771		827									821				331			
27	700	771		827									821				331			
28	700	771		827									821				331			
29	700	771		827									821				331			
30	700	771		827									821				331			
31																				

700 *Walrus, Swordfish I S/P, Seafox I, Fulmar I*

771 *Swordfish, Skua II, Roc I, Maryland, Henley III, Blenheim I*

802 *Martlet I, Martlet III (to Audacity)*

809 *Fulmar II (Victorious)*

821 *Swordfish I*

827 *Albacore I*

832 *Albacore I (from Victorious to Victorious)*

880 *Sea Hurricane Ib (to Sumburgh)*

253 *Hurricane IIA, IIB (to Castletown)*

331 *Hurricane II B (Norwegian, from Castletown)*

1941 October

	Hatston					Grimsetter	Twatt		Skeabrae
1	700	771	827				821		331
2	700	771	827				821		331
3	700	771	827				821		331
4	700	771	827				821		331
5	700	771	827				821		331
6	700	771	827				821		331
7	700	771	827				821		331
8	700	771	827				821		331
9	700	771	827				821		331
10	700	771					821		331
11	700	771					821		331
12	700	771					821		331
13	700	771					821		331
14	700	771					821		331
15	700	771					821		331
16	700	771					821		331
17	700	771					821		331
18	700	771					821		331
19	700	771					821		331
20	700	771					821		331
21	700	771					821		331
22	700	771					821		331
23	700	771					821		331
24	700	771					821		331
25	700	771					821		331
26	700	771		817	832			809	331
27	700	771		817	832			809	331
28	700	771		817	832		821	809	331
29	700	771		817	832		821	809	331
30	700	771		817	832		821	809	331
31	700	771		817	832		821	809	331

700 Walrus, Swordfish I S/P, Seafox I, Fulmar I

771 Skua II, Roc I, Maryland, Henley III, Blenheim I

809 Fulmar II (from Victorious)

817 Albacore I (from Donibristle)

821 Swordfish I (to Machrihanish; return to Twatt)

827 Albacore I (to Indomitable)

832 Albacore I (from Victorious)

331 Hurricane IIB (Norwegian)

1941 November

	Hatston								Grimsetter			Twatt				Skeabrae			
1	700	771	817	832	820							809	821			331			
2	700	771	817	832	820							809	821			331			
3	700	771			820							809	821			331			
4	700	771			820							809	821			331			
5	700	771			820							809				331			
6	700	771			820							809				331			
7	700	771			820							809				331			
8	700	771			820							809				331	801		
9	700	771			820							809				331	801		
10	700	771			820							809				331	801		
11	700	771			820							809				331	801		
12	700	771			820							809				331	801		
13	700	771			820							809				331	801		
14	700	771			820							809				331	801		
15	700	771			820							809				331	801		
16	700	771			820							809				331	801		
17	700	771			820							809				331	801		
18	700	771			820							809				331	801		
19	700	771			820							809				331	801		
20	700	771			820							809				331	801		
21	700	771			820							809				331	801		
22	700	771			820							809				331	801		
23	700	771			820							809				331	801		
24	700	771			820							809				331	801		
25	700	771			820							809				331	801		
26	700	771			820							809				331	801		
27	700	771			820							809				331	801		
28	700	771			820							809				331	801		
29	700	771			820							809				331	801		
30	700	771	817		820							809				331	801		
31																			

700 *Walrus, Swordfish I S/P, Seafox I*

771 *Skua II, Roc I, Maryland, Henley III, Blenheim I, Sea Gladiator*

801 *Sea Hurricane Ia, Ib (from St. Merryn)*

809 *Fulmar II*

817 *Albacore I (to Victorious; to Hatston)*

820 *Albacore I*

821 *Swordfish I (to Sumburgh)*

832 *Albacore I (to Victorious)*

331 *Hurricane II B (but converted to Spitfire IIA during this month; Norwegian)*

1941 December

	Hatston								Grimsetter	Twatt				Skeabrae			
1	700	771	817		820					809				331	801		
2	700	771	817		820					809				331	801		
3	700	771	817	832	820					809				331	801		
4	700	771	817	832	820					809				331	801		
5	700	771	817	832	820					809				331	801		
6	700	771	817	832	820					809				331	801		
7	700	771	817	832	820					809				331	801		
8	700	771	817	832	820					809				331	801		
9	700	771	817	832	820					809				331	801		
10	700	771	817	832	820					809				331	801		
11	700	771	817	832	820					809				331	801		
12	700	771	817	832	820					809				331	801		
13	700	771	817	832	820					809				331	801		
14	700	771	817	832	820					809				331	801		
15	700	771	817	832	820					809				331	801		
16	700	771	817	832	820					809				331	801		
17	700	771	817	832	820					809				331	801		
18	700	771	817	832	820					809				331	801		
19	700	771	817	832	820					809				331	801		
20	700	771	817	832	820					809				331	801		
21	700	771	817	832	820					809				331	801		
22	700	771	817	832	820					809				331	801		
23	700	771			820					809				331	801		
24	700	771												331	801		
25	700	771												331	801		
26	700	771												331	801		
27	700	771												331	801		
28	700	771												331	801		
29	700	771												331	801		
30	700	771												331	801		
31	700	771												331	801		

700 Walrus, Swordfish I S/P, Seafox I

771 Skua II, Roc I, Maryland, Henley III, Blenheim I, Sea Gladiator

801 Sea Hurricane Ib

809 Fulmar II (to Victorious)

817 Albacore I (to Victorious)

820 Albacore I (to Victorious)

832 Albacore I (Victorious)

331 Spitfire IIA (Norwegian)

1942 January

	Hatston								Grimsetter			Twatt				Skeabrae			
1	700	771		820								_809_				331	801		
2	700	771	817	820								_809_				331	801		
3	700	771	817	820								_809_				331	801		
4	700	771	817	820								_809_				331	801		
5	700	771	817	820								_809_				331	801		
6	700	771	817	820								_809_				331	801		
7	700	771	817	820								_809_				331	801		
8	700	771	817	820								_809_				331	801		
9	700	771	817	820								_809_				331	801		
10	700	771	817	820								_809_				331	801		
11	700	771	817	820								_809_				331	801		
12	700	771	817	820								_809_				331	801		
13	700	771	817	820								_809_				331	801		
14	700	771	817	820								_809_				331	801		
15	700	771	817	820								_809_				331	801		
16	700	771	817	820								_809_				331	801		
17	700	771		820								_809_				331	801		
18	700	771		820												331	801		
19	700	771		820												331	801		
20	700	771														331	801		
21	700	771														331	801		
22	700	771														331	801		
23	700	771														331	801		
24	700	771														331	801		
25	700	771														331	801		
26	700	771														331	801		
27	700	771		822									819			331	801		
28	700	771		822									819			331	801		
29	700	771		822									819			331	801		
30	700	771		822									819			331	801		
31	700	771		822									819			331	801		

700 *Walrus, Swordfish I S/P, Seafox I*

771 *Skua II, Roc I, Maryland, Henley III, Blenheim I, Sea Gladiator*

801 *Sea Hurricane Ib*

809 *Fulmar II (Victorious)*

817 *Albacore (to Victorious)*

819 *Swordfish I (from Crail)*

820 *Albacore I (to Machrihanish)*

822 *Swordfish II (from Gosport)*

331 *Spitfire II A (Norwegian)*

1942 February

	Hatston								Grimsetter			Twatt				Skeabrae			
1	700	771	822									819				331	132		
2	700	771	822									819				331	132		
3	700	771	822									819				331	132		
4	700	771	822									819				331	132		
5	700	771	822									819				331	132		
6	700	771	822									819				331	132		
7	700	771	822									819				331	132		
8	700	771	822									819				331	132		
9	700	771	822									819				331	132		
10	700	771	822									819				331	132		
11	700	771	822									819				331	132		
12	700	771	822									819				331	132		
13	700	771	822									819				331	132		
14	700	771	822									819				331	132		
15	700	771	822									819				331	132		
16	700	771	822									819				331	132		
17	700	771	822									819				331	132		
18	700	771	822									819				331	132		
19	700	771	822									819				331	132		
20	700	771	822									819				331	132		
21	700	771	822									819				331	132		
22	700	771	822			819										331	132		
23	700	771	822	817	832	819										331	132	416	
24	700	771	822	817	832	819										331	132		
25	700	771	822	817	832	819										331	132		
26	700	771	822	817	832	819										331	132		
27	700	771	822	817	832	819										331	132		
28	700	771	822	817	832	819										331	132		
29																			
30																			
31																			

700 *Walrus, Seafox I, Kingfisher I*

771 *Skua II, Roc I, Maryland, Henley III, Blenheim I, Sea Gladiator*

801 *Sea Hurricane Ib (to Tain)*

817 *Albacore I (from Victorious)*

819 *Swordfish I*

822 *Swordfish II*

832 *Albacore I (from Victorious)*

132 *Spitfire IIB (from Peterhead)*

331 *Spitfire IIA (Norwegian)*

416 *Spitfire 12 x IIA, 1 x IIb (Australian): (from Peterhead) reinforcement for special convoy passing through Pentland Firth*

1942 March

	Hatston							Grimsetter	Twatt	Skeabrae	
1	700	771	822	817	832		819			331	132
2	700	771	822	817	832		819			331	132
3	700	771	822	817	832		819			331	132
4	700	771	822				819			331	132
5	700	771	822				819			331	132
6	700	771	822				819			331	132
7	700	771	822				819			331	132
8	700	771	822				819			331	132
9	700	771	822				819			331	132
10	700	771	822				819		809	331	132
11	700	771	822		832		819		809	331	132
12	700	771	822		832		819		809	331	132
13	700	771	822		832		819		809	331	132
14	700	771	822		832		819		809	331	132
15	700	771	822		832		819		809	331	132
16	700	771	822		832		819		809	331	132
17	700	771	822		832		819		809	331	132
18	700	771	822		832		819		809	331	132
19	700	771	822				819		809	331	132
20	700	771	822				819		809	331	132
21	700	771			832	833	819		809	331	132
22	700	771			832	833	819			331	132
23	700	771			832	833	819			331	132
24	700	771			832	833	819			331	132
25	700	771			832	833	819			331	132
26	700	771			832	833				331	132
27	700	771			832	833				331	132
28	700	771			832	833			809	331	132
29	700	771			832	833			809	331	132
30	700	771			832	833			809	331	132
31	700	771			832	833			809	331	132

700 Walrus, Seafox I, Kingfisher I

771 Skua II, Roc I, Maryland, Henley III, Blenheim I, Sea Gladiator

809 Fulmar II (Victorious)

817 Albacore I (to Victorious)

819 Swordfish I (to Donibristle)

822 Swordfish II (to Crail)

832 Albacore I (Victorious)

833 Swordfish I (from Crail)

132 Spitfire IIB

331 Spitfire VB (Norwegian)

1942 April

	Hatston								Grimsetter			Twatt			Skeabrae			
1	700	771	833										809		331	132		
2	700	771											809		331	132		
3	700											771	809		331	132		
4	700											771	809		331	132		
5	700	AG7	AG7	AG7								771	809		331	132		
6	700	AG7	AG7	AG7								771	809		331	132		
7	700	AG7	AG7	AG7								771	809		331	132		
8	700	AG7	AG7	AG7								771	809		331	132		
9	700	AG7	AG7	AG7	832							771	809		331	132		
10	700	AG7	AG7	AG7	832							771	809		331	132		
11	700	AG7	AG7	AG7	832							771	809		331	132		
12	700	AG7	AG7	AG7								771	809		331	132		
13	700	AG7	AG7	AG7								771			331	132		
14	700	AG7	AG7	AG7								771			331	132		
15	700	AG7	AG7	AG7								771			331	132		
16	700	AG7	AG7	AG7								771			331	132		
17	700	AG7	AG7	AG7								771			331	132		
18	700	AG7	AG7	AG7	832							771	809		331	132		
19	700	AG7	AG7	AG7	832							771	809		331	132		
20	700	AG7	AG7	AG7								771	809		331	132		
21	700	AG7	AG7	AG7								771	809		331	132		
22	700	AG7	AG7	AG7								771	809		331	132		
23	700	AG7	AG7	AG7								771	809		331	132		
24	700	AG7	AG7	AG7								771	809		331	132		
25	700	AG7	AG7	AG7								771	809		331	132		
26	700	AG7	AG7	AG7								771	809		331	132		
27	700	AG7	AG7	AG7								771	809		331	132		
28	700	AG7	AG7	AG7								771	809		331	132		
29	700	AG7	AG7	AG7								771	809		331	132		
30	700	AG7	AG7	AG7								771	809		331	132		

700 Walrus, Seafox I, Kingfisher I

771 Skua II, Roc I, Maryland, Henley III, Blenheim I, Sea Gladiator (from Hatston to Twatt)

809 Fulmar II (Victorious)

833 Swordfish I (to Machrihanish)

832 Albacore I (Victorious)

132 Spitfire 16 x VB

331 Spitfire 15 X VB (Norwegian)

AG7 Vought Vindicator, Douglas Devastator, Grumman Duck (from USS Wasp)

N.B. USS *Wasp* arrived in Scapa on 5th April and disembarked three squadrons of Air Group 7 to Hatston for training while vessel sailed to Malta with Spitfires; 771 Squadron transferred to Twatt to make way for them and remained there for the duration of the war.

1942 May

Day	Hatston								Grimsetter			Twatt			Skeabrae		
1	700	AG7	AG7	AG7								771	809		331	132	
2	700	AG7	AG7	AG7								771	809		331	132	
3	700	AG7	AG7	AG7								771	809		331	132	
4	700	AG7	AG7	AG7								771	809			132	164
5	700	AG7	AG7	AG7								771	809			132	164
6	700	AG7	AG7	AG7								771	809			132	164
7	700	AG7	AG7	AG7								771	809			132	164
8	700	AG7	AG7	AG7								771	809			132	164
9	700	AG7	AG7	AG7								771	809			132	164
10	700	AG7	AG7	AG7								771	809			132	164
11	700											771	809			132	164
12	700											771	809			132	164
13	700											771	809			132	164
14	700											771	809			132	164
15	700											771	809			132	164
16	700											771				132	164
17	700											771				132	164
18	700											771				132	164
19	700											771				132	164
20	700											771				132	164
21	700											771				132	164
22	700											771				132	164
23	700											771				132	164
24	700											771				132	164
25	700											771				132	164
26	700											771				132	164
27	700											771				132	164
28	700											771				132	164
29	700											771				132	164
30	700											771				132	164
31	700											771				132	164

700 *Walrus, Seafox I, Kingfisher I*

771 *Swordfish, Skua II, Roc I, Maryland, Henley III, Blenheim I, Sea Gladiator, Chesapeake I*

809 *Fulmar II*

132 *Spitfire 16 x VB, 1VC*

164 *Spitfire 16 x VA (from Peterhead)*

331 *Spitfire 17 x VB, 1 x IIa, Norwegian (to North Weald)*

AG7 *Vought Vindicator, Douglas Devastator, Grumman Duck (to USS Wasp)*

1942 June

	Hatston					Grimsetter	Twatt				Skeabrae			
1	700						771				132	164		
2	700						771				132	164		
3	700						771				132	164		
4	700						771				132	164		
5	700	825					771				132	164		
6	700	825					771				132	164		
7	700	825					771				132	164		
8	700	825					771				132	164		
9	700	825					771				132	164		
10	700	825					771				132	164		
11	700	825	835				771					164		
12	700	825	835				771					164		
13	700	825	835				771					164		
14	700	825	835				771					164		
15	700	825	835				771					164		
16	700	825	835	817	832		771		809			164		
17	700	825	835	817	832		771		809			164		
18	700	825	835	817	832		771		809			164		
19	700	825	835	817	832		771		809			164		
20	700	825	835	817	832		771		809			164		
21	700	825	835	817	832		771		809			164		
22		825	835	817	832		771	700	809			164		
23	885	825	835	817	832		771	700	809			164		
24	885	825	835	817	832		771	700	809			164		
25	885	825	835	817	832		771	700	809			164		
26	885	825	835	817	832		771	700	809			164		
27	885	825	835	817	832		771	700	809			164		
28		825	835	817	832		771	700	809			164		
29		825	835				771	700				164		
30		825	835				771	700				164		

700 *Walrus, Seafox I, Kingfisher I (from Hatston to Twatt)*

771 *Swordfish, Skua II, Roc I, Maryland, Henley III, Blenheim I, Sea Gladiator, Chesapeake I, Defiant TT.1*

809 *Fulmar II (Victorious)*

817 *Albacore I (Victorious)*

825 *Swordfish I, Swordfish II (from Machrihanish)*

832 *Albacore I (Victorious)*

835 *Swordfish I (from Lee)*

885 *Sea Hurricane Ib (from Machrihanish to Victorious)*

132 *Spitfire VB, VC*

164 *Spitfire VA*

1942 July

	Hatston							Grimsetter			Twatt				Skeabrae			
1	825		835					132			700	771			164			
2	825		835					132			700	771			164			
3	825		835					132			700	771			164			
4	825		835					132			700	771			164			
5	825		835					132			700	771			164			
6	825		835					132			700	771			164			
7	825	832	835					132			700	771			164			
8	825	832	835					132			700	771			164			
9	825	832	835					132			700	771			164			
10	825	832	835	817	885			132			700	771	809		164			
11	825	832	835	817	885			132			700	771	809		164			
12	825	832	835	817	885			132			700	771	809		164			
13	825	832	835	817	885			132			700	771	809		164			
14	825	832	835	817	885			132			700	771	809		164			
15	825	832	835	817	885			132			700	771	809		164			
16	825	832	835	817	885			132			700	771	809		164			
17	825	832	835	817	885			132			700	771	809		164			
18	825	832	835	817	885			132			700	771	809		164			
19	825	832	835	817	885			132			700	771	809		164			
20	825	832	835	817	885			132			700	771	809		164			
21	825	832	835	817	885	884		132			700	771	809		164			
22	825	832	835	817	885	884		132			700	771			164			
23		832	835	817	885			132			700	771			164			
24		832	835	817	885			132			700	771			164			
25		832	835	817	885			132			700	771			164			
26		832	835	817	885			132			700	771			164			
27		832	835	817	885			132			700	771			164			
28		832	835	817	885			132			700	771			164			
29		832	835	817	885			132			700	771			164			
30			835		885			132			700	771			164			
31			835					132			700	771						

700 Walrus, Seafox I, Kingfisher I

771 Swordfish, Skua II, Roc I, Maryland, Henley III, Blenheim I,
Sea Gladiator, Chesapeake I, Defiant TT.1

809 Fulmar II (Victorious)

817 Albacore I (Victorious)

825 Swordfish I (to Avenger)

832 Albacore I (Victorious)

835 Swordfish I

884 Fulmar II (from Turnhouse to Victorious)

885 Sea Hurricane Ib (Victorious)

132 Spitfire VB, VC

164 Spitfire VA

1942 August

	Hatston								Grimsetter			Twatt				Skeabrae				
1			835						132			700	771			164				
2			835						132			700	771			164				
3			835						132			700	771			164				
4			835						132			700	771			164				
5	825		835						132			700	771			164				
6	825		835						132			700	771			164				
7	825		835						132			700	771			164				
8	825		835						132			700	771			164				
9	825		835						132			700	771			164				
10	825		835						132			700	771			164				
11	825		835						132			700	771			164				
12	825		835						132			700	771			164				
13	825		835						132			700	771			164				
14	825		835						132			700	771			164				
15	825		835						132			700	771			164				
16	825		835						132			700	771			164				
17	825	802	835						132			700	771			164				
18	825	802	835						132			700	771			164				
19	825	802	835						132			700	771			164				
20	825	802	835						132			700	771			164				
21	825	802	835						132			700	771			164				
22	825	802	835						132			700	771			164				
23	825	802	835						132			700	771			164				
24	825	802	835						132			700	771			164				
25	825	802	835						132			700	771			164				
26	825	802	835						132			700	771			164				
27	825	802	835	883					132			700	771			164				
28		802	835	883					132			700	771			164				
29		802	835	883					132			700	771			164				
30		802	835	883					132			700	771			164				
31		802	835	883					132			700	771							

700 *Walrus, Seafox I, Kingfisher I*

771 *Swordfish, Skua II, Roc I, Maryland, Henley III, Blenheim I, Sea Gladiator, Chesapeake I, Defiant TT.1*

802 *Sea Hurricane Ib (from Machrihanish)*

825 *Swordfish II (Avenger)*

835 *Swordfish I*

883 *Sea Hurricane Ib (from Avenger)*

132 *Spitfire VB, VC*

164 *Spitfire VA*

1942 September

	Hatston				Grimsetter		Twatt			Skeabrae		
1	802	835	883		132		700	771		164		
2	802	835	883		132		700	771		164		
3		835			132		700	771		164		
4		835			132		700	771	807	164		
5		835			132		700	771	807	164		
6		835			132		700	771	807	164		
7		835			132		700	771	807	164		
8		835			132		700	771	807	164		
9		835			132		700	771		164		
10		835			132		700	771		164		
11	807	835		823	132		700	771			602	
12	807	835		823	132		700	771			602	
13	807	835		823	132		700	771			602	
14	807	835		823	132		700	771			602	
15	807	835		823	132		700	771			602	
16	807	835		823	132		700	771			602	
17	807	835		823	132		700	771			602	
18	807	835		823	132		700	771			602	
19	807	835		823	132		700	771			602	
20		835		823	132		700	771			602	
21		835		823	132		700	771			602	
22				823	132		700	771			602	
23			800	823		129	700	771			602	
24			800	823		129	700	771			602	
25	883		800			129	700	771			602	884
26	807	825	800			129	700	771			602	884
27	807	825	800			129	700	771			602	884
28	807	825	800			129	700	771			602	884
29	807	825	800			129	700	771			602	884
30	807		800			129	700	771			602	884
31												

700 Walrus, Seafox I, Kingfisher I

771 Swordfish, Skua II, Roc I, Maryland, Henley III, Blenheim I, Sea Gladiator, Chesapeake I, Defiant TT.1

800 Sea Hurricane Ib, IIb (from Lee)

802 Sea Hurricane Ib (to Avenger)

807 Seafire Ib, L.IIc (Furious)

822 Albacore I (from Furious to Machrihanish)

823 Albacore I (from Furious)

825 Swordfish I (Avenger)

835 Swordfish I (to Stretton)

883 Sea Hurricane Ib, IIb (to Avenger)

884 Fulmar II, Spitfire Va (from Lee)

129 Spitfire VB, VC, VI (from Thorney Island)

132 Spitfire VB, VC (to Martlesham Heath)

164 Spitfire VA (to Peterhead)

602 Spitfire VI (from Peterhead)

1942 October

	Hatston							Grimsetter			Twatt				Skeabrae			
1	883							129			700	771	822		602	884	882	
2	883							129			700	771	822		602	884	882	
3	883							129			700	771	822		602	884	882	
4	883							129			700	771	822		602	884	882	
5	883							129			700	771	822		602	884	882	
6	883	893						129			700	771	822		602	884		
7	883	893						129			700	771	822		602	884		
8	883	893	888		800			129			700	771	822		602	884		
9	883	893	888					129			700	771	822		602	884		
10	883	893	888	820				129			700	771			602	884		
11	883	893	888	820				129			700	771			602	884		
12	883	893	888	820				129			700	771			602	884		
13	883	893	888	820				129			700	771			602	884		
14	883	893	888	820				129			700	771			602	884		
15	883	893	888	820				129			700	771			602	884		
16		893	888	820				129			700	771			602	884		
17		893	888	820				129			700	771			602	884		
18		893	888	820				129			700	771			602	884		
19		893	888	820				129			700	771			602	884		
20			888	820				129			700	771			602	884		
21								129			700	771			602			
22								129			700	771			602			
23								129			700	771			602			
24								129			700	771			602			
25								129			700	771			602			
26								129			700	771			602			
27								129			700	771			602			
28	819							129			700	771			602			
29	819							129			700	771			602			
30	819							129			700	771			602			
31	819							129			700	771			602			

700 Walrus, Kingfisher I

771 Swordfish, Skua II, Roc I, Maryland, Henley III, Blenheim I, Sea Gladiator, Chesapeake I, Defiant TT.1

800 Sea Hurricane Ib, IIb (from Lee to Biter)

819 Swordfish I, Swordfish II (from Thorney Island)

820 Albacore I (to Formidable)

822 Albacore I (to Machrihanish)

882 Martlet I, II, IV (from Donibristle to Victorious)

883 Sea Hurricane Ib, IIb (to Avenger)

884 Fulmar II, Spitfire Va, Spitfire Vb (to Victorious)

888 Martlet II (to Formidable)

893 Fulmar I, Martlet I, II (to Formidable)

129 Spitfire VB, VC, VI

602 Spitfire VI

1942 November

	Hatston							Grimsetter			Twatt					Skeabrae			
1	819							129			700	771				602			
2	819							129			700	771				602			
3	819	812						129			700	771				602			
4	819	812						129			700	771				602			
5	819	812						129			700	771				602			
6	819	812						129			700	771				602			
7	819	812						129			700	771				602			
8	819	812						129			700	771				602			
9	819	812						129			700	771				602			
10	819	812						129			700	771				602			
11	819	812						129			700	771				602			
12	819	812						129			700	771				602			
13	819	812						129			700	771				602			
14	819	812						129			700	771				602			
15	819	812						129			700	771				602			
16	819	812						129			700	771				602			
17	819	812						129			700	771				602			
18	819	812	837					129			700	771				602			
19	819	812	837					129			700	771				602			
20	819	812	837	880				129			700	771				602			
21	819	812	837	880				129			700	771				602			
22	819	812	837	880				129			700	771				602			
23	819	812	837	880	882			129			700	771	884			602			
24	819	812	837	880	882			129			700	771	884			602			
25	819	812	837	880	882			129			700	771				602	884		
26	819	812	837	880	882			129			700	771				602	884		
27	819	812	837	880	882			129			700	771				602	884		
28	819	812	837	880	882			129			700	771				602	884		
29	819	812	837	880	882			129			700	771				602	884		
30	819	812	837	880	882			129			700	771				602	884		
31																			

700 Walrus, Kingfisher I

771 Swordfish, Skua II, Roc I, Maryland, Henley III, Blenheim I,
Sea Gladiator, Chesapeake I, Defiant TT.1

812 Swordfish I, II (from Bircham Newton)

819 Swordfish I, II

837 Swordfish I, II (from St.Merryn)

880 Spitfire Vb, Seafire IIc (from Argus)

882 Martlet II, IV (from Machrihanish)

884 Spitfire Vb, Vb (hooked), Seafire IIc (Victorious)

129 Spitfire VB, VC, VI

602 Spitfire VI

1942 December

	Hatston								Grimsetter			Twatt				Skeabrae			
1	837	880	819	812		882			129			700	771			602	884	1476	
2	837	880	819	812		882			129			700	771			602	884	1476	
3	837	880	819	812		882			129			700	771			602	884	1476	
4	837	880	819	812		882			129			700	771			602	884	1476	
5	837	880	819	812		882			129			700	771			602	884	1476	
6	837	880	819	812		882			129			700	771			602	884	1476	
7	837	880	819	812		882			129			700	771			602	884	1476	
8	837	880	819	812		882			129			700	771			602	884	1476	
9	837	880	819	812		882			129			700	771			602	884	1476	
10	837	880	819	812		882			129			700	771			602	884	1476	
11	837	880	819	812		882			129			700	771			602	884	1476	
12	837	880	819	812		882			129			700	771			602	884	1476	
13	837	880	819	812		882			129			700	771			602	884	1476	
14	837	880	819	812			817		129			700	771			602		1476	
15	837	880	819	812			817		129			700	771			602		1476	
16	837	880		812	899		817		129			700	771			602		1476	
17	837	880		812	899		817		129			700	771			602		1476	
18	837	880		812	899	811	817		129			700	771			602		1476	
19	837	880			899	811	817		129			700	771			602		1476	
20	837	880			899	811	817		129			700	771			602		1476	
21	837	880			899	811	817		129			700	771			602		1476	
22	837	880			899	811	817		129			700	771			602		1476	
23	837	880			899	811	817		129			700	771			602		1476	
24	837	880			899	811	817		129			700	771			602		1476	
25	837	880			899	811	817		129			700	771			602		1476	
26	837	880			899	811	817		129			700	771			602		1476	
27	837	880			899	811	817		129			700	771			602		1476	
28	837	880			899	811	817		129			700	771			602		1476	
29	837	880			899	811	817		129			700	771			602		1476	
30		880			899	811	817		129			700	771			602		1476	
31		880			899	811			129			700	771			602		1476	

700 *Walrus, Kingfisher I, Sea Otter*

771 *Swordfish, Skua II, Roc I, Maryland, Henley III, Blenheim I, Sea Gladiator, Chesapeake I, Defiant TT.1, Havoc I*

811 *Swordfish II (from Thorney Island)*

812 *Swordfish I (disbanded to 811)*

817 *Albacore I (from Furious)*

819 *Swordfish I (to Fearn)*

837 *Swordfish I, II (to Crail)*

880 *Spitfire Vb, Seafire IIc*

882 *Martlet II, IV*

884 *Seafire IIc (to Turnhouse)*

899 *Seafire IIc (formed at Hatston)*

129 *Spitfire VB, VC, VI*

602 *Spitfire VI*

1476 *Anson (Advanced Ship Recognition Flight)*

1943 January

	Hatston					Grimsetter			Twatt		Skeabrae		
1	899	831	811	880	817	129			700	771		602	1476
2	899	831	811	880	817	129			700	771		602	1476
3	899	831	811	880	817	129			700	771		602	1476
4	899	831	811	880	817	129			700	771		602	1476
5	899	831	811	880	817	129			700	771		602	1476
6	899	831	811	880	817	129			700	771		602	1476
7	899	831	811	880	817	129			700	771		602	1476
8	899	831	811	880	817	129			700	771		602	1476
9	899	831	811	880	817	129			700	771		602	1476
10	899	831	811	880	817	129			700	771		602	1476
11	899	831	811	880	817	129			700	771		602	1476
12	899	831	811	880	817	129			700	771		602	1476
13	899	831	811	880	817	129			700	771		602	1476
14	899	831	811	880	817	129			700	771		602	1476
15	899	831	811	880	817	129	800		700	771		602	1476
16	899	831	811	880	817	129	800		700	771		602	1476
17	899	831	811	880	817	129	800		700	771		602	1476
18	899	831	811	880	817	129	800		700	771		602	1476
19	899	831	811	880	817		800		700	771	129		1476
20	899	831	811	880	817		800		700	771	129		1476
21	899	831	811	880	817		800		700	771	129		1476
22	899	831	811	880	817		800	234	700	771	129		1476
23	899	831	811	880	817		800	234	700	771	129		1476
24	899	831	811	880	817		800	234	700	771	129		1476
25	899	831	811	880	817		800	234	700	771	129		1476
26	899	831	811	880	817		800	234	700	771	129		1476
27	899	831	811	880	817		800	234	700	771	129		1476
28	899	831	811	880	817		800	234	700	771	129		1476
29	899	831	811	880	817		800	234	700	771	129		1476
30	899	831	811	880	817		800	234	700	771	129		1476
31	899	831	811	880	817		800	234	700	771	129		1476

700 *Walrus, Kingfisher I, Sea Otter*

771 *Swordfish, Skua II, Roc I, Maryland, Henley III, Blenheim I, Sea Gladiator, Chesapeake I, Defiant TT.1, Havoc I*

800 *Sea Hurricane IIc (from Machrihanish to Argus)*

811 *Swordfish I and II, Wildcat IV*

817 *Albacore I*

831 *Albacore I, Barracuda I (from Lee)*

880 *Spitfire Vb, Seafire IIc*

899 *Seafire IIc*

129 *Spitfire VB, VC, VI*

234 *Spitfire VB, VC, VI (from Perranporth)*

602 *Spitfire VI (to Perranporth)*

1476 *Anson (Advanced Ship Recognition Flight)*

1943 February

	Hatston								Grimsetter		Twatt			Skeabrae			
1	899	831	811	880	817				800	234	700	771		129		1476	
2	899	831	811	880	817				800	234	700	771		129		1476	
3	899	831	811	880	817				800	234	700	771	804	129		1476	
4	899	831	811	880	817				800	234	700	771	804	129		1476	
5	899	831	811	880	817				800	234	700	771	804	129		1476	
6	899	831	811	880	817				800	234	700	771	804	129		1476	
7	899	831	811	880	817				800	234	700	771	804	129		1476	
8	899	831	811	880	817				800	234	700	771	804	129		1476	
9	899	831	811	880	817				800	234	700	771	804	129	66	1476	
10	899	831	811	880	817				800	234	700	771	804	129	66	1476	
11	899	831	811	880	817	822			800	234	700	771	804	129	66	1476	
12	899	831	811	880		822			800	234	700	771	804	129	66	1476	
13	899	831	811	880		822			800	234	700	771	804		66	1476	
14	899	831	811	880		822			800	234	700	771	804		66	1476	
15	899	831	811	880		822			800	234	700	771	804		66	1476	
16	899	831	811	880		822			800	234	700	771	804		66	1476	
17	899	831	811	880	804	822	894		800	234	700	771			66	1476	
18	899	831	811	880	804	822	894		800	234	700	771			66	1476	
19	899	831	811	880	804	822	894		800	234	700	771			66	1476	
20	899	831		880	804	822	894		800	234	700	771			66	1476	
21					804	822	894		800	234	700	771			66	1476	
22					804	822	894		800	234	700	771			66	1476	
23					804	822	894		800	234	700	771			66	1476	
24					804	822	894		800	234	700	771			66	1476	
25					804	822	894		800	234	700	771			66	1476	
26	816	891		_837_	804	822	894		800	234	700	771			66	1476	
27	816	891		_837_	804	822	894		800	234	700	771			66	1476	
28	816	891		_837_	804	822	894		800	234	700	771			66	1476	

700 Walrus, Sea Otter

771 Swordfish, Skua II, Roc I, Maryland, Henley III, Blenheim I, Sea Gladiator, Chesapeake I, Defiant TT.1, Havoc I

800 Sea Hurricane IIc

804 Sea Hurricane IIc (from Ouston to Dasher)

811 Swordfish II, Wildcat IV (to Biter)

816 Swordfish II (from Dasher)

817 Albacore I (to Furious)

822 Albacore I (from Furious)

831 Albacore I, Barracuda I (to Machrihanish)

837 Swordfish I, II (from Dasher)

880 Spitfire Vb, Seafire IIc (to Machrihanish)

891 Sea Hurricane IIc (from Dasher)

894 Martlet IV (from Machrihanish)

899 Seafire IIc (to Machrihanish)

66 Spitfire VA, VB, VC (from Ibsley)

129 Spitfire VB, VC, VI (to Ibsley)

234 Spitfire VB, VC, VI

1476 Anson (Advanced Ship Recognition Flight)

1943 March

	Hatston							Grimsetter		Twatt		Skeabrae	
1	816	891		837	804	894	822	800	234	700	771	66	1476
2	816	891		837	804	894	822	800	234	700	771	66	1476
3	816	891		837	804	894		800	234	700	771	66	1476
4	816	891		837	804	894		800	234	700	771	66	1476
5	816	891		837	804	894		800	234	700	771	66	1476
6	816	891		837	804	894		800	234	700	771	66	1476
7	816	891		837	804	894		800	234	700	771	66	1476
8	816	891		837	804	894		800	234	700	771	66	1476
9	816	891		837	804	894		800	234	700	771	66	1476
10	816	891		837	804	894		800	234	700	771	66	1476
11	816	891		837	804	894		800	234	700	771	66	1476
12	816	891		837	804	894			234	700	771	66	1476
13	816	891		837	804	894			234	700	771	66	1476
14	816	891		837	804	894			234	700	771	66	1476
15	816	891		837	804	894			234	700	771	66	1476
16	816	891		837	804	894			234	700	771	66	1476
17	816	891		837	804	894			234	700	771	66	1476
18	816	891		837	804	894			234	700	771	66	1476
19	816	891		837	804	894			234	700	771	66	1476
20	816	891		837	804	894			234	700	771	66	1476
21		891		837	804	894			234	700	771	66	1476
22	887			837	804	894			234	700	771	66	1476
23	887			837	804	894			234	700	771	66	1476
24	887			837	804	894			234	700	771	66	1476
25	887			837	804	894			234	700	771	66	1476
26	887			837	804	894			234	700	771	66	1476
27	887	881		837	804	894			234	700	771	66	1476
28	887	881	890	837	804	894			234	700	771	66	1476
29	887	881	890		804	894			234	700	771	66	1476
30	887	881	890		804	894			234	700	771	66	1476
31	887	881	890		804	894			234	700	771	66	1476

700 *Walrus, Sea Otter*

771 *Swordfish, Skua II, Roc I, Maryland, Henley III, Blenheim I, Sea Gladiator, Chesapeake I, Defiant TT.1, Havoc I*

800 *Sea Hurricane IIc (to Machrihanish)*

804 *Sea Hurricane IIc*

816 *Swordfish II (to Machrihanish)*

822 *Albacore I (to Furious)*

837 *Swordfish I, II (to Dunino)*

881 *Martlet II (to Furious)*

887 *Seafire Ib, IIc (from St.Merryn)*

890 *Martlet IV (from Donibristle)*

891 *Sea Hurricane IIc (to Machrihanish)*

894 *Spitfire Vb, Seafire Ib, IIc, L.IIc*

234 *Spitfire VB, VC, VI*

66 *Spitfire VA, VB, VC*

1476 *Anson (Advanced Ship Recognition Flight)*

1943 April

	Hatston							Grimsetter			Twatt				Skeabrae			
1	887	881	890			804	894	234			700	771			66	1476		
2	887	881	890			804	894	234			700	771			66	1476		
3	887	881	890			804	894	234			700	771			66	1476	254	
4	887	881	890			804	894	234			700	771			66	1476	254	
5	887	881	890			804	894	234			700	771			66	1476	254	
6	887	881	890	801			894	234			700	771			66	1476	254	
7	887	881	890	801			894	234			700	771			66	1476	254	
8	887	881	890	801			894	234			700	771			66	1476	254	
9	887	881	890	801			894	234			700	771			66	1476	254	
10	887	881	890	801	822		894	234			700	771			66	1476		
11	887	881	890	801	822		894	234			700	771			66	1476		
12	887	881	890	801	822		894	234			700	771			66	1476		
13	887	881	890	801	822		894	234			700	771			66	1476		
14	887	881	890	801	822		894	234			700	771			66	1476		
15	887	881	890	801	822		894	234			700	771			66	1476		
16	887	881	890	801	822		894	234			700	771			66	1476		
17	887	881	890	801	822		894	234			700	771			66	1476		
18	887	881	890	801	822		894	234			700	771			66	1476		
19	887	881	890	801	822		894	234			700	771			66	1476		
20	887	881	890	801	822		894	234			700	771			66	1476		
21	887	881	890	801	822		894	234			700	771			66	1476		
22	887	881	890	801	822		894	234			700	771			66	1476		
23	887	881	890	801	822		894	234			700	771			66	1476		
24	887	881	890	801	822		894				700	771			66	1476	234	
25	887	881	890	801	822		894				700	771			66	1476	234	
26	887	881	890	801	822		894				700	771			66	1476	234	
27	887	881	890	801	822		894				700	771			66	1476	234	
28	887	881	890	801			894				700	771			66	1476	234	
29	887	881	890	801			894				700	771			66	1476	234	
30	887	881	890				894				700	771			66	1476	234	

700 Walrus, Sea Otter

771 Swordfish, Skua II, Roc I, Maryland, Henley III, Blenheim I, Sea Gladiator, Chesapeake I, Defiant TT.1, Havoc I

801 Seafire IIc (Furious)

804 Sea Hurricane IIc (to Charlton Horethorne)

822 Albacore I (Furious)

878 Martlet IV (from Lee)

881 Martlet IV

887 Seafire IIc (to Machrihanish)

890 Martlet IV

894 Spitfire Vb, Seafire IIc

66 Spitfire VA, VB, VC

234 Spitfire VB, VC, V1

254 Beaufort Strike (North Coates)

1476 Anson (Advanced Ship Recognition Flight)

1943 May

	Hatston							Grimsetter			Twatt				Skeabrae			
1	878	881	890	894							700	771			66	234	1476	
2	878	881	890	894							700	771			66	234	1476	
3	878	881	890	894	840	842					700	771			66	234	1476	
4	878	881	890	894	840	842					700	771			66	234	1476	
5	878	881	890	894	840	842	884				700	771			66	234	1476	
6	878	881	890	894	840	842	884				700	771			66	234	1476	
7	878	881	890	894	840	842	884				700	771			66	234	1476	
8	878	881	890	894	840	842	884				700	771			66	234	1476	
9	878	881	890	894	840	842	884				700	771			66	234	1476	
10	878	881	890	894	840	842	884				700	771			66	234	1476	
11	878	881	890	894	840	842	884				700	771			66	234	1476	
12	878	881	890	894	840	842	884				700	771			66	234	1476	
13	878	881	890	894	840	842	884				700	771			66	234	1476	
14	878	881	890	894	840	842					700	771			66	234	1476	
15	878	881	890	894	840	842					700	771			66	234	1476	
16	878	881	890	894	840	842					700	771			66	234	1476	
17	878	881	890	894	840	842					700	771			66	234	1476	
18	878	881	890	894	840	842					700	771			66	234	1476	
19	878	881	890	894	840	842					700	771			66	234	1476	
20	878	881	890	894	840	842					700	771			66	234	1476	
21	878	881	890	894	840	842					700	771			66	234	1476	
22	878	881	890	894	840	842					700	771			66	234	1476	
23	878	881	890	894	840	842					700	771			66	234	1476	
24	878	881	890	894	840	842					700	771			66	234	1476	
25	878	881	890	894		842					700	771			66	234	1476	
26	878	881	890	894	840	842					700	771			66	234	1476	
27	878	881	890	894	840	842					700	771			66	234	1476	
28	878	881	890	894							700	771			66	234	1476	
29	878	881	890	894							700	771			66	234	1476	
30	878	881	890	894							700	771			66	234	1476	
31	878	881	890	894							700	771			66	234	1476	

700 *Walrus, Sea Otter*

771 *Swordfish, Roc I, Skua II, Maryland, Henley III, Blenheim I, Sea Gladiator, Chesapeake I, Defiant TT.1, Havoc I*

840 *Swordfish II (from Machrihanish to Avenger to Machrihanish.)*

842 *Swordfish II (Machrihanish)*

878 *Martlet IV*

881 *Martlet II*

884 *Seafire IIc (from Drem)*

890 *Martlet IV*

894 *Seafire IIc, Seafire L.IIc,*

66 *Spitfire VA, VB, VC*

234 *Spitfire VB, VC, VI*

1476 *Anson (Advanced Ship Recognition Flight)*

1943 June

	Hatston								Grimsetter		Twatt				Skeabrae			
1	878	881	890		842	894					700	771			66	234	1476	
2	878	881	890		842	894					700	771			66	234	1476	
3	878	881	890		842	894					700	771			66	234	1476	
4	878	881	890		842	894					700	771			66	234	1476	
5	878	881	890		842	894					700	771			66	234	1476	
6	878	881	890		842	894					700	771			66	234	1476	
7	878	881	890		842	894					700	771			66	234	1476	
8		881			842						700	771			66	234	1476	
9		881			842						700	771			66	234	1476	
10		881			842						700	771			66	234	1476	
11		881			842						700	771			66	234	1476	
12		881			842						700	771			66	234	1476	
13		881			842						700	771			66	234	1476	
14	801	881	825		842						700	771			66	234	1476	
15	801	881	825		842						700	771			66	234	1476	
16	801	881	825		842						700	771			66	234	1476	
17	801	881	825		842						700	771			66	234	1476	
18	801	881	825	830	842						700	771			66	234	1476	
19	801	881	825	830	842						700	771			66	234	1476	
20	801	881	825	830	842						700	771			66	234	1476	
21	801	881	825	830	842						700	771			66	234	1476	
22	801	881	825	830	842						700	771			66	234	1476	
23	801	881	825	830	842						700	771			66	234	1476	
24	801	881	825	830	842						700	771			66	312	1476	
25	801	881	825	830	842						700	771			66	312	1476	
26	801	881	825	830	842						700	771			66	312	1476	
27	801	881	825	830							700	771			66	312	1476	
28	801	881	825	830							700	771				312	1476	
29	801	881	825	830							700	771				312	1476	
30	801	881	825	830							700	771				312	1476	

700 *Walrus, Sea Otter*

771 *Swordfish, Roc I, Skua II, Maryland, Henley III, Blenheim I, Sea Gladiator, Chesapeake I, Defiant TT.1, Havoc I*

801 *Seafire Ib, IIc (from Furious)*

825 *Swordfish II (from Furious)*

830 *Barracuda II (from Lee)*

842 *Swordfish II (to Machrihanish)*

878 *Martlet IV (to Machrihanish)*

881 *Martlet II, IV*

890 *Martlet IV*

894 *Seafire IIc, L.IIc (to Machrihanish)*

66 *Spitfire VA, VB, VC (to Churchstanton)*

234 *Spitfire (to Churchstanton)*

312 *Spitfire VB, VC, VI (from Churchstanton)*

1476 *Anson (Advanced Ship Recognition Flight)*

1943 July

	Hatston								Grimsetter			Twatt				Skeabrae			
1	801	881	825		830							700	771			312			
2	801	881	825		830							700	771			312			
3	801	881	825		830							700	771			312			
4	801	881			830							700	771			312			
5	801	881	825		830							700	771			312			
6		881	825		830							700	771			312			
7		881	825		830							700	771			312			
8		881	825		830							700	771			312			
9		881	825		830							700	771			312			
10		881	825		830							700	771			312			
11		881	825		830							700	771			312			
12		881	825		830							700	771			312			
13		881		845	830							700	771			312			
14		881		845	830							700	771			312			
15		881		845	830							700	771			312			
16		881		845	830							700	771			312			
17		881		845	830							700	771			312			
18		881		845	830							700	771			312			
19		881		845	830	860						700	771			312			
20		881		845	830	860						700	771			312			
21		881		845	830	860						700	771			312			
22		881		845	830	860						700	771			312			
23		881		845	830	860						700	771			312			
24		881		845	830	860						700	771			312			
25		881		845	830	860						700	771			312			
26				845	830	860						700	771			312			
27				845	830	860						700	771			312			
28		846		845	830	860						700	771			312			
29		846		845	830	860						700	771			312			
30		846		845	830	860						700	771			312			
31		846		845	830	860						700	771			312			

700 Walrus, Sea Otter, Swordfish

771 Swordfish, Roc I, Skua II, Maryland, Henley III, Sea Gladiator, Chesapeake I, Defiant TT.1, Havoc I

801 Seafire Ib (to Stretton: to Stornoway: to Stretton)

825 Swordfish I, II (less 4 to HMS Furious)

830 Barracuda II

845 Avenger I (from Machrihanish)

846 Avenger I (from Machrihanish)

860 Swordfish I (from Donibristle)

881 Martlet IV (less 7 to HMS Furious)

312 Spitfire VB, VC (Czech.)

1943 August

	Hatston									Grimsetter			Twatt				Skeabrae			
1	846	845	830	860									700	771			312			
2	846	845	830	860									700	771			312			
3	846	845	830	860									700	771			312			
4	846	845	830	860									700	771			312			
5	846	845	830	860									700	771			312			
6	846	845	830	860									700	771			312			
7	846	845	830	860									700	771			312			
8	846	845	830	860									700	771			312			
9	846	845	830	860									700	771			312			
10	846	845	830	860									700	771			312			
11	846	845	830	860									700	771			312			
12	846	845	830	860									700	771			312			
13	846	845	830	860									700	771			312			
14	846	845	830	860									700	771			312			
15	846	845	830										700	771			312			
16	846	845											700	771			312			
17	846	845											700	771			312			
18	846	845											700	771			312			
19	846	845											700	771			312			
20	846	845											700	771			312			
21	846	845											700	771			312			
22	846	845											700	771			312			
23	846	845											700	771			312			
24	846	845											700	771			312			
25	846	845											700	771			312			
26	846	845											700	771			312			
27	846	845											700	771			312			
28	846	845											700	771			312			
29	846	845											700	771			312			
30	846	845											700	771			312			
31	846	845											700	771			312			

700 *Walrus, Sea Otter, Swordfish*

771 *Swordfish, Roc I, Skua II, Maryland, Henley III, Sea Gladiator, Chesapeake I, Defiant TT.1, Havoc I, Martinet TT.I*

830 *Barracuda II (to Machrihanish)*

845 *Avenger I*

846 *Avenger I*

860 *Swordfish I (to Dunino)*

312 *Spitfire VB, VC (Czech.)*

1943 September

	Hatston								Grimsetter			Twatt				Skeabrae			
1	846	845										700	771			312			
2	846	845										700	771			312			
3	846	845										700	771			312			
4	846	845										700	771			312			
5	846	845	*USS Ranger in Scapa Flow*									700	771*			312			
6	846	845										700	771			312			
7	846	845										700	771			312			
8	846	845										700	771			312			
9	846	845										700	771			312			
10	846	845										700	771			312			
11	846	845										700	771			312			
12	846	845										700	771			312			
13	846	845										700	771			312			
14	846	845										700	771			312			
15	846	845										700	771			312			
16	846	845										700	771			312	801		
17	846	845										700	771			312	801		
18	846	845										700	771			312	801		
19	846	845										700	771			312	801		
20	846	845										700	771			312	801		
21	846	845										700	771				801		
22	846	845										700	771				801		
23	846	845										700	771				801		
24	846	845										700	771				801		
25		845							846			700	771				801		
26	832	845							846			700	771				801		
27	832	845							846			700	771				801		
28	832	845							846			700	771				801		
29	832	845							846			700	771				801		
30	832	845							846			700	771				801		

700 *Walrus, Sea Otter, Swordfish*

771 *Swordfish, Roc I, Skua II, Maryland, Sea Gladiator,*
      Chesapeake I, Havoc I , Martinet TT.I

801 *10 x Seafire Ib (from Machrihanish)*

832 *Avenger TBF-1, Avenger I (from Victorious)*

845 *Avenger I*

846 *Avenger I*

312 *Spitfire VB, VC (Czech.) (to Ibsley)*

* N.B. US Avengers embarked at Twatt for part of this month

1943 October

	Hatston								Grimsetter			Twatt				Skeabrae			
1	845	832							846			700	771			801			
2	845	832							846			700	771			801			
3	845	832							846			700	771			801			
4	845	832							846			700	771			801			
5	845	832							846			700	771			801			
6	845	832							846			700	771			801			
7	845	832							846			700	771			801			
8	845	832							846			700	771			801			
9	845	832							846			700	771			801			
10	845	832							846			700	771			801			
11	845	832							846			700	771			801			
12	845	832							846			700	771			801			
13	845	832							846			700	771			801			
14	845	832							846			700	771			801			
15	845	832							846			700	771				453		
16	845	832							846			700	771				453		
17	845	832							846			700	771				453		
18	845	832							846			700	771				453		
19	845	832							846			700	771				453		
20	845	832							846			700	771				453		
21	845	832							846			700	771				453		
22	845	832							846			700	771				453		
23	845	832							846			700	771				453		
24	845	832										700	771				453		
25	845	832										700	771				453		
26	845	832										700	771				453		
27	845	832										700	771				453		
28	845	832										700	771				453		
29	845	832										700	771				453		
30	845	832										700	771				453		
31	845	832										700	771				453		

700 Walrus, Sea Otter, Swordfish

771 Swordfish, Roc I, Skua II, Maryland, Sea Gladiator,
 Chesapeake I, Havoc I, Martinet TT.I

801 Seafire Ib (to Machrihanish)

832 Avenger TBF-1, Avenger I

845 Avenger I

846 Avenger I (to Machrihanish)

453 Spitfire (Australian)

1943 November

	Hatston									Grimsetter			Twatt				Skeabrae			
1	832	845												700	771			453			
2	832	845												700	771			453			
3	832	845												700	771			453			
4	832	845												700	771			453			
5	832	845												700	771			453			
6	832	845									848			700	771			453			
7	832	845									848			700	771			453			
8	832	845	_888_								848			700	771			453			
9	832	845	_888_								848			700	771			453			
10	832	845	_888_								848			700	771			453			
11	832	845	_888_								848			700	771			453			
12	832	845	_888_								848			700	771			453			
13	832	845									848			700	771			453			
14	832	845									848			700	771			453			
15	832	845									848			700	771			453			
16	832	845									848			700	771			453			
17	832	845									848			700	771			453			
18	832	845									848			700	771			453			
19	832	845									848			700	771			453			
20	832	845									848			700	771			453			
21	832	845									848			700	771			453			
22	832	845									848			700	771			453			
23	832	845									848			700	771			453			
24	832	845												700	771			453			
25	832	845	848								849			700	771			453			
26	832	845	848								849			700	771			453			
27	832	845	848								849			700	771			453			
28	832	845	848								849			700	771			453			
29	832	845	848								849			700	771			453			
30	832	845	848								849			700	771			453			

700 *Walrus, Sea Otter, Swordfish*

771 *Swordfish, Roc I, Skua II, Maryland, Sea Gladiator,*
Chesapeake I, Havoc I , Martinet TT.I

832 *Avenger TBF-1, Avenger I*

845 *Avenger I*

848 *Avenger I (from Ayr)*

849 *12 x Avenger I (from Speke)*

888 *Martlet IV (Formidable)*

453 *Spitfire (Australian)*

1943 December

	Hatston							Grimsetter			Twatt					Skeabrae			
1	832		845					849			700	771				453			
2	832		845					849			700	771				453			
3	832		845					849			700	771				453			
4			845					849			700	771				453			
5			845					849			700	771				453			
6	801	827	845	848	830			849			700	771				453			
7	801	827	845	848	830			849			700	771				453			
8	801	827	845	848	830			849			700	771				453			
9	801	827	845	848	830			849			700	771				453			
10			845	848				849			700	771				453			
11			845	848				849			700	771				453			
12			845	848				849			700	771				453			
13			845	848				849			700	771				453			
14	827	830	845	848				849	1770		700	771				453			
15	827	830	845	848				849	1770		700	771				453			
16	827	830	845	848				849	1770		700	771				453			
17	827	830	845	848				849	1770		700	771				453			
18	827	830	845	848				849	1770		700	771				453			
19	827	830	845	848				849	1770		700	771				453			
20	827	830	845	848				849	1770		700	771				453			
21	827	830	845	848				849	1770		700	771				453			
22	827	830	845	848				849	1770		700	771				453			
23	827	830	845	848				849	1770		700	771				453			
24	827	830	845	848				849	1770		700	771				453			
25	827	830	845	848				849	1770		700	771				453			
26			845	848				849	1770		700	771				453			
27			845	848				849	1770		700	771				453			
28			845	848				849	1770		700	771				453			
29			845	848				849	1770		700	771				453			
30			845	848				849	1770		700	771				453			
31			845					849	1770		700	771				453			

700 *Walrus, Sea Otter, Swordfish*

771 *Swordfish, Roc I, Skua II, Maryland, Sea Gladiator, Chesapeake I, Havoc I, Martinet TT.I*

801 *Seafire Ib (Furious)*

827 *Barracuda II (Furious)*

830 *Barracuda II (Furious)*

832 *Avenger I (to Machrihanish)*

845 *Avenger I*

848 *Avenger I (to Gosport)*

849 *Avenger I*

1770 *Firefly I (from Yeovilton)*

453 *Spitfire (Australian)*

1944 January

Day	Hatston			Grimsetter		Twatt		Skeabrae		
1	845	827	830	849	1770	700	771	453		
2	845	827	830	849	1770	700	771	453		
3	801	827	830	849	1770	700	771	453		
4	801	827	830	849	1770	700	771	453		
5	801	827	830	849	1770	700	771	453		
6	801	827	830	849	1770	700	771	453		
7	801	827	830	849	1770	700	771	453		
8	801	827	830	849	1770	700	771	453		
9	801	827	830	849	1770	700	771	453		
10		827	830	849	1770	700	771	453		
11	831	827	830	849	1770	700	771	453	801	
12	831	827	830	849	1770	700	771	453	801	
13	831	827	830	849	1770	700	771	453	801	
14	831	827	830	849	1770	700	771	453	801	
15	831	827	830	849	1770	700	771	453	801	
16	831	827	830	849	1770	700	771	453	801	
17	831	827	830	849	1770	700	771	453	801	
18	831	827	830	849	1770	700	771	453	801	602
19	831	827	830	849	1770	700	771		801	602
20	831	827	830	849	1770	700	771		801	602
21	831	827	830	849	1770	700	771		801	602
22	831	827	830	849	1770	700	771		801	602
23	831	827	830	849	1770	700	771		801	602
24	831	827	830	849	1770	700	771		801	602
25	831	827	830	849	1770	700	771		801	602
26	831	827	830	849	1770	700	771		801	602
27	831	827	830	849	1770	700	771		801	602
28	831	827	830	849	1770	700	771		801	602
29	831	827	830	849	1770	700	771		801	602
30	831	827	830	849	1770	700	771		801	602
31	831	827	830	849	1770	700	771		801	602

700 *Walrus, Sea Otter*

771 *Swordfish, Roc I, Skua II, Maryland, Sea Gladiator, Chesapeake I, Havoc I , Martinet TT.I*

801 *Seafire Ib*

827 *Barracuda II (from Furious)*

830 *Barracuda II (from Furious)*

831 *Barracuda II (from Machrihanish)*

845 *Avenger I (to Machrihanish)*

849 *Avenger I*

1770 *Firefly I*

453 *Spitfire (Australian) to Detling*

602 *Spitfire IX (from Detling)*

1944 February

	Hatston				Grimsetter		Twatt		Skeabrae		
1	831	827	830		849	1770	700	771	602	801	
2	831	827	830		849	1770	700	771	602	801	
3	831	827	830		849	1770	700	771	602	801	
4	831	827	830		849	1770	700	771	602	801	
5	831	827	830		849	1770	700	771	602	801	
6	831	827	830		849	1770	700	771	602	801	880
7	831	827	830		849	1770	700	771	602	801	880
8	831				849	1770	700	771	602		
9	831				849	1770	700	771	602		
10	831				849	1770	700	771	602		
11					849	1770	700	771	602		
12	816				849	1770	700	771	602		
13	816		830		849	1770	700	771	602		
14	816		830			1770	700	771	602	801	
15	816		830	1770			700	771	602	801	
16	816		830	1770			700	771	602	801	880
17	816		830	1770			700	771	602	801	880
18	816		830	1770			700	771	602	801	880
19	816		830	1770			700	771	602	801	880
20	816		830	1770			700	771	602	801	880
21	816		830	1770			700	771	602	801	880
22	816		830	1770			700	771	602	801	880
23	816		830	1770			700	771	602	801	880
24				1770			700	771	602		
25				1770			700	771	602		
26				1770			700	771	602		
27				1770			700	771	602		
28				1770			700	771	602		
29		827	830	1770			700	771	602	801	880

700 *Walrus, Sea Otter*

771 *Swordfish, Roc I, Skua II, Maryland, Sea Gladiator, Chesapeake I, Havoc I , Martinet TT.I*

801 *Seafire Ib (Furious)*

816 *Swordfish II (Chaser)*

827 *Barracuda I (Furious)*

830 *Barracuda II (Furious)*

831 *Barracuda II (to Machrihanish)*

849 *Avenger I (to Maydown)*

880 *Seafire L.IIc, Spitfire I (Furious)*

1770 *Firefly I*

602 *Spitfire IX*

1944 March

	Hatston						Grimsetter			Twatt				Skeabrae			
1	827	830	1770							700	771				801	880	602
2	827	830	1770							700	771				801	880	602
3	827	830	1770							700	771				801	880	602
4	827	830	1770							700	771				801	880	602
5	827	830	1770	807						700	771				801	880	602
6	827	830	1770	807						700	771				801	880	602
7	827	830	1770	807						700	771			118	801		602
8	827	830	1770	807						700	771			118	801		602
9	827	830	1770	807						700	771			118	801		602
10	827	830	1770							700	771			118	801		
11	827	830	1770							700	771			118	801		
12	827	830	1770							700	771			118	801		
13	827	830	1770							700	771			118	801		
14	827	830	1770							700	771			118	801		
15	827	830	1770							700	771			118	801		
16	827	830	1770							700	771			118	801		
17			1770							700	771			118			
18			1770							700	771			118			
19			1770							700	771			118			
20			1770							700	771			118			
21			1770							700	771			118		880	
22	827	830	1770								771			118		880	
23	827	830	1770								771			118		880	
24	827	830	1770				1834				771			118		880	
25	827	830	1770				1834				771			118		880	
26	827	830	1770				1834				771			118		880	
27	827	830	1770				1834				771			118			
28	827		1770				1834				771			118			
29	827		1770				1834				771			118			
30			1770								771			118			
31			1770								771			118			

700 *Walrus, Sea Otter (disbanded)*

771 *Swordfish, Roc I, Skua II, Maryland, Sea Gladiator, Chesapeake I, Havoc I , Martinet TT.I, Walrus*

801 *Seafire Ib (to Furious)*

807 *Seafire L.IIc (from Turnhouse to Hunter)*

827 *Barracuda II (Furious)*

830 *Barracuda II (to Donibristle)*

880 *Seafire L.IIc, F.III (Furious)*

1770 *Firefly I*

1834 *Corsair II (from Machrihanish to Vic.)*

118 *Spitfire VB, IX (from Detling)*

602 *Spitfire IX (to Detling)*

N.B. Squadrons left Hatston end March/ beginning April and embarked to bomb *Tirpitz* in in Kaa Fjord, Norway.

	Hatston						Grimsetter	Twatt	Skeabrae		
1				1770				771	118		
2				1770				771	118		
3				1770				771	118		
4				1770				771	118		
5				1770				771	118		
6	800	804	882	1770	896		842	771	118		
7	800	804	882	1770	896		842	771	118	801	880
8	800	804	882	1770	896		842	771	118	801	880
9	800	804	882	1770	896		842	771	118	801	880
10	800	804	882	1770	896		842	771	118	801	880
11	842			1770				771	118	801	880
12	842			1770			824	771	118	801	880
13	842			1770			824	771	118	801	880
14	842	846		1770			824	771	118	801	880
15	842	846	882	1770	898		824	771	118	801	880
16	842	846	882	1770	898		824	771	118	801	880
17	842		882	1770	898		824	771	118	801	880
18				1770			824	771	118	801	880
19				1770			824	771	118	801	880
20				1770			824	771	118		
21				1770			824	771	118		
22				1770			824	771	118		
23				1770			824	771	118		
24				1770			824	771	118		
25				1770			824	771	118		
26				1770			824	771	118		
27				1770			824	771	118		
28	800	804	827	1770	898	830	824	771	118		
29	800	804	827	1770	898	830	824	771	118		
30	800	804	827	1770	898	830	824	771	118		

771 Swordfish, Roc I, Skua II, Maryland, Sea Gladiator, Chesapeake I, Havoc I , Martinet TT.I, Blenheim IV, Sea Otter, Walrus

800 Hellcat I (Emperor)

801 Seafire Ib, L.IIc (Furious)

804 Hellcat I (Emperor)

824 Swordfish II, Sea Hurricane IIc (from Striker))

827 Barracuda II (from Furious)

830 Barracuda II (from Furious)

842 Swordfish II, Wildcat V (Fencer)

846 Avenger I (from Tracker to Machrihanish)

880 Seafire L.IIc, F.III (Furious)

882 Wildcat V (from Searcher to Fencer)

896 Wildcat V (Pursuer)

898 Wildcat V (Searcher

1770 Firefly I

118 Spitfire VB, IX

N.B. Squadrons again left Hatston for bombing attacks on enemy shipping off Norway, part of *Operation Fortitude North*, a plan to deceive Germany that the invasion of the continent of Europe was begin in Norway.

1944 May

Day	Hatston								Grimsetter			Twatt				Skeabrae			
1	800	804	827	1770	898	830						771				118	801	880	
2	800	804	827	1770	898	830						771				118	801	880	
3	800	804	827	1770		829						771				118			
4	800	804	827	1770		829						771				118			
5	800	804		1770		829						771				118			
6				1770		829						771				118			
7				1770		829						771				118	801	880	
8				1770		829						771				118	801	880	
9	824			1770		829						771				118	801	880	
10	824			1770		829						771				118	801	880	
11	824	882		1770		829						771				118			
12		882		1770		829			829			771				118			
13		882		1770		829			829			771				118			
14		882		1770	899				829			771				118			
15		882		1770	899				829			771				118			
16		882		1770					829	899		771				118			
17	824	882		1770					829	899		771				118			
18	824	882	830			827			829	899		771				118	801	880	
19	824	882	830			827			829	899		771				118	801	880	
20	824	882	830			827				899		771				118	801	880	
21	824	882	830			827				899		771				118	801	880	
22	824	882	830			827				899		771				118	801	880	
23	824	882	830			827				899		771				118	801	880	
24	824	882	830			827				899		771				118	801	880	
25	824	882	830			827				899		771				118	801	880	
26	824	882	830			827				899		771				118	801	880	
27	824	882	830			829				899		771				118	801		
28	824	882				829				899		771				118	801		
29	824	882				829				899		771				118	801		
30	824	882				829				899		771				118	801		
31	824	882				829						771				118	801		

771 Swordfish, Roc I, Maryland, Sea Gladiator, Havoc I , Martinet TT.I, Blenheim IV, Sea Otter, Walrus, Hurricane FB.IIc

800 Hellcat I (to Emperor)

801 Seafire Ib, L.IIc, L.III (Furious)

804 Hellcat I (to Emperor)

824 Swordfish II, Sea Hurricane IIc (to Striker)

827 Barracuda II (Furious)

829 Barracuda II (Victorious)

830 Barracuda II (Furious)

880 Seafire F.III (Furious)

882 Wildcat V (from Searcher)

898 Wildcat V 9to Searcher)

899 Seafire L.III (from Khedive)

1770 Firefly I (to Indefatigable)

118 Spitfire VB, IX

	Hatston								Grimsetter			Twatt			Skeabrae			
1	882	898	829						824			771			118	801		
2	882	898	829						824			771			118	801		
3	882	898	829									771			118	801		
4	882	898	829									771			118	801		
5	882	898	829									771			118	801		
6	882	898	829									771			118	801		
7		898	829									771			118			
8			829									771			118			
9			829									771			118			
10												771			118			
11												771			118			
12												771			118			
13												771			118			
14	824											771			118			
15	824											771			118			
16	824											771			118			
17	824		827									771			118	801	880	881
18	824		827									771			118	801	880	881
19			827									771			118	801	880	881
20			827									771			118	801	880	881
21			827									771			118	801	880	
22			827									771			118			
23		830	827									771			118	801	880	
24		830	827									771			118	801	880	
25	824	830	827									771			118	801	880	
26	824	830	827						842			771			118	801	880	
27	824	830	827						842			771			118	801	880	
28	824	830	827						842			771			118	801	880	
29	824	830	827						842			771			118	801	880	
30	824	830	827						842			771			118	801	880	

771 *Swordfish, Maryland, Sea Gladiator, Havoc I , Martinet TT.I, Blenheim IV, Sea Otter, Walrus, Hurricane FB.IIc*

801 *Seafire Ib, L.IIc (Furious)*

824 *Sea Hurricane IIc, Wildcat V (Striker)*

827 *Barracuda II (from Furious)*

829 *Barracuda II (to Victorious)*

830 *Barracuda II (from Furious)*

842 *Swordfish II, Wildcat V (from Fencer)*

880 *Seafire F.III (Furious)*

881 *Wildcat V, Wildcat VI (from Drem to Fencer)*

882 *Wildcat V (to Searcher)*

898 *Wildcat V (to Searcher)*

118 *Spitfire VB, IX*

N.B. From 10th to 13th June there were no aircraft stationed at Hatston or Grimsetter; they had embarked on the aircraft carriers *Victorious* and *Searcher* to support the Normandy landings. This was the last occasion that *Victorious* appeared in Orkney waters.

1944 July

	Hatston							Grimsetter			Twatt				Skeabrae			
1	824	827	830					842			771				118			880
2	824	827	830	1770				842			771				118			880
3	824	827	830	1770				842			771				118			880
4	824	827	830	1770				842			771				118			880
5	824	827	830	1841		820	826	842	1770		771				118			880
6	824	827	830	1841	1840	820	826	842	1770		771				118		887	880
7	824	827	830	1841	1840	820	826	842	1770		771				118			880
8	824	827	830	1841	1840	820	826	842	1770		771				118			880
9	824	827		1841		820	826	842			771				118			880
10	824	827						842			771				118			
11		827						842			771				118	313		
12		827						842			771					313		
13		827						842			771					313		
14								842			771					313		
15								842			771					313		
16								842			771					313		
17								842			771					313		
18								842	894		771					313		
19		827	830	842	1840	1841			894		771					313		880
20		827	830	842	1840				894		771					313		880
21		827	830	842	1840				894		771					313		880
22		827	830	842	1840				894		771					313		880
23		827	830	842	1840				894		771					313		880
24		827	830	842	1840						771					313		880
25		827	830	842	1840	1770					771					313		880
26		827	830	842	1840						771					313		880
27		827	830	842	1840						771					313		880
28		827	830	842	1840						771					313		880
29		827	830	842	1840						771					313		880
30		827	830	842	1840						771					313		880
31		827	830	842							771					313		880

771 Swordfish, Maryland, Havoc I , Martinet TT.I, Blenheim IV,
    Sea Otter, Hurricane FB.IIc

820 Barracuda II (Indefatigable)

824 Wildcat V (to Striker)

826 Barracuda II (Indefatigable)

827 Barracuda II (Formidable)

830 Barracuda II (from Formidable)

842 Wildcat V

880 Seafire F.III (Furious)

887 Seafire F.III, L.III (transit to Indefatigable)

894 Seafire F.III (Indefatigable)

1770 Firefly I (from Indefatigable to Grimsetter to Hatston
    (transit) to Donibristle
1840 Hellcat I (from Furious to Form.)
1841 Corsair II (Formidable)
118 Spitfire VB, IX (to Detling)
313 Spitfire VII (Czech.) (from Lympne)

N.B. Squadrons leave Hatston in a further but abortive attempt to bomb *Tirpitz* in Kaa Fjord.

	Hatston				Grimsetter		Twatt	Skeabrae		
1		827	830	842			771	313		
2	712	827	830	842			771	313		
3	712	827	830	842			771	313		
4	712	827	830	842			771	313		
5	712	827	830	842			771	313		
6	712	827	830	842			771	313		
7	712	827	830	842	826		771	313	880	801
8	712	827	830		826		771	313	880	801
9	712	827	830		826		771	313	880	
10	712	827	830		826		771	313	880	
11	712	827	830		826		771	313	880	
12	712	827	830		826		771	313	880	
13	712	827	830		826		771	313	880	
14	712	827	830	1842	826	841	771	313	1841	
15	712	827	830	1842		841	771	313	1841	
16	712	827	830	1842		841	771	313	1841	
17	712	827	830	1842		841	771	313	1841	
18	712	827	830			841	771	313	1841	
19	712	827	830			841	771	313		
20	712	827	830				771	313		
21	712	827	830				771	313		
22	712	827	830				771	313		
23	712	827	830				771	313		
24	712	827	830				771	313		
25	712	827	830				771	313		
26	712	827	830	852			771	313		
27	712	827	830	852			771	313		
28	712	827	830	852			771	313	801	880
29	712	827	830	852			771	313	801	880
30	712	827	830	852			771	313	801	880
31	712	827	830	852			771	313	801	880

712 Expeditor, Dominie I, Sea Otter, Traveller I (formed at Hatston as a Communications Squadron out of 'B' flight 771 Sqdn.)

771 Swordfish, Maryland, Havoc I, Martinet TT.I, Blenheim IV, Sea Otter, Hurricane FB.IIc, Boston III

801 Seafire L.III (Furious)

814 Barracuda II (from Stretton)

826 Barracuda II (to Formidable)

827 Barracuda II

830 Barracuda II

841 Barracuda II (Formidable)

842 Wildcat V (to Stornoway)

852 Wildcat V, VI (from Nabob to Trumpeter)

880 Seafire F.III (Furious)

1841 Corsair II (Formidable)

1842 Corsair II x 18 (Formidable)

313 Spitfire VII (Czech.)

1944 September

	Hatston							Grimsetter			Twatt				Skeabrae			
1	712	827		852	814	1840					771				313	801	880	
2	712	827		852	814			826			771				313	801	880	
3	712	827		852	814			826			771				313	801	880	
4	712	827		852	814			826			771				313	801	880	
5	712	827		852	814			826			771				313	801	880	
6	712	827		852	814			826	1770		771				313	801	880	
7	712	827		852	814			826	1770		771				313	801	880	
8	712	827		852	814			826	1770		771				313	801	880	
9	712	827		852	814			826	1770		771				313	801	880	
10	712	827		852	814			826	1770		771				313	801	880	
11	712				814			826	1770		771				313	801		
12	712		856		814			826	1770		771				313	801		
13	712	827	856	852	814	830		826	1770		771				313	801	880	
14	712	827	856	852	814	830		826	1770		771				313	801	880	
15	712	827	856	852	814	830		826	1770		771				313	801	880	
16	712	827	856	852	814	830	846	826	1770		771				313			
17	712	827	856	852	814	830	846		1770		771				313			
18	712	827	856	852	814	830	846				771				313			
19	712	827	856	852	814	830	846				771				313			
20	712	827	856	852	814	830	846				771				313			
21	712	827	856	852	814	830	846				771				313			
22	712	827	856	852	814	830	846				771				313			
23	712	827	856	852	814	830					771				313			
24	712	827	856	852	814	830					771				313	894		
25	712	827	856	852	814	830					771				313	894		
26	712	827	856	852	814	830					771				313	894		
27	712	827	856	852	814	830					771				313	894		
28	712	827	856	852	814	830					771				313	894		
29	712	827	856	852	814	830					771				313	894		
30	712	827	856	852	814	830					771				313	894		

712 *Expeditor, Dominie I, Sea Otter, Traveller I*

771 *Swordfish, Maryland, Havoc I , Martinet TT.I, Blenheim IV, Sea Otter, Hurricane FB.IIc, Boston III*

801 *Seafire L.III (from Furious to Machrihanish)*

814 *Barracuda II*

826 *Barracuda II (from Formidable to Indefatigable)*

827 *Barracuda II (Furious)*

830 *Barracuda II (from Furious)*

846 *Wildcat VI (Trumpeter)*

852 *Wildcat VI*

856 *Wildcat VI (Premier)*

880 *Seafire F.III (Furious to Machrihanish)*

887 *Seafire F.III (from Indefatigable)*

894 *Seafire F.III (from Indefatigable)*

1770 *Firefly I (from Indefatigable to Ayr)*

1840 *Hellcat I, II (from Indefatigable to Eglinton)*

313 *Spitfire VII (Czech.)*

1944 October

	Hatston							Grimsetter		Twatt	Skeabrae			
1	712	814	827	852	830					771	313		894	887
2	712	814	827	852	830					771	313		894	887
3	712	814	827	852	830					771	313		894	887
4	712	814	827	852						771		611	894	887
5	712	814	827	852						771		611	894	887
6	712	814	827	852	846					771		611	894	887
7	712	814	827	852	846					771		611	894	887
8	712	814	827	852	846					771		611	894	887
9	712	814	827	852	846					771		611	894	887
10	712	814	827	852	846					771		611	894	887
11	712	814		852	846					771		611	894	887
12	712	814		852	846					771		611	894	887
13	712	814	827	852						771		611	894	887
14	712	814	827	852						771	841	611	894	887
15	712	814	827	852						771	841	611		
16	712	814	827	852				887	894	771		611		
17	712	814	827	852						771		611		
18	712	814	827		846					771		611		
19	712	814	827		846					771		611		
20	712	814	827		846					771		611		
21	712	814	827		846	828				771	841	611		
22	712	814	827		846	828				771	841	611		
23	712	814	827			828				771		611		
24	712	814	827							771		611		
25	712	814	827							771		611	801	
26	712	814	827							771		611	801	
27	712	814	827							771		611	801	880
28	712	814	827							771		611	801	880
29	712	814	827							771		611	801	880
30	712	814	827					881		771		611	801	880
31	712	814	827		1820	828	841	881		771		611	801	880

712 Expeditor, Dominie I, Sea Otter

771 Swordfish, Martinet TT.I, Blenheim IV, Sea Otter, Hurricane FB.IIc, Boston III, Corsair II

801 Seafire L.III (from Machrihanish)

814 Barracuda II

827 Barracuda II (Furious)

828 Barracuda II (Implacable)

830 Barracuda II (disbanded)

841 4 x Barracuda II (Implacable)

846 Avenger I, Wildcat VI (Trumpeter)

852 Wildcat VI (disbanded)

880 Seafire F.III (from Machrihanish)

881 Wildcat VI (from Pursuer)

887 Seafire F.III. L.III (to Implacable)

894 Seafire F.III (to Implacable)

1820 Helldiver I (from D'bristle)

313 Spitfire (Czech.) (to North Weald)

611 Spitfire VII (from Bradwell Bay)

1944 November

	Hatston							Grimsetter	Twatt	Skeabrae			
1	712	1820	828	814	841		827	881	771	611	801	880	
2	712	1820	828	814	841		827	881	771	611	801	880	
3	712	1820	828	814	841		827	881	771	611	801	880	841
4	712	1820	828	814	841		827	881	771	611	801	880	841
5	712	1820	828	814	841		827		771	611	801	880	
6	712	1820	828	814	841		827		771	611	801	880	
7	712	1820	828	814	841	1771	827		771	611	801	880	841
8	712	1820	828		841	1771	827		771	6111			841
9	712	1820	828		841	1771	827		771	611			
10	712	1820	828		841	1771			771	611			
11	712	1820	828		841	1771			771	611			
12	712	1820	828		841	1771			771	611			
13	712	1820	828		841	1771			771	611			
14	712	1820	828		841	1771			771	611			
15	712	1820	828		841	1771			771	611			
16	712	1820	828		841				771	611			
17	712	1820	828		841				771	611			
18	712	1820	828		841				771	611			
19	712	1820	828		841				771	611			
20	712	1820	828		841				771	611			
21	712	1820	828		841				771	611			
22	712	1820	828		841				771	611			
23	712	1820	828		841				771	611			
24	712	1820	828		841				771	611			
25	712	1820	828		841		835		771	611			
26	712	1820	828	856	841		835		771	611			
27	712	1820	828	856	841		835	881	771	611			
28	712	1820	828	856	841*		835		771	611			
29	712	1820		856		1771	835		771	611	801	880	
30	712	1820		856		1771			771	611	801	880	
31													

712 Expeditor, Dominie I, Sea Otter

771 Swordfish, Martinet TT.I, Blenheim IV, Sea Otter, Hurricane
FB.IIc, Boston III, Corsair II

801 Seafire L.III (Implacable)

814 Barracuda II (to Fearn)

828 Barracuda II (to Implacable)

835 Wildcat VI (Nairana)

841* Barracuda II (N.B. detachment to Skeabrae; all later
disbanded into 828 at Hatston)

856 Avenger II(from Premier)

880 Seafire F.III (to Implacable)

1771 Firefly I (Implacable)

1820 Helldiver I (to Donibristle)

611 Spitfire VII

	Hatston						Grimsetter	Twatt	Skeabrae		
1	712	853		856	1771		881	771	611	801	880
2	712	853		856	1771		881	771	611	801	880
3	712	853		856	1771		881	771	611	801	880
4	712	853		856	1771		881	771	611	801	880
5	712	853		856			881	771	611	801	880
6	712	853		856			881	771	611		880
7	712	853		856			881	771	611		880
8	712	853					881	771	611		880
9	712	853	828		1771		881	771	611	801	880
10	712	853	828		1771		881	771	611	801	880
11	712	853	828		1771		881	771	611	801	880
12	712	853	828		1771		881	771	611	801	880
13	712	853	828		1771		881	771	611	801	880
14	712	853	828		1771		881	771	611	801	880
15	712	853	828		1771		881	771	611	801	880
16	712	853	828		1771		881	771	611	801	880
17	712	853	828		1771		881	771	611	801	880
18	712	853	828		1771		881	771	611	801	880
19	712	853	828		1771		881	771	611	801	880
20	712	853	828		1771		881	771	611	801	880
21	712	853	828		1771		881	771	611	801	880
22	712	853	828		1771		881	771	611	801	880
23	712	853	828	856	1771		881	771	611	801	880
24	712	853	828	856	1771		881	771	611	801	880
25	712	853	828	856	1771		881	771	611	801	880
26	712	853	828	856	1771		881	771	611	801	880
27	712	853	828	856	1771		881	771	611	801	880
28	712	853	828	856	1771	835	881	771	611	801	880
29	712	853	828	856	1771	835	881	771	611	801	880
30	712	853	828	856	1771	835	881	771	441	801	880
31	712	853	828	856	1771	835	881	771	441	801	880

712 Expeditor, Dominie I, Sea Otter

771 Swordfish, Martinet TT.I, Blenheim IV, Sea Otter, Hurricane FB.IIc, Boston III, Corsair II, Corsair III

801 Seafire L.III (Implacable)

828 Barracuda II (from Implacable)

835 Wildcat VI (Nairana)

853 Avenger II, Wildcat VI (from Tracker in Clyde)

856 Avenger II(Premier)

880 Seafire F.III

881 Wildcat VI (Fighter Flight)

1771 Firefly I (Implacable)

441 Spitfire (RCAF) (to Hawkinge)

611 Spitfire VII (to Hawkinge)

1945 January

	Hatston							Grimsetter			Twatt	Skeabrae		
1	712	828	856		853		1771	881			771	441	801	880
2	712	828	856		853		1771	881			771	441	801	880
3	712	828	856		853		1771	881			771	441	801	880
4	712	828	856		853		1771	881	801		771	441		880
5	712	828	856	835	853	746	1771	881	801		771	441		880
6	712	828	856	835	853	746	1771	881	801		771	441		880
7	712	828	856	835	853	746	1771	881	801		771	441		880
8	712	828	856	835	853	746		881	801		771	441		880
9	712	828	856	835	853	746		881	801		771	441		880
10	712	828	856	835	853	746		881	801		771	441		880
11	712	828	856	835	853	746		881	801		771	441		880
12	712	828	856	835	853	746		881	801		771	441		880
13	712	828	856	835	853	746		881	801		771	441		880
14	712	828	856	835	853	746		881	801		771	441		880
15	712	828	856	835	853	746		881	801	880	771	441		
16	712	828	856	835	853	746		881	801	880	771	441		
17	712	828	856	835	853	746		881	801	880	771	441		
18	712	828	856	835	853	746		881	801	880	771	441		
19	712	828	856	835	853	746	813	881	801	880	771	441		
20	712	828	856	835	853	746	813	881	801	880	771	441		
21	712	828	856	835	853	746	813	881	801	880	771	441		
22	712	828	856	835	853	746	813	881	801	880	771	441		
23	712	828	856	835	853	746	813	881	801	880	771	441		
24	712			835	853	746	813	881	801	880	771	441		
25	712			835		746		881	801	880	771	441		
26	712			835		746		881	801	880	771	441		
27	712			835		746		881	801	880	771	441		
28	712			835		746			801	880		441	881	
29	712			835		746			801	880	771	441	881	65
30	712			835		746			801	880	771	441	881	
31	712			835		746			801	880	771	441	881	

712 Expeditor, Dominie I, Sea Otter

746 Firefly INF, Firefly NF.II (A Flight)

771 Swordfish, Martinet TT.I, Blenheim IV, Sea Otter, Hurricane FB.IIc, Boston III, Corsair II, Corsair III, Hoverfly I

801 Seafire L.III

813 Wildcat VI (Campania)

828 Barracuda II, Avenger I

835 Wildcat VI (Fighter Flight) (from Nairana)

853 Avenger II, Wildcat VI (to Queen)

856 Avenger II (to Premier)

880 Seafire 22 x F.III

881 14 x Wildcat VI

1771 Firefly I

65 Mustang III x 9 from Banff: (diverted here from Norwegian operation after encountering severe weather)

441 Spitfire (RCAF)

	Hatston							Grimsetter			Twatt				Skeabrae			
1	712	835	746					801	880		771				441	881		
2	712	835	746					801	880		771				441	881		
3	712	835	746					801	880		771				441	881		
4	712	835	746					801	880		771				441	881		
5	712	835	746	_821_				801	880		771				441	881		
6	712	835	746	_821_				801	880		771				441	881		
7	712	835	746	_821_				801	880		771				441	881		
8	712	835	746	_821_				801	880		771				441	881		
9	712	835	746	_821_				801	880		771				441			
10	712	835	746	_821_				801	880		771				441			
11	712	835	746					801	880		771				441			
12	712	835	746	821				801	880		771				441			
13	712	835	746	821				801	880		771				441			
14	712	835	746	821				801	880		771				441	881		
15	712	835	746	821				801	880		771				441	881		
16	712	835	746	821				801	880		771				441	881		
17	712	835	746					801	880		771				441			
18	712	835	746					801	880		771				441			
19	712	835	746					801	880		771				441			
20	712	835	746					801	880		771				441			
21	712	835	746					801	880		771				441			
22	712	835	746					801	880		771				441			
23	712	835	746		856			801	880		771				441			
24	712	835	746		856			801	880		771				441			
25	712	835	746	821	856			801	880		771				441	881		
26	712	835	746	821	856			801	880		771				441	881		
27	712	835	746	821	856			801	880		771				441	881		
28	712	835	746	821	856			801	880		771				441	881		
29																		
30																		
31																		

712 *Expeditor, Dominie I*

746 *Firefly INF, Firefly NF.II, Hellcat IINF (A Flight) (from Ford)*

771 *Swordfish, Martinet TT.I, Blenheim IV, Sea Otter, Hurricane FB.IIc, Boston III, Corsair II/III, Hoverfly*

801 *Seafire L.III*

821 *Barracuda II, TR III x 12 (Puncher)*

835 *Wildcat VI (Nairana)*

856 *Avenger II*

880 *Seafire F.III, L.III*

881 *Wildcat VI (Puncher)*

441 *Spitfire*

* 801 and 880 had 24 aircraft in each squadron: on at least one occasion at Grimsetter, all 48 aircraft were airborne at the same time

1945 March

#	Hatston								Grimsetter			Twatt					Skeabrae			
1	712	746	821	835		856			801	880		771					441	881		
2	712	746	821	835	881	856			801	880		771					441			
3	712	746	821	835	881	856			801	880		771					441			
4	712	746	821	835	881	856			801	880		771					441			
5	712	746	821	835	881	856			801	880		771					441			
6	712	746	821	835	881	856			801	880		771					441			
7	712	746	821	835	881	846			801	880		771					441			
8	712	746	821		881	846			801	880		771					441			
9	712	746	821		881	846				880		771					441			
10	712	746	821		881	846				880		771					441			
11	712	746	821		881	846				880		771					441			
12	712	746	821	828	881	846				880		771					441			
13	712	746	821		881	846				880		771					441			
14	712	746	821		881	846				880		771					441			
15	712	746	821	835	881	846						771					441			
16	712	746		835	881							771					441			
17	712	746		835	881							771					441			
18	712	746		835	881							771					441			
19	712	746		835	881							771					441			
20	712	746		835	881							771					441			
21	712	746		835	881							771					441			
22	712	746		835	881							771					441			
23	712	746										771					441			
24	712	746										771					441			
25	712	746										771					441			
26	712	746										771					441			
27	712	746										771					441			
28	712	746										771					441			
29	712	746	821	835	853							771					441			
30	712	746	821	835	853	846			_825_	882		771					441			
31	712	746	821	835	853				_825_	882		771					441			

771 *Swordfish, Martinet TT.I, Blenheim IV, Sea Otter, Hurricane FB.IIc, Boston III, Corsair II, Stinson Reliant, Corsair III, Hoverfly I*

801 *Seafire L.III (to Implacable)*

821 *Barracuda II, TR III (Puncher: to Fearn)*

825 *Wildcat VI (Wildcat flight) (from Campania)*

828 *Avenger I (to Implacable)*

835 *Wildcat VI (Nairana) (disbanded)*

846 *Wildcat VI (Trumpeter)*

853 *Avenger II, Wildcat VI (Queen)*

856 *Avenger II*

880 *Seafire F.III*

881 *Wildcat VI (to Pursuer)*

882 *Wildcat VI (Searcher)*

441 *Spitfire (RCAF)*

1945 April

	Hatston								Grimsetter			Twatt				Skeabrae			
1	712	746	846		853				825	882		771				441			
2	712	746	846		853				825	882		771				441			
3	712	746	846							882		771				329			
4	712	746	846							882		771				329			
5	712	746										771				329			
6	712	746										771				329			
7	712	746										771				329			
8	712	746										771				329			
9	712	746										771				329			
10	712	746										771				329			
11	712	746										771				329			
12	712	746										771				329			
13	712	746	846	821	853				825	882		771				329			
14	712	746	846	821	853				825	882		771				329			
15	712	746	846	821	853				825	882		771				329			
16	712	746	846	821	853				825	882		771				329			
17	712	746	846	821	853				825			771				329			
18	712	746	846	821	853				825			771				329			
19	712	746	846	821	853				825	882		771				329			
20	712	746	846	821	853				825	882		771				329			
21	712	746	846	821	853				825			771				329			
22	712	746	846	821	853				825			771				329			
23	712	746	846	821	853				825			771				329			
24	712	746	846	821	853				825			771				329			
25	712	746	846	821	853				825			771				329			
26	712	746	846	821	853				825			771				329			
27	712	746										771				329			
28	712	746										771				329			
29	712	746										771				329			
30	712	746										771				329			
31																			

712 *Expeditor, Dominie I*

746 *Firefly INF, Firefly NF.II, Hellcat IINF (A Flight)*

771 *Swordfish, Martinet TT.I, Blenheim IV, Sea Otter, Hurricane FB.IIc, Boston III, Corsair II, Stinson Reliant, Corsair III, Hoverfly I*

821 *Barracuda II, TR III x 12, Wildcat VI x 6 (from Fearn)*

825 *Wildcat VI (Flight) (Puncher: to Stretton)*

846 *Wildcat VI (Trumpeter)*

853 *Avenger II, Wildcat VI (Queen)*

882 *Wildcat VI (Searcher)*

329 *Spitfire IX, XVI (Free French) (from Turnhouse.)*

441 *Spitfire (RCAF) to Hawkinge*

1945 May

	Hatston								Grimsetter			Twatt					Skeabrae				
1	712	746										771					329				
2	712	746										771					329				
3	712	746										771					329				
4	712	746										771					329				
5	712	746										771					329				
6	712	746										771					329				
7	712	746										771					329				
8	712	746										771					329				
9	712	746										771					329				
10	712											771					329				
11	712											771					329				
12	712											771					329				
13	712											771					329				
14	712											771					329				
15	712											771					329				
16	712											771					329				
17	712											771					329	451			
18	712											771					329	451			
19	712		856									771					329	451			
20	712		856									771					329	451			
21	712		856									771					329	451			
22	712		856									771					329	451			
23	712		856									771					329	451			
24	712		856									771					329	451			
25	712		856									771						451			
26	712		856									771						451			
27	712		856									771						451			
28	712		856									771						451			
29	712		856									771						451			
30	712		856									771						451			
31	712		856									771						451			

712 *Expeditor, Dominie I*

746 *Firefly INF, Firefly NF.II, Hellcat IINF (A Flight) (to Ford)*

771 *Martinet TT.I, Blenheim IV, Sea Otter, Boston III, Corsair III, Stinson Reliant, Hoverfly I*

856 *Avenger II (from Premier)*

329 *Spitfire XI, XVI (Free French) (to Harrowbeer)*

451 *Spitfire (Australian)*

1945 June

	Hatston								Grimsetter			Twatt					Skeabrae			
1	712		856									771					451			
2	712		856									771					451			
3	712		856									771					451			
4	712		856									771					451			
5	712		856									771					451			
6	712		856									771					451			
7	712		856									771					451			
8	712		856									771					451			
9	712		856									771					451			
10	712		856									771					451			
11	712		856									771					451			
12	712		856									771					451			
13	712		856									771					451			
14	712		856									771						603			
15	712		856									771						603			
16	712											771						603			
17	712											771						603			
18	712											771						603			
19	712	846										771						603			
20	712	846										771						603			
21	712	846										771	802					603			
22	712	846										771	802					603			
23	712	846										771	802					603			
24	712	846										771	802					603			
25	712	846										771	802					603			
26	712	846										771	802					603			
27	712	846										771	802					603			
28	712	846										771	802					603			
29	712	846										771	802					603			
30	712	846										771	802					603			
31																				

712 *Expeditor, Dominie I*

771 *Martinet TT.I, Sea Otter, Boston III, Corsair III, Stinson Reliant, Hoverfly I*

802 *24 x Seafire L.III (from Arbroath)*

846 *9 x Avenger II (from Stretton)*

856 *Avenger II (disbanded)*

451 *Spitfire (Australian) to Lasham*

603 *Spitfire XVI (from Drem)*

1945 July

	Hatston								Grimsetter			Twatt				Skeabrae			
1	712	846										771	802			603			
2	712	846										771	802			603			
3	712	846										771	802			603			
4	712	846										771	802			603			
5	712	846										771	802			603			
6	712	846										771	802			603			
7	712	846										771	802			603			
8	712	846										771	802			603			
9	712	846										771	802			603			
10	712	846										771	802			603			
11	712	846										771	802			603			
12	712	846										771	802			603			
13	712	846										771	802			603			
14	712	846										771	802			603			
15	712	846										771	802			603			
16	712	846										771	802			603			
17	712	846										771	802			603			
18	712	846										771				603			
19	712	846										771				603			
20	712											771	846			603			
21	712											771	846			603			
22	712											771	846			603			
23	712											771	846			603			
24	712											771	846			603			
25	712												846			603			
26	712												846			603			
27	712												846			603			
28	712												846						
29	712												846						
30	712												846						
31	712												846						

712 *Expeditor, Dominie I*

771 *Martinet TT.I, Sea Otter, Boston III, Corsair III, Hoverfly I*
   (to Zeals)

802 *24 x Seafire L.III (to Ayr)*

846 *9 x Avenger II (to Crail)*

603 *Spitfire XVI (to Turnhouse)*

1945 August

	Hatston								Grimsetter			Twatt			Skeabrae			
1	712																	
2	712																	
3	712																	
4	712																	
5	712																	
6	712																	
7	712																	
8	712																	
9	712																	
10	712																	
11	712																	
12	712																	
13	712																	
14	712																	
15	712																	
16	712																	
17	712																	
18	712																	
19	712																	
20	712																	
21	712																	
22	712																	
23	712																	
24																		
25																		
26																		
27																		
28																		
29																		
30																		
31																		

712 Expeditor, Dominie I (disbanded)

ABOUT TERN

March—April 1945 :: **Price 6d**

'The cover of the last issue of *About Tern*, the monthly magazine produced at HMS *Tern*, RNAS Twatt.

A recent photograph of the three RNAS Twatt photographers who have left us with such a fine visual record of their station: Left to Right: Celia Pemberton (née Green), Walter (Bing) Crosby and Mary Kiddie.

List of Abbreviations

CAP	Combat Air Patrol
Cdr.	Commander
CO	Commanding Officer
CPO	Chief Petty Officer
D/F	Direction Finding
ENSA	Entertainments National Services Association
FAA	Fleet Air Arm
FAAM	Fleet Air Arm Museum
Fl.Lt.	Flight Lieutenant
FRU	Fleet Requirements Unit
IWM	Imperial War Museum
Lt.Cdr.	Lieutenant Commander
MAC	Merchant Aircraft Carrier
NAAFI	Navy, Army and Air Force Institute(s)
PCB	Protected Control Building
PO	Petty Officer
PRO	Public Record Office
RNAS	Royal Naval Air Station
RNVR	Royal Naval Volunteer Reserve
RNZNVR	Royal New Zealand Naval Volunteer Reserve
Sqdn.Ldr.	Squadron Leader
Sub.Lt.	Sub Lieutenant
TAG	Telegraphist Air Gunner
TBR	Torpedo Bomber Reconnaissance
TT	Target Towing
USS	United States Navy
W/T	Wireless Transmission
WAAF	Women's Auxiliary Air Force
WRNS	Women's Royal Naval Service

References

The Ship's Log of Hatston (HMS *Sparrowhawk*), Twatt (HMS *Tern*) and Grimsetter (HMS *Robin*) were destroyed after the war: the history of these stations has had to be built up from information in the Public Record Office at Kew and from personal reminiscences. Material relating to Grimsetter as a RAF Station is practically non-existent. The Operations Record Books (Station Diaries) of RAF Skeabrae and Wick (later FSH Kirkwall) are complete and quite detailed.

AIR1 453: Marine Operations Vol. 5.
      1. f100: Scapa 1918, Aircraft Repairs Base and Storage Depot
      2. f110: Smoogro, 1918
      3. f144: Loch Stenness, 1918: Seaplane Station, Nos. 309, 310 and 311 Flights

AIR20 262: Photo Index, Scapa Flow

AIR28 712: Operations Record Book, Skeabrae

AIR28 917: Operations Record Book, Fighter Sector Headquarters, Wick (later FSH Kirkwall)

ADM1 3574: Naval Air Stations in Scotland: (report 1942 - 1943)

ADM116 3831: Scapa Flow, Photo Index

ADM116 5790: Scapa Flow, Photo Index

ADM1 10210: Fleet Air Arm War Base in Orkney (1938 - 1939)

ADM1 10736: 1939 - 1940: Skeabrae Aerodrome, Orkneys: construction

ADM1 10737: Defence of Orkney and Shetland: provision of fighter squadrons, 1939 -1940

ADM1 11192: Construction of Additional Aerodrome at Twatt, Orkney, 1940 - 1941

ADM1 11725: New Royal Naval Air Stations: fighter direct office, telephone arrangements (1942 -1945)

ADM1 13587: Share facilities for FAA and subsequent transfer to RN

ADM1 13627: RN Air Station, Grimsetter, layout

ADM1 16024: Improvement of Radar Cover in Orkney against low flying aircraft (1944)

ADM1 16427: MFQ 61/16 RN Air Station, Twatt (Map, 4' x 2½')

ADM1 16427: MFQ 61/8 RN Air Station, Grimsetter

ADM1 16427: MF 61/18 RN Air Station, Hatston (Map, 18" x 13")

ADM1 16464: Acquisition of Helicopters by FAA for A/S work, 1942 -1944

ADM1 16481: RN Air Station, Twatt, Orkney: expansion scheme and layout

ADM1 17033: Helicopters for the RN, 1943-44

ADM1 17423: RN Air Stations in the Scottish Highlands and Islands: discussions on post war requirements and future policy (1945)

ADM1 17429: Decision to close down Scapa as Fleet Base after defeat of Germany and reduce facilities to a minimum: proposals on future use of Orkney Air Stations in the area (1945)

ADM1 65790: (Chronology): especially Chapter V *The Naval Air Stations*

ADM53 109896: Log of HMS *Nelson*, August 1939

ADM187 2-4: Pink Lists: location of HM Ships at 1600 hours each day

WO199 2712: Decoy Sites, September 1940 - February 1943

WO199 2713: Ground Defence of Grimsetter Aerodrome, July 1941 - July 1943

WO199 2715: Defence of Aerodromes, January 1941 - 1943

Beaver, Paul: *The British Aircraft Carrier*, Patrick Stephens, Wellingborough, Northants, 1987

Bradford, Ernle: *Siege: Malta 1940-1943*

Brown, David: *Carrier Fighters*, Macdonald and Co. Ltd., London, 1975

Brown, David: *Carrier Operations in World War II Vol.I, The Royal Navy*: Ian Allan Ltd, London, 1968

Brown, Eric: *Wings of the Navy*, Airlife Publishing Ltd., Shrewsbury, 1987

Burns M. G.: *Bader, the Man and his Men*, Cassell, London, 2001 (several chapters given over to the lives and deaths of members of 880 Sqdn.**)**

Churchill, Winston: *The Gathering Storm*, Houghton Mifflin Company, Boston, 1948

Clostermann, Pierre: *The Big Show*, Chatto and Windus, London, 1951

Crosley, Cmdr. R. Mike: *They gave me a Seafire*, Airlife Publishing Ltd., Shrewsbury, 1986

Department of the Navy, Naval History Division: *Dictionary of American Naval Fighting Ships*, Washington

Foster David: *Wings Over the Sea*, Harrop Press, Canterbury, 1990 (deals with 849 Sqdn..)

Gordon, Dr. T. Crouther: *Early Flying in Orkney: seaplanes in World War I*, BBC Radio Orkney, 1985

Halley, James J.: *Squadrons of the Royal Air Force*, Air-Britain, 1980

Hamilton, Duncan: *Touch Wood*, Duncan Hamilton & Co. Ltd., Bagshot, Surrey, 1990

Hewison, W. S.: *This Great Harbour Scapa Flow*, The Orkney Press, Stromness, Orkney, 1985

Judd, Donald: *Avenger from the Sky*, William Kimber & Co Ltd., London, 1985

Liskutin A.: *Challenge in the Air; a Spitfire pilot remembers*, William Kimber, London, 1988; (refers to Skeabrae)

Moore W. G.: *Early Bird*, Putnam, London, 1963 (Moore was Second-in-Command to Dunning)

Nicholl G. W. R.: *The Supermarine Walrus*, G. T. Foulis & Co. Ltd., London, 1966

Norris Geoffrey *The Royal Flying Corps, a history,* Muller, London, 1965.

Partridge, R. T. (Major): *Operation Skua*, Fleet Air Arm Museum, Yeovilton, Somerset, 1983

Poolman, Kenneth: *Allied Escort Carriers of World War Two*, Blandford Press, London, 1988

Robertson, Bruce: *British Military Aircraft Serials*, 1878-1987, Midland Counties Publications, Earl Shilton, Leicester, 1987

Rawlings, John D. : *Fighter Squadrons of the RAF and their Aircraft*, MacDonald and Co., London, 1969

Roskill, Capt. Stephen W.: *The War at Sea, 1939-1945*, HMSO, London, 1976.

Roskill, Capt. Stephen W.: *Documents Relating to the Naval Air Service, Vol. I, 1908-1918*, Navy Records Society, 1969

Ross Catherine: *Battledress*, Eyre Methuen, London, 1979. (This novel is based on the writer's experience as a WAAF at Skeabrae during World War II; it has a good plot and succeeds in giving a realistic account of life on an RAF Station at that time.)

Rotherham, G. A. (Capt.): *"It's Really Quite Safe"*, Hangar Books, Belville, Ontario, Canada, 1985

Schroder, Virginia: *Bloody Orkney?*, Bellavista Publications, Kirkwall, Orkney, 2006

Scott, Desmond: *One More Hour*, Century Hutchinson Ltd, London, 1989

Smith, David J.: *Action Stations, 7. Military Airfields of Scotland, the North-East and Northern Ireland*, Patrick Stephens Ltd., Wellingborough, Northamptonshire, 1989

Smith, David J.: *British Military Airfields, 1939-45*, Patrick Stephens Ltd., Wellingborough, Northamptonshire, 1989

Stahl, Peter: *The Diving Eagle; a Ju-88 Pilot's Diary*

Sturtivant, Ray: *Squadrons of the Fleet Air Arm*, Air-Britain (Historians) Ltd., Tonbridge, Kent, 1984

Times (The): *Return to the Orkneys*, May 1946

Winton, John: *Carrier Glorious, the life and death of a carrier*, Leo Cooper, 1986

Young, John M.: *Britain's Sea War, a diary of ship losses, 1939-1945*, Patrick Stephens Ltd., Wellingborough, Northamptonshire, 1989

Index

Note that the Index <u>excludes</u> references in the Aircraft Crash Records and Aviation War Diary

Squadrons

3 85, 87, 103
43 49, 52, 54, 103
124 87
164 92, 93,100
253 86, 87, 90, 143, 144, 154
254 55, 84, 94
271 139, 141
312 139
331 90, 91, 92, 93, 98
504 33
602 93, 96, 140
603 37, 103
605 32, 49, 53, 55, 100
700 19, 35, 59, 69, 70, 83, 84, 86, 99, 105, 117, 154, 165, 174, 183
771 30, 34-36, 48, 56, 59, 61, 63-67, 69, 70, 74, 83, 84, 89, 90, 99, 103, 105, 121-123, 139, 150, 151, 154, 155, 157, 162, 166, 168, 178, 179
800 30, 52-55, 59, 85, 105, 107
801 59, 91, 92, 94, 105, 107, 119, 122, 123, 125, 126, 131, 134, 135, 139, 150, 153, 156, 161
802 150, 153, 156
803 32, 48, 49, 52, 53, 54, 105, 106, 107
804 32, 49, 50, 53, 54, 5685, 95, 105, 118, 125
806 55
809 143, 153
819 53, 107
821 55
823 55, 141
828 56, 59, 83, 107, 109, 123, 126
845 35, 119, 121, 124
846 35, 36, 37, 103, 121, 125, 126, 132, 138
880 153
881 159
884 77, 118
1476 94
1494 93

*Denotes aircraft

Air Transport Auxiliary 150
*Albacore 56, 76, 83, 107-110, 113, 117, 118
Argentine-British 93
Army Cooperative Exercises 63
Auskerry 57, 99
*Avenger 35, 37, 103, 119, 121, 124-126, 130, 132, 133, 137
Barrage Balloons 49, 50, 83, 89, 90, 122
*Beechcraft Expeditor 175
Bellman Hangar 29

Bergen (see also Norway) 53, 55, 56, 87, 109
Binscarth, Firth 56
Birsay 32, 35, 67, 71, 72, 90, 95, 103, 104, 117, 144, 167, 177, 178, 184
Bismarck 53, 56, 107, 109, 113
*Boston 68, 71, 75, 84
*Blenheim 55, 67, 68, 69,71, 84, 87, 90
Burn of Grid, Birsay, Decoy Airfield, 35
Burray 54, 57
Caldale 20
Caldale Air Station 21
Castletown 33, 87, 103
Churchill, Winston 20, 31, 48-50, 91, 103, 105, 115
Churchill Barriers 64
Cinemas 151, 152, 158, 169
Coastal Command 32, 36
*Condor 87
Contraband 33, 84, 87
Control Tower, Twatt, 42-45
Convoy JW53 118
Convoy PQ12 113
Convoy PQ18 116
Convoy RA59 61,122
Copinsay 49, 54
*Corsair 68, 70, 74, 80, 84, 122, 123
Cot-on-Hill, Decoy Airfield 35
Crail, Fife 37, 103, 126
Crown Prince Olaf 91
Crowther-Gordon 27
*Curtiss Flying Boat 26, 27
Czech Squadron 95, 96
*Dakota 37
Deasbreck, Birsay, Decoy Airfield 35
Decoy Airfields 35
Deerness 56, 93, 118
*Defiant 61, 76, 83, 89
Denmark 95
*Devastator 115, 117, 122
Distler 19, 139
Dounreay 36
Dramatic Societies 50, 151, 153
*Do-17 53
Duke of Kent 36
Dunning, E., Cdr. 24-26
Ely, Eugene 19
ENSA 151, 153, 167, 181
Evanton 30
Fair Isle 27, 83, 87
Fancourt H. St. J., Capt. 36, 114-116, 121
Faroes 84, 93
*Felixstowe Flying Boat 27
Festigarth, Sandwick 33
Fighter Direction Centre, Twatt 67, 72, 104, 117
Fighter Direction School, Twatt 67, 73
Fighter Direction Station, Kirkwall 34, 35

*Firefly 123
Flotta 57
Forbes, Admiral 47, 50
Free French 95, 103
*Fulmar 79, 109-113, 125
Garson Farm, Sandwick 29, 32
*Gladiator 32, 49, 50, 54, 95, 105, 106, 107, 114, 115
Goddard Noel 56
Gosport 29
Grimsetter 32, 34, 35, 38, 39, 67, 84, 85, 93-95, 105, 117, 122, 123, 125, 126, 140, 150, 153, 166, 168, 169
Grind, Sandwick 32
*Grumman Martlet 33, 78, 85, 118, 119, 127, 128, 137
Hammerclait, Sandwick 29, 32
*Handley Page Harrow 33, 99, 139
Harray Loch 29
Harriman Averell 165
Hatston 29, 31-33, 36, 37, 48, 50, 52-54, 59-61, 66, 67, 69, 77, 79, 80, 83-85, 94, 100, 105-107, 109, 110, 112-119, 121-126, 128, 132, 138, 139, 141, 143, 144, 146, 148, 150, 151, 153-156, 158-160, 162, 163, 165, 167-171, 173-175, 178, 179, 184-186
Hatston Industrial Estate 37
*Hawker Hart 57
*Hawker Henley 44, 155
*Heinkel IIIs 50, 54, 106
HMS *Africa* 19
HMS *Arethusa* 100
HMS *Ark Royal* 30, 48, 49, 105, 106, 107, 109
HMS *Argonaut* 67
HMS *Atmah* 53
HMS *Aurora* 48
HMS *Avenger* 67, 116, 117, 119
HMS *Bermuda* 88, 89
HMS *Birmingham* 86
HMS *Campania* 23, 126
HMS *Carlisle* 100
HMS *Ceylon* 66
HMS *Courageous* 48
HMS *Dreadnought* 18
HMS *Duke of York* 67, 120, 121
HMS *Edinburgh* 86, 113
HMS *Euryalus* 86
HMS *Fencer* 61
HMS *Furious* 23, 25, 94, 105-107, 109, 110, 117-119, 121, 122, 123
HMS *Galatea* 100
HMS *Glasgow* 49, 70
HMS *Hermes* 20
HMS *Hermes* 28
HMS *Hood* 49
HMS *Indomitable* 67, 118, 119
HMS *Iron Duke* 48

HMS *King George V* 67, 78, 120
HMS *Nelson* 48, 67
HMS *Newcastle* 49, 70
HMS *Norfolk* 50, 86
HMS *Pegasus* 84
HMS *Premier* 125, 126, 137
HMS *Quiberon* 103
HMS *Robin* 36, 95
HMS *Rodney* 49, 122
HMS *Royal Oak* 48, 83, 105
HMS *Sheffield* 49, 70, 83
HMS *Shropshire* 83, 100
HMS *Southampton* 49, 70
HMS *Sparrowhawk* 31, 53, 117
HMS *Suffolk* 55
HMS *Tern* 34
HMS *Tern II* 36, 37
HMS *Trumpeter* 123, 125, 126, 132
HMS *Victorious* 77, 84, 107-110 112, 113, 116-118, 123, 129
HMS *Vindex* 126, 136
Holm 139
Hotspur Glider 57
Houton Kite Balloon Station 23
Houton 20, 28
*Hurricane 32, 33, 67, 83, 84, 86, 87, 90, 92, 100, 103, 106, 107, 116, 118, 119
Hyval, Sandwick 33
Iceland 39, 110, 111, 116, 118, 121
Inganess Bay 49, 87
Instrument Landing System
Irish Labourers 85
Isbister, James 50
Jellicoe 139
Jördens, Wilhelm 18, 19, 139
Jutland 27
*JU-88 48, 55, 85, 87, 90, 93, 95, 99, 119
King George VI 48, 86, 123, 129, 130
Kirkness, John 29
Kirkwall Airport 37
Königsberg 107
Kite Balloon 20, 21, 22
Lamb, Theodore F/Lt. 20
Larsen Reiser, Admiral
Leuchars, Fife 99
*Liberator 103
Link Trainer 67, 73, 74,
Loch Erribol 69, 78, 122
*Lockheed Hudson I 36
Longhope 27, 106
Lossiemouth 37
Lucy, William Lt. 52, 106
Luftwaffe 32, 47-48, 49, 50, 52-54, 56, 57, 87, 95, 106, 115
Lyness 47, 85, 143, 150
*Lysander 93, 95, 119
MAC Ships 84
*Maryland 54, 56, 66
Menuhin, Yehudi 153
*Messerschmitt 96, 98, 110,
Met Flights 65, 66, 100
Metzger, Ernst 18, 19
*Miles Whitney Straight 84
Military Airfields, Orkney 46

Moore Geoffrey 25
Montgomery, Field Marshal 165, 174
Mortimer Lt.Cdr. 30
Murmansk 61, 165
NAAFI 34, 150, 151, 157, 162, 169
NATO 39
Nether Scapa 20
Newhall, Sandwick 33
North Ronaldsay 27
North Sea Oil 39
North Newhall, Sandwick 33
Norway (see also Bergen) 32, 56, 61, 63, 86, 91, 92, 93, 95, 105-107, 109, 110, 116, 121-123, 134, 135
Norwegians 90, 91-93, 98, 139
Norwegian Army 68, 103
Odiham 29
Old Man of Hoy 154, 155
Operation D.X. 105
Operation Fortitude North 122
Operation Goodwood 123
Operation Leapfrog 86
Operation Mascot 123
Operation Overlord 123
Operation Pedestal 116, 117
Operation Tindall 159
Operation Torch 84, 105, 117, 118
Operation Tungsten 121, 122
Orphir 26
Partridge, R. T., Major 50
Plain of Fidge, Sanday, Decoy Airfield 35
Power Station, Linklater, Sandwick 45
Prien Günther Lt. 48
Protected Area 50
Quoyburray 29
Radar 52, 66, 69, 84, 87, 90, 98, 99, 106, 120, 127
Ramsay, Admiral 165, 174
Rescue Launch, Hatston 32
RNAS Grimsetter (see also Grimsetter) 9
RNAS Hatston (see also Hatston) 30, 49, 50
RNAS Houton 21
RNAS Stenness 26,
RNAS Twatt (see also Twatt) 35, 39, 40, 41, 43
*Roc 32, 44, 60, 61, 63, 64, 99, 106
Rotherham, Hank, Cdr. 36, 56
Rousay 35
Royal Flying Corps 20
Royal Hotel 49
Sacquoy Head, Rousay, Decoy Airfield 35
Samson, C. R. Lt. 19
Sanday 35, 56, 91, 109, 139
Sandwick (see also Skeabrae) 29, 47, 55, 74
Scapa Barrage 50, 55
Scapa Pier 77
Scottish Airways 29, 168
*Seafire 77, 94, 117-119, 122, 123, 125, 126, 134, 135, 150
*Sea Otter 59, 83, 84, 86, 94
Shapinsay 35

Shetland (see also Sumburgh) 84, 87, 90
*Short Seaplane 26, 27
*Sikorsky R-4 67, 81, 82
Skeabrae 29, 32, 33, 37, 38, 39, 55, 57, 67, 84-87, 90-105, 115, 117, 119, 122, 123, 125, 131, 134, 135, 139, 140, 141, 144, 146, 150, 151, 152, 154-156, 161-165, 167, 169, 170, 172, 173, 177, 185
Skogar, Sandwick 33, 149
*Skua 30, 32, 50, 52, 55, 56, 61, 92, 100, 105, 106
Smoogro 23, 25
SMS *Hindenberg* 28
South Ronaldsay 52, 57, 63
St. Magnus Chapel, Twatt 151, 152
Sumburgh (see also Shetland) 84, 87, 99, 100, 109
*Sopwith Pup 23, 24
*Spitfire59, 87, 92, 93-100, 102, 103, 115, 124, 131, 139, 178
S.S. *Daghestan* 49
S.S. *Danmark* 49
S.S. *Loch Maddy* 49
S.S. *Voltaire* 48
Stack Skerry 83, 88, 120
Standing Stones Hotel 26
Stavanger 87
Stenness 27, 50
Stromness 49, 61, 70, 83
Stronsay 49, 98, 99, 118,
Sule Skerry 57
*Supermarine Southampton III 27
Swan, Oliver Capt. 27
Swanbister 27
Swedish Mercenary 91
*Swordfish 30, 53, 55, 61, 75, 83, 84, 92, 105-107, 109, 113, 116, 118, 121, 122, 136
Tankerness 29
Twatt (see also Birsay) 32-34, 36, 37, 39, 59, 61, 63-70, 72-76, 78-84, 86, 87, 90, 91, 93-95, 99, 102-105, 109-113, 121, 122, 125, 126, 138, 139-144, 146-154, 156-157, 161-169, 172, 175, 178, 179, 183, 184
U-Boat 27, 48, 78, 83, 87, 111, 126
U-47 48
USS *Ranger* 36, 117, 121
USS *Wasp* 34, 59, 113-116, 121
VE Day 169, 181
WAAFs 34, 100, 103, 104, 140, 142, 150, 152, 168, 169, 179, 181
*Walrus 49, 70, 78, 83, 84, 88, 89, 91, 93
Weather Willie 99
Westray 78
Wick 32, 49, 55, 56, 100, 103, 120
Wideford 29
*Wildcat 77, 80, 115, 121-123, 125, 137
Wood, James 29
Wrens 46, 66, 79, 81, 100, 103, 104, 139, 140, 142, 145, 146, 148-150, 151-154, 156, 157, 161, 162, 164, 168, 169, 172, 179, 185